Truth Commissions

PENNSYLVANIA STUDIES IN HUMAN RIGHTS

Bert B. Lockwood, Jr., Series Editor

Truth Commissions

Memory, Power, and Legitimacy

Onur Bakiner

PENN

UNIVERSITY OF PENNSYLVANIA PRESS

PHILADELPHIA

Published by
University of Pennsylvania Press
Philadelphia, Pennsylvania 19104-4112
www.upenn.edu/pennpress

Printed in the United States of America
on acid-free paper

1 3 5 7 9 10 8 6 4 2

Library of Congress Cataloging-in-Publication Data

Bakiner, Onur, author.
   Truth commissions : memory, power, and legitimacy / Onur Bakiner.
      pages cm. — (Pennsylvania studies in human rights)
   ISBN 978-0-8122-4762-6 (alk. paper)
   1. Truth commissions—Political aspects—Case studies.   2. Political crimes and
offenses—Investigation—Case studies.   3. Reconciliation—Political aspects—Case
studies.   4. Memory—Political aspects—Case studies.   I. Title.   II. Series:
Pennsylvania studies in human rights.
JC580.B35 2016
323.4'9—dc23

                                                                2015006392

CONTENTS

Truth Commissions

Introduction

The National Theater of Guatemala City hosted an unusual crowd on February 25, 1999. The Commission for Historical Clarification, Guatemala's truth commission, was going to hand over its final report to the nation's president, Álvaro Arzú, before an audience of high-ranking civilian and military officials and a number of victims' groups and human rights organizations. Members of the political elite must have been comfortable enough, thinking that the truth commission, systematically deprived of resources and juridical powers to carry out its mandate, would present relatively uncontroversial results. However, the chair of the truth commission, Christian Tomuschat, took the stage to present the findings that little by little took the comfort away from political leaders: findings that referred to some of the atrocities the military committed against the Mayan population during the civil war as acts of genocide; findings that excited the victims' groups in the audience to such an extent that they began to clamor for "justicia!" At the end of the ceremony President Arzú, surprised and upset, refused to take the commission's final report directly from Tomuschat's hands and sent his peace secretary to receive the report instead.[1]

South Africa's famous Truth and Reconciliation Commission was facing accusations of bias since its inception. Opposition figures kept insisting that the African National Congress (ANC) established the panel to discredit political rivals and impose its interpretation of history as the official truth. When the commission completed its task, the expectation was that ANC's opponents, especially the members of the outgoing apartheid regime, would object to the final report, while the ANC would endorse it wholeheartedly. The opposition did not surprise the observers. However, some sectors within the ANC leadership, disappointed to learn that the commission had implicated their movement in past atrocities, sought a last-minute political maneuver to prevent the final report from getting published. It was only Nelson Mandela's personal intervention in favor of the commission that saved the report.[2]

*   *   *

Political-institutional mechanisms to come to terms with the past have swept across the globe since the early 1980s. Pieces of the past flew out of dusty archives, echoed in prison walls and presidential palaces, and erupted onto the political stage, sometimes through the choking voice of an old woman searching for a lost son, other times in the solemn words of a politician apologizing for past wrongs, and yet other times in the form of angry protests against the "unpatriotic" human rights defenders. Although it does not enjoy the status of universal consensus, the demand that every polity confront its past in an open-minded and critical fashion has become widely accepted. Human rights violators in Argentina and Rwanda, Guatemala and Serbia, face domestic or international courts; legislatures all around the world recognize genocides and impose punitive measures against denial; governments apologize for past abuses to rectify historical injustice; and victims receive material and symbolic reparations in many countries. All these measures address but a fraction of all political violence and human rights violations, and the forces of impunity and amnesia still prevail in most cases, but, arguably, individual and civil society advocacy in the wake of atrocities elicits official responses at a greater rate than any other period in human history.

One novel institution that appears to embody this zeitgeist of coming to terms with the past is called "the truth commission." Incoming democratic governments have been establishing truth commissions since the early 1980s to investigate grave human rights violations committed under previous regimes. Even after the third wave of democratization ebbed, consolidated democracies like those in Uruguay and South Korea and reformist authoritarian regimes such as the one in Morocco resorted to truth commissions to set the historical record straight.

A glance at the news over the last few years shows that truth commissions are here to stay. Côte d'Ivoire and Thailand established truth commissions in 2010 and 2011 respectively to examine recent political violence; Venezuela's government and opposition agreed to do the same in early 2014.[3] A section of the Basque Left (*izquierda abertzale*) called for an international truth commission in Spain's Basque region in 2012,[4] and the UN high commissioner for human rights, Navi Pillay, asked the same for Zimbabwe.[5] Some politicians and the media are testing the waters for a commission in Northern Ireland.[6]

Of course, not every truth commission initiative ends in success. Civic groups and legislators have recently proposed to establish commissions, to no avail, in settings as diverse as Indonesia and the United States, Mexico and Turkey. Nepal's Supreme Court blocked an attempt to establish a truth commission in 2013 out of fear that such a panel would grant amnesties for serious crimes. A similar proposal met the same fate at the hands of the Legislative Assembly in Bolivia the same year. Yet, even failed attempts reveal the extent to which this institutional response to past atrocities (and disagreements over the meaning of *truth, justice, memory, reconciliation, recognition*, and *forgiveness*) has become central to the political controversies of today.

The introductory anecdotes from Guatemala and South Africa point to a simple fact: truth commissions are *political*, that is to say, they are sites of contestation over material and symbolic resources. Outgoing and incoming politicians, government and opposition parties, victims' groups, human rights organizations, transnational advocacy networks, the judiciary, state security institutions, rebel groups, and the media participate in truth commission processes to achieve multiple, and often contradictory, objectives. The fact that commissions are the stage on which the complexity of interests, incentives, and values associated with nation building and truth telling is played out does not mean that commissioners and the staff simply replicate the political and ideological struggles taking place in society. Commissions are attentive, but not servile, to the broader political context. What makes them essentially political is that the commissioners and the staff constantly make choices when they define such basic objectives as truth, reconciliation, justice, memory, reparation, and recognition, and decide how those objectives should be met and whose needs should be served. Inevitably there will be winners and losers in a truth commission process. Thus, assessing the achievements and shortcomings of truth commissions requires identifying the complex set of actors, interests, values, and expectations that play into the politics of truth commissions and also recognizing commissions' agency as a crucial factor.

The anecdotes reveal an important pattern: truth commissions can be subversive. Politicians often lend them initial support in the hope of taming the societal pressure for justice and historical truth and imposing their vision of nation building. Yet, commissions have managed to surprise and upset powerful individuals and institutions many times. Even when they legitimize an incoming regime by laying bare the crimes of the previous one, their findings and conclusions may prove inconvenient for the new leaders, as the example of South Africa demonstrates. Of course, commissions are neither fully subversive nor fully docile. Comparative analysis should account for the unintended and unforeseen consequences of a truth commission process and explain why some commissions influence politics and society the way they do, whereas others do not. This is what this book sets out to do.

Truth Commission Impact

As more countries adopt truth commissions, human rights trials, victim-centered reparations, and purges of human rights violators from public office, the ability of these institutional mechanisms to deliver on their promises of justice, restitution, reconciliation, historical truth, and democratic strengthening is increasingly questioned. For national governments and foreign donors, the question of impact is closely related to funding choices, as transitional justice measures often compete with other state- and nation-building initiatives during difficult transitions. Furthermore, reckoning with past wrongs can be politically sensitive, controversial, even destabilizing. Therefore, incoming regimes want to weigh the expected political benefits and costs before jumping on the global transitional justice bandwagon. Finally, the ethical stakes of invoking truth, justice, and reparation in the face of individual trauma and social dissolution necessitate studies of transitional justice impact.

Scholars and practitioners in the fields of transitional justice and peace studies often disagree on the very definition of such essentially contested concepts as *justice, reconciliation*, and *truth*. Even if normative disagreements are suspended, empirical research on the effectiveness of transitional justice yields widely divergent results, reflecting the deep epistemological and methodological divisions across disciplines. Are we observing a "justice cascade" increasingly overpowering obstacles to human rights accountability,[7] or should we adjust our expectations to some form of justice "in balance" with amnesty?[8] Do truth commissions promote reconciliation between victims and perpetrators and/or between former enemies, or is reconciliation an unrealistic conclusion given that commissions often leave behind dissatisfied victims and unapologetic perpetrators? Should governments and foreign donors sequence their policy and funding decisions in search of a future political context conducive to human rights accountability, or should they stand firm in support of human rights and the rule of law from the start, ignoring the short-term political costs of such support? Some answers come from detailed case studies, whereas others rely on comparative data from many countries. In the end, however, the enormous divergence in the answers and the difficulty of initiating dialogue across methodological and disciplinary boundaries limit our ability to make sense of the achievements and short-comings of transitional justice. After decades of journalistic and scholarly work on coming to terms with past human rights violations, it seems that we know a lot, but understand little.

This book offers a deeper understanding of truth commissions, one of the chief mechanisms of postconflict justice and repair in today's world. The motivation comes from three key observations. First, many truth commissions have published findings, historical explanations, and recommendations that proved inconvenient to endorse and implement into policy for the political leaders, as explained above. Second, some of the bolder and more comprehensive truth commissions have generated surprisingly little impact in terms of policy reform and the public acknowledgment of human rights violations by key political actors. And third, even when some commissions have failed to generate observable policy impact, they have managed to inspire civil society activism in unanticipated ways by triggering the creation of new victims' organizations, promoting public debates over social memory, and inducing civil society actors to monitor the country's human rights policy.

The motivating question is: What are the practical and normative implications of a truth commission for a society coming to terms with a violent and divisive past? This is an admittedly ambitious quest, which I divide into smaller, more manageable questions throughout the course of the book: In what ways do truth commissions facilitate policy reform, human rights accountability, and the public recognition of human rights violations? What is the nature of state–civil society interactions during a commission's work? To what extent have truth commissions maintained, challenged, or transformed public discourses on memory, truth, justice, reconciliation, recognition, nationalism, and political legitimacy? What explains cross-national variation in their impact on politics and society? In what ways do truth commissions take part in the struggles for social memory in societies deeply divided over the meaning of past political violence? What does the popularity of truth commissions say about the relationship between truth and politics in today's world?

Democratization and transitional justice scholars have posed similar questions. Under what conditions do governments establish truth commissions? How does the political balance of power shape these commissions? How do commissions serve, if at all, justice, truth, and reconciliation? This book has developed out of thought-provoking academic debates around these questions. However, its scope, as well as central concern, is distinctive. It documents the ways in which truth commissions not only reflect the balance of power during delicate political transitions but also unsettle this balance in unforeseen ways. It seeks to explain commissions' impact on policy, political attitudes, judicial behavior, and social norms by embedding commissions in the context of societal and political struggles over historical truth and justice, yet also acknowledging the independent agency of commission members.

Truth commissions should be rethought as an inherently conflictive space for action and reflection by virtue of the tensions and contradictions built into their institutional design. They are established as investigatory bodies free from direct political intervention—at least ideally. Politicians and the commissioners themselves often portray a commission's task as the ethical and practical reconstruction of the nation. Commissions' autonomy, political efficacy, and transformative potential are therefore crucial for understanding what they expect to accomplish in contemporary societies. Yet, the very conditions under which commissions are set up, supported, and endorsed reveal their dependence on, and vulnerability before, influential decision makers and institutions that set limits on commissions' ability to transform politics and society. The tension between agency and vulnerability defies simplistic explanations of what truth commissions should or can achieve.

Truth commissions arise from, and generate impact through, complex political and social processes. Naturally, the sponsoring institution (frequently the government, but also the parliament, courts, or international organizations) pursues a narrow, if not entirely self-serving, set of political goals. The willingness of incoming governments to set up commissions has led critical commentators to label these bodies as instruments of political legitimation. In addition, the widespread resort to truth commissions during negotiated transitions where the outgoing authoritarian elites enjoy significant de facto and de jure power has led many observers to portray commissions as a second-best policy option to criminal prosecution. Accordingly, incoming democratic governments take into consideration the popular demand for the prosecution of human rights violators, but the threat of an authoritarian backlash prevents them from pursuing retributive justice. Instead, they adopt the less controversial policy of establishing a truth commission to satisfy the demands of victims, victims' relatives, and human rights organizations. Thus, truth commissions are modeled as a policy outcome reflecting the interests and balance of power across influential political and social actors.

However, the convenience that truth commissions offer political elites is only part of the story. The findings, historical narratives, and recommendations of truth commissions frequently surprise, upset, and delegitimize influential individuals and organizations, including the sponsors and advocates of the commission. Furthermore, the changes truth commissions have produced in policy and political attitudes do not necessarily conform to the anticipations of politicians, human rights advocates and scholars. Governments sometimes implement commissions' recommendations, but politically driven impact often falls short of the original aspirations, as governments can ignore the recommendations or implement them selectively. Despite the near-universal expectation that commissions should promote reconciliation, they have instead heightened tensions over the meaning of the national past, at least in the short run. Perpetrators and their political allies have acknowledged their responsibility for past abuses and sought reconciliation only in a small number of countries, and only if they are given material incentives (such as amnesty) or if the long-term political and judicial transformations make such a gesture necessary. Likewise, prosecutors have made use of the findings of a truth commission only in a small number of countries where the legal, political, and institutional context is auspicious. Nonetheless, even if truth commissions do not contribute to retributive justice everywhere, it is also true that they do not undermine human rights accountability: the enormous controversy over the South African amnesty hearings notwithstanding, most truth commissions do not grant or recommend amnesty provisions, and even where they do (as in South Africa and Liberia), most perpetrators fail to qualify for amnesty.

While truth commissions do not always generate impact in expected ways, their unanticipated effects need to be acknowledged. A commission may trigger civil society mobilization around its findings and recommendations, so much so that even after the commission disbands, the societal struggles over historical memory, human rights accountability, and victim-centered reparations may reference the commission as a focal point. Civic pressures have resulted in the delayed adoption of recommendations into policy in several countries where governments initially ignored the commission's work. Civil society mobilization has been stronger in cases where domestic and international human rights organizations and victims' groups take active part in structuring the commission.

Since truth commission impact is by and large determined by a commission's capacity to exercise agency, as well as its reception by politicians and civil society actors, variation across truth commissions in terms of agency and reception should be explained. This book documents sources of variation in truth commission impact at every stage of a commission process: (1) the creation of a commission, a process in which the basic goals and procedures are decided on, and the commissioners are appointed; (2) the commission process itself, shaped by dynamics of collaboration *and* conflict between the commissioners, the political elite, state bureaucracies, and civil society actors; and (3) the post-commission process, in which these numerous actors acknowledge or deny, adopt or ignore, the findings and recommendations of a commission.

A note of caution: nothing would be more misleading than to suppose that all truth commissions operate uniformly. There is considerable variation across commissions in terms of power dynamics, stated objectives, actual processes, and outcomes. Throughout the book *truth commissions* refer to ad hoc panels with characteristics similar enough to make conceptualization and comparative analysis possible, while acknowledging the need to account for variation across experiences.

History, Ethics, and Politics

An examination of truth commissions' impact on contemporary societies should not be limited to questions of causal effect on policies and attitudes. The worldwide popularity of truth commissions is the clearest manifestation of a greater phenomenon of memory politics, that is to say, contestations over the meaning of past atrocities committed by states and violent nonstate actors. As official propaganda is increasingly challenged by societal demands for accurate and truthful representations of the past, and as self-reflective and critical historiographies counter conventional views of history as a source of national glory, truth commissions face the difficult task of policing the boundaries of truth and lie, fact and opinion, and past and present. Therefore, this book seeks to explain why factual and historical truth have become so central to contemporary politics, and how the construction of *truth* in truth commissions shapes, and is shaped by, this new relationship between history, ethics, and politics.

Truth commissions offer a peculiar solution to one of the key problems of contemporary politics: recovering the factual truth about past violations and narrating national history in the context of nation (re)building. Their prominence in today's world reflects the hope, shared by many citizens, civil society activists, intellectuals, and politicians, that a self-critique of the past will help rebuild a divided nation on the basis of shared values. Therefore, understanding the role of truth commissions in contemporary politics requires an examination of their participation in struggles over social memory.

How, if at all, do truth commissions shape efforts to come to terms with the past? Situating truth commissions in the historical dialectic of modern politics offers some key insights. Commissions have come into existence when the nation-state's hegemony over history was increasingly facing challenges. Despite their claims to equal citizenship and social inclusion, nation-states and nationalism have almost always reproduced existing patterns of exclusion and marginalization and created new forms of vulnerability. Social cleavages along the lines of class, ethnicity, race, gender, and region were further aggravated in the second half of the twentieth century, when violent internal conflict was accompanied in most countries by state-led efforts to mislead the public about the causes, patterns, and consequences of violence through propaganda and deliberate lying. The acquiescence and complicity of judicial institutions created a situation whereby the defense of human rights was taken up by victims' associations and human rights organizations, which, through relentless and courageous activism, pushed the recovery of factual truth and an honest discussion about past violations onto the center stage of national politics during transitions. Truth commissions reflect this aspiration for a fact-based, critical, and national (but not nationalist) notion of factual-cum-historical truth that should reorient the nation and the nation-state in light of a new ethics of political conduct. As a result, most commissions to date have combined human rights investigation with a historical narrative on the causes, patterns, and consequences of political violence and violations.

The tremendous challenge of articulating an ethics of national reconstruction in a transitional context exposes the ambiguities and limitations built into truth commissions. They seek to recuperate the status of facts in politics, but their findings have limited or no legal sanction. Some of them reference international legal and moral norms to address the nation-state's failures, but their scope, limited to the nation both as object and audience, prevents them from advocating a postnational political project. Ultimately, even in the case of commissions that produce comprehensive narratives and make broad recommendations, the striving for a supra-political, ethical "founding moment" for the nation is unlikely to move politicians, state bureaucracies, and many citizens toward a radical rethinking of the country's political institutions and dominant identity perceptions.

I do not mean to downplay truth commissions' enormous contributions to the recovery of factual truth and the use of history as a source of critique by exposing these ambiguities and limitations. Rather, I hope to initiate a debate on the implications of today's obsession with memory and truth for political practice and legitimacy. We live in an age of international tribunals, official apologies, state-sanctioned truth commissions, human rights memorials, and victim-centered reparations programs. It is the age of "never again!" Many of us hope that acknowledgment, reflection, and repair will help us build a future society that is better, less violent, and more just than before. Yet, for all that was done, there is reason to be skeptical about whether contemporary societies, and especially their leaders, take the lessons from history seriously enough. Some postconflict societies are indeed less violent, but hardly more just. Others suffer from recurrent atrocities in part as a result of their failure to address the underlying causes of previous conflicts. It is questionable whether the victim-centered policies have brought the much-desired voice, empowerment, and healing to those who endured physical and structural violence.

Transformative potential and modest impact: truth commissions' achievements and shortcomings say a lot about how we are coming to terms with the past, what has been accomplished, and what needs to be done. This book is, therefore, an empirical and normative inquiry into the role of truth commissions in contemporary societies.

Outline of the Book

Part I sets the conceptual and theoretical framework for understanding truth commissions' place in contemporary struggles for justice, truth, and recognition. It is about the material and symbolic power relations in and around truth commissions. Chapter 1 offers a precise definition of truth commissions and provides a conceptual history by exploring commissions' evolution since the 1980s. For purposes of conceptual clarity, truth commissions should be distinguished from similar investigatory, judicial, or commemorative practices and institutions, such as parliamentary human rights commissions, courts, monitoring institutions, and nongovernmental organizations' (NGOs') truth-finding efforts. It is also important to acknowledge that some truth commissions were disbanded before they could finish their work, or that civil society initiatives to set up an official panel were frustrated in the first place. Furthermore, the idea of *truth commissions* has evolved over time. The procedures, methodologies, timing, and political functions of truth commissions have undergone profound changes, producing two generations of *transitional* commissions, as well as recent *nontransitional* ones.

Chapter 2 explores the politics of truth commissions, that is, the interactions and power relations between political decision makers, civil society actors, and the commissioners. Commissions are neither state bureaucracies nor civil society organizations, and they find themselves facing the task of mediating between the state and a portion of society. Their liminal position vis-à-vis the state requires a deeper understanding of state–civil society dynamics in commission processes. Furthermore, cooperative and competitive interactions among nonstate actors have become so central to contemporary truth-finding efforts that the vague notion of "civil society" should be analyzed in further detail.

The chapter challenges many of the taken-for-granted explanations about the relation of truth commissions to the state and civil society actors. Even if political elites tend to see commissions as tools of political legitimation and national reconstruction, the independent agency of commissioners often frustrates narrow political calculations. Commissions create a field of political struggle, that is to say, a site of contestation for material and symbolic power over questions of truth, memory, and justice. By its very nature the field is pluralistic, provisional, limited in its time horizon, and uncertain with respect to its expected impact on politics and society.

Chapter 3 expands the sociopolitical analysis to situate truth commission narratives in the broader context of struggles for social memory. The historical context chapters in truth commissions' final reports reflect, to some extent, the memory tropes circulating in society, but they also often redefine the terms of the societal debate. Truth commissions constantly renegotiate the tension between their authoritative status enabling them to produce *the* truth over the past and the need to persuade those who question their truthfulness and overall legitimacy. This tension drives many commissions to

develop narrative strategies at the intersection of embeddedness and transformation with respect to the field of social memory. Truth commissions adjudicate between contending positions by confirming or rejecting certain
narratives and explanations that hold sway in public debates; at times, they
simply avoid the contentious issue at hand; they claim to give voice to memories and experiences that are systematically excluded from public debates;
and finally, they transform the public debate by producing narratives and
explanations that unsettle the terms of social engagement. A truth commission's final report may combine some or all of these positions. Furthermore, the conscious and unconscious exclusions of a truth commission
narrative (that is, its silences) may be as constitutive of historiography as
the written text.

Part II is devoted to empirical studies of truth commissions' effects on
policy, judicial attitudes, social norms, and struggles for memory. Chapters 4
and 6 are about all transitional truth commissions, while Chapters 5 and 7
provide a detailed comparison of the Chilean and Peruvian panels based on
my field research in these countries.

Chapter 4 outlines the specific ways in which truth commissions impact
policy, judicial behavior, and social norms. Academic scholarship has offered
various explanations for how truth commissions should or can produce
changes in politics and society; yet a rigorous assessment of these explanations is lacking. In light of all transitional truth commissions that have produced a final report, I identify several causal mechanisms linking truth
commissions to social and political outcomes. Some of the causal explanations of truth commission impact, despite their popularity, do not hold: commissions do not promote immediate reconciliation between victims and
perpetrators, and their contribution to human rights accountability (or impunity) is limited. Truth commissions generate impact in most cases through
government adoption of truth commission findings and recommendations
into policy (direct political impact), and delayed policy adoption due to pressure on the part of human rights activists and victims' groups (civil society
mobilization).

Chapter 5 explains why some truth commissions produce more direct
political impact, while others tend to rely on civil society mobilization to
generate impact. The commission creation process that sets a commission's
goals, mandate, and composition is an initial factor that explains variation in
terms of politically driven and socially driven impact. The more control key
political decision makers (the government or a governing coalition) exercise

over the design and mandate of a commission by excluding political rivals and civil society groups, the more likely that the truth commission will produce a final report in line with these decision makers' expectations, and, consequently, the more likely that impact will be through the endorsement of the commission's final report and adherence to its recommendations (direct political impact). However, the exclusionary commission creation process is likely to alienate civil society groups and reduce the likelihood of civil society mobilization around the commission. By contrast, an all-inclusive initial negotiation process tends to allow the commission to exercise greater political agency, independently of the interests and expectations of the political elite.

Chapter 5 offers in-depth comparison of two commissions, namely, those in Chile and Peru, to explain why different truth commissions elicit such divergent responses from politicians and civil society groups. A high degree of government control in the creation of Chile's National Commission on Truth and Reconciliation (1990–1991) ensured greater political-institutional adherence in the post-commission setting, as the government endorsed the commission's final report and implemented major policy recommendations. However, the absence of civil society participation in the process resulted in a low degree of societal reception of the commission report and the dissolution of the Chilean human rights network in the early 1990s. In contrast, Peru's Truth and Reconciliation Commission (2001–2003) was established through a participatory process in which human rights organizations set the terms under which the commission operated. The commissioners produced a comprehensive history of political violence and proposed broad recommendations and a reparations program. Successive governments by and large ignored these findings and recommendations, while victims' groups and human rights organizations continued to mobilize around the social and political goals set by the commission.

Complementing the comparison of Chile and Peru, Chapter 6 zooms out to expand the comparison to fifteen transitional truth commissions established in the 1980s, 1990s, and early 2000s in Africa, Asia, and Latin America. This chapter offers a critical rereading of scholarly and journalistic accounts by paying specific attention to the conditions under which commissions have produced politically driven and civil society–led impact in Argentina, Uganda, Nepal, Chad, El Salvador, Sri Lanka, Haiti, South Africa, Guatemala, Nigeria, Timor-Leste, Sierra Leone, and Liberia. The findings confirm the influence of the commission creation process on a commission's mandate, composition, procedures, and, eventually, impact. The chapter also addresses some of the alternative explanations of variation in truth commission impact, like the type of political transition and the timing of a commission. While all of these factors seem to play a role, they influence a commission's impact only through the commission creation process and the subsequent operation of the commission.

Chapter 7 compares the historical narratives found in the Chilean and Peruvian commissions' final reports. It explains why the Chilean commission produced a relatively circumscribed memory of past violence, while its Peruvian counterpart took full advantage of its mandate to write a comprehensive social history of violence and violations. In accordance with the theoretical framework in Chapters 5 and 6, I find that the National Commission on Truth and Reconciliation in Chile, established under a high degree of government control in the interest of reconciliation between opposing political camps, produced a limited account of the underlying causes of political violence and violations, blaming the political radicalization and polarization of the 1960s and early 1970s for the nation's failures. By contrast, the Peruvian commission's comprehensive and politically sophisticated historical explanation proved more difficult to integrate into the political mainstream than its Chilean counterpart. The end of the chapter revisits the silences of truth commission narratives in light of the Chilean and Peruvian experiences.

Part III zooms out once again to rethink truth commission experiences in the trajectory of modernity. Chapter 8 examines how truth commissions problematize and transform the ways in which citizens of contemporary societies think and speak about historical truth, memory, justice, reconciliation, recognition (of victimhood and violations), and official historiography. Drawing on the works of Hannah Arendt, Pierre Nora, and Jürgen Habermas on factual truth, the public use of history, the ethics of national reconstruction, and collective memory, the chapter provides a new perspective on truth commissions. Truth commissions have opened a critical space to resignify the complex relations between history and memory, the past and the present, ethics and practical considerations, and nationalism and the postnational context. They have recovered basic facts about human rights violations and for the most part forced societies to rethink the violence and exclusion inherent in the political history of the nation. Consequently, commissions have produced a new dynamic whereby the state seeks to legitimize its central position between history and politics only by accepting a high degree of societal penetration into the production and diffusion of official national history. The problematization of the link between historiography and state sovereignty is evidenced by the incorporation of individual and social memory narratives into the production of truth commission histories, which occupy a quasi-official position.

The concluding remarks suggest that a truth commission's contributions should be understood not merely as a matter of policy success but also in terms of an ethical commitment to equal participation. Commissions should open a space for every person who wants to take part in reflecting on past violence and violations but should also take into account the power asymmetries resulting from the same violations in question, as well as other violations and injustices that effectively force many experiences and memories into silence and oblivion. Finally, the book concludes with an overview of the lessons learned from past truth commissions in the hope of providing useful guidelines for future truth projects.

A Note on Data Sources and Methodology

I conducted a total of 107 semistructured interviews with political decision makers, NGO activists, intellectuals, victims of political violence, and their relatives in Santiago (Chile), Lima (Peru), and the city centers of Ayacucho and Huanta (Peru) between September 2008 and July 2009. I complemented the interviews with archival research on press reports, human rights documentation, and memoirs of key social and political actors. Toward this end, I conducted archival research at the Vicaría de la Solidaridad's Center of Documentation (Chile), the Information Center for Collective Memory and Human Rights (Peru), and the press archives of the Association for Human Rights (APRODEH), a leading Lima-based human rights organization (Peru). I also maintained e-mail communication with a number of experts on transitional justice.

I use interview and archival data to explain (1) how and why key actors decided to create a truth commission; (2) which actors were excluded from decision-making processes; (3) how the commission operated within the constraints of its mandate; (4) aspects of the commission's work that satisfied, surprised, legitimized, or delegitimized important political, military, and judicial institutions; (5) the extent to which the government endorsed the final report and implemented its recommendations; and (6) the degree of civil society mobilization around the commission.

I complement the original empirical research on Chile and Peru with information on all truth commissions that took place during a political transition. Commissions' own final reports contain valuable information. In addition, I use secondary sources, which include academic scholarship, journalistic accounts, and human rights reports. Some of these sources analyze broad patterns for a large number of truth commissions, such as the United States Institute of Peace (USIP) Truth Commission Digital Collection, Priscilla B. Hayner's articles and books, and transitional justice databases. I also rely upon case studies, which provide in-depth information about one commission or a small number of them.

Reliance on secondary data may pose a major methodological problem if the sources are biased. For example, overreliance on the press bulletins of human rights NGOs may lead the researcher to overstate the efficacy of the human rights movement in pressuring the government and achieving policy outcomes. Media coverage might likewise suffer from pro- or anti-commission biases. Many of the personal accounts of truth commission processes come from the commissioners and the staff themselves. All these accounts need to be treated as invaluable yet partial contributions for a deeper understanding of truth commission processes.

Another major problem with conducting cross-national analysis concerns deficiencies in data. Truth commissions disband after producing the final report; therefore, they cannot monitor the social and political developments in the post-commission period. The media usually focus on the visible and dramatic aspects of truth commissions, thus hiding from view the subtle and longer-term effects of unanticipated processes during and after the commission's operation. International NGOs often transfer resources and personnel at the end of the truth commission process, which reduces their capacity to monitor truth commission impact. Academic literature has the merit of providing conceptual clarity in presenting data. However, since each scholar poses a specific research question that generates a particular set of conceptual and analytical categories, reliance on previous academic work may limit the conceptual tools and available information unnecessarily.

A further difficulty has to do with the asymmetry of available information across truth commission cases. Some commissions have attracted a large number of academic and nonacademic observers (e.g., Argentina, Chile, Guatemala, and South Africa), while little has been written about others (e.g., Chad and Nepal). The perceived importance of a country in world politics makes a difference, as well as its official language—commissions of English-

and Spanish-speaking countries have been covered more widely. Contextual factors are crucial, too: commissions operating in the midst of political violence (e.g., Sri Lanka) are less likely to be reported on, as journalists and NGO activists flee for security or get deported.

I acknowledge all the potential problems that might arise in my analysis due to these data deficiencies. However, instead of abandoning the task of providing a cross-national analysis of truth commissions altogether, my research strategy is to keep the information sources as varied as possible to amplify access to data, overcome bias in data collection, and achieve precision in evaluating the validity of concepts and causal relations. I incorporate data from as many resources as possible for each commission.

To justify the research methodology employed in this book, it is essential to give an account of the shortcomings of the existing methodological approaches. Chapter 4 provides an in-depth analysis of the strengths and weaknesses of alternative research methods. Large-N statistical analyses seek to isolate the truth commission effect by controlling for a number of alternative hypotheses. However, the number of commissions is relatively small compared to the large number of explanatory variables to justify statistical analysis; data collection problems abound; differences in model specification yield diametrically opposed results even for the same outcome of interest; and the dissimilar processes of transitional and nontransitional commissions (and differences between truth commissions and nongovernmental truth-finding efforts, which are lumped together for the purpose of increasing observation points) are often not taken into consideration. Other transitional justice scholars turn to case studies, either of a single commission or a small number of them. The ethnographic insights into the multilayered power dimensions pervading truth commissions and contextualized explanations of truth commission impact are the key contributions of the case study approach. The difficulty arising from case studies is the loss of a comparative framework to make sense of the conditions under which truth commissions produce changes in policy, courts, and social norms.

Therefore, I advocate a research strategy that explains truth commission impact comparatively, but without losing sight of the context-specific insights gained in case studies. I conduct comparative case studies to analyze the extent to which, and the specific mechanisms through which, a truth commission produces politically and socially driven impact. I use a process-tracing approach to examine within-case data collected in Chile and Peru. The technique of data analysis known as "process tracing" refers to a variety of

procedures that perform different functions. Some scholars use it to analyze evidence in a case to build a general theory, while others test existing
theories by exploring whether the observable implications of the theory fit the
empirical evidence.[9] Historical explanations based on process tracing may
be formulated as general theories, or, conversely, the technique may illumi-
nate the unique, even idiosyncratic, features of a case that resists generaliza-
tion.[10] Process tracing is closely associated with qualitative data collection
methods, which leads many scholars to think that the technique promotes
interpretive social-scientific epistemology, but it has been argued that process
tracing is compatible with quantitative data collection, as well as a positivistic
outlook on theory generation and theory testing.[11]

I use comparative process tracing to build and assess my theory of truth
commission impact because process tracing can provide comparative insights
into causal mechanisms across cases, even though it is primarily a within-
case analysis method.[12] Finally, I choose both cases from Latin America to
control for geographic, historical, and cultural similarities and to limit the
risk of confounding the explanatory framework with unrelated causal patterns. Through process tracing, I identify the mechanisms through which the
pre-commission process, that is to say, the political bargain that sets the mandate and appoints the commissioners, shapes the commission's capacity to
generate impact in the post-commission process. Process tracing also helps
to assess the plausibility of various causal explanations of truth commission
impact (Chapter 4), and eliminate rival explanations of cross-national variation in impact, such as the nature of the democratic transition (Chapter 6).

PART I

Truth, Power, and Legitimation
in Truth Commission Processes

PART I explores the place of truth commissions in today's struggles for memory, justice, and reconciliation during political transitions. It addresses the following questions: What are truth commissions? What explains their global popularity? Are they different from other fact-finding projects? What is their relationship to the state? In what ways do civil society groups mobilize for or against a truth commission's work? Who are the members of a truth commission and what role do they play during political transitions? To what extent do truth commissions mediate or transform the struggles over the meaning of the past? What are the narrative strategies they employ while rewriting the nation's history?

Part I sets a theoretical framework by engaging academic and policy debates in three interrelated areas: conceptual issues surrounding truth commissions and other fact-finding initiatives (Chapter 1), the politics of establishing, operating, and endorsing a truth commission (Chapter 2), and commissions' role in the struggles for social memory (Chapter 3). While differences between commissions are highlighted, these chapters focus more on what is common across the multitude of experiences. State-society relations, political legitimation, civil society participation, commission autonomy, divisions over social memory, and the tension between forensic investigation and historiography are common themes that all truth commissions find themselves grappling with. Part I explores these themes and thus sets the stage for the empirical analyses of truth commission impact in Part II, where variation across truth commissions is analyzed in further detail.

CHAPTER 1

Definition and Conceptual History of Truth Commissions: What Are They? What Have They Become?

Few ideas have gained as much international attention in such a short time span as the concept of the *truth commission*. Successful and failed initiatives to set up ad hoc panels called "truth commissions" to investigate patterns of human rights violations abound. In addition, in some countries single incidents of violence have led to calls for a commission when the facts about the event remained in the dark for decades. Two examples that come to mind are the 1985 siege and fire in Colombia's Palace of Justice[1] and the 1994 bombing of the Israeli-Argentine Mutual Association in Buenos Aires.[2] Perhaps more surprisingly, so-called truth commissions or truth and reconciliation commissions were proposed to tackle issues that had little or nothing to do with massive political violence, such as banking practices in England,[3] sexual abuse by a television presenter,[4] educational achievement in New York City,[5] and doping scandals in international cycling.[6] The fashion of naming all sorts of investigatory panels "truth commissions" poses two challenges: (1) setting conceptual boundaries to enable research and discussion on postconflict truth initiatives and to avoid "concept misformation,"[7] and (2) explaining how the idea of the truth commission has evolved over time to encompass such a wide variety of topics, procedures, and expectations.

In the following section, I offer a definition to set truth commissions apart from similar institutions and practices, such as governmental commissions of inquiry, civil society truth projects, courts, and human rights monitoring organizations. Next, I will introduce the notions of "incomplete truth commissions" and "frustrated truth commission attempts" to distinguish failed truth commission efforts from successfully completed ones and then employ

Louis Bickford's notion of "unofficial truth projects" to refer to nongovernmental truth-finding initiatives. Once the definitional characteristics are clarified, I will outline the ways in which the idea of the truth commission has evolved. The procedures, methodologies, timing, and political functions of truth commissions have undergone profound changes over time. Initially, governments established them with limited mandates during political transitions. The increasing role of international organizations in later transitions, along with domestic and international NGOs, brought the idea and practice of truth commissions into worldwide significance. Some of the newer commissions became increasingly more ambitious with respect to their goals and better funded compared to earlier commissions. Recently, truth commissions have been created by consolidated democracies (or authoritarian regimes not undergoing transition), rather than transitional regimes, to investigate violations that had taken place decades ago, rather than in the recent past.

Truth Commission: Definition

A truth commission is a temporary body established with an official mandate to investigate past human rights violations, identify the patterns and causes of violence, and publish a final report through a politically autonomous procedure.[8]

The definition above specifies five fundamental characteristics that distinguish a truth commission from other investigatory bodies. First, it operates for a limited amount of time. Permanent organizations like human rights NGOs or parliamentary human rights commissions are therefore not truth commissions.

Second, a truth commission publishes a final report summarizing the main findings and making recommendations. Usually, the report is submitted first to the political institution that had issued the commission mandate, such as the office of the president, but it is common practice to make the final report available to the general public, as well.[9] Some scholars include those truth commissions that were disbanded before publishing a final report (e.g., Bolivia's 1982 National Commission of Inquiry into Disappearances and Ecuador's 1996 Truth and Justice Commission) in their truth commission lists. It is problematic to include these commissions without qualification because the failure to publish a final report simply violates the essential task of a truth commission, namely, to disclose information on human rights violations. In addition, a final report does not only offer publicity; its existence also affirms the autonomy of a truth commission from direct political intervention. A political authority that disbands a commission or conceals its final report interferes with the publication and dissemination of facts about human rights violations and eliminates a commission's chances of influencing policy or social norms through its findings and recommendations. Those commissions that fail to publish a public report should be named "incomplete truth commissions." Recognizing these commissions as a separate category corrects for biases arising from conceptual stretching and enables a deeper understanding of the conditions under which truth commission projects fail to publicize their findings and recommendations. Thus, studies of truth commission impact should either not include incomplete truth commissions in their accounts or be specific about how they are expected to generate impact on human rights policy, attitudes, and norms.

Third, a truth commission examines a limited number of past events and violations that occurred over a period of time, investigating not only incidents of violence and violations but patterns, causes, and consequences, as well.[10] In other words, it establishes a circumscribed historical record. The remit may be extended to the study of a vast array of human rights violations and structural inequalities (e.g., Peru) or restricted to events and violations that affected the lives of a few hundred individuals (e.g., Paraguay). Likewise, the time period under scrutiny may be as long as forty-five years (e.g., Kenya) or as short as three years (e.g., Haiti).[11] What matters for definitional purposes is that the remit and periodization are stated in the mandate establishing the commission. The bounded character of the investigation separates truth commissions from official and nongovernmental monitoring institutions that investigate ongoing violations.

Fourth, a truth commission enjoys autonomy from direct intervention by political actors. It is possible to confuse presidential or parliamentary investigatory commissions with truth commissions, as truth commissions are also established by presidential (e.g., Argentina and Chile), parliamentary (e.g., Ecuador), or United Nations (e.g., Timor-Leste) mandate. The question of who establishes the commission (or to what political institution it is accountable) is not immediately relevant for determining procedural autonomy. Rather, a truth commission's mark of distinction is that its operation and final report are independent of the authority that establishes it. Mark Freeman is right to point out that truth commission autonomy is analogous to judicial autonomy in that appointment by the state does not undermine the independence of a body as long as it enjoys operational autonomy.[12]

The crucial test for autonomy is whether or not the political decision makers alter the content of the final report, either during or after the commission process. Most truth commissions defend their autonomy in the face of political encroachment. For example, the South African Truth and Reconciliation Commission (TRC) ensured that neither the governing African National Congress nor any other political actor succeeded in revising the content of its final report, despite the fact that many of the findings had delegitimizing consequences for the postapartheid government and the opposition.[13] A contrasting example is the final report of Uruguay's 1985 parliamentary commission of inquiry called the Investigative Commission on the Situation of Disappeared People and Its Causes. A commentator writes: "the final statement of the commission on the disappeared was negotiated between the participating parties," that is to say, between members of the parliament representing different political parties.[14] Thus, the South African commission qualifies as a truth commission, while the Uruguayan one does not. Needless to say, the commissioners and the staff, aware of the political stakes involved, take into account the reactions of powerful actors. In other words, autonomy is not isolation: the criterion of autonomy asks for freedom from *direct* political intervention, but not inattentiveness to the political context.

Truth commission autonomy introduces a caveat that concerns the professional profile and prior political activism of commissioners. Commissions usually try to avoid appearing like partisan bodies, which separates them from bipartisan or multiparty parliamentary commissions, like Uruguay's 1985 Investigative Commission or Germany's 1992 Commission of Inquiry for the Assessment of History and Consequences of the SED Dictatorship. Individual merit (a combination of professional standing and moral impeccability) is emphasized as the fundamental criterion for designating commissioners. Nevertheless, it is important to note that most commissioners come from a background of political activism or public service. Notable exceptions notwithstanding, politicians and bureaucrats usually resign government jobs before taking part in the commission process.[15] In other words, the principles of nonpartisanship and individual merit guide all truth commissions, but in each process the principles are interpreted differently.

Fifth, truth commissions are official in character, in the sense that a state institution or an international organization authorizes the commissioners to undertake the truth-finding task. Nongovernmental fact-finding bodies are not truth commissions. It cannot be denied that efforts to come to terms with the legacy of political violence usually originate with civil society actors, prior to the establishment of official commissions. For example, the meticulous documentation of abuses by human rights groups in Argentina, Chile, Guatemala, and Peru under high-risk conditions laid the groundwork for truth commissions in those countries, while similar civil society projects in other Latin American countries, like Brazil, Uruguay, and Paraguay, contributed to the preservation of historical memory when governments refused to establish official truth commissions. The enormous impact of some civil society initiatives cannot be overemphasized: as the "Never Again" reports in Uruguay and Brazil suggest, nonofficial investigations can substitute for the lack of political initiative in addressing the public demand for the truth concerning human rights violations. In procedural terms, however, civil society investigations are not truth commissions because they lack an official mandate, and their findings do not carry the promise of official endorsement.

Table 1 presents a list of truth commissions. Incomplete truth commissions, as well as parliamentary commissions of inquiry are excluded from this list in light of the criteria explained above. As of late 2014 there were thirty-three national truth commissions that had completed their work, two

Table 1. Complete and Ongoing Truth Commissions

Country	Name of Truth Commission	Years of Operation	Context of Commission[1]
Argentina	National Commission on the Disappearance of Persons	1983–1984	Transitional (democratization)
Uganda	Commission of Inquiry into Violations of Human Rights	1986–1994	Transitional (end of conflict)
Nepal	Commission on Inquiry to Locate the Disappeared Persons During the Panchayat Period	1990–1991	Transitional (democratization)
Chile	National Commission on Truth and Reconciliation	1990–1991	Transitional (democratization)

(continued)

Table 1 (continued)

Country	Name of Truth Commission	Years of Operation	Context of Commission[1]
Chad	Commission of Inquiry into the Crimes and Misappropriations Committed by the Ex-President Habré, His Accomplices, and/or Accessories	1991–1992	Transitional (democratization)
El Salvador	Commission on the Truth for El Salvador	1992–1993	Transitional (end of conflict)
Sri Lanka	Commission of Inquiry into the Involuntary Removal or Disappearance of Persons	1994–1997	Transitional (democratization)
Haiti	National Commission for Truth and Justice	1995–1996	Transitional (democratization)
South Africa	Truth and Reconciliation Commission	1995–1998; 1998–2002	Transitional (democratization)
Guatemala	Commission to Clarify Past Human Rights Violations and Acts of Violence That Have Caused the Guatemalan People to Suffer	1997–1999	Transitional (end of conflict)
Nigeria	Human Rights Violations Investigation Commission	1999–2002	Transitional (democratization)
Uruguay	Commission for Peace	2000–2003	Nontransitional
South Korea	Presidential Truth Commission on Suspicious Deaths of the Republic of Korea	2000–2004	Nontransitional
Panama	Panama Truth Commission	2001–2002	Nontransitional
Peru	Truth and Reconciliation Commission	2001–2003	Transitional (democratization)
Grenada	Truth and Reconciliation Commission	2001–2004	Nontransitional
Ghana	National Reconciliation Commission	2002–2004	Nontransitional

(continued)

Table 1 (continued)

Country	Name of Truth Commission	Years of Operation	Context of Commission[1]
Timor-Leste	Commission for Reception, Truth, and Reconciliation	2002–2005	Transitional (end of conflict)
Sierra Leone	Truth and Reconciliation Commission	2002–2004	Transitional (end of conflict)
Chile	National Commission on Political Imprisonment and Torture	2003–2004	Nontransitional
Morocco	Equity and Reconciliation Commission	2004–2006	Nontransitional
Paraguay	Truth and Justice Commission	2004–2008	Nontransitional
Indonesia and Timor-Leste	Commission for Truth and Friendship	2005–2008	Nontransitional
South Korea 2005	Truth and Reconciliation Commission, Republic of Korea	2005–2010	Nontransitional
Colombia	Historical Memory Group	2005–2013	Nontransitional
Liberia	Truth and Reconciliation Commission	2006–2009	Transitional (end of conflict)
Ecuador	Truth Commission	2007–2010	Nontransitional
Mauritius	Truth and Justice Commission	2009–2013	Nontransitional
Solomon Islands	Truth and Reconciliation Commission	2009–2013	Nontransitional
Togo	Truth, Justice, and Reconciliation Commission	2009–2012	Transitional (end of conflict)
Kenya	Truth, Justice, and Reconciliation Commission	2009–2013	Transitional (end of conflict)
Canada	Truth and Reconciliation Commission of Canada	2009–	Nontransitional
Brazil	Truth Commission	2011–	Nontransitional
Thailand	Truth and Reconciliation Commission	2010–2012	Nontransitional
Côte d'Ivoire	Dialogue, Truth, and Reconciliation Commission	2012–2014	Nontransitional

[1] A truth commission is transitional if it is created within one to three years following the transition from authoritarianism to democracy and/or from conflict to peace.

ongoing commissions, and five incomplete commissions that had disbanded without producing a final report. Of the completed commissions, seventeen were established during transitions from authoritarianism to democracy and/or from internal conflict to peace,[16] while sixteen were nontransitional. Both of the ongoing commissions are nontransitional.

Incomplete Truth Commissions

Not all truth commissions succeed in producing a publicly available record of human rights violations. Some commissions fail to publish a final report, and in other cases social and political actors' attempts to establish a truth commission fail in the first place. Failed attempts should not be named "truth commissions" in the interest of sustaining conceptual clarity. Rather, the processes leading up to their failure should be addressed in further research. Those truth commissions that were disbanded before publishing a final report should be called "incomplete truth commissions." The existence of an incomplete commission means that the idea of a truth commission had considerable societal appeal, which had to be acknowledged by decision makers, but that the project fell short of realization for reasons that may shed light on that country's politics around postconflict truth and justice.

Five countries set up panels that could not publicize their findings and recommendations at all. In Bolivia (1982), Ecuador (1996), and the former Yugoslavia (2001), the commissions disbanded before completing their job; in Uganda (1974) and Zimbabwe (1983), the final reports, presented to presidents who had no interest in promoting human rights accountability, did not see the light of day. Below I provide a brief description of how and why these commission attempts were frustrated, in chronological order.

Although many governments that sponsored truth commissions were reluctant to commit to the goals of truth finding and justice, arguably none was as uncommitted to the human rights norm as Idi Amin's regime. The Commission of Inquiry into the Disappearances of People in Uganda Since 25 January 1971 was remarkably bold in its documentation of forced disappearances. The final report (1974) was not made public, and the recommendations were entirely ignored. The chair of the commission, an expatriate Pakistani judge, lost his government job after the commission, while another was sentenced to death over a murder allegation.[17]

Bolivia's 1982 National Commission for Investigation for Forced Disappearances, chaired by the undersecretary of ministry of the interior of the incoming government, brought together members of the human rights community. Forced disappearances that took place between 1964 and 1982 were to be investigated. However, the commission was dissolved before completing its work, and no final report was released.[18]

Robert Mugabe set up the Commission of Inquiry into the Matabeleland Disturbances in 1983 to collect information about the human rights violations that took place when government forces countered the Zimbabwe People's Revolutionary Army in Matabeleland. The commission completed its work, but the final report was not released. Human rights groups (the Catholic Commission for Justice and Peace and the Legal Resources Foundation) released their own report in 1997, called "Breaking the Silence, Building True Peace: A Report on the Disturbances in Matabeleland and the Midlands, 1980–1988." Its recommendations have been ignored to this day.[19]

Ecuador's Truth and Justice Commission managed to collect information about three hundred cases of human rights violations that took place between 1979 and 1996 in the five months of its operation, but the overall political instability of the country took its toll on the commission, which came to an abrupt end. A new truth commission was established in 2007 to complete the work initiated by the disbanded one.[20]

President Vojislav Koštunica established the Yugoslav Truth and Reconciliation Commission in 2001, arguably to offer an alternative to the International Criminal Tribunal for the Former Yugoslavia's narrative of the dissolution of Yugoslavia.[21] Some of the leading figures of the South African TRC (like Alex Boraine) counseled the newly elected Koštunica and the commissioners with advice. Yet, the commission was disbanded one year after its creation, as the political leadership did not succeed in setting a mandate.[22] During the operation of the commission, most members took the task of explaining why Yugoslavia fell apart more seriously than investigating individual violations, as there was little political support for a commission that cared primarily about human rights investigation rather than historical reinterpretation.[23]

In conclusion, failed truth commission attempts teach two valuable lessons. First, a minimal degree of government support is necessary to have any truth commission at all. In all of the cases covered above, politicians were either deeply confused about what a commission was supposed to do (the former Yugoslavia) or were entirely cynical when it came to human rights initiatives (Uganda and Zimbabwe), or political instability eliminated the modest achievements of investigatory bodies (Bolivia and Ecuador). Second, none of these commissions produced any discernible political, social, or judicial impact, which suggests that even if commissions influence politics and society through their *process* as well as *product*,[24] a commission that fails (or is not allowed) to publish its final report produces no process-driven impact. That is in part because the content of a commission's final report matters: politicians and public officials make use of the findings and recommendations for policy reform either willingly or under pressure from civil society actors. Furthermore, the failure to produce a final report probably indicates a faulty commission process in which the commissioners and staff did not work in peace and autonomy for the duration of their investigation.

All in all, these frustrated efforts were forced to fail, but human rights activism around new truth-telling initiatives bore fruits in the form of later truth commissions (Uganda in 1986 and Ecuador in 2007) or nongovernmental truth-finding efforts (Zimbabwe in 1997) in three of these cases.

Unofficial Truth Projects and Frustrated Truth Commission Attempts

The definition of truth commissions provided above distinguishes between NGO truth-finding efforts and officially mandated truth commissions. Instead of confounding civil society truth-finding efforts with truth commissions or ignoring them altogether, I recommend using Louis Bickford's notion of "unofficial truth projects" to distinguish civil society projects from truth commissions.[25] Such alternative truth projects capture the extent of civil society pressure on governments to establish truth commissions and reveal the discrepancy between the social appeal of the idea of a "truth commission" in a country and the government's incapacity to satisfy that demand.[26] Thus, distinguishing NGO commissions from truth commissions would allow scholars to better appreciate the independent political and social impact of different kinds of truth-finding projects.

Another category of observations concerns cases of frustrated truth commission attempts, when civil society actors lobby for a truth commission, but the government response is negative. In those cases, the absence of a truth commission cannot be attributed to society's unawareness of, or indifference to, the idea. Rather, the frustrated attempt points to the discrepancy between a social demand and its political fulfillment. For example, the Uruguayan civil society pressured the government for the official recognition of a variety of human rights violations through an investigatory body upon return to democracy in 1985. Ultimately the government's refusal to establish a truth commission and the dissatisfaction with the parliamentary commission on disappearance led civil society actors to publish an NGO report on human rights violations that "seem[ed] to mimic truth commissions,"[27] especially the Argentine one. The failure of a similar truth commission attempt in Paraguay in 1989 reveals that the aspiration to establish a truth commission swept through the Southern Cone between the 1983 Argentine National Commission on the Disappeared and the 1990 Chilean National Commission on Truth and Reconciliation, but the official responses tended to be negative. A similar trend is observed in the entire Western Hemisphere in the 2000s, as proposals to establish a truth commission came to naught in Mexico, Venezuela, and the United States.

The categories of incomplete truth commissions and frustrated truth commission attempts point to the need for rigorous case studies to examine the role of truth commissions in world politics as a popular transitional justice mechanism. Exclusive focus on completed truth commissions may understate the demand for truth in countries where no observable truth commission took place. The final product, namely a public report, is the main objective of all truth-finding processes, but the significance of these processes cannot be reduced to the product. The enormous normative appeal and mobilization potential of the truth commission *as an idea* shape the values, interests, and strategies of civil society actors and politicians. Complete, incomplete, and frustrated truth commission projects help transnational activists and local human rights and victims' groups to develop financial, organizational, and intellectual links.

Thus far, the chapter developed a concise definition that treats *truth commission* as a static concept in order to delineate those procedural characteristics that apply to all commissions and used this definition to distinguish truth commissions from similar investigatory mechanisms, as well as from incomplete or frustrated truth commission attempts. The next section pays close attention to the dynamic nature of truth commission practices across the world, analyzing the transformations the concept has undergone since its emergence in the early 1980s.

Transitional and Nontransitional Truth Commissions

Truth commission is a fluid and evolving concept. Politicians, civil society actors, and scholars have come to associate with it a variety of procedures and objectives under changing circumstances. For example, Argentina's 1983 National Commission on the Disappeared, insofar as it sought to complement criminal prosecution with human rights investigation, fashioned itself as a truth-*and*-justice mechanism. This holistic approach to transitional justice slowly gave way in the 1990s to "balancing the ethical imperatives"[28] of justice and political expediency in academic and political circles, thanks to the lobbying effort that took the Chilean National Commission on Truth and Reconciliation as the model. Innovations in techniques and procedures, such as statistical data imputation methods and public hearings, have also transformed the functions of truth commissions in transitional settings.

Three identifiable types of truth commissions have emerged in the context of democratic transitions and peace processes around the globe: first-generation transitional, second-generation transitional, and nontransitional.

The first-generation transitional commissions were established to investigate human rights violations under military dictatorship. The commissions in Argentina, Uganda (1986), Nepal, Chile, and Chad, and the incomplete truth commissions in Uganda (1974), Bolivia, and Zimbabwe fall under this category. Presidential initiative proved critical to the establishment of these commissions, and the preferred legal instrument to set up the mandate was presidential decree. This period in the history of truth commissions was marked by civil society mobilization around alternative unofficial truth projects. The dissatisfaction with the parliamentary commission of inquiry led the Uruguayan civil society group Servicio Paz y Justicia (SERPAJ) to publish the "Uruguay Never Again" report. In Brazil and Paraguay, human rights organizations and the church took the initiative to establish unofficial truth commissions when the government failed to respond to their demands.[29] In other words, the first generation was associated with a relatively high number of frustrated and incomplete truth commissions, as well as unofficial truth projects.

All the first-generation transitional commissions were established within the first year of the democratic transition. It seems that discovering the truth about human rights violations was a pressing need. In that sense, the dynamics of uncertain transitions explain the quandaries of many of these early commissions. Each relevant actor had a particular sense of what truth commissions could and should achieve, and that often led to contradictory expectations. The key problematic was to determine the relationship between the truth commission and criminal proceedings against presumed perpetrators. Democratic governments did have an interest in settling accounts with the outgoing military dictatorship, provided that coming to terms with the past did not jeopardize democratic stability. In short, these commissions were framed as transitional justice tools.

The early truth commissions were characterized by methodological parsimony. The immediacy of establishing the historical record on death and forced disappearance set limits on the investigatory phase. Other serious human rights violations, such as torture, illegal imprisonment, sexual violence, and forced exile, were either not investigated at all or discussed in generic terms. The truth commission processes in the 1980s and early 1990s did not have the performative aspects (public hearings, lengthy victims' testimonies, and televised sessions) associated with many of the later truth commissions, most notably the South African one. Likewise, the potential for rewriting the nation's history was not fully utilized by these early commissions, as explanations of the causes and consequences of political violence did not extend beyond short context chapters. The first-generation transitional truth commissions conceived of truth as factual, rather than historical; the methodology was limited, rather than comprehensive; and the process was technical, rather than performative.

Most second-generation truth commissions, set up between the mid-1990s and 2000s, addressed civil war and internal armed conflict between the government forces and insurgent groups. El Salvador, Sri Lanka, Haiti, South Africa, Guatemala, Nigeria, Peru, Timor-Leste, Sierra Leone, and Liberia established truth commissions to dig deeper into violent pasts in which domestic conflict had continued through several democratic and/or authoritarian regimes. UN-backed peace accords set the scene for some of these commissions (El Salvador, Guatemala, Timor-Leste, Sierra Leone, and Liberia), while in other contexts incoming democratic regimes, often under pressure from international organizations and NGOs, set up commissions in the wake of internal conflict and authoritarianism (Sri Lanka, Haiti, South Africa, Nigeria, and Peru).[30]

The second-generation transitional commissions shared the sense of immediacy with their first-generation counterparts: almost all of them came into existence within one year of transition to peace and/or democracy. Some of these commissions received significant foreign funding, and they invited foreign human rights activists and experts to serve as commissioners or functionaries. Finally, the second generation broadened the scope of investigation beyond death and disappearance to encompass a wide array of violations.

How did the idea of *truth commission* change? The mid-1990s were the critical years during which truth commissions acquired worldwide popularity in policy and intellectual circles. This increased the speed of ideational change. Throughout the 1990s, advocates of the truth commission idea published books, organized conferences, lobbied governments, and trained civil society groups. With the South African experience, truth commissions began to attract global media attention. The irruption of interest in truth commissions meant that the institutional form could be transported across geographies; therefore, the second generation contributed to the transformation of the truth commission from a domestic project to an international, even transnational, one. The ideational change also meant the birth of a genre that attracted an enormous variety of hopes, expectations, grievances, social movements, cultural sensitivities, artistic approaches, and so on.[31]

In the context of Latin America, the differences between the Salvadoran, Guatemalan, and Peruvian commissions exemplify this transformation. El Salvador's 1992 Commission on the Truth fits uneasily between the first and the second generation of transitional truth commissions. As the first internationally directed truth-finding effort, this UN-backed commission initiated the internationalization (and transnationalization) of truth commissions. Much like the Argentine and Chilean predecessors, however, its mandate limited the investigation to the most serious human rights violations only.[32] Like its predecessors, and very much unlike the later commissions, the Salvadoran panel did not seize the opportunity to write a comprehensive historical narrative.

In contrast, Guatemala's 1998 Commission for Historical Clarification and Peru's 2001 Truth and Reconciliation Commission decided to produce comprehensive histories of national tragedy. Both societies confronted the enormous task of explaining the historical and structural roots of political violence, such as intersecting class and ethnic cleavages, which had played out in the perpetuation of inequality, marginalization, and exclusion. Furthermore, the combination of neglect and coercion that marked the relationship between the state and parts of the territory under its sovereign control complicated both truth commissions' work, as the commissioners themselves had difficulty accessing the rural and ethnolinguistically diverse populations that had been devastated during the internal conflict. The commissioners realized that reaching out for victims meant nothing less than bridging the enormous geographical, social, and emotional gaps between the vulnerable populations in the periphery and the cultural-political centers. Despite all the difficulties, they decided to undertake the ambitious project of rewriting the nation's history with an inclusionary gesture toward the vulnerable groups. They embodied the aspirations of many, but not all, second-generation transitional commissions: investigating a broad range of violations, accompanied by lengthy historical narratives analyzing the underlying causes of political violence, and proposing comprehensive recommendations.

A further transformation came in the 2000s: truth commissions were established under consolidated democracies in Uruguay, South Korea, Panama, Grenada, Ghana, Chile, Paraguay, Ecuador, Mauritius, the Solomon Islands, Brazil, and Canada. In Morocco, a commission was created under a monarchical authoritarian regime.[33] Colombia initiated a truth commission-like process in the context of limited demobilization that fell short of a comprehensive peace accord. Indonesia and Timor-Leste created a joint truth commission as part of a larger diplomatic move to strengthen bilateral relations. These nontransitional commissions address a period of human rights violations that had ended more than a decade earlier (with the exception of the joint Indonesian and East Timorese commission, where the time lag between the transition and the commission was six years). In this sense they are retrospective in character, and they signify the transformation of truth commissions from transitional justice tools to post-transitional institutions.

Uruguay, Paraguay, and Brazil produced official accounts of human rights violations after more than a decade of democratic rule, building on civil society truth-finding efforts and earlier official attempts. Panama and Grenada took the first steps toward establishing the historical record about events that had taken place decades ago. In Ghana, change of government (but not regime) in 2001 created the impulse for a commission. Ecuador's 2007 truth commission was meant to replace the commission that was disbanded in 1997. The Chilean National Commission on Political Imprisonment and Torture (2003) reflected the emerging awareness that the 1990 truth commission had not dealt adequately with torture, illegitimate political imprisonment, sexual violence, and the mistreatment of minors. South Korea established two consecutive commissions, expanding the time period under investigation to the entire twentieth century in the latter one. Mauritius began to unearth the legacies of colonialism and slavery through a commission, while Canada tackled abusive and discriminatory schooling policies toward indigenous children. In other words, truth commissions expanded from transitional to nontransitional regimes, from the developing to the developed world, and from investigating a narrow set of violations to a broad range of injustices.

The striking characteristic of the nontransitional commissions is the capacity to reach politically conservative sectors. While the first- and second-generation commissions were mostly established by centrist or center-left presidents, or through peace accords between state forces and guerrillas, the third-generation commissions incorporate a broader spectrum of political actors and ideologies. Leftist and center-left presidents established nontransitional truth commissions in Chile (Ricardo Lagos), Ecuador (Rafael Correa), Brazil (Luiz Inácio Lula da Silva), and Uruguay (Julio María Sanguinetti). In contrast, Panama's truth commission was established by a conservative president (Mireya Moscoso), and the parliament that set up Paraguay's 2004 commission was dominated by the same Colorado Party that had collaborated with the military dictatorship for decades. King Mohammed VI of Morocco established the Moroccan Equity and Reconciliation Commission to investigate the abuses during the reign of his father, Hassan II, without making significant changes on the structure of the regime.

Table 2 presents a list of truth commissions by generation, illustrating the essential characteristics, such as the timing of the commission's creation, the context in which the violations under investigation took place, the remit, and the sponsoring individuals and institutions.

Conclusion

Truth commissions are no passing fashion. Between 2009 and 2012, three countries transitioning from internal conflict (Kenya, Togo, and Côte d'Ivoire), two consolidated democracies (Canada and Brazil), and one country facing regime instability (Thailand) established national truth commissions. The panel in Tunisia was about to begin its work as of late 2014. Many other countries have flirted with the idea of a truth commission recently, although ultimately the decision makers chose not to establish one. As one-party rule came to an end in Mexico, incoming President Vicente Fox promised to establish a truth commission to investigate the 1968 massacre

Table 2. Truth Commissions by Type

First-generation transitional

	Argentina (1983)	Uganda (1986)	Nepal (1990)	Chile (1990)	Chad (1991)
Timing	Within first year of transition	Within first year of transition	Within first year of transition	Within first year of transition	Within first year of transition
Context of violations	Military dictatorship	Military and civilian dictatorships	The Panchayat system	Military dictatorship	Civilian dictatorship
Remit	Forced disappearance	Broad range of violations	Forced disappearance	Extrajudicial killings and forced disappearance	Broad range of violations and other crimes
Sponsor(s)	President Raúl Alfonsín	President Yoweri Museveni	Nepali Congress government	President Patricio Aylwin	President Idriss Déby

Second-generation transitional

	El Salvador (1992)	Sri Lanka (1994)	Haiti (1995)	South Africa (1995)	Guatemala (1997)
Timing	Within first year of transition	Within first year of democratization	Within first year of transition	Within first year of transition	Within first year of transition
Context of violations	Internal conflict	Internal conflict	Military dictatorship	Apartheid	Internal conflict
Remit	Broad range of violations	Involuntary removal and disappearance	Broad range of violations	Broad range of violations	Broad range of violations
Sponsor(s)	Salvadoran government; FMLN (guerrilla organization); United Nations	President Chandrika Bandaranaike Kumaratunga	President Jean-Bertrand Aristide	African National Congress government	Guatemalan government; URNG (guerrilla organization); United Nations

(continued)

Table 2 (continued)

	Nigeria (1999)	Peru (2001)	Timor-Leste (2002)	Sierra Leone (2002)	Liberia (2006)
Timing	Within first year of transition	Within first year of transition	Within first year of international recognition	Within three years of peace accords	Within two years of peace accords
Context of violations	Military dictatorship and civil unrest	Internal conflict and civilian dictatorship	Indonesian occupation, internal conflict	Internal conflict	Internal conflict
Remit	Broad range of violations	Broad range of violations	Broad range of violations	Broad range of violations	Broad range of violations
Sponsor(s)	President Olusegun Obasanjo	Presidents Valentín Paniagua and Alejandro Toledo	UN Transitional Administration in East Timor	Sierra Leone government; RUF (armed insurgency)	Liberian Transitional Legislative Assembly

	Kenya (2009)	Togo (2009)	Côte d'Ivoire (2012)
Timing	Two years after violence	Four years after transition	Two years after transition
Context of violations	Election-related violence	Military dictatorship; civilian dictatorship; limited democracy	Civil war; postelection violence
Remit	Broad range of violations	Politically motivated crimes	Broad range of violations
Sponsor(s)	Parliament	Government	President Alassane Ouattara

Nontransitional

	Uruguay (2000)	South Korea (2000)	Panama (2001)	Grenada (2001)	Ghana (2002)	Chile (2003)
Timing	Fifteen years after transition	Thirteen years after transition	Twelve years after transition	Ten years after period of violence	Nine years after transition	Thirteen years after transition
Context of violations	Military dictatorship	Military dictatorship	Military dictatorships	Revolution, military dictatorship, foreign invasion	Military dictatorships	Military dictatorship
Remit	Forced disappearance	Suspicious deaths	Broad range of violations	Extrajudicial killings	Broad range of violations	Torture and political imprisonment
Sponsor(s)	President Jorge Battle	President Kim Dae-Jung	President Mireya Moscoso	Governor-general Daniel Charles Williams	President John Kufuor	President Ricardo Lagos

	Morocco (2004)	Paraguay (2004)	Indonesia and Timor-Leste (2005)	South Korea (2005)
Timing	Five years after monarchical succession	Fifteen years after transition	Six years after the independence of Timor-Leste	Eighteen years after transition
Context of violations	Monarchical authoritarianism	Military dictatorship	Indonesian occupation, internal conflict	Military dictatorship; foreign occupation
Remit	Forced disappearance and arbitrary detention	Broad range of violations	Broad range of violations	Broad range of violations
Sponsor(s)	King Mohammed VI	Congress (dominated by Colorado Party)	Presidents Yudhoyono (Indonesia) and Ramos-Horta (Timor-Leste)	Parliament

(continued)

Table 2 (continued)

	Colombia (2005)	Ecuador (2007)	Mauritius (2009)	Solomon Islands (2009)	Thailand (2010)
Timing	Ongoing conflict	Nineteen years after end of repressive period	Consolidated democracy	Six years after transition to peace	Democratic succession
Context of violations	Internal conflict under democratic regimes	Democratic regime	Colonial rule	Ethnic violence	Monarchical democracy
Remit	Broad range of violations	Broad range of violations	Slavery and indentured labor under colonialism	"People's traumatic experiences"	Election violence
Sponsor(s)	Government-appointed National Reparation and Reconciliation Commission	President Rafael Correa	National Assembly	Government	Cabinet

Ongoing (as of January 2015)

	Canada (2009)	Brazil (2011)
Timing	Consolidated democracy	Twenty-six years after transition
Context of violations	Democratic regimes	Military dictatorship
Remit	Human rights abuses in the residential school system	Broad range of violations
Sponsor(s)	Government of Canada; Assembly of First Nations	Chamber of Deputies and Senate

of protesting students in the Tlatelolco Square, Mexico City. Soon after, however, he abandoned the idea and instead appointed a special prosecutor for the case.[34] A similar development took place in Venezuela, where parliament pressure to establish a truth commission about the April 2002 coup against Hugo Chávez was overturned by Chávez himself. In the United States, President Barack Obama rejected proposals by Senator Patrick Leahy and Congressman John Conyers to establish a truth commission to investigate crimes under the outgoing Bush administration. Fiji's proposed Reconciliation and Unity Commission was scrapped after the 2006 military coup. In Philippines, President Benigno Aquino's proposal to establish a truth commission in 2010 was overturned by the Supreme Court.[35] Likewise, the Supreme Court of Nepal suspended a truth commission project in 2013.[36] Calls to create a truth commission in Turkey find no response in the context of an ongoing insurgency, although the recent peace negotiations between the government and the Kurdish rebels may change the prospects for truth-finding initiatives. In Iraq and Algeria, the demand from external actors, such as Human Rights Watch, was ignored. In short, politicians and judges are not always convinced about a truth commission's usefulness and convenience. Nonetheless, the idea has such normative appeal that its advocates promote it under a variety of political configurations (transitional democracies as well as established ones, right-wing governments as well as left-wing ones) to investigate many types of violations (crimes against humanity, massacre, torture, sexual violence, coup attempt, assassination, colonialism, and slavery, among others).

Several recent commissions were set up in consolidated democracies (or nontransitioning authoritarian regimes) as a means of coming to terms with the distant, rather than immediate, past. A major implication is that nontransitional commissions should be investigated with conceptual tools that differ from those of the transitional justice paradigm.[37] Understanding the actors' motivations and expectations in crafting a truth commission as a nontransitional or post-transitional tool will be a worthwhile challenge for future journalism and research.

The enormous variety of responsibilities and functions attributed to truth commissions across time and space militates against reaching simplistic judgments on the role truth commissions play in contemporary politics. The following chapters will combine theoretical insights into transitional justice and politics of memory with case studies to understand and explain what it is that truth commissions claim to do and what they do *in fact*.

CHAPTER 2

Speaking Truth to Power? The Politics of Truth Commissions

Chapter 1 identifies autonomy as a key element of what makes a truth-finding panel a *truth commission*. Politicians may establish commissions with self-serving motives, but it is far from obvious that the commissioners share those motives. Commissions are neither state bureaucracies nor pure civil society initiatives. Rather, they come into existence and carry out their tasks through interactions between politicians, bureaucracies, supportive and hostile civil society actors, and the commissioners themselves. This chapter explores these complex state-society dynamics.

First, this chapter identifies the decision points before and during a commission process, and the interactions between the commissioners and the broader political context, to map out the multiple layers of power relations at every stage of a commission's operation. The stakes involved in grassroots human rights activism, the political decision to establish a commission with a specific mandate, and the contestations among the commissioners and the staff have powerful effects on the processes and outcomes of every truth commission. An official mandate sets the commission's goals and appoints commissioners, but once they begin their work, the commissioners and the staff use considerable discretion in deciding the panel's goals, procedures, and findings. Each decision reflects the politics *around* the commission, as well as *within* it.

I then address the question: under what conditions do commissions assume autonomy and agency with respect to the interests and expectations of key political decision makers? Portraying truth commissions as a policy tool that legitimizes the incoming regime, a common tendency among transitional justice scholars, is too simplistic and misses the fact that many commissions have defended their autonomy from political intervention and published findings that surprised and delegitimized the same politicians who had established the commission in the first place. The relation between the political elite and a truth commission is one of elective affinities, rather than instrumentalization.

This discussion is followed by the argument that truth commissions make a bold attempt to insert themselves into state-society relations as mediators. The historical backdrop of massive human rights violations makes such a mediating role possible. Truth commissions tend to be attentive to the struggles for power and legitimacy that take shape between various political and social actors in the context of a regime transition, but their independent agency has to be acknowledged, too. Commissioners' professional and intellectual backgrounds, values, goals, and ideas reveal a lot about the specific ways in which they seek to build bridges between the state and victims, as well as society in general.

Opening the Black Box: The Politics of Truth Commissions

Truth commissions stand out as an institutionalized means of coming to terms with the past. As such, they mediate between political decision makers and vulnerable sectors of the population (in particular the victims of human rights violations), regulate disagreements among political and cultural elites over the violent past, and create a space of contestation at the interstices of grassroots activism and governmental institutions. Therefore, power relations permeate truth commissions. Exploring the interaction of bottom-up and top-down processes is useful in understanding what truth commissions set out to achieve.

My approach is partly inspired by Richard Ned Lebow's framework for the study of institutional memory in the introduction chapter of a coedited volume on the politics of memory in postwar Europe.[1] He maps the study of memory politics onto three levels: individual, collective, and institutional. The individual level is the subject matter of psychology and psychoanalysis, while the study of collective memory falls within the scope of cultural sociology and history. The level of institutional memory, understood as the study of how individual memory can be shaped by political elites, is a proper political science topic. At this level, scholars should challenge the implicit and explicit assumptions that treat social memory like the common heritage of a culturally homogeneous collective and uncover the ways in which relations of power pervade the institutional construction of memory. Lebow suggests that studying the interaction of top-down and bottom-up processes is a fruitful approach, as layers of grassroots organizing and elite involvement shape politically relevant fact-finding and commemorative projects. My approach refines Lebow's general framework by examining the possibility that institutional fact-finding and memory projects, such as truth commissions, take on a life of their own by acting somewhat autonomously from the broader political context. In addition, I show that relations of power operate *on* institutional memory projects, as well as *within* them.

The interplay of power relations takes place at three levels in a truth commission process: (1) civil society activism around a truth commission, (2) the political decision-making process that establishes the commission with a mandate, and (3) the politics within the truth commission.

Civil Society and Truth Commissions

Defined broadly, *civil society* refers to spheres of activity outside the state. What is included in this formulation is of course debatable. Is civil society synonymous with the NGO sector? Are markets part of it? Do illiberal or violent movements count as members of the civic sector? While this book is not primarily about civil society, the importance attributed to civic movements in the literature on human rights (including in this book) makes it necessary to clarify what is understood by *civil society*.

In the context of postconflict truth and justice initiatives, *civil society* refers to the totality of nongovernmental groups organizing around human rights policy, retributive and restorative justice, and the preservation of historical memory. NGOs are the most visible elements of civil society, but it should be acknowledged that some of the most influential social movements originate from less organized citizens' initiatives, like victims' groups. Furthermore, there is nothing intrinsically pro-rights about civil society: it is impossible to understand why and how a country's justice and truth initiatives are created, amended, and disbanded without taking into consideration the individual and organizational actors with a hostile attitude toward such initiatives. Even though civil society groups that matter for truth commissions tend to be domestic and international human rights organizations and associations of victims and victims' relatives, the human rights sector is not the exclusive agent of civil society mobilization. Throughout this book *civil society mobilization* refers to organized action in favor of a truth commission's findings and recommendations, since this is the dominant form of activism concerning truth-finding initiatives, but mobilization against a truth commission is also taken into consideration.

Civil society actors' contributions to truth finding, justice, reconciliation, and the preservation of historical memory should be assessed rather than assumed.[2] Without grassroots interest in confronting the past, truth commissions simply would not have existed.[3] Victim-survivors, victims' relatives, and human rights activists have pioneered efforts to create truth commissions for the investigation, official acknowledgment, and dissemination of the facts about violations.[4] They valorize the right to truth about violations both for its own sake and as the first step toward criminal justice and reparations. The truth commission idea provides a platform for cooperation across diverse human rights initiatives. Many commissions, and especially the later ones, came into existence as a result of network-building encounters such as seminars, training programs, and demonstrations that brought together domestic and international civil society actors and members of previous commissions. For example, advice from the members of the Chilean commission was influential in shaping South Africa's transitional justice agenda in the mid-1990s; later, some of the South African commissioners and civil society activists became the chief promoters of truth commissions and other transitional justice initiatives elsewhere in the world, especially through their participation in the creation of the International Center for Transitional Justice in 2001.

Once established, a truth commission presents opportunities for domestic and international human rights groups to work together. Collaboration across various NGOs involves the interchange of information, ideas, knowhow, and funds. Human rights activists based at the national and provincial centers seek effective and innovative ways to reach out for victims' relatives and victim-survivors. The effect of mobilization outlives the commission itself when human rights organizations monitor the country's human rights situation in light of the commission's findings and recommendations, scholars and activists conduct studies to evaluate the commission's achievements and shortcomings, and the networks established during the commission process are maintained. In some cases, human rights organizations espouse the truth commission's message to such an extent that they celebrate the day on which the commission's final report came out (e.g., Peru) as a platform for raising awareness about the country's human rights record. In short, truth commission processes can generate synergies for human rights activism beyond the duration of the commission itself.

Finally, the societal reception of a commission's findings depends as much on the government as grassroots publicity campaigns. If a commission fails to publish a final report, or the final report fails to satisfy civil society actors, unofficial truth projects may substitute for the failed official effort. Furthermore, truth commissions emerge, advance and produce results in those countries where victims' associations, as well as the domestic and international human rights organizations, pressure the political decision makers successfully with their demands for historical truth.

The interactions between international NGOs, their national counterparts, and people without NGO affiliation may be mutually supportive, but the potential for conflict should not be ignored.[5] The exchange of funds, information, and know-how is often based on unequal power relations. The perceptions, policy priorities, and budgetary concerns of international NGOs may frustrate the expectations of their local partners. International organizations and NGOs are often criticized for having short time horizons, limited engagement with local actors, and one-size-fits-all policy suggestions.

The problematization of international NGOs should not be understood as embracing the "local" uncritically. The grassroots level is not free from power relations. International organizations and NGOs seek domestic partners for their human rights campaigns. Victims' experiences, memories, and demands pass through leading individual and organizational actors. Therefore, domestic human rights activists compete with one another over clientele, funds, and recognition. Competition introduces leadership positions for those individuals and organizations that enjoy privileged access to resources (time, funds, governmental protection, and so on). At the individual level, "norm entrepreneurs"[6] pioneer in the mobilization of grievances around memory, truth, and justice, devising strategies to bring those grievances to public attention. In those regions where historical exclusion and marginalization have deprived indigenous populations of access to the country's resources, such basic capacities as literacy set an individual apart from his or her fellow citizens as a community leader.

At the organizational level, the concentration of skills, expertise, and resources in particular NGOs generates a differentiation between more and less powerful actors within the broad human rights coalition. Access to local information is crucial, as are connections with governmental, intergovernmental, and nongovernmental institutions, to acquire and maintain leadership at the grassroots level. Ultimately, only those NGOs that are recognized by governmental and/or international actors as leaders succeed in sitting at the negotiation table to establish a truth commission and have the opportunity to push their agenda in an official truth-telling project. Furthermore, the politics of local civil society is not merely a competition over funds and recognition; local groups have serious disagreements about what truth, justice, and reconciliation entail. For example, faith-based initiatives that emphasize reconciliation and social healing might run up against international NGOs' (and many victims') insistence on the criminal accountability norm.[7] In conclusion, even those civil society groups that may agree on a similar set of substantive goals compete as much as collaborate during and after a truth commission process.

The Politics of the Decision to Establish a Truth Commission

Once the civil society pressures succeed in forcing the government to commit itself to creating a truth commission, a number of decision makers participate in issuing a mandate that delineates the basic tasks and the organizational structure of the commission. The political decision-making process creates the truth commission, designates some or all the commissioners and the staff, and sets the rules on how much discretionary power to grant the commission.[8] In most countries the government establishes the mandate, but parliaments, high courts, or international organizations (such as the United Nations) have also sponsored truth commissions. Civil society groups may or may not find the opportunity to voice their interests and values in the initial negotiation process establishing the truth commission. Opposition parties, insurgent groups, the military, and courts often participate in the process, if not as decision makers, at least as key veto players. The inclusivity of the commission creation process is the key determinant of truth commission impact, dictating to a great extent the goals, composition, and procedures of a truth commission.

The commission mandate settles organizational and logistical issues, such as the duration of the commission and sources of funding. More important, those who establish the mandate make key political decisions, such as the determination of the commission's *goals*, specification of the crimes and violations under investigation (the *remit*), the *periodization* of political violence and violations, and the delimitation of the commission's *judicial powers* (to subpoena, to name perpetrators, and so on). At times, the mandate even sets limits on the nature of the truth commission's historical narrative, for example, when it prohibits the commission from passing judgment on certain historical events and periods—a topic examined in detail in Chapter 3. It is also possible that the political mandate leaves many of the logistical and substantive issues to be decided by the commissioners themselves. Finally, the decision makers decide on the *composition* by appointing the commissioners. Combined, the mandate and composition decisions determine the extent to which, and the specific ways in which, a truth commission exercises agency in discovering facts and narrativizing the violent past.

Typically, the establishing mandate specifies a set of violations to be examined by the truth commission. In some cases only one category of serious human rights violations, such as forced disappearance, is investigated (e.g., Argentina). In other cases a small set of violations, such as forced disappearance, cases of torture resulting in death, and attacks on state agents by the armed opposition, is under scrutiny (e.g., Chile). Yet other truth commissions, typically the later ones, are mandated to study a wide array of violations (e.g., Peru). Sometimes the limitations of a truth commission's mandate create discontent among the victims and human rights organizations, who expect a more comprehensive investigation of the full horrors of an outgoing regime. For example, the exclusion of torture and exile from the mandate of Chile's 1990 National Commission on Truth and Reconciliation was seen as a serious shortcoming by human rights activists and motivated them to address torture and exile in subsequent official and unofficial truth projects. The decision to include a wide range of violations in the mandate is certainly in line with the quest for a comprehensive notion of truth, but it requires a longer duration for the commission, as well as more resources.

Delimiting the period of investigation is another political constraint on the truth commission. Periodization serves to bracket political violence and human rights violations on both ends. The left-hand bracket punctures linear temporal progression by separating the pre-violence political community from one that is torn apart by the multiple effects of violence, failure of state institutions, and the loss of shared cultural and political meanings. The right-hand bracket marks the beginning of a presumed return to post-violence normality in which the promise of national reconstruction lies ahead. As such, periodization affects not only which crimes are covered by the commission's mandate but also the kind of historical narrative that can be produced.

The limits on periodization almost always create controversy. If the human rights violations took place at a massive scale under a military dictatorship or military-backed civilian government, as in the Southern Cone throughout the Cold War, the mandate asks the commission to examine precisely the period of undemocratic rule. In Chile, the objection to the truth commission's periodization came from the defenders of Augusto Pinochet's regime, who asked for the investigation of the acts of political violence before the military coup of 1973. In cases of civil conflict, it may be difficult to determine when the hostilities began, and, equally important, the assumption that the conflict did in fact come to an end might be unrealistic. The ideologically motivated Shining Path insurgency was defeated by the Peruvian state in 1992, but breakaway factions reorganized themselves as a narcotraffic network, and incidents of violence have continued to the present day. Yet, the truth commission set the limit for its investigation at 2000, when Alberto Fujimori's civilian-authoritarian regime collapsed. The issue of setting time limits on violence and violations is even more complicated when a series of democratic governments were involved in the conflict or democratic and authoritarian regimes alternated, as in El Salvador, Nigeria, and Peru. Individual politicians, military and paramilitary leaders, and political parties take part in the periodization debate in an effort to exclude those periods that may bring up unwanted memories and compromise their present reputation and interests.

Political decision makers simultaneously enable and constrain the truth commission in another way: they appoint the commissioners. The social pressure to establish an impartial truth-finding procedure introduces a new set of actors to the political stage. Most commissioners to date were jurists and social workers, but international diplomats (e.g., El Salvador), religious authorities (e.g., South Africa), and social scientists (e.g., Peru) also served on commissions. Truth commissions are defined as much by who composes them as who is left out. The implicit and explicit criteria for exclusion vary across commissions. They may exclude active-duty members of the military or guerrilla organizations. Sometimes victims and victims' relatives are excluded to sidestep accusations of bias (e.g., Chile). Some countries exclude foreigners, even if viable candidates do exist (e.g., Peru), while others designate only nonnational commissioners, arguing that domestic actors introduce bias and security concerns (e.g., El Salvador). Some commissions try to represent the country's ethnocultural diversity (e.g., South Africa and Guatemala), while others choose not to do so (e.g., Peru). Implicit and explicit exclusion practices, insofar as they block direct access to a wide range of experiences, memories, opinions, values, and interests, deeply influence the ways in which a truth commission makes sense of that nation's history of political violence.

The Politics Within the Truth Commission

The fact that a commission is limited by a politically established mandate may invite the criticism that truth commissions appropriate the past in the service of narrow political goals. This instrumentalist critique captures the political limitations of truth commissions but misses the fact that commissions enjoy significant discretion once the mandate sets the basic framework. Commissioners usually appoint the staff, redefine the objectives and tasks, select cases to investigate, imitate and innovate methodological approaches, establish informational networks with civil society organizations, and seek external funding.

The commission process is not devoid of political contestation: commissioners reach consensus on many points, but they also disagree. Truth commissions try hard to fight off direct political pressures, but they certainly take into account the legal, political, and cultural contexts in which they operate. Since commissions do not publish their minutes, our knowledge of debates and disagreements within commissions comes from commissioners' memoirs and public statements. For example, the commissioners and staff in Peru are known to have engaged in long discussions about whether "truth" should be understood as a forensic matter or part of a broader social history of the nation. In South Africa, the question of granting amnesty to the ANC leaders created tensions between the Truth and Reconciliation Commission and the Amnesty Committee that operated under it. When disagreements emerge, some commissions try to find the least common denominator: the Chilean commission, for example, sought unanimity, but keeping in mind that the memories of the military coup of 1973 still divided the nation (and the commissioners), the final report stated that people could "agree to disagree" over such issues. The Peruvian commission tended to agree on most findings, explanations, and recommendations, but one of the members (a retired general) publicized his reservations in a letter to the country's president.

Truth Commissions and Political Legitimation: A Complex Relationship

The political constraints on a truth commission's work bring into question the extent to which commissions serve the political actors who create them. It has been suggested that truth commissions tend to legitimate the incoming regime[9] and the hegemonic socioeconomic order.[10] If powerful political actors create commissions as a means of promoting national reconstruction and unity, how could commissions possibly avoid catering to the interests and expectations of those actors? Why do politicians agree to establish truth commissions if they do not expect that the findings will serve their interests? How can truth commissions produce a historical narrative, which they hope will receive official recognition, without instrumentalizing the past? If they in fact cater to political interests, then why do so many politicians deny their findings and ignore their recommendations for reform?

Throughout this book I claim that the forensic and historical truth produced by truth commissions is not necessarily an instrumental appropriation of the past and that they have surprised and delegitimized political decision makers in many countries. In fact, their autonomy partly explains why societies invented or emulated truth commissions as ad hoc truth-finding bodies in the first place. The raison d'être of a truth commission is to establish an honest and impartial account of past events and reconstruct historical memory where conventional state institutions, such as courts and parliamentary committees, have failed to do so. The commissioners and staff who make up a truth commission are expected not to represent a government, institution, or party position. Instead, the criteria for selection tend to focus on political impartiality, intellectual honesty, and moral uprightness. Ultimately, truth commission findings, narratives, and recommendations do not necessarily advance the interests of power holders. Political exigencies delimit and partially condition what commissions produce, but they cannot determine the final outcome.

Truth commissions frequently surprise and upset politicians, including those who had established the commission in the hope of advancing their political interests. The findings of the South African Truth and Reconciliation

Commission delegitimized not only the representatives of the apartheid regime, but also some politicians within the incoming African National Congress government, so much so that some party members tried to stop the publication of the final report the day before it was submitted to President Mandela. After listening to the summary of the final report's contents, Guatemala's president refused to receive the report from the hands of the commission chair at the delivery ceremony. In Peru and Guatemala, among other cases, the enormously high estimates of the death toll surprised the political class. The publication of the death toll in turn slowed down the incorporation of the commissions' recommendations (including a victim-centered reparations program) into policy in both countries. Furthermore, both commissions pointed to structural racism and socioeconomic inequality at the root of nation building and, consequently, widespread political violence. Thus, the recommendations went beyond institutional reform, encompassing radical changes in social organization and dominant political discourses—clearly not an easy (and for some political sectors, not even desirable) reform plan for respective governments. In Nigeria, where the government expected the underfunded and unsupported commission to produce no effect, observers were surprised by the number of cases covered.

Do truth commissions serve to legitimize the incoming government? Yes and no. The commissioners' interests, goals, and ideologies may match those of political decision makers, but they may just as well be in conflict. If and when a truth commission legitimizes the incoming democratic regime, the mechanism that ensures the convergence between the interests of the incoming political elite and the truth commission should be analyzed in further detail. The relative autonomy of a truth commission from direct political intervention means that the concurrence of the truth commission with the incoming regime is explained by elective affinities,[11] rather than crude instrumental appropriation.[12] In other words, the core values informing a commission's work may (or may not) be conducive to the legitimation of the political order.

Truth commissions tend to concur with the incoming political elite in that the prevention of violence is essential for social peace and political stability. Ideally, a commission provides citizens with the assurance that the political community is being reconstructed through the exclusion of violence and the affirmation of the rule of law. In a way, a truth commission "exorcises" terror[13] in line with the aspirations of the incoming regime to establish a stable and peaceful polity. Furthermore, incoming governments invoke the normative discourses of democracy, political liberalism, the rule of law, and human rights to distinguish the new political order from the preceding one and to muster support from domestic and international audiences. Insofar as truth commissions develop historical narratives and propose recommendations for institutional reform in accordance with such normative aspirations, the commission agenda may serve to legitimize the new regime. A high degree of control exercised by key decision makers in establishing the commission makes it likelier that the commission's findings and recommendations will satisfy those political actors.

Critics have documented the degree of concurrence between truth commission narratives and the legitimation discourses of incoming political elites. Historian Greg Grandin analyzes truth commissions in Argentina, Chile, and Guatemala to develop a general critique of their achievements and limitations. He notes that truth commissions tend to promote a particular political project: "state-sanctioned investigations into past episodes of political terror were one part of this transition's agenda to cultivate a notion of liberal citizenship that viewed the state not as a potential executor of social justice but as an arbiter of legal disputes and protector of individual rights."[14] The affirmation of liberal constitutionalism through the memories of political violence is in fact an exercise in forgetfulness, as socialist and social democratic visions of building a just and democratic society, a viable alternative to the liberal democratic project, are left to oblivion.[15]

Grandin criticizes the depoliticization of history by truth commissions: "In most truth commissions, history was not presented as a network of causal social and cultural relations but rather as a dark backdrop on which to contrast the light of tolerance and self-restraint."[16] History as a source of critique and radical transformation is abandoned in favor of a "parable" that affirms liberal principles of tolerance and elimination of illegitimate violence. Moreover, Grandin notes that societies have not moved far beyond the nationalist genre of historical narrative: "truth commissions serve as modern-day instruments in the creation of nationalism and embody what Benedict Anderson describes as nationalism's enabling paradox: the need to forget acts of violence central to state formation that can never be forgotten."[17]

Grandin's critique of truth commissions captures the political stakes of writing history in early transitions. I agree that the Argentine and Chilean truth commissions served to highlight the merits of a liberal notion of democracy in a way that discouraged the pursuit of socioeconomic and political transformations in the name of social justice. My research in Chile reveals that the truth commission narrativized political violence as the product of political radicalism and ideological polarization, ignoring the deeper economic and historical reasons behind political conflict. However, as Grandin himself is careful to note in the example of Guatemala's Commission for Historical Clarification, not all truth commissions have adopted historical narratives that affirm democratic capitalism uncritically. In fact, human rights activists and social scientists participated as commissioners to analyze the history of structural marginalization and exclusion of indigenous populations in Peru and the violent origins of state building in Guatemala. Consequently, the political class expressed dissatisfaction with these highly critical accounts.

In other words, the mutually reinforcing relationship between truth commission narratives and the incoming regime should not be taken for granted. New governments sometimes criticize the findings and historical explanations of a truth commission that they set up themselves (e.g., South Africa) or reject the validity of a commission altogether (e.g., Guatemala). The affirmation of the principles of the rule of law, political liberalism, and the human rights norm may serve to legitimize the new regime, but these principles also set a standard against which to evaluate a government's human rights policy. Domestic and international NGOs have been publishing reports to evaluate the national government's compliance with the truth commission's recommendations in some countries (e.g., Sri Lanka and Peru); successive governments' failure to live up to those standards undermines the initial legitimacy drawn from the self-declared willingness for reform.

Sometimes the legitimizing discourses of the incoming regime are reappropriated by a truth commission to propose an alternative national reconstruction project. The Guatemalan commission, for example, takes advantage of politicians' constant references to democracy and national unity to advance an alternative vision for the country. The peace accord between the government and the guerrillas makes reference to broad and relatively uncontroversial political aspirations such as "peace and national harmony," "observance of human rights," and democracy. The commission redefines these goals in a way that does not necessarily follow the logic of the political mandate that established it. The prologue of the commission's final report reads: "Knowing the truth of what happened will make it easier to achieve national reconciliation, so that in the future Guatemalans may live in an authentic democracy, without forgetting that the rule of justice as the means for creating a new State has been and remains the general objective of all."[18] The stated goal is not merely democracy, but *authentic* democracy, for the attainment of which justice is deemed crucial. Likewise, the report resignifies the notion of national unity, which had been used to justify the exclusion and eventual decimation of the indigenous peoples for decades, if not centuries: "To bring about a reconstruction of Guatemala's social fabric, based on lasting peace and reconciliation, it is vital to foster an authentic sense of national unity among the diversity of peoples that make up the nation."[19] Authenticity is not defined clearly, but the language of the report suggests that the affirmation of diversity is the first step for building an authentically unified nation, one that is presented in contrast to an earlier model of nation building that equated unity with the suppression, stigmatization, and criminalization of ethnolinguistic and cultural differences.

To sum up: commissions sometimes legitimate the incoming regime by employing a liberal democratic discourse of nonviolence and tolerance. However, many truth commissions are not simple tools of political legitimation, thanks to their critical and autonomous character. Some commissions have severely criticized, to the point of delegitimizing, outgoing as well as incoming political elites and set alternative normative standards to reconfigure transitional politics thanks to their attentiveness to emerging global human rights sensitivities. In other words, the normative import of truth commissions goes beyond regime legitimation.[20] Given their capacity to surprise and upset their political sponsors, the legitimation offered by truth commissions should be examined contextually and within the framework of elective affinities between the commission and the incoming elites rather than simple instrumentalization.

Bridging the Gap? The Agency of Truth Commission Members

The prominence of truth commissions in contemporary transitional politics highlights the agency of commissioners and the staff. Who are they? What kind of an ethical and political function do they fulfill at the margins of state institutions? Do they represent the state? Why do societies bestow upon them critical postconflict tasks? It is impossible to schematize the commissioners as a monolithic whole because there is enormous variation with respect to the professional, ideological, gender, national, and ethnolinguistic composition of truth commissions. Ideally, professional and moral standing is the primary criterion for the selection of commissioners. Their designation does not conform to the procedures of electoral politics because unlike the executive and legislative branches, commissioners are not elected officials, nor are they selected on the basis of partisan commitments. They are not bureaucrats in the strict sense, either, since they are appointed for a temporary (and often pro bono) job with a vague set of tasks and objectives.

As they are not elected politicians, the commissioners cannot claim to represent the demands of constituencies. Rather, they assume the responsibility to bridge between the state and the victims. Truth commissions have emerged and acquired such popularity in part because conventional mechanisms of human rights investigation and provision of justice (chief among them, judicial institutions) had failed to meet the demands of post-violence reconstruction. Truth commissions foster a victim-focused approach, aiming to reintegrate those sectors of the population that have suffered the most from authoritarian rule and internal conflict. They are guided by the notion that the reintegration of victims into society as equal members worthy of recognition, respect, and compensation is the precondition of a peaceful and functional society. Moreover, commissions often encourage the state and larger society to acknowledge violations, recognize the victimhood of fellow citizens, ask for forgiveness, and provide recompense through mechanisms of material and symbolic reparation.[21]

An additional task of truth commissions—a crucial yet ignored dimension—is to mediate between (some sectors of) society and the state, and not just between victims and perpetrators.[22] The state needs to reassert itself as an impartial and disinterested arbiter of social and political conflict after a period of violence during which representatives of the state had violated citizens' fundamental rights and/or failed to protect these rights against attacks by armed groups. An important sector of society, including the victim-survivors, victims' relatives, and some opposition groups, cannot easily restore their trust in state officials and institutions (even if there was any trust to begin with). Years of conflict have seen not only the violation of fundamental rights at the hands of the coercive apparatus of the state but also basic protection mechanisms like habeas corpus rights have been systematically ignored by courts. Lawmakers and enforcement agencies have often actively aggravated the violations. Furthermore, in many countries the need to restore trust and legitimacy goes beyond undoing the harm caused by the most recent wave of violence: vulnerability, exclusion, and violence have characterized state-society relations in the form of repression of political dissent, practices of expropriation and coercion, and systematic neglect of social demands for centuries.

Truth commission members insert themselves as mediators between state and society against such a historical backdrop. During the individual and public testimonial procedures of the Peruvian Truth and Reconciliation Commission, for example, the commissioners always put a Peruvian flag on the table around which they met the victims. The staging of the testimonial process sought to reassert state sovereignty in parallel to the recognition of the deponents' victimhood. It has been suggested that the citizenship of victims is constituted performatively through truth telling in commissions.[23] The commissioners act as agents of an economy of mutual recognition in which society as a whole is expected to reaffirm the state as the sovereign political power through the good offices of the truth commission, while the state is expected to recognize and redress the vulnerability and victimization of social sectors in return. The presumed truthfulness, accuracy, and goodwill of a truth commission thus entitles it to an elevated ethical status that, albeit temporarily, subjects the state to a mediation process. The mutual recognition is accentuated if the state heeds the truth commission's recommendations and puts into operation restorative and retributive justice mechanisms, which would presumably serve to imagine the state as an arbiter of social and political conflict again.

The bridging of the past with the future, individual suffering with national reconstruction, and the state with society generates tensions. Truth commissions are typically established as victim-oriented mechanisms to achieve acknowledgment, social peace, and some kind of reconciliation. However, the tasks of producing a truthful account of the past, promoting the recognition of victimhood, and forging social peace and reconciliation might be at odds with one another. Victims do not simply forgive and forget for the sake of enabling dialogue with perpetrators. Presumed perpetrators do not necessarily agree with the categorization of victims and victimizers, and even when they do, they tend to portray themselves as the actual victims of the violent process.[24] The quest for bridging the emotional and informational gap between the state and victims forces the truth commissioners to take a stance in favor of victims, while the task of adjudicating on historical memory pushes them to avoid taking sides. Truth, justice, and reconciliation may not be mutually reinforcing objectives. This accentuates the polyvalent, if not outright contradictory, character of the mediating role assumed by commissioners.

The professional profile, socioeconomic and cultural background, and political views of commissioners shape the commission's goals, findings, historical narratives, and recommendations. Chile's 1990 National Commission on Truth and Reconciliation was staffed by human rights lawyers who opposed Pinochet's regime and high-profile individuals with links to that regime, and the commission reflected this political balance. Peru's 2001 Truth and Reconciliation Commission was the brainchild of left-leaning urban intellectuals whose striving to understand and transform the social reality left its mark on the commission's goals, definitions, findings, narratives, and recommendations (see Chapter 5 for a detailed analysis of the commissions in Chile and Peru). Desmond Tutu's vision of forgiveness shaped the South African Truth and Reconciliation Commission's discourse in general and, arguably, provided philosophical justification for its amnesty program.

Naturally, commissioners' profiles and political connections spark controversy. Some members of Uganda's 1986 Commission of Inquiry into Violations of Human Rights were criticized for their alleged links to incoming President Museveni's regime. The Salvadoran commissioners, by contrast, had no domestic connections, much to the detriment of the commission in many ways. The charge that the commissioners are part of a human rights "elite" that caters to the interests and expectations of international NGOs and their domestic partners rather than the majority of the people they claim to serve has troubled most commissions. Of course, commissioners' connections have implications for the values, interests, and resources they bring to a commission. However, even those commissions that were closely associated with the government, like those in Uganda and Nigeria, or with the NGO sector, like those in Peru and Sierra Leone, have managed to move beyond the narrow confines of their connections by discovering facts that are inconvenient for governments and unleashing forms of civil society activism unforeseen by NGOs.

Conclusion

Critics from different political persuasions have wildly discrepant perceptions of what truth commissions do. A communist conspiracy or an appendage to democratic neoliberalism; a tool of regime legitimation or the big thorn in the government's side; the epitome of the victim-centered approach to transitional justice or an escape valve for perpetrators; and everything in between.

Of course, some interpretations have more truth in them, and some carry the spirit of constructive criticism more than others, but still, how is it possible that these temporary institutions invoke so much passion and controversy?

The answer lies in the multiplicity of interests, incentives, and values that play into institutional mechanisms of coming to terms with the past. Truth commissions have been established as an institutionalized response to the problem of confronting the violent past in divided societies. They have an enormously difficult task to accomplish: to convey individual memories of suffering and trauma to the public within the framework of human rights and generate normative and practical transformations in politics and society. They are constituted as much by bottom-up pressures as by top-down decision making. Interactions at multiple levels simultaneously enable and constrain a truth commission, and power relations and dynamics of political contestation develop within the commission itself.

The view of truth commissions as an uncontroversial alternative to adversarial models of fact-finding and justice, such as the courtroom, is wrong: commissions reflect and seek to transform societal disagreements over past atrocities, which makes their work political and adversarial. They choose among the many possible ways of approaching the past. Their choices are shaped in great part by power relations between major political actors (like the incoming and outgoing governments and armed actors), as well as national and international human rights organizations, victims' groups, social sectors that are unsympathetic to a truth commission, and, of course, the bystanders. Yet, truth commissions cannot be reduced to the broader political context because the political, intellectual, and professional profiles of the commissioners shape a truth commission's perspectives on the past.

Thus, truth commission processes are at once highly structured by the contents of the mandate and the selection of the commissioners *and* open to surprising twists because the mandate can be intentionally or unintentionally vague and because commissioners make a difference with their backgrounds, interests, experiences, worldviews, and skills. All commissions deal with the complex interactions between incoming and outgoing regime forces, state institutions (such as the military and the judiciary), civil society organizations, and the commission members themselves. Almost all of them deviate from narrow political constraints, but some do so more than others. The reason for this variation is explained in Chapters 5 and 6.

CHAPTER 3

One Truth Among Others?
Truth Commissions' Struggle for
Truth and Memory

One of the ways history is not merely professional or
a matter of research is that it undertakes to create a
critically tested, accurate memory as its contribution to
a cognitively and ethically responsible public sphere.
—Dominick LaCapra, *Writing History, Writing Trauma*

Most truth commissions combine human rights investigation with a historical narrative explaining the causes and patterns of violence and violations.
However, their historiographical function has been generally overlooked
by transitional justice scholars, as well as historians.[1] It is understandable
that temporary panels established primarily for human rights investigation, rather than the publication of professional historiography, fail to
draw attention to their engagement with the past. In addition, not all truth
commissions complement forensic investigation with a historical narrative.
Nonetheless, many truth commissions do take part in academic and nonacademic controversies over the causes, patterns, and consequences of political violence: "The historical narrative written by a truth commission
constitutes an important foundational text inserted in the mosaic of cultural memory. Thus, truth commissions produce a counterweight to other
narratives circulating in public discourse."[2] They make a strong claim in
favor of remembrance and truth as the precondition of individual and social
processes of healing, reconciliation, and peace building. Furthermore, truth

commissions are sponsored by governments and sometimes by the United Nations and international NGOs. In other words, their verdict on history carries the promise of official endorsement. Even though commissions' historical narratives do not enjoy the status of professional historiography, their capacity to shape processes of societal contestation over the meaning of the past suggests that their historiographical function should be taken seriously.

This chapter explores the ways in which truth commissions reconstruct the national past. How do truth commissions combine forensic investigation with a historical narrative about past political violence? What entitles the commissioners and the staff, lacking the credentials of professional historians, to assume the responsibility to write history? In what ways do they participate in the debates over social memory? What are the common narrative strategies that allow truth commissions to interact with existing representations of the past circulating in public discourse?

Truth commissions have emerged in political contexts where societies' conventional mechanisms for investigating serious crimes and writing unbiased accounts of the past (the judiciary and the media, chief among them) had ceased to function. They face the twofold task of discovering forensic facts and forging societal consensus over the meaning of the past. On the one hand, political decision makers grant them, at least ideally, the authority to publicize *the* truth about the nation's past, above and beyond political and societal debates. On the other hand, commissions are firmly embedded in the social struggles over memory and history, which makes the reception of their findings and narratives dependent on larger political and societal processes. They produce one truth among others.

Commissions constantly negotiate the boundaries between legal-forensic and narrative-historical notions of truth to validate their claim to truth (an authoritative account of the past) *and* memory (a shared account of the past). Furthermore, their methodologies, social functions, and forms of public reception force observers to rethink the relationship between history and memory. They take a strong moral, political, and epistemological stance in favor of *truth* against the possibility of denial and relativization, which leads them to consider (individual and social) memory and history to be deeply intertwined. It is through their moral interest in history that truth commissions seek to overcome the positivist separation of the strong truth claim attributed to history and collectively shared meanings attributed to social memory.

Truth commissions are at once socially embedded and transformative. They are embedded in the sense that they draw their factual and discursive sources from the existing field of social memory: they use prior human rights documentation and forensic investigation, as well as narratives and memory tropes circulating in the public. Their transformative potential comes from their self-declared objective to move beyond the confines of existing accounts of political violence by publicizing hitherto unacknowledged violations and providing novel explanations for the causes and consequences of violence.

The tension between the social embeddedness of truth commissions and their claim to move beyond social and political cleavages in the name of truth forces the commissioners and the staff to make strategic choices to interpret the past. I identify four such strategies: they might (1) adjudicate between contending positions by confirming or rejecting certain narratives and explanations that hold sway in public debates; (2) avoid contentious issues; (3) claim to give voice to memories and experiences that are systematically excluded from public debates; and (4) transform the public debate by producing narratives and explanations that unsettle the existing accounts of the past.

A specific truth commission may make use of one, some, or all of these strategies. Furthermore, truth commission narratives are produced as much by the exclusions as the written content. I develop an analysis of the silences of truth commissions to better understand the ways in which they reconstruct the past and provide illustrative examples of various commissions' narrative strategies and exclusions.

Writing History in Truth Commissions

A major source of disagreement among historians concerns the epistemological status of the relationship between history and collective memory.[3] Historical positivism finds memory's claim to truth rather weak. It asserts that memory belongs to the domain of fiction and myth, where social, ideological, and aesthetic concerns take precedence over the claim to represent the past truthfully. The relationship between history and memory is one of opposition between fact and fiction, science and myth, "hard" data and anecdotal evidence. Contrasting this position, other historians rightly point to the interdependent nature of this relationship: memory, whether in the form of oral history or written memory stored in archives, is the raw material of history, which in turn informs, and is at times challenged by, collective remembrance.[4] The standard of truth, let alone establishing the epistemological superiority of history over memory, in fact points to the dependence of the former on the latter for its truth claim: "we have no other resource, concerning our reference to the past, except memory itself."[5]

The self-stated objectives of, and expectations from, truth commissions lead them to blur the distinctions between history and memory at every step of their investigatory and historiographical endeavor. They are expected to uphold a high standard of accuracy and truthfulness and simultaneously produce a historical narrative to forge agreement over the meaning of the past among most, if not all, citizens—a shared memory. As I explain below, their double claim to truth and memory is riven by tension.

The primary task of truth commissions is to provide the full picture of human rights violations. Commissioners and the staff collect testimonial data from victims, observers, and occasionally, perpetrators.[6] Although the human rights investigation is not conducted primarily for historiographic purposes, *forensic truth*, which can be defined as the totality of corroborated facts about human rights violations, is not wholly separable from *historical truth*, which incorporates these facts into explanations about conflict onset, patterns of violations, and their consequences.[7] Historical explanation is a crucial step for interpreting the data on violations within a broader context and connecting individual stories of suffering to national tragedy. Furthermore, the claim that confronting past wrongs prevents future conflict, a foundational premise for truth commissions, requires knowledge about the circumstances that made violence and violations possible in the first place. Therefore, truth commissions write context chapters to analyze the proximal causes of conflict onset as well as its deeper roots.

There is considerable variation across truth commissions in terms of how they combine human rights investigation with historical explanation. All truth commissions contribute to the historiography of political violence, at least minimally, by publicizing the facts of human rights violations. Identifying patterns of violations and responsible institutional actors is another historiographical operation that most, if not all, truth commissions undertake. There is greater variation across truth commissions in whether or not they put the atrocities in historical context. Of the twenty-three truth commissions that produced a publicly available final report as of 2014, seventeen have undertaken the task of writing a historical narrative. Among them, some prioritize rigorous forensic investigation over historical narrative, devoting a short chapter (e.g., Chile) or several paragraphs (e.g., Argentina) to situating political violence in context. Others limit the human rights investigation to a number of illustrative cases and pay closer attention to general patterns of violence (e.g., El Salvador). Some truth commissions highlight the outgoing dictator's personal disposition for brutality and corruption as the chief cause of national tragedy (e.g., Chad). Others produce several volumes to make sense of conflict and violence from political-institutional, economic, legal, and sociohistorical perspectives (e.g., Guatemala and Peru). Some explicitly reject the challenge of rewriting the nation's history within the confines of a truth commission (e.g., El Salvador), while others embrace it fullheartedly (e.g., Guatemala). Some commissions declare themselves unfit to pass moral and political judgment on particularly divisive and controversial historical events (e.g., Chile), while others consciously tackle the sources of bitter divisions in social memory (e.g., Peru). In short, there is no common historiographical approach across truth commissions.

Moral and political considerations shape the ways in which truth commissions make strategic decisions about the relative weight and interconnectedness of forensic investigation and historical narrative. Forensic data are costly and difficult to obtain; yet publicizing the facts of forced disappearance, massacre, torture, sexual violence, and forced recruitment evokes the public's indignation against perpetrators and makes it difficult for the latter to question the commission's legitimacy.[8] Focusing on forensic data, therefore, boosts the moral standing and political legitimacy of the truth commission in a way that historical explanation, typically considered a matter of opinion, cannot. However, overreliance on forensic data may have alienating effects for victims, who want the public to understand why they were targeted. The choice of not contextualizing political violence or assigning individual and/or institutional responsibility for violations reduces forensic data to a set of isolated and incomplete truths,[9] devoid of logical connection and meaning. A commission misses the opportunity to convey the message that policies designed to promote civic and political repair should address the root causes of political violence. At the extreme, the failure to respond to the questions that matter to society about political violence and violations may drive a truth commission to irrelevance. Therefore, most truth commissions, even the most forensically oriented ones, provide at least minimal historical explanation.

The claim to truth carries enormous political and moral weight.[10] Deponents (especially surviving victims and victims' relatives, but sometimes perpetrators and bystanders, as well) want the commissioners and larger society to treat their memories as reflecting *the* sad truth, *the* real experience of violence. They do not regard testimony as an idiosyncratic account of episodes straddling fact and fiction. Rather, the testimonial process is an act of witnessing and truth telling that links individual suffering to political repression and social breakdown. The timing and staging of the truth commission at the moment of political transition and reconstruction accentuates the moral and political character of truth commission narratives.

The demand for truth forces commissioners and the staff to take on the role of historians and social scientists,[11] but truth commission reports are addressed to the general public, rather than to the academic community. The public judges their historical narratives less on the merit of scholarship than on the basis of perceptions of their truthfulness, accuracy, and usefulness for a number of social and political ends. As the societal reception of a commission's findings, narratives, and recommendations involves the text of the final report as well as performative and commemorative practices, the commission's role in guiding public discussion goes well beyond the text: "The work of truth commissions is memory work, the creation of collective history and national memory."[12]

The twofold claim to truth and social memory places truth commissions in an ambiguous position. Ideally, societies bestow upon them the authority to tell the truth, even if temporarily. Yet their social embeddedness means that the same processes of societal contestation over historical memory, which truth commissions purportedly mediate and even suspend in the name of overcoming biases arising from social divisions and political interests, deliver the ultimate judgment on their authority. Powerful political and military actors may impede truth-finding efforts to protect their personal reputation or uphold political stability founded upon social amnesia. Likewise, many citizens who did not participate in committing violations may mistrust human rights defenders, victims, and the commission staff for various reasons. Thus, they may see a truth commission's narrative as one historical interpretation among others, enjoying no special authority to interpret the nation's past. The tension between a commission's authority to produce *the* truth, beyond and above the social and political circumstances that paralyze other institutions charged with the task of truth finding (chief among them, the judiciary and the media), and its social reception as *one* claim to truth among others, motivates the question: under what conditions do truth commissions overcome, mediate, suspend, initiate, or conclude societal conflicts over the meaning of the past?

Truth commissions are best understood as privileged participants in social struggles over memory, or what Eviatar Zerubavel famously calls "mnemonic battles,"[13] that is to say, processes of social contestation over the veracity and moral-political significance of various reconstructions of the past. Even though the commissioners and the staff share with historians, journalists, prosecutors, and social scientists the quest for truth, their authority on truth is somewhat different. Truth commissions' legitimacy is found in the interstices of procedural authority (truth is an effect of the procedures that bring it into being), and personal authority (the truth value of a narrative is shaped by the moral and social standing of the narrator), the latter highlighting the impartiality and moral impeccability of the commissioners. Oftentimes truth commissions complement these two notions of legitimacy with a third principle: the orientation toward witnesses, especially victims, as the sufferers and narrators of personal and national tragedy.[14]

Commissions' ad hoc authority on forensic and historical truth and their embeddedness in social struggles over the meaning of the past result in a constant tension. The struggle for social memory typically precedes the truth commission process. Periods of political violence result from, and reproduce, irreconcilable interests and values, contending social demands, and rival social memories. The presence of alternative memory narratives and "frameworks of memory"[15] simultaneously enable and constrain a commission's construction of historical truth. Insofar as the interpretive frameworks, anecdotes, patterns, causal explanations, and memory tropes employed by a truth commission originate in the process of social interaction, the field of social memory enables the commission. However, the social embeddedness of the truth commissions is also a constraint because the commissioners and staff cannot step outside the hermeneutics of social interaction to produce a completely independent narrative.

Truth commissions operate in the already existing field of social memory, yet their involvement may alter the field itself. While the social embeddedness of truth commissions creates a strong tendency toward conformity with existing representations of the past in scholarship and social memory narratives, truth commissions' capacity to transcend taken-for-granted meaning frameworks should be acknowledged. The raison d'être of truth commissions is to uncover facts and provide new perspectives on national history.[16] Their sponsors (politicians, civil society groups, and international agencies) assume, implicitly or explicitly, that before the intervention of truth commissions, the social contestation around the past had been impaired by incomplete information, the presence of actors too biased to acknowledge the complete truth, and the absence of procedures and institutions to generate agreement over the facts as a precondition of public deliberation. Therefore, many truth commissions have incentives to redefine the terms of the debate to challenge the ongoing reconstructions of the past circulating in the public sphere.

As is often witnessed during political transitions, the perpetrators and beneficiaries of violations prefer to live on as though past crimes did not matter. Likewise, bystanders might choose to turn the page on history in the name of political stability or a narrow notion of social reconciliation.[17] Many victims are no longer alive and victim-survivors are likely to face social exclusion. Under those circumstances, truth commissions rupture the forced normalization of social and political life by advocating a process of coming to terms with the violent and divisive past as a precondition of recovering a shared, uncoerced public space.

The need to rupture the operation of the existing field of memory requires an external framework of reference, as the existing hegemonic frameworks cannot foster societal agreement without deceit or violence.[18] Truth commissions problematize the past in ways that may upset some sectors of the population, especially the presumed perpetrators and a significant portion of uninvolved bystanders, although one important measure of truth commission success is the ability to persuade precisely those potentially hostile sectors. To overcome the forced silencing of alternative memory narratives, commissions endow victim-survivors and victims' relatives with a historically unprecedented role in making meaning of the past. Yet, their empathetic engagement does not translate into full identification with the victims, as truth commission narratives often diverge from victims' own explanations of causes and consequences, thereby failing to fully satisfy victims' expectations.[19] Thus, commissions risk alienating all concerned actors while trying to satisfy them all.

In other words, the simultaneous processes of working through existing memory narratives *and* suspending them complicate truth commissions' social function. The authority associated with their claim to truth is transfigured into the need for legitimation through persuasion and agreement over the meaning of the past. Toward that end, truth commissions make strategic choices to produce historical narratives that disrupt existing meaning frameworks without destroying the possibility of mutual understanding altogether and without compromising the claim to truth.

Truth Commissions' Narrative Strategies

Truth commission narratives make strategic interventions into the struggles for social memory, in dialogue (and contestation) with official statements, media coverage, scholarship in history and the social sciences, and the memory narratives of civil society groups, state security institutions, (in some cases) nonstate armed actors, and political parties. Truth commissions take part in the ongoing social debates by employing four main strategies: adjudication, avoidance, the claim to giving voice, and transformation. A truth commission's final report may combine some or all of these positions.

The specific provisions of a commission's mandate set limits on what it can say. Sometimes the commissioners are discouraged from adjudicating politically contentious memory debates (e.g., El Salvador), whereas in other cases they are either explicitly encouraged by the mandate (e.g., Peru) or the silences of the mandate can be interpreted by the commissioners as a window of opportunity for historical interpretation (e.g., Guatemala). Furthermore, a commission's forensic investigation is powerfully shaped by the judicial attributes granted (and more often, not granted) by the mandate. While acknowledging the mandate constraints on commissions, however, I hold that commissioners and the staff exercise considerable agency in their choice of narrative strategies. Many commissions have surprised and even upset the political decision makers who established them as limited fact-finding panels through their shocking findings, comprehensive historical narratives, and recommendations. Therefore, I treat commissions' narrative strategies as semiautonomous decisions made by commissioners and the staff under constraining circumstances.

Adjudication

Part of truth commissions' memory work requires the adjudication of contending social memories. The truthfulness and accuracy of existing historical interpretations are scrutinized, and commissions confirm or disconfirm some or all the elements that make up various reconstructions of the past.

Truth commissions almost always refute the official propaganda circulating under authoritarianism and internal conflict. Guatemala's Commission for Historical Clarification debunked the state's claim that the guerrillas posed a serious threat to the military.[20] Another example comes from Uruguay's Commission for Peace, which found that the majority of the victims did not participate in subversive acts and were killed after the armed insurgency was defeated; therefore, it concluded that the practices of torture and disappearance were not in response to insurgency.[21]

Aside from refuting propaganda, some truth commissions also correct widely held misperceptions. The Peruvian Truth and Reconciliation Commission rejected the widespread belief that the Shining Path was a typical Latin American guerrilla organization using Guevarist methods to achieve its objectives.[22] The social scientists working for the commission explained that the inspiration behind the Shining Path movement came from the Chinese Cultural Revolution, and that the group adopted a totalitarian version of Maoist doctrine, similar to the Pol Pot doctrine in Cambodia[23]—an explanation that confirmed earlier studies on the Shining Path.[24]

The adjudication function is not limited to exposing official lies and misperceptions. Truth commissions incorporate or exclude elements from a rich array of social memories. To the extent that they adjudicate between contending memory narratives, their judgment risks political controversy. Argentina's National Commission on the Disappeared provides contextual background on the pre-coup violence with a single sentence, written by Ernesto Sábato in the prologue: "During the 1970s, Argentina was torn by terror from both the extreme right and the far left."[25] The sentence has sparked such reaction from the relatives of leftist victims that after decades of controversy, it was deleted from the prologue of the 2006 edition of the final report. Chile's National Commission on Truth and Reconciliation intervenes in the public debate over the legacy of the democratic socialist Unidad Popular government (1970–1973) experience that ended with the military coup. Drafted by the conservative historian and commission member Gonzalo Vial,[26] the commission's context chapter sides with the right-wing memory camp that sees decline, crisis, and potential for violence in the socialist experiment. The leftist memories of political mobilization and social transformation are entirely absent from the commission's narrative. Nonetheless, the context chapter refutes the military regime's characterization of the postcoup period as an internal conflict.[27]

Avoidance

Commissions sometimes make the explicit decision not to take sides. Mandate limitations may force the commissioners to avoid judgment. At times, commissioners themselves prefer not to take a stance: the issue at hand may be considered irrelevant to the commission's work; the commissioners may declare themselves unfit to assert their points of view; or the commission may find the issue too controversial to take the risk of making a judgment.

Avoidance should not be understood as the absence of historiography. A truth commission's decision not to intervene into the debates over social memory defines issue areas in which the commission puts no restrictions on the struggle for social memory. Divergent positions enjoy equal legitimacy and truth-value from the commission's perspective. In other words, if commissions are asked to "draw the moral bottom line"[28] by setting limits on what can be said, then the strategy of avoidance identifies those parts of the past for which it sets no moral or political limits on what can be said.

For example, El Salvador's Commission on the Truth (1992–1993), established by the peace accords signed at Chapultepec, Mexico on January 16, 1992, that ended the conflict between the government and the guerrillas, was composed of nonnationals. As a result, the commissioners devoted themselves to documenting abuses, confining historical explanation to several paragraphs. They simply declared the commission uninterested (or unable) to pass judgment on Salvadoran history.[29]

Chile's National Commission on Truth and Reconciliation decided not to comment on the legitimacy of the military coup of 1973 and the accomplishments or failures of the military regime. The final report declares that Chileans can have "legitimate disagreements" on those issues.[30] Presumably, the polarization of the Chilean society around the legacy of the Pinochet dictatorship led the commissioners to take a cautious approach. In fact, the composition of the commission itself reflects the deep divisions over memory: the truth commission was split between centrist or left-leaning human rights advocates and sympathizers of the Pinochet regime. The commissioners sought to ensure consensus within the panel by refraining "from taking a stand on whether the use of force on September 11, 1973, and immediately thereafter was legitimate."[31]

Giving Voice

One of the key claims of truth commissions is to give voice to those experiences and memories that were forced into silence and oblivion. The appeal of truth commissions as tools of transitional justice and the preservation of historical memory owes partly to the fact that postconflict societies face serious obstacles to instituting processes of dialogue free of intimidation, exclusion, and manipulation. The systematic exclusion of persons and social groups from struggles for memory threatens the very truthfulness of publicly circulated narratives. Ideally, commissions take into account the relations of political, cultural, and socioeconomic domination that deny victimized individuals and communities access to state institutions, civil society organizations, the media, and academia. In other words, they seek to transcend the existing field of social memory by granting access and visibility to hitherto silenced individuals and social groups.

Commissions frequently bring into light those voices that otherwise remain excluded from public debates: "those largely in favour of the [South African] TRC, argue that the TRC will heal the wounds of the past through survivors telling their stories to sympathetic individuals who, for the first time, will acknowledge their real pain."[32] Almost every final report has chapters devoted to addressing the needs and grievances of victims. A number of procedures, including confidential testimony-taking sessions and public hearings, are specifically designed to give voice to victim-survivors and victims' relatives.[33]

Commentators note commissions' considerable (if limited) success in promoting official recognition of victimhood by incorporating the narratives of affected persons into national memory.[34] Fiona Ross notes that "individual experiences of suffering were harnessed to the imaginative work of forging a new public imaginary and sociality" in the work of the South African TRC.[35] Elizabeth Lira argues that "the Report of the National Commission of Truth and Reconciliation [in Chile] built a bridge between private suffering and social policies."[36] Based on their observations in Peru, Lisa Laplante and Kimberly Theidon note that, for many victims, the truth commission was the first (and probably only) platform where "they received recognition from a state entity, and were treated with interest and respect."[37]

Parallel to their orientation toward victims, truth commissions offer a platform for perpetrators to come forward to testify. Confessional narratives can be thought of as "giving voice" in a different way: they bring new voices into the public debate by overcoming self-concealment rather than forced silence and exclusion. Even under auspicious circumstances, however, a small number of perpetrators testify before truth commissions. Among those who do, many reproduce self-justifying tropes of heroism and sacrifice, while a few others add elements of confession, repentance, and apology into their narratives, thereby unsettling fixed positions on the struggles for social memory.[38] Despite the prevalence of the reconciliation discourse that emphasizes mutual respect and acknowledgment between victims, perpetrators, and bystanders as a crucial step for forging lasting peace, the majority of individual and institutional actors implicated in past abuses have either kept silent or reacted to commissions' findings and conclusions in angry and dismissive statements. As a result, truth commissions remain a predominantly victim-driven transitional justice mechanism.

Transformation

Truth commissions do not merely address existing memory narratives, causal explanations, and justifications. They sometimes *transform* the public debate by incorporating novel vocabularies, narratives, and explanations. As stated earlier, the transformative potential allows a truth commission to challenge the limitations arising from its social embeddedness.

In what ways do truth commission narratives try to move beyond the constraints intrinsic to the circumstances of their creation? The primary source for the transformative narrative strategy is the moral and legal language of human rights and transitional justice. Definitions and sensitivities regarding the global human rights norm shape, and are in turn shaped by, truth commissions. For example, the incorporation of material and symbolic reparations as a restorative justice mechanism correlates strongly with truth commission recommendations for monetary reparations, health and education benefits for victims, and commemoration measures as symbolic reparation.[39] The consciousness around truth commissions has also resulted in the inclusion of the *right to truth* as a human right that governments and courts are obliged to uphold in customary international law.[40] If *truth, memory,* and *reconciliation* have become so central to postconflict justice and reconstruction efforts in the contemporary period, truth commissions can claim much of the credit.

As truth commissions shape the human rights discourse in various ways, the evolution of the human rights discourse also creates new mentalities and sensitivities that truth commissions attend to. For example, Guatemala's Commission for Historical Clarification has attempted to transform the public debate through its conclusion that the military committed "acts of genocide" against the Mayan population.[41] The final report makes direct reference to the Convention on the Prevention and Punishment of the Crime of Genocide to reach this conclusion. It also assigns responsibility to the Guatemalan state for failing to prosecute the perpetrators of genocide. The commission's assertion that state agents committed "genocidal acts" against indigenous populations reflects the emerging consciousness that many atrocities should be re-conceptualized as genocide or politicide in today's world. The moral force of the word *genocide* accentuates the commission's suggestion that Guatemalans rethink the racist, discriminatory and violent foundations of the political order.[42] This novel moral and legal vocabulary found support among some sectors of the judiciary, too. In 2011, Guatemala's former military ruler Óscar Mejía Victores was indicted on genocide charges, a category of crime not covered by the amnesty law, in great part thanks to this emerging consciousness. Likewise, former president Efraín Ríos Montt was found guilty of genocide in May 2013, but the Constitutional Court annulled the verdict soon after and called for a retrial in 2015.

Another prominent example of truth commissions' attentiveness to emerging global human rights norms has to do with the way different commissions have dealt with sexual violence across time. While earlier truth commissions largely ignored the issue of sexual violence on the grounds that this category of crimes did not fall within their mandate,[43] the worldwide recognition of sexual violence as a distinct category of human rights violations throughout the 1990s led some of the later truth commissions (e.g., South Africa, Guatemala, Peru, and Chile) to address the issue specifically.[44]

For example, Chile's 1990 National Commission on Truth and Reconciliation did not conduct a separate investigation on sexual violence, as the commission's mandate limited the remit of investigation to forced disappearance, extrajudicial killings, and lethal torture. By contrast, the final report of Chile's 2003 Commission on Political Imprisonment and Torture devotes a section to sexual violence and two shorter sections to violence against women and the mistreatment of minors during the military rule. The commission attempts to overcome the silence on sexual violence with a mixture of *transforming* lack of discussion on rape and sexual torture and *giving voice* to the victims.

The Silences of Truth Commission Narratives

The silences of a text should not be considered the absence of narrative; to the contrary, conscious and unconscious exclusions may be as constitutive of historiography as the written text. In fact, the commissioners and the staff adopt specific case selection and analysis methods to conduct forensic investigation, make sense of the data through particular meaning frameworks and vocabularies, and shape historical narratives with their values, worldviews, and interests.[45] Therefore, the final reports necessarily exhibit selective and exclusionary features—with significant variation across truth commissions.

The decision makers who set a truth commission's mandate partly account for historiographical exclusions. Most mandates do not allow the final report to identify perpetrators. Therefore, commissions usually produce something less than the "complete truth," that is, the identification of the criminal act, the harmed individuals, and the perpetrators.[46] Narrow definitions of human rights violations may also bias the reconstruction of the past. For example, the mandate of South Africa's TRC allows the investigation of only those crimes that had been committed with a "political motive." This definition facilitates the recognition of political activists in the resistance movement as victims, but not the sufferers of the everyday functioning of apartheid.[47] Limitations on the remit may likewise create gender bias:[48] a truth commission asked to investigate cases of death and disappearance exclusively is likely to put emphasis on young male victims, which in turn means that women's experiences of suffering and vulnerability (for example, as widows and orphans facing poverty and social exclusion) are written out of history.

Periodization plays an enormous role in shaping the historical narratives, as well. For example, the truth commissions in Chad, Sri Lanka, and Haiti have analyzed only a portion of the acts and patterns of political violence because their mandates imposed firm restrictions on the start date of investigation. Arbitrary cutoff dates inevitably produce truncated histories of violence[49] and trigger the suspicion of intentional bias. Social and political actors dispute a specific periodization because it has implications for which violations are under investigation, which individual and institutional actors are held responsible for the violations, and how the commission will narrativize the past. For example, Nigeria's Human Rights Violations Investigation Commission was initially asked to investigate violations under the previous military governments between 1984 and 1999, which excluded the dictatorial first term of the president-elect Olusegun Obasanjo. Pressure from the human rights community forced the government to extend the periodization.[50]

Mandate constraints notwithstanding, the commissioners and the staff exercise considerable discretion over the content of the historical narrative and, consequently, its exclusions. Their decision often determines whether or not a truth commission will produce a comprehensive and inclusionary historical narrative. For example, the members of Chile's 1990 commission decided to write a short context chapter on the immediate causes of the military coup, overlooking the possibility of explaining the socioeconomic, political-institutional, and cultural factors underlying political conflict. In contrast, Peru's Truth and Reconciliation Commission, bringing together famous social scientists and human rights advocates as commissioners, produced a comprehensive and methodologically pluralistic social history of the country, interconnected by a central narrative and spanning nine volumes.[51]

Some exclusions happen when commissions fail to give voice despite their best intentions to be all-inclusive and empowering, especially toward the victims. Technical difficulties make it impossible to reach all the affected. For example, the Peruvian commission failed to take testimonies in faraway Andean villages. The social climate of fear and mistrust also prevents victims from testifying in those regions recovering from a prolonged period of violence. The lack of resources forced Chad's truth commission to set up its offices in a former secret police detention center, where an important amount of torture and killings had taken place. As a result, many victims did not come forward to testify.[52] Furthermore, relations of social domination may block vulnerable persons' access to a commission, as their social superiors claim the right to speak for them. The Regional Commission in East Timor (2002–2005) could not contact women during the testimonial process because, when the commissioners arrived at villages, male heads of household directed them.[53] Complicating the picture is the fact that commissioners sometimes fail to understand the nature of victimization and to devise strategies to reach out for victims. Early commissions' failure to conceptualize sexual violence as a category of violation distinct from torture is one such example.

This limited capacity to discover and publicize memories of individual suffering has led some commentators to claim that commissioners are better equipped for capturing "macro truth" (patterns of mass violence) than "micro truth" (individual narratives).[54] Nonetheless, most commissions have been criticized for ignoring systemic violence. The South African TRC's lack of engagement with institutionalized racism is a case in point.[55] The tendency to create hierarchies of violations has led most commissions to prioritize civil/political rights at the expense of socioeconomic rights, although the final reports in Guatemala, Peru, Sierra Leone, and Timor-Leste have moved beyond this narrow framework.[56]

Several commentators have criticized truth commissions on the grounds that their historical narratives focus too much on individualized criminal acts, to the exclusion of the mundane operation of violations and injustice. Mahmood Mamdani points out that "from the outset, there was a strong tendency in the [South African] TRC not only to *dehistoricize* and *decontextualize* the story of apartheid but also to individualize the wrongs done by apartheid."[57] Millions of citizens who had suffered from the regime's practices of coerced labor, forced removal, and racial discrimination were excluded from the TRC's broader historical narrative.

Mamdani's criticism sheds light on a greater phenomenon that seems to have afflicted most truth commissions: overemphasis on forensic investigation excludes from historiographical interpretation those cultural, socioeconomic, ethnolinguistic, racialized, and gendered social hierarchies and relations of domination that produce, maintain, and perpetuate inequality, discrimination, and violence. As Mamdani notes, the apartheid system violated "subsistence rights" as much as "bodily integrity rights"; yet the TRC fails to acknowledge this aspect of repression. Similarly, the Southern Cone dictatorships in the 1970s and 1980s committed massive violations of bodily integrity rights in the context of ambitious economic liberalization projects that left significant portions of society under conditions of poverty, unemployment, and vulnerability.[58] However, truth commissions in Argentina, Chile, and Uruguay have not addressed these social and economic factors as either the underlying cause of or motivation for political repression.

Another major source of exclusion for truth commission narratives is their methodological nationalism.[59] The political and symbolic space designated by truth commissions is the nation (and the nation-state). Political violence and human rights violations are defined as a national problem. Therefore, data collection and historical analysis take place primarily at the national level, with the goal of promoting nationwide self-reflection and reconciliation. Methodological nationalism generates serious exclusions. First and foremost, regional and global political factors are rarely taken into account. Even when the forensic investigation points to a high degree of regional cooperation across repressive regimes (e.g., the Southern Cone in the 1970s) and the responsibility of nonnational actors, such as multinational corporations or foreign governments, most commissions do not broaden their factual investigation beyond the national scope. At most, they mention the responsibility of foreign actors in passing.[60]

Some of the silences expose the limits of coming to terms with the past through truth commissions. For all the emphasis on *voice* in today's victim-centered approaches to memory and justice, those affected by large-scale violence use strategic silences in institutional as well as noninstitutional settings to be able to reconstruct their everyday lives.[61] The selectivity of memory narratives sets boundaries on how much "truth" can be recovered through the truth commission testimonies. Furthermore, truth commissions' reliance on written archives to store individual and social memory means that they lose sight of embodied and performative acts of voice and silence. Preserving memory may require witnessing as a living and affective engagement on the part of the listener, which is more than what formal truth-telling measures can offer.[62]

This summary of the shortcomings and exclusions of truth commissions takes the discussion of this chapter back to where it started: truth commissions are established, usually during political transitions, as a mechanism for coming to terms with a violent and divisive past, and as such, they are part of a larger national reconstruction project. As critics of the transitional justice paradigm suggest, the context in which truth commissions produce historical narratives is one of "nation-building and a hegemonic project of state formation."[63] One can argue that the potential for political and discursive violence is lurking at this founding moment of national reconstruction.[64] Various commissions have excluded key events, historical figures, and forms of human suffering from their historical accounts, which raises the suspicion that the project of nation building through remembrance is a contemporary version of Ernest Renan's famous association of willed forgetting and national (re)imagination.

However, it is also crucial to take into account those truth commissions that try to produce the most inclusionary and complex historical narrative possible. Many commissions, even those established for narrow political ends, have surprised and upset their sponsors with their findings, historical explanations, and recommendations—as demonstrated in this chapter. Rather than losing faith in truth commissions altogether, explaining variation across commissions offers a deeper understanding of the conditions under which truth commissions assume a transformative role in reinterpreting the nation's history.

Conclusion

This chapter explores the ways in which truth commissions make sense of the past. Almost all commissions have dealt with the challenges of understanding and narrativizing violent and potentially divisive pasts, although there are differences across commissions in terms of the political and historical circumstances under which they work and the strategies they employ. Historically truth commissions emerged when the social communication over the meaning of the past failed. Some people did not know about the basic facts of human rights violations, either because facts were concealed or because they chose to ignore them. Even when the facts were known, radical disagreement over their meaning threatened mutual understanding. Life-shattering experiences of a significant portion of the citizenry were considered by their compatriots to be minor events—collateral damage of political conflict. The beneficiaries and sufferers of the past simply did not have venues for dialogue and contestation, not least as a result of the asymmetries of power. The politically troubling implications of the breakdown in social communication led decision makers, often under civil society pressure, to intervene indirectly by endowing a temporary body, the truth commission, with the moral and procedural authority to discover and publicize the truth about the past.

Truth commissions take their truth claim seriously, not only as a scholarly but also as a moral and political matter. This moral-political character explains why truth commission narratives activate society-wide processes of contestation in democracies and democratizing regimes. However, those same processes of social contestation may threaten the legitimacy of such hegemonic truth-finding institutions as truth commissions. In other words, truth commissions expose the ethical and political implications of historiography, but this undertaking paradoxically puts their own basis of legitimacy at stake.

Thus, truth commissions constitute their legitimacy *performatively* as they narrativize the nation's past. The realization that larger society does not grant them a priori legitimacy leads them to make efforts to bridge the breach between those political and social actors who establish and advocate them and those who question their accuracy, legitimacy, and usefulness. The authoritative claim to truth goes hand in hand with the need for persuasion as the basis of legitimacy, which drives many commissions to develop narrative strategies in the interstices of embeddedness and transcendence with respect to the field of social memory.

Critics have rightly pointed out that some commissions have risked putting the quest for historical truth in the service of the political project of national reconstruction and reconciliation. While it should be acknowledged that the strategic interventions and silences of commissions have ruled out many alternative memories (and along with them, visions of future), it is also wrong to reduce commission narratives to politically usable reconstructions of the past. Even when an incoming government and a truth commission tended to share a narrow and politically expedient notion of reconciliation (e.g., Chile and South Africa) or a government intentionally deprived the commission of resources to curb its authority (e.g., Guatemala and Nigeria), the commissioners and staff surprised and upset governments, as well as other political and military leaders, through their findings, historical explanations, and recommendations. It is not their social and political embeddedness, or their deconstructive and transformative potential, but rather the interplay of these forces that characterizes truth commissions' struggle for truth and memory.

I make use of these broad insights to explore the ways in which the Chilean and Peruvian truth commissions have reinterpreted the history of political violence differently in Chapter 7.

PART II

Zooming In: Political and
Social Change Through
Truth Commissions

PART II makes use of Part I's broad outline of truth commissions' place in contemporary societies in order to understand the variety of ways in which specific truth commissions change (or fail to change) politics and society. The theoretical discussions of state-society relations, legitimation, commission autonomy, and social memory are observed in action. Do truth commissions influence policies, judicial decisions, and social attitudes? If yes, what are the specific mechanisms through which they achieve their goals? Why do political decision makers endorse a commission's final report and implement a good number of its recommendations in some countries, whereas a commission's impact depends critically on the continued mobilization of supportive civil society actors in others? What are the twists and turns in the course of a commission's creation, operation, and post-commission impact? Why do some commissions explain the underlying causes of human rights violations in relatively short passages, whereas others seek to transform citizens' relationship to the national past with comprehensive historical narratives?

Part II pays close attention to the differences across truth commissions in terms of structure, goals, process, and outcome. Detailed analyses of truth commission process and impact in Argentina, Uganda, Nepal, Chad, El Salvador, Sri Lanka, Haiti, South Africa, Guatemala, Nigeria, Timor-Leste, Sierra Leone, and Liberia (Chapters 4 and 6) complement the findings of my research in Chile and Peru (Chapters 5 and 7). This way I address whether and how truth commissions change politics and society (Chapter 4), why the commissions in Chile and Peru have generated impact in different ways (Chapter 5), whether the pattern observed in Chile and Peru conforms to a more general theory of politically driven and civil society–driven truth commission impact (Chapter 6), and the different ways in which the commissions in Chile and Peru problematize the nation's history (Chapter 7).

CHAPTER 4

Truth Commission Impact:
An Assessment of How Commissions Influence Politics and Society

In what ways do truth commissions influence policy, human rights accountability, and social norms? The transitional justice literature suggests various mechanisms through which truth commissions are expected to achieve a set of moral and political objectives in peace-building and democratization contexts. However, only a handful of studies have explored the commission *and* post-commission processes to assess claims of truth commission impact. In this chapter I explain whether or not, and the specific ways in which, truth commissions *in fact* transform the lessons from history into policy, human rights accountability, and changes in shared social norms. In short, this chapter is about how truth commissions do (or do not) change politics and society and why addressing this question is important.

Truth commission impact is the effect of truth commissions on government policy, judicial processes, and social norms, operating independently of the simultaneous effects of postconflict institution building, as well as other transitional justice and conflict resolution measures. I employ a two-step research strategy to assess impact: first, I identify all plausible causal explanations of how truth commissions are likely to produce impact, and, second, I assess those explanations in light of evidence from all transitional truth commission experiences. Some of the taken-for-granted explanations of truth commission impact hold in none or only a few of the cases, whereas others apply more broadly.

Drawing upon the existing literature, I identify seven explanations for truth commission impact: direct political impact, indirect political impact

through civil society mobilization, vetting, delegitimation, immediate reconciliation, impact on social norms, and (positive/negative) judicial impact.
Political impact refers to a commission's capacity to make the key decision
makers acknowledge human rights violations publicly and to influence policy in the areas of institutional reform and human rights policy through its
findings and recommendations. Almost all truth commissions have produced
political impact, albeit to different degrees. I distinguish between *direct* and
indirect impact to separate those cases in which the government demonstrates
the political will to implement truth commission recommendations immediately from other situations where the government is pressured to adopt policy. The distinction is important because civil society mobilization around a
truth commission is an important contributor to policy reform when political will is weak or nonexistent. Although there is little systematic treatment
of civil society mobilization in the literature, it is a crucial element that drives
much cross-national variation in policy adoption once a commission's work
comes to an end.

Truth commissions' role in human rights accountability or impunity is a
controversial issue. Of course, commissions have no authority to punish, and
few of them enjoy subpoena and seizure powers. Nonetheless, some commissions have produced *positive judicial impact*, understood as the use of findings
for prosecution. This kind of impact often takes place with a delay, highlighting the significance of an auspicious political and judicial context, as well
as continued civil society activism, for human rights accountability. They are
also claimed to promote *impunity* through amnesty procedures built into the
commission in a small number of cases. Despite the widespread tendency
to associate truth commissions with amnesties, only two commissions (in
South Africa and Liberia) have actually granted or recommended immunity
from prosecution. Although the amnesties benefited hundreds, it should be
noted that the beneficiaries represent a fraction of the total number of perpetrators. In other words, the overall failure of human rights accountability
cannot be attributed to truth commissions only, even in the two countries
where commissions promoted amnesty.

All truth commissions have tried to delegitimize at least some perpetrators and faced angry reactions from those individuals and organizations representing or in alliance with violent actors. However, it is unclear whether
the *delegitimation* of perpetrators and the backlash have produced significant and lasting political effects. *Vetting* (the policy of removing perpetra-

tors from public office) as a result of a truth commission process has taken place only in El Salvador.

Most truth commissions have tried to transform social norms by cultivating nonviolence and respect for human rights (and other norms, depending on the specific context) among the political elite as well as the broader population, but the results of these efforts remain inconclusive, in great part because normative change takes place over a very long period of time and as a consequence of many factors. Case studies and surveys (such as James L. Gibson's surveys on the South African Truth and Reconciliation Commission)[1] provide compelling evidence for the achievements and shortcomings of reconciliation in specific countries, but the evidence for cross-national normative change is suggestive at best.

Assessing Truth Commission Impact: What Is Missing? How Can It Be Done Better?

Truth commissions are expected to contribute to human rights conduct and democratic strengthening.[2] Ideally commissions acknowledge the victimhood of those affected by the human rights violations during an outgoing regime and/or internal conflict by providing a platform for truth telling[3] and setting the stage for symbolic and material reparations.[4] They rewrite the nation's history of political violence and human rights violations, focusing on the patterns, causes, and consequences, in order to forge a shared historical memory and draw lessons from history.[5] They make recommendations for institutional reform to create the legal, political and cultural framework conducive to peace and democratic strengthening.[6] Some commissions facilitate the removal of those public officials responsible for violence and violations.[7] Furthermore, commissions may serve national reconciliation, a "healthy social catharsis,"[8] as former enemies reach common understandings, the incentives for revenge diminish, and society is reunited through tolerance and forgiveness. For some, genuine reconciliation ought to be based on the full disclosure of past atrocities and the provision of criminal justice: truth, justice, and reparations complement one another.[9] Others point to the looming threat of renewed violence or military coups during fragile transitions and conceptualize the relationship between criminal justice and the other objectives of transitional justice, in particular democratic stability, as a trade-off. Accordingly, truth commissions' success rests upon their ability to sidestep retributive justice and promote restorative justice and social reconciliation—what one commentator names "compromise justice."[10]

The abundance of expectations has triggered scholars to evaluate truth commissions' achievements and shortcomings.[11] International organizations and international NGOs have been publishing manuals to assess truth commissions' role in promoting postconflict peace and reconciliation using the best practice approach.[12] Recently, scholars have turned to statistical, survey, experimental, and ethnographic methods, as well as mixed-method strategies. Those studies that evaluate truth commission impact tend to focus on the country's human rights conduct,[13] democratic stability,[14] social reconciliation,[15] and the rule of law.[16] Although case studies of one or several truth commissions had initially dominated the field,[17] recent studies increasingly use large-N regression analysis.[18]

A striking characteristic of the existing literature is the coexistence of competing, if not outright contradictory, theories about truth commission impact.[19] For example, Tricia D. Olsen, Leigh A. Payne, and Andrew G. Reiter (2010) find that truth commissions, when used alone, "have a significant, negative effect" on democracy and human rights, but yield positive outcomes when combined with trials and amnesties.[20] Hunjoon Kim and Kathryn Sikkink (2010), on the other hand, argue that truth commissions have a positive independent effect on human rights conduct, which increases in magnitude if accompanied by prosecutions.[21] Others find truth commissions to have weak negative impact,[22] or no observable impact at all,[23] on democracy and human rights.

What explains the divergent results between studies that explore the same causal relationship? Qualitative and quantitative research strategies are known to produce systematically different results in human rights research.[24] Moreover, even studies using the same data collection and analysis method (for example, large-N regression analysis) arrive at divergent results due to differences in their conceptualization of key variables, codification and collection of data, and model specification. Below I discuss the sources of scholarly disagreement over truth commission impact. These methodological and epistemological debates are not just intramural disagreements among social scientists: victims' groups, human rights organizations, politicians, international donors, and concerned citizens want to make sure that the time, energy, money, and hope invested in transitional justice mechanisms, such as truth commissions, are not misplaced. Whether truth commissions get things done and, if so, how are therefore relevant questions that need to be addressed rigorously.

Definition and Codification

Scholarly disagreement over the definition of a truth commission has implications for coding data and testing theories. Transitional justice databases often codify the same procedure under different categories, which in part explains divergent outcomes. Some scholars count parliamentary investigation commissions (such as Uruguay's 1985 Investigative Commission on the Situation of Disappeared People and Its Causes, and Germany's 1992 Commission of Inquiry for the Assessment of History and Consequences of the SED Dictatorship) as truth commissions, whereas others object to this classification, noting that a truth commission should have sufficient autonomy from the executive and the legislative branches. Commissions that were dissolved before terminating their work (such as Bolivia's 1982 National Commission of Inquiry into Disappearances and Ecuador's 1996 Truth and Justice Commission) are particularly divisive, since unfinished commissions raise conceptual and empirical questions about whether a commission *process*, regardless of the *outcome*, can generate substantial political and social change (as discussed in Chapter 1). Furthermore, some studies identify a relatively large number of investigative or deliberative procedures as truth commissions, with little or no attention to definitional criteria. For example, the Transitional Justice Data Base Project sets the number of truth commissions established between 1970 and 2007 at sixty,[25] while the figure ranges between twenty-eight and forty in all other studies.[26]

Theory

Once the concepts are defined and data codified, the specification of relevant variables can generate differences, too. For example, two recent studies of human rights accountability disagree over the evidence for the "justice cascade" (that is, unprecedented human rights accountability) in the 1990s and 2000s: while Kim and Sikkink (2010) get statistically significant results supporting the theory, Olsen, Payne, and Reiter (2010) argue that the incorporation of amnesty laws into the statistical model eliminates the overwhelming support for the justice cascade. Given the extremely complex nature of causal relations among relevant variables, statistical analyses of large-N data sets are particularly prone to the omitted variable bias, that is to say, the likelihood that ignoring relevant factors generates biased and inconsistent results.

Coexistence of Alternative Explanations (Multicollinearity)

Another set of complications arises from the intrinsic difficulty of measuring truth commission impact.[27] Critics rightly warn against confounding other causal processes with the independent impact of truth commissions.[28] It makes intuitive sense to expect improvements in human rights conduct and democratic governance during and after the truth commission process in great part because truth commissions are likely to be established during democratic transitions and when the human rights situation has already improved, at least to the extent that transitional justice becomes a viable possibility.

The reverse case, that is, when the truth commission process is followed by increasing levels of violence and instability, does not offer much analytical leverage, either: countries that have undergone civil wars are more likely to suffer from future violent conflict than countries with peaceful pasts,[29] but truth commissions' role in provoking such conflict is unclear. Therefore, the variety of factors that might lead to democratic strengthening and nonviolence (which in turn makes the creation of a truth commission possible) or renewed conflict should not be conflated with the independent effect of truth commissions.

Insufficient Attention to Causal Explanation

Many scholars prefer regression analysis to draw causal inferences on the independent effect of truth commissions on democracy and human rights. Causal inference may indeed address troublesome methodological challenges (such as endogeneity, multicollinearity, and counterfactual reasoning), but its successful implementation depends critically on using a large and accurate data set, and, as important, on correct model specification. Statistical analyses should first have a consistent theory of how and why a transitional justice mechanism (or a combination of them) produces outcomes and then proceed to testing. Insufficient attention to causal processes may aggravate the methodological problems of omitted variable bias, endogeneity, and multicollinearity and yield misleading substantive results.

Defining and Explaining Impact: A Methodological Guide

Truth commission impact refers to the causal effect of a truth commission process on individuals' and institutions' decisions, interests, beliefs, and values. The epistemological and methodological challenges of establishing causality are well known. In social sciences and humanities, one rarely observes "smoking gun" evidence that confirms one hypothesis beyond doubt, while discarding alternative explanations.[30] Transitional justice scholarship has recently taken steps to address the question of causality by conducting large-N regression analysis to assess the impact of transitional justice tools on outcome variables (the shortcomings of this approach to causal inference are discussed above). Studies in the qualitative tradition, on the other hand, seek to establish causal connections by getting the causal mechanism right, which raises the evidentiary standards for linking transitional justice processes to outcomes.

What kinds of data would amount to "smoking gun" evidence in explaining truth commission impact? Two examples come to mind: first, a political leader declaring that he or she was urged, influenced, or inspired *exclusively* by a truth commission to enact a policy; second, a representative sample of the population telling researchers that their views on human rights or reconciliation changed *exclusively* or *primarily* as a result of the commission process. However, such unambiguous evidence on decisions and values is lacking in most cases, and the existing evidence is insufficient for cross-national comparison.

These challenges should not produce pessimism. Although irrefutable evidence is often lacking, it is possible to set a reasonably high standard for establishing causal impact if the collected evidence satisfies two tests. For example, if there are two hypothesized causal explanations—$TC \rightarrow A \rightarrow I$ and/or $TC \rightarrow B \rightarrow I$—where a truth commission process (TC) generates impact (I) through the intermediary steps A and/or B, confirming the veracity of a causal explanation requires that (1) I should be observed—policies and judicial processes after a truth commission should reflect its findings and recommendations; and (2) only A, only B, or both A and B should be observed—the researcher should find empirical evidence for the intermediate steps (that is, intervening variables) that connect a truth commission to the outcomes of interest to confirm or disconfirm contending hypotheses.

The second test is crucial for overcoming problems of equifinality (the likelihood that an outcome results from a causal mechanism other than that hypothesized by the researcher) and multicollinearity (the failure to account for the interactions between various factors that lead to an outcome). There may be more than one mechanism to produce similar impact: as I show in the following section, in some countries the recommendations of truth commissions are incorporated into policy because politicians take the initiative to implement them, whereas in other cases the implementation takes place *despite* the reluctance, or even hostility, of the political leadership, as a result of continuous civil society mobilization. Assessing impact, therefore, requires accounting for all the intermediate steps in the causal process.

What causes a truth commission to generate impact in the first place? This chapter is a descriptive account of the causal mechanisms that connect a truth commission to post-commission outcomes. The causes for the causes, that is, the sources of variation in impact across countries, are explained in Chapter 5. Nonetheless, it is important to highlight two factors that play into the direction and magnitude of impact by shaping the pre-commission and commission processes. First, a truth commission is simultaneously enabled and constrained by its mandate, which determines its tasks, powers, and organizational structure. Second, the commissioners and staff exercise considerable agency in terms of how they interpret the mandate, how they identify and carry out their tasks, what they choose to include in the final report, and how they interact with victims, presumed perpetrators, politicians, bureaucrats, armed actors, and civil society organizations. Part of their impact is attributable to the product, that is, the final report, which contains findings, a historical narrative, and recommendations. In addition, the commission process itself is credited for giving voice to the victims of human rights violations (and, occasionally, perpetrators) and building linkages between various civil society actors.[31]

One observes a constant struggle between forces that seek to delimit and predetermine a commission's capabilities and the commission's striving for autonomy and transformative agency. In great part as a result of this interplay of mandate and agency, various decision makers and civil society actors endorse, reject, mobilize around, or ignore a truth commission's findings and recommendations. Impact is constituted by the content of the final report and by the process itself. It is shaped, but not predetermined, by the mandate limits.

Empirical Evidence for Truth Commission Impact

Several causal mechanisms have been proposed to evaluate commissions' capacity to produce changes in policy, judicial practices, and social norms. Most accounts pay attention only to some parts of the causal chain that links the initial conditions to the outcomes of interest. I draw upon the literature on truth commissions, from enthusiasts as well as skeptics, to outline these mechanisms in full here, but if the existing explanations have missing causal links, I identify those missing parts as well. I also provide evidence for cases where policy change may be wrongly attributed to a commission's direct or indirect impact in order to avoid conflating commission impact with similar causal processes. Table 3 presents these causal mechanisms, along with their observable implications (what we should expect to see if the causal explanation were true) and supporting empirical evidence from the history of truth commissions, if any. Table 4 provides a detailed summary of truth commission impact in fifteen transitional countries.

Direct Political Impact

The most straightforward causal effect is when the findings and recommendations of a truth commission's final report are incorporated into policy. If a government acknowledges the commission's final report, legislates reparations for victims, and establishes watchdog institutions for human rights protection, then these reforms are likely to lead to progress in democratic governance and human rights conduct. Direct political impact depends crucially on political decision makers' ability and willingness to implement a commission's recommendations. Only in El Salvador and Sierra Leone did the commission mandate stipulate that the recommendations would be binding on all parties, and even then politicians enjoyed a high degree of discretion on which reform proposals to adopt.

Given that truth commissions make context-specific recommendations, and given that the quality of policy implementation can be quite varied,[32]

Table 3. Explanations of Truth Commission Impact

Name of Causal Mechanism	Causal Process	Observable Implications	Empirical Evidence
Direct political impact	Findings and recommendations → official publication, acknowledgment, and implementation	• Political will to implement commission recommendations • Immediate publication, acknowledgment, and policy implementation	• Most commissions produce direct political impact • Variation across commissions
Indirect political impact through civil society mobilization	Civil society mobilization around the commission → pressure on government → delayed official implementation	• Civil society mobilization • Delayed policy implementation under civil society pressure	• Some commissions produce political impact through civil society mobilization • Variation across commissions
Vetting	Vetting recommended → official implementation	• Recommendation for vetting • Political will to implement	• El Salvador (1993; limited) only
Delegitimation	Commission delegitimizes perpetrators → civil society mobilization around the commission → pressure on government → exclusion or self-exclusion of perpetrators, and reaction from perpetrators	• Civil society mobilization for formal or informal vetting • Hostile reaction from perpetrators and institutions representing them	• All commissions try to delegitimize • Most commissions face hostile reaction

Immediate reconciliation	Commission as a democratic and participatory platform → consensus and reconciliation between victims, perpetrators, and bystanders	• Consensus and reconciliation soon after truth commission	• No evidence for immediate reconciliation • Counterevidence: lack of consensus immediately after truth commission
Impact on social norms	Publicity and incorporation into educational curriculum → widespread acceptance of commission norms → norm change	• Public awareness of truth commission's message • Incorporation into educational curricula	• Some commissions may have produced normative change • Variation across commissions
Positive judicial impact	Findings → judges and prosecutors use in proceedings, immediately or delayed	• Use of truth commission report in court proceedings	• Delayed and limited use of some commissions' findings in domestic and foreign courts
Negative judicial impact	Commissions accompany amnesty laws or promote amnesty → impunity for perpetrators Commissions dampen the demand for retribution → impunity for perpetrators	• Amnesty built into, or legislated along with, truth commission • Impunity resulting from truth commission • Civil society demobilization	• Conditional amnesty built into commission (South Africa, Liberia); most perpetrators not covered • Counterevidence: amnesty law to offset truth commission impact (Nepal and El Salvador) • No evidence of civil society demobilization

comparative measures are bound to be imperfect. Nevertheless, one observes near-universal demand for certain policies and political gestures, which I employ as indicators of direct political impact: (1) public endorsement of the commission's work by government leadership; (2) government publication of the commission's final report; (3) implementation of a reparations program (this measure is applicable in twelve cases where the truth commission recommended reparations); and (4) the creation of follow-up institutions to carry out the recommended reforms and monitor progress.[33]

It is important to note that a government might implement human rights policies whether or not it abides by a truth commission's recommendations. *Direct political impact* captures only the truth commission-induced political change. It is often confounded with the country's overall human rights improvement, leading to the under- or overstatement of truth commission impact. The measures described above refer to political change relative to the commission's recommendations for reform. In conducting cross-national comparisons, I take into account variations in discursive and policy change relative to the expectations of each country's truth commission, rather than variation in overall political reform. Thus the independent effect of truth commissions is disentangled from the broader reform processes during democratic transition by distinguishing the cases in which reform results from the commission's findings and recommendations from those cases in which this does not happen.

Direct political impact is the chief mechanism through which commissions influence policy, but the implementation is always selective. Table 4 shows that every transitional truth commission except the one in Nepal has produced some direct political impact. Of the fifteen transitional truth commissions that completed their work before 2013, ten published the final report within one year of the commission's termination. Presidents, backed by the governments they represented, endorsed the commission's work upon receiving the final report in Argentina,[34] Chile,[35] South Africa,[36] Guatemala,[37] and Nigeria,[38] and Peru. Acknowledgment did not take place in eight countries, and in Sierra Leone, it happened only after a new president assumed office. Uganda,[39] Chile,[40] Sri Lanka,[41] Haiti,[42] Timor-Leste,[43] Sierra Leone,[44] and Liberia[45] immediately established follow-up institutions to monitor the post-commission reform process, whereas eight countries did not. The least favored policy by the governments was reparations: twelve truth commissions demanded compensation for victims, and only the Chilean government initiated a reparations program without delay. Governments in El Salvador,[46]

Haiti, Nigeria,[47] and Liberia[48] ignored the recommendation for reparations completely.

Indirect Political Impact Through Civil Society Mobilization

A truth commission can improve a country's human rights record by drawing attention to past violations.[49] Domestic and international actors, most notably human rights organizations and victims' associations, may build sufficient pressure on politicians and state functionaries to reform human rights policy and behave in conformity with a truth commission's recommendations. What distinguishes indirect from direct political impact is that decision makers adopt truth commission recommendations and related human rights initiatives only as a result of civil society pressure. Thus, implementation is typically delayed, although such delay does not prove the existence of civil society mobilization in and of itself. Therefore evidence of civil society pressure is necessary to confirm the specific impact mechanism outlined here.

Indirect political impact results from civil society mobilization around a truth commission. *Civil society mobilization* refers to a truth commission's ability to motivate human rights activism, especially in the post-commission period. I use two indicators to account for civil society mobilization: (1) nongovernmental initiatives to publish and/or disseminate the commission's final report if the government fails to do so; and (2) activism on the part of local, national, and international NGOs to monitor the progress of the implementation of recommendations, especially the reparations program.

Generally, domestic human rights groups make alliances with international organizations and transnational networks to hold governments accountable to the human rights norm.[50] Whether domestic human rights activism originates with or merely follows the transnational actors is a matter of controversy. Some see transitional advocacy networks' capacity to pressure governments by naming and shaming them in the international arena as crucial, whereas others point to the predominantly domestic nature of norm change.[51] In the case of truth commission recommendations, I observe that even when international actors initiate the commission process, the success of the reform process ultimately depends on pressure built by domestic human rights groups. Beth Simmons's brilliant formulation in the case of international treaty ratification applies to truth commissions, too: "Nobody cares more about human rights than the citizens potentially empowered" by these efforts.[52]

Civil society mobilization, a key causal step in policy change, only measures the capacity of a commission to motivate civil society actors. Human rights activism may exist independently of, and conceivably in opposition to, a truth commission. Civil society mobilization around a truth commission does not capture the overall quality of civic relations (i.e., social capital); it instead focuses on those civic groups most likely to pursue the truth commission's agenda and maximize its impact, since the primary concern is to explain the precise mechanisms through which truth commissions produce impact. Finally, the model of civil society advocacy presented here does not make a priori assumptions about state-civil society relations—it does not claim right away that they are antagonistic or mutually reinforcing. It is plausible to expect that impact driven by political will and impact through civil society mobilization are both high, both low, or in an inverse relationship in any given country. Nonetheless, in practice politicians and civil society actors have more often than not had contrasting views on a truth commission.

Several, but not all, truth commissions have provided a platform for domestic and international human rights groups to make demands on the government and evaluate policy progress. There is evidence of civil society mobilization around the truth commission in ten countries, albeit to varying degrees. In some countries where governments initially chose not to publish the final report or adopt reparations programs, human rights activism led to delayed policy change. In South Africa,[53] Guatemala,[54] Peru,[55] Sierra Leone,[56] and Timor-Leste[57] reluctant governments found themselves pressured into legislating reparations programs, although the speed and efficiency with which the reparations were actually disbursed generated discontent in most cases.

In Nepal,[58] Sri Lanka,[59] and Haiti,[60] it took domestic and/or international human rights organizations several years of pressuring to get the government to publish the commission's final report, and in Nigeria, private initiative undertook the publication.[61] Civil society groups were also crucial in publishing abridged versions of the final report in Peru, Timor-Leste,[62] and Sierra Leone.[63]

Not every policy in the area of human rights can be attributed to a truth commission's recommendations or its capacity to mobilize civil society. In Chad, human rights groups successfully campaigned for reparations even though the truth commission had not recommended the policy. In Argentina, reparations laws were enacted more than a decade after the commission's work and without any clear indication that the commission's recommendation prompted their legislation.[64] Likewise, there is no evidence suggesting that Sri Lanka's compensatory policies were in response to the truth commission.

Vetting

Truth commissions might recommend the removal of presumed perpetrators and their political supporters from public office through vetting. Also known as "lustration," this transitional justice tool has often been used in the absence of a truth commission, especially in the Central and Eastern European transitions of the early 1990s. Here I seek to identify not all vetting initiatives, but only those recommended by truth commissions.

Despite commissions' best efforts, recommending vetting/lustration has not produced significant impact.[65] Although four of the fifteen transitional truth commissions demanded the removal of presumed perpetrators from office, only one government met this demand partially (El Salvador),[66] whereas in Chad, Timor-Leste, and Liberia, the call for vetting was disregarded. In one of the countries where vetting was used (Nigeria), the truth commission had not recommended the measure. In other words, evidence does not support the claim that removal of violators follows from the recommendation of a truth commission.

Delegitimation

Another causal explanation states that truth commissions improve democratic governance and human rights conduct by exposing, shaming, or delegitimizing antidemocratic and violent actors, even when they do not make a plea for official vetting.[67] All commissions have pointed to those individual and institutional actors responsible for human rights violations, albeit with varying levels of specificity: a number of commissions have named individual perpetrators, while others have described in detail the systematic and institutional nature of human rights violations under the outgoing regime. Unlike vetting, which relies on explicit recommendation and direct political implementation, this causal mechanism usually relies on civil society backing and media cooperation to further delegitimize violent actors.

Some scholars have argued that the delegitimation effect might work against democratic strengthening and social peace. Those individuals and

institutions that have the most to fear from human rights accountability often seek to steer the course of national debates away from truth and justice.
Alleged perpetrators and their allies have tended to not participate in truth
commission processes, tried to obstruct truth-finding efforts, and been
quick to condemn commission findings. The denial of the truth commission
findings often accompanies the defamation of the commissioners, so much
so that commissioners and collaborating social activists in many countries
have suffered various threats and attacks against their lives and well-being
during and after a truth commission process.[68]

If the opponents of a commission succeed in swaying key decision makers
and the broader public, they might see their position strengthened in the context of a fragile democracy. Furthermore, some of those actors might engage
in extralegal activities to defend their power, further undermining democratic
stability and the rule of law.[69] The failure of a truth commission to mobilize
civil society is likely to aggravate the failure of delegitimation. In other words,
explanations based on the delegitimizing effect of truth commissions need to
conceptualize the post-commission political developments as a dynamic and
open-ended process that involves a multiplicity of political and social actors
contesting and reconstructing political legitimacy in the short and long runs.

Delegitimation and reaction to delegitimation pose serious challenges to
research on truth commissions. First, the quantitative criteria for successful
delegitimation are unclear. How many of those individuals who deserve public opprobrium actually face unofficial sanction? Is there a cut-off number to
evaluate success and failure? In many cases one sees the delegitimation, even
prosecution, of some violent actors, whereas other individuals who should
have faced similar treatment seem to enjoy political clout. The second challenge, related to the first, is that delegitimation is a long-term, dynamic, and
society-wide process, which can only be measured via periodical and consistent surveys on representative samples. Added to the difficulty is that many
individuals lose the public's favor independently of the naming and shaming by truth commissions, say, as a result of corruption scandals, so the
independent effect of truth commissions might be conflated with other
processes of delegitimation.

Eight of the transitional commissions published the names of individual
perpetrators, and at least in one other case (Argentina), the list of perpetrators
was leaked to the press. Beyond individuals, truth commissions also criticize
organizational actors, such as the military, police, nonstate armed groups, political parties, and judicial institutions, for committing or condoning human

rights violations and contributing to a political context in which violations would happen. They often refute self-justificatory discourses of violent actors.[70] The angry responses to the commissions' findings on the part of military institutions almost everywhere, high courts (e.g., Chile and El Salvador), and political parties (e.g., South Africa's major parties, including the African National Congress) show that truth commissions are capable of *delegitimizing* institutional actors and, consequently, the individuals representing those institutions.

There is anecdotal evidence to confirm both delegitimation of *and* backlash on the part of presumed perpetrators. Much less clear is whether delegitimation translates into change of personnel within institutions or a nationwide attitude change toward human rights. The military and high courts in Chile did not undergo significant change in the first seven years following the publication of the truth commission report. Augusto Pinochet was the retired commander in chief, with full honors, and lifelong senator, when he was arrested in London in October 1998. In Guatemala, the political repercussions of human rights awareness were deeply felt when various courts ruled against former dictator and presumed human rights violator Efraín Ríos Montt's bid for the presidency in 2004, a process that brought his opponents and supporters into bitter conflict. Ríos Montt participated in the presidential election, lost, and ran a successful campaign for a seat in Congress in 2007. In Peru, former president Alberto Fujimori was sentenced for human rights violations in 2009, but his political downfall had begun before the truth commission, and, in fact, the commission became possible only after Fujimori's corrupt civilian-authoritarian regime collapsed in 2000. Following collapsed transitions (e.g., Argentina, Uganda, Chad, Haiti, Peru, among others) commissions have further discredited former dictators by publicizing the abuses and corruption under their regime, but it is impossible to disentangle truth commissions' role in discrediting deposed and widely hated dictators. In conclusion, there is suggestive evidence for the delegitimation of perpetrators and their allies, as well as their reaction to delegitimation, but the specific mechanisms that affect their stature are too complex to attribute to the independent effect of truth commissions only.

Reconciliation Through Consensus

The promise of overcoming social conflict through truth commissions has captured the imagination of transitional justice scholars. Ideally the potential for renewed conflict decreases because the inclusion of victims and victims' relatives in the human rights investigation reduces their incentives for revenge;[71] the creation of a participatory space through truth commissions results in the affirmation of democratic values; victims, perpetrators, and bystanders engage in dialogue;[72] perpetrators and victims learn to live under "contentious coexistence";[73] and the rewriting of official history allows society to reach consensus about human rights violations and the meaning of the national past.[74] The idea of reconciliation is so engrained as an expectation that many investigatory bodies are called "truth and reconciliation commissions."

If such reconciliation were to take place, one would expect to observe that the individuals representing different viewpoints with respect to past violence converge on the accuracy and significance of a truth commission's work. Military and insurgency leaders, politicians across the political spectrum, and high-court judges would acknowledge the facts of human rights violations, and perhaps even make mea culpa statements.

The idea that truth commissions produce consensus and reconciliation between victims, perpetrators, and bystanders draws no empirical support. This causal explanation misses the potential for increased social and political conflict (although not necessarily violence) resulting from the reactions of individual and organizational actors accused of conducting and/or abetting human rights violations, as well as victims' own frustrations with the truth-telling process.[75] Far from acknowledging violations and seeking reconciliation, presumed perpetrators and their political allies resort to rejecting the findings and conclusions of the commission, discrediting the moral authority of the commissioners and victims, and in extreme cases, threatening the political system with instability. In Chile, El Salvador, Guatemala, and Peru, military leaders were quick to reject the truth commission's work in angry words. The Supreme Court of Chile went so far as to declare that the commission's final report put the country's institutional stability in danger. In South Africa and Peru, political parties voiced serious disagreements with the truth commission and certainly did not make a gesture toward apology, forgiveness, or reconciliation. If anyone has extended a gesture of acknowledgment and apology toward victims, it has been the leadership of the incoming government and not those individuals and institutions responsible for past violence.

In conclusion, the release of a commission's final report invariably leads to disagreement and a tense political environment, at least in the short run.[76] Institutions responsible for repression acknowledged and apologized for violations in Argentina, Chile, Timor-Leste, but only years after the publication of the commission's final report.[77] The commission may have played an important role by providing the factual basis upon which to build a politics of recognition and forgiveness, but this role should be evaluated in the context of long-term normative and political transformations, rather than immediate reconciliation. Consensus-based models of truth commission impact need to be abandoned in favor of explanations that acknowledge the conflict potential of coming to terms with a violent and divisive past. Reconciliation is a complex and multivalent process that defies quick closure.[78]

It should be also noted, however, that there is no evidence linking a truth commission to the recurrence of violence. The termination of the commission's work coincided with large-scale violence in Sri Lanka, but no observer has attributed to the commission process a causal role.

Impact on Social Norms

Truth commissions' efforts at ruling out violence and promoting democratic participation might produce long-term effects by cultivating a civic culture based on nonviolence and human rights.[79] Truth commissions do not advocate the exact same set of norms everywhere. For example, the South African TRC stands out for its emphasis on forgiveness, while the Guatemalan commission is known for its defense of socioeconomic and cultural equality. Nonetheless, the call for nonviolent political conduct and respect for human rights is prevalent across commissions.

It is notoriously difficult to measure long-term normative changes, let alone determine if they were caused by truth commissions' transformative potential. Nonetheless, assuming that broad-based exposure to a truth commission's ideas increases social groups' likelihood of internalizing nonviolence and respect for human rights, two intermediary processes should be observed: (1) widespread access to, and readership of, the truth commission's final products (the report as well as audiovisual documentation), measured by governmental and nongovernmental efforts to disseminate the commission's work; and (2) the incorporation of the commission's findings and recommendations into school curricula.[80]

A satisfactory cross-national analysis of truth commissions' impact on social norms would require nothing less than conducting cross-national standardized surveys on the change of social and political values as a result of truth commissions. The best available data come from case studies, including my fieldwork in Chile and Peru, and the only available proxies for impact on social norms, albeit imperfect, are the data on the dissemination of a truth commission's final work. Evidence shows that some truth commissions have devised ways to increase public awareness of their findings and recommendations, such as publishing the final report as a marketable book or in a newspaper, producing an accessible version of the final report for adults and/or children (Peru, Timor-Leste, and Sierra Leone), organizing outreach activities, and so on.

Governments have been invariably unsupportive of truth commissions' dissemination efforts other than publishing the final report. Even the official publication was not available to most citizens in Uganda, Sri Lanka, Haiti, and Nigeria. Domestic and international civil society organizations have spearheaded efforts to incorporate the commissions' findings and lessons into educational curricula, but only Guatemala,[81] and to a lesser extent South Africa have taken steps to implement curriculum reform. Several of my interviewees in Peru stated that educational incorporation was one of the major goals of local civil society groups in Ayacucho and Huancavelica in the face of political disinterest at the local and national levels. Finally, incorporation might be burdensome for teachers, who find themselves in a position to adjudicate historical controversies with the aid of a truth commission's report, potentially to the dismay of school authorities and parents.

In conclusion, truth commissions' contribution to society-wide normative change is inconclusive, but civil society mobilization to popularize the commission's work is likely to increase its visibility and normative force.

Judicial Impact: Accountability and Impunity

Do truth commissions contribute to human rights accountability? Commissions are not allowed to deliver sentences, but their findings may be used during criminal proceedings, as either evidence or contextual information.[82] Judicial impact depends as much on the powers granted by the truth commission mandate as on judges' and prosecutors' willingness to incorporate commission findings, the existence of laws, and conditional amnesty procedures that precede or operate simultaneously with the commission, and civil society mobilization around the commission.[83] There is variation across commissions with respect to their search and subpoena powers and the power to name perpetrators. Setting mandate limits on commissions' judicial attributes is justified on the grounds of fair trial guarantees.[84]

Yet agency during and after a commission may challenge the structural limits imposed by the mandate. Commissioners may or may not choose to refer cases to courts—a decision that depends critically on civil society agendas. Prosecutors may be willing or, more likely, unwilling to use findings to initiate lawsuits against alleged perpetrators, claiming in the latter case that commission procedures fail to satisfy the evidentiary standards of the courtroom.

Skeptics have long noted the possibility that truth commissions, far from contributing to justice, in fact serve to perpetuate impunity, as they provide an imperfect substitute for human rights trials. It is generally assumed that a truth commission is a moderate transitional justice tool to meet the victims' demands in the context of a negotiated political transition.[85] Jon Elster, for example, notes that a new democratic regime may have to "choose between justice and truth."[86] Mark Osiel takes the opposition between truth commissions and prosecution to an extreme when he claims that most commissions' inability to take testimonies from perpetrators not only undermines justice but defeats the justification for the existence of the truth commission, which is to establish the historical truth, which involves the full disclosure of violations and names of perpetrators.[87] Some claim that commissions promote *impunity through amnesty* through amnesty laws built into the truth commission or legislated as a result of the commission's work. The South African TRC especially has raised serious concerns about the extent to which truth commissions serve to sidestep accountability because a specialized amnesty committee granted amnesty to those perpetrators who fully confessed to their crimes, and the commission itself constantly invoked the language of forgiveness and reconciliation.[88]

Finally, other skeptics argue that the spectacle of a truth commission creates a distraction from prosecution. More specifically, the recognition of victimhood and the provision of material and symbolic reparations through truth commissions may assuage the public demand for truth and some kind of justice.[89] Furthermore, some argue, the decision to establish a truth commission itself is a sad admission of the country's inability to prosecute, which undermines the rule of law at the outset of a democratic transition.[90] Therefore, the public demand for prosecutions would fall, and/or civil society groups advocating retributive justice would get demobilized during and after the truth commission process.

Several commissions have generated judicial impact, but the magnitude remains small.[91] The commissions in Argentina, Chile, Chad, El Salvador, Sri Lanka, Guatemala,[92] Nigeria, and Peru saw their findings incorporated into a small number of domestic or foreign lawsuits as contextual information. For example, in Argentina, the commission transferred files to prosecutors, which resulted in the "conviction and imprisonment of five generals."[93] A commission's judicial impact is typically delayed: even the preliminary investigation for prosecution takes place several years after the publication of the final report. Often one observes surprising turns, in which a commission acquires renewed significance thanks to changing domestic and international circumstances. For example, the final report of Chad's commission "unexpectedly took on new importance," more than a decade after its publication, "as rights advocates turned to it as a primary source of information in an effort to prosecute Habré at the international level. It was still the only detailed record of rights crimes under Habré, and was thus critical in providing leads to witnesses for a trial."[94]

In none of the cases did judicial impact extend beyond one or two high-profile cases, such as the arrest of Pinochet (Chile), the indictment of Hissène Habré (Chad), and the conviction of Fujimori (Peru). This brings up normative and practical questions about prioritizing accountability for the "big fish" rather than the rank and file. Arguably, the design of truth commissions, which curtails their judicial powers, accounts for their relative insignificance in judicial processes. However, evidence suggests that even when commissions have made full use of their capacity to facilitate prosecutions, courts have neglected their findings. The Special Court for Sierra Leone, for example, had the power to force the Truth and Reconciliation Commission to share the information at its disposal, but the prosecutor rejected the possibility.[95] In the end, commissions produce limited judicial impact, but this is not necessarily their own fault.

Do truth commissions promote impunity, then? There is a tendency to exaggerate the prevalence of amnesty laws accompanying truth commissions as a result of the attention given to the South African TRC's amnesty procedures.[96] South Africa and Liberia are the only countries where an amnesty-for-truth option was built into the commission,[97] but it would be unfair to fault the amnesty procedure for the obstruction of justice: the South African TRC rejected about 88 percent of the 7,112 amnesty applications, and many perpetrators did not testify at all.[98] Thus, the majority of perpetrators were and are available for prosecution.[99] Peace accords in Guatemala and

Sierra Leone[100] had amnesty provisions initially, but pressure from the international community and domestic NGOs forced the exclusion of serious charges, such as genocide and crimes against humanity, from the amnesty laws.[101] In other words, the failure to prosecute results less from amnesty laws accompanying truth commissions than other factors, such as the unwillingness of the judiciary or political pressures.

In Chile and Sri Lanka, amnesty laws preceded the truth commission by over a decade. Chile's amnesty law dates back to 1978, and Sri Lanka's to 1982—long before the respective truth commissions of 1990 and 1994. El Salvador and Nepal are the only countries where a truth commission resulted in amnesty, but precisely as counterevidence for the *impunity through amnesty* hypothesis: an amnesty law was passed hastily in each country as the release of the final report generated the fear of prosecution among the political and military elite.[102] The post-commission amnesties in Argentina served to stop criminal accountability, but they were not recommended by, or established as a subcommittee of, the commission: 1986 Full Stop Law halted the prosecution of most perpetrators, and Carlos Menem's 1989 presidential pardon of military officers accused of violations further undermined retributive justice.

There is no empirical evidence to show that the actors who actively seek prosecution get "distracted" by the nonretributive promises of truth commissions, like healing, reconciliation, or monetary compensation. My fieldwork reveals that commissions have restructured their investigation methods to respond to the persistent advocacy for trials (e.g., Peru) or have found themselves severely criticized for failing to respond to this demand (e.g., Chile). While it is true that many politicians, military leaders, and armed groups have accepted the creation of truth commissions under the impression that those panels would replace prosecutions, commissions have neither advocated impunity nor dampened the energies of activists who sought trials. The failure to prosecute has resulted from many other factors, but not from the existence of truth commissions.

Conclusion

Truth commissions discover facts of human rights violations, and their primary goal is to contribute to the country's human rights conduct. Yet, they do not invariably contribute to, or inhibit, retributive justice or overall progress

Table 4. Truth Commission Impact in Fifteen Transitional Countries

	Reparations Recommended / Immediately Implemented	Immediate Publication of Final Report	Official Endorsement	Immediate Creation of Follow-up Institutions	Recommended Reparations Implemented as a Result of Civil Society Mobilization	Publication of Final Report as a Result of Civil Society Mobilization
Argentina (1983)	Yes/no	Yes	Yes	None	No (reparations: 2004)	Immediate policy
Uganda (1986)	No/no	No	No	Ugandan Human Rights Commission	No reparations	No publication
Nepal (1990)	No/no	No	No	None	No reparations	Yes (1994)
Chile (1990)	Yes/yes	Yes	Yes	National Corporation for Reparation and Reconciliation	Immediate policy (1992)	Immediate policy
Chad (1991)	No/no	Yes	No	None	No reparations	Immediate policy
El Salvador (1992)	Yes/yo	Yes	No	None	No reparations	Immediate policy
Sri Lanka (1994)	Yes/yes	No	No	Presidential Commission on Ethnic Violence	Yes (reparations: 1998)	Yes (2001)
Haiti (1995)	Yes/no	No	No	Office of the Public Prosecutor	No reparations	Yes (1998)
South Africa (1995)	Yes/no	Yes	Yes (government divided)	None	Yes (reparations: 2003)	Immediate policy
Guatemala (1997)	Yes/no	Yes	Yes	None	Yes (reparations: 2005)	Immediate policy
Nigeria (1999)	Yes/no	No	Yes	None	No reparations	Yes (2005; unofficial)
Peru (2001)	Yes/no	Yes	Yes	None	Yes (reparations forthcoming)	Immediate policy
Timor-Leste (2002)	Yes/no	Yes	No	Technical Secretariat	Yes (reparations: 2010)	Immediate policy
Sierra Leone (2002)	Yes/no	Yes	No (delayed endorsement)	National Commission for Social Action	Yes (reparations: 2008)	Immediate policy
Liberia (2006)	Yes/no	Yes	No	Independent National Commission on Human Rights	Ongoing civil society campaign	Immediate policy

	New Human Rights NGOs Established to Monitor Post-Commission Policy	Nongovernmental Efforts to Disseminate Truth Commission Report	Vetting Recommended/ Implemented	Judicial Impact	Amnesty Law Legislated During or Immediately After the Truth Commission
Argentina (1983)	No	No	No/no	Domestic courts; immediate and delayed	No
Uganda (1986)	No	No	No/no	None	No
Nepal (1990)	No	No	No/no	None	Yes (1991; de facto)
Chile (1990)	No	No	No/no	Domestic and foreign courts; delayed	No
Chad (1991)	No	No	Yes/no	Foreign courts; delayed	No
El Salvador (1992)	No	No	Yes/yes (1993; partial)	Foreign courts; delayed	Yes (1993; blanket)
Sri Lanka (1994)	No	No	No/no	Domestic courts; immediate and delayed	No
Haiti (1995)	No	No	No/no	None	No
South Africa (1995)	Institute for Justice and Reconciliation (2000)	Yes	No/no	None	Yes (built-in; partial)
Guatemala (1997)	No	Yes	No/no	Domestic and foreign courts; delayed	No
Nigeria (1999)	No	No	No /yes (1999)	Domestic courts; immediate	No
Peru (2001)	Movimiento Ciudadano Para Que No Se Repita (2003)	Yes	No/no	Domestic courts; immediate and delayed	No
Timor-Leste (2002)	No	Yes	Yes/no	None	No
Sierra Leone (2002)	Transitional justice branch of the Campaign for Good Governance	Yes	No/no	None	No
Liberia (2006)	Post-TRC Transitional Justice Initiative under the Transitional Justice Working Group	Yes	Yes/no	None	Yes (built-in; partial)

in human rights conduct. The mandate limits interact with a variety of other factors, such as the degree of judicial autonomy, the presence of amnesty laws, judges' willingness to pursue human rights cases, political will, and civil society activism, to determine the net impact of truth commissions on accountability. It is safe to argue that truth commissions are not designed to pursue human rights accountability by assuming court-like functions even under auspicious circumstances, although the claim that truth commissions serve to undermine justice is also misleading.

The complexity of the relationship between truth commissions and human rights conduct suggests that truth commission impact cannot be reduced to the immediate implementation of recommendations. Focusing on immediate results has fueled misperceptions about what truth commissions can achieve, as many individual victims were led to believe that truth commissions would by themselves provide restorative, if not retributive, justice.[103] The findings in this chapter warn against making unrealistic demands on these ad hoc panels with no policy-making powers. In spite of their limited impact on policy change, it should also be noted that the social, political, and judicial processes triggered by a truth commission experience may generate unanticipated changes at the level of civil society mobilization, the reinvigoration of societal debates over historical memory, and changes in how the human rights norm is conceived and put into practice.

This chapter conceptualizes *truth commission impact* as a set of political, institutional, societal, and judicial transformations resulting from a truth commission. The processes that generate the largest effects are *direct political impact* and *indirect political impact through civil society mobilization*. The former points to the quasi-official character of truth commissions, while the latter is a reminder of the need for continued civil society activism to keep politicians accountable to nonbinding recommendations. Civil society mobilization is a crucial factor in generating long-term judicial and normative impact, as well. Truth commissions are neither state institutions nor civil society organizations; their liminal position vis-à-vis public authorities necessitates a broader discussion of their agency and vulnerability, stated goals, and unanticipated consequences. It is through the relations of cooperation and competition, autonomy and dependence, legitimation and delegitimation between politicians, domestic and international human rights activists, and commissioners that truth commissions generate impact.

The discussion above discards commission-induced *vetting* (effective only in El Salvador) as a significant impact mechanism. In addition, commissions do not bring about immediate consensus and closure. Their *positive judicial impact* (i.e., human rights accountability) tends to appear several years after the commission's termination, in great part as a result of broader changes in politicians' and judges' attitudes on human rights trials; and *negative judicial impact* (i.e., impunity) favors only a small subsection of perpetrators, while the overall climate of impunity is likely caused by factors other than truth commissions' amnesty procedures. Evidence from various countries suggests that truth commissions and courts are not necessarily in an antagonistic relationship: it is not a question of *whether* they can work together, but rather *how*.[104]

Truth commissions *delegitimize* perpetrators and produce long-term impact on social norms, but the evidence for impact is suggestive rather than conclusive, since a host of contextual factors produces political and societal normative changes in conjunction with the effect of truth commissions. As the normative impact of truth commissions on politics and society is undeniable, researchers should devise innovative and precise data collection and analysis tools to assess the magnitude, direction, and specific causal mechanism of cross-national variation in normative change. Therefore I give a detailed account of these causal processes in my case studies of Chile and Peru in Chapter 5.

In conclusion, truth commissions do produce significant changes, and in favor of human rights accountability more often than not, but the magnitude of the change should not be exaggerated. Their ad hoc and nonbinding character limits their potential for impact. Nevertheless, sustained post-commission pressure on the part of human rights associations and victims' groups, where it happens, compensates for the intrinsic weakness of commissions to some extent.

CHAPTER 5

Explaining Variation in Truth Commission Impact (I): Chile and Peru

> The approach of democratic leaders in such difficult transitional situations should, then, be based on the ethical maxim that Max Weber lucidly characterized in his famous lecture, *Politics as a Vocation*: Political leaders should be guided by the ethics of responsibility, as opposed to the ethics of conviction.
>
> —José Zalaquett, "Balancing Ethical Imperatives"

> The notion of a nation lying prostrate before the victims is closely related to that notion of reconciliation. We meant to be the first, though not the sole, representatives of the state making that gesture of recognition. The Truth Commission, through its *Final Report*, would be the starting point for a new kind of relation between the Peruvian state and its excluded citizens.
>
> —Salomón Lerner Febres, interview

This chapter zooms into truth commissions in two neighboring countries to examine in detail the creation, procedures, and outcomes of truth-finding panels. The first case is Chile's 1990 National Commission on Truth and Reconciliation (popularly known as the "Rettig Commission" after its president, Raúl Rettig), and the second case is Peru's 2001 Truth and Reconciliation Commission (popularly known by its Spanish acronym, "CVR"). The Chilean commission, established by the president and his advisers in the absence of considerable civil society participation, faced mandate constraints. The findings and recommendations satisfied the expectations of the government and were mostly incorporated into political practice. However, the commission generated little civil society mobilization. In contrast, the Peruvian commission was created through massive domestic and transnational human rights mobilization under conditions of political collapse. The far-reaching conclusions and comprehensive recommendations of this highly autonomous commission were by and large ignored by successive governments, and the reparations program has made little progress. Nevertheless, the commission's work unleashed intense human rights mobilization and novel forms of activism on the part of the victims. Society-wide reconciliation did not take place in the immediate aftermath of the truth commission in either country, as the perpetrators and their political allies refused to acknowledge human rights violations.

The chapter's organization follows the causal and chronological sequence. The first section offers a theoretical framework to explain variation in truth commission impact. The following sections then look at varying aspects of the Chilean and Peruvian commissions: the commission creation processes; the operation, findings, and recommendations of each commission; the institutional and societal responses to the commissions' final reports; and the long-term trajectory of justice, memory, and reparation efforts in the wake of the commissions. The conclusion addresses the plausibility of alternative explanations of variation, such as the nature of the political transition and the timing of the truth commissions in Chile and Peru.

Explaining the Variation in Truth Commission Impact: A Theoretical Framework

Why do some truth commissions receive endorsement and support from the political leadership, while others rely on the mobilization of civil society actors to produce impact? The variation starts from the *commission creation process* (i.e., the initial political decision-making process that establishes a truth commission), which shapes whether or not, and the extent to which, the findings and recommendations generate impact in politics and society. The more control key political decision makers (especially the government) exercise over the initial process, the more likely that they will set a limited mandate, appoint the commissioners in line with their political expectations, and empower the commission to the extent that it satisfies those decision makers. A commission creation process undertaken solely by the government leadership is called *exclusionary*.

Such a commission will be constrained in terms of how much agency it can exercise, and it will be more likely to produce a final report in line with the government's expectations. Consequently, the government will endorse the final report by acknowledging its findings, and it will implement its recommendations, even if selectively. Thus, the commission is likely to generate direct political impact, although the degree of policy change depends on the government's willingness to implement recommendations. Evidence suggests that exclusionary commission creation processes may produce relatively high direct political impact (as in Argentina, Chile, and Sri Lanka), but it is also likely that dependence on government endorsement and adoption leads to low impact in cases where the decision makers choose to ignore the commission (examples include Uganda and Nigeria). The exclusionary process is likely to alienate civil society groups and reduce the likelihood of civil society mobilization around the commission.

In contrast, a *participatory* commission creation process enables a broader set of politicians, civil society actors, the commissioners, and the commission staff to exercise agency with respect to the commission's goals, procedures, and methodology. Especially if transnational advocacy networks join the effort, more funding will be available from more diverse sources, and the commission will be empowered in terms of know-how. Such a high-capacity and high-autonomy commission is likely to produce a more comprehensive and critical account of political violence and human rights violations and make demanding recommendations. The findings and recommendations may surprise and upset decision makers, perhaps delegitimizing the same politicians who sponsored the commission. Such a truth commission may or may not generate considerable direct political impact, as politicians will be unwilling to endorse the final report and implement the recommendations. Yet those civil society actors who participated in the commission process will mobilize to disseminate the report, have the recommendations implemented into policy, and pressure the government for delayed implementation. Policy changes are likely to result through this indirect and longer-term influence.

Although the commission creation process sets limits on what a commission can do and how its findings are likely to be received, constraints on the commission are only part of the story. The commissioners' autonomous work and their interactions with the state and nonstate actors influence truth commission impact, as well. The argument presented here points to the coexistence of path dependence and independent agency before, during, and after a commission's operation.

Chile's Commission Creation Process

When Augusto Pinochet's military dictatorship (1973–1990) was coming to an end, the idea of establishing an official truth-finding body to investigate human rights violations, along the lines of Argentina's 1983 National Commission on the Disappeared, resonated with the democratic politicians and human rights activists. It was José Zalaquett, an ardent advocate of truth commissions as the most suitable mechanism to uncover violations and design reparations, who convinced the government to establish the National Commission on Truth and Reconciliation in 1990.[1] As a young lawyer, he had directed the legal assistance department of Comité pro Paz immediately after the coup.[2] When the military regime adopted an openly hostile stance toward this interfaith human rights initiative, he was arrested along with 111 members of the Comité in November 1975, and soon thereafter he was deported to France. He devoted himself to human rights defense abroad, joining the executive committee of Amnesty International in 1979. When he returned to Chile before the 1989 elections, he participated in efforts to develop the newly elected Concertación coalition's human rights strategy.[3] When Patricio Aylwin assumed the presidency and quickly realized the practical and legal obstacles to criminal justice, he called upon Zalaquett to establish a commission.[4] Aylwin would have much rather established a commission mandated by the legislature, but the weight of Pinochet supporters (Pinochetistas) in the Senate[5] undermined any possibility that human rights initiatives could go through the legislative route.[6] The Rettig Commission, therefore, was established by a presidential decree.[7]

Mandate

Supreme Decree No. 355 limited the investigation of human rights violations to incidents that resulted in death. Leaving out torture, illegal imprisonment, mass layoffs, and exile, the mandate decided to forgo the opportunity to reveal the nature of repression under the dictatorship in its full horror.[8]

Pinochet's Amnesty Decree Law of 1978 had moved almost all crimes committed by state agents in the first five years of the dictatorship outside the reach of courts.[9] The formation of the truth commission coincided with a legislative proposal by the right-wing politician Ricardo Rivadeneira to extend amnesty to all political crimes committed between September 11, 1973, and March 11, 1990. The socialists, social democrats, and a section of the Christian Democrats defeated the bill in the Chamber of Deputies. Meanwhile, President Aylwin had to admit that the derogation of the Amnesty Law, stated in the governing coalition's political program, had to be abandoned in the face of the right-wing majority in the Senate.[10] In other words, the Rettig Commission operated under conditions that did not entirely block the route to criminal justice, but there were few inroads.[11]

The mandate was shaped by Zalaquett's careful approach to transitional justice that sought to balance the "ethical imperatives" of justice and the "political constraints" of a negotiated transition.[12] Article 2 of Supreme Decree No. 355 stated that the commission could not assume jurisdictional functions. By corollary, it was not allowed to name perpetrators, as this would violate the standards of procedural fairness. However, if "the Commission received evidence about actions that appear to be criminal" during its operation, "it will immediately submit it to the appropriate court."[13] The commission was not granted subpoena powers, either. Instead, it relied on voluntary participation to collect information regarding death and disappearance.[14] Although the establishing decree obliged all government officials and agencies to "offer the Commission all the collaboration it may request, furnish the documents it may need, and provide access to such places as it may determine necessary to visit,"[15] there was no penalty attached to noncooperation.

The mandate stipulated that the commissioners produce the complete picture about death and disappearance, including the fate and whereabouts of the disappeared persons, make recommendations for a reparations program, and suggest legal and administrative measures to prevent the repetition of such grave acts. It did not expect the commissioners to present a broader account of the causes and consequences of the military coup and the subsequent political repression and human rights violations, but neither did it explicitly prevent them from doing so. As explained in its final report, the commission used discretion when it "decided to include with these accounts [of most serious human rights violations] some observations it believed to be essential to a better understanding of this matter." The decision to study the "climate" before and after September 11, 1973,[16] the commissioners argued, would serve to prevent violations from happening again.

Composition

President Aylwin carefully selected eight commissioners and the chair, Raúl Rettig, from among "highly respected people with moral authority in our country."[17] Thus, the criterion of selection was individual moral and professional merit rather than participation in a political party or civil association. However, analyzing only the outcome without due attention to the appointment process may be misleading. Moral authority became the primary criterion of selection only because Aylwin's initial plan to recruit commission members directly from political parties, especially from the right-wing opposition, had been frustrated. Aylwin was dedicated to the idea of a representative commission that would satisfy diverse constituencies of the political spectrum, unite them under the moral imperative of recognizing human rights violations, and minimize objections to the commission. As the leftists and the Christian Democrats already endorsed human rights defenders like José Zalaquett and Jaime Castillo,[18] he did not face pressure from those sectors. In order to include the Right in the process, he invited Francisco Bulnes and Ricardo Rivadeneira from the National Renovation Party (RN) to join the commission, and both refused. Guillermo Pumpin, close to the Independent Democratic Union (UDI), also declined.[19]

Therefore, Aylwin turned to Ricardo Martín, José Luis Cea, Gonzalo Vial, and Laura Novoa Velázquez, individuals known to represent right-wing sectors but without formal party commitment.[20] The president's minimal precondition to name right-wing individuals was either an attitude of self-distancing vis-à-vis the military regime or at least some indication of sensitivity towards the human rights issue.[21] It should be noted that victims' organizations had no representation. Also absent were the representatives of the military, who in any case expressed no interest in joining the commission. Perhaps Aylwin considered the military and victims' organizations as interested parties whose participation would be perceived as compromising the impartial nature of the commission's truth-finding work.[22] The outcome, only partially Aylwin's choice, was a commission that adopted as its operating principle a peculiar notion of political representation whereby some commissioners represented political ideologies but not political parties.[23] The striving for ideological balance reflected the prospect of reaching a negotiated and terminal solution to the problem of human rights violations by promoting reconciliation between the Left and the Right.[24]

Peru's Commission Creation Process

When the Fujimori regime began to crumble in early 2000, the organized human rights movement did not miss the opportunity to negotiate the terms of the political transition. Human rights defense was highly institutionalized in Peru—perhaps a surprising fact given the duration of the internal conflict (1980–1992) and the atomization of civil society[25] under Fujimori's civilian-authoritarian regime.[26] In the civil sector, the National Coordinator of Human Rights (Coordinadora Nacional de Derechos Humanos) had been serving as an umbrella coalition of more than sixty national and regional nongovernmental human rights organizations since 1985. Peru's ombudsman's office (Defensoría del Pueblo), established under the 1993 constitution, was designed to serve as an official, yet politically autonomous, human rights agency. A number of nongovernmental associations were specialized in the areas of legal assistance to victims of human rights violations.[27]

Human rights defenders had begun to communicate with politicians during the last months of the Fujimori regime through their participation in the Dialogue Roundtable (Mesa de Diálogo)[28] that brought representatives of the regime together with the opposition under the auspices of the Organization of American States in 2000.[29] The political prospects of the Roundtable took a dramatic turn during the fateful events from September to November 2000, when the corruption scandal that erupted around the figure of Fujimori's intelligence chief, Vladimiro Montesinos, precipitated the decline of the regime.[30] As other political institutions rapidly lost legitimacy, the Roundtable "became the locus of real decisionmaking power during the final days of the Fujimori government, almost becoming a parallel congress before the Peruvian opposition could win control of the congress and form an interim government."[31] Soon after, Fujimori fled to Japan, and the Congress elected Valentín Paniagua, an opposition member of the Roundtable from the Acción Popular political party, as interim president. The acquaintances established during the Roundtable meetings proved crucial for fortifying the relations between the transition's political leadership and the human rights movement. So much so that, when Paniagua established the truth commission in mid-2001, he designated his colleagues from the Roundtable, Sofía Macher and Beatriz Alva, as commissioners, and Luis Bambarén was later added as an observer to the commission.[32]

The architects of the Peruvian commission did not have to worry about the reaction of powerful military, political, and judicial institutions at the initial stage. The collapse of the Fujimori regime and the dissolution of the corruption network that involved top politicians, military leaders, and judges meant that the political scene was temporarily cleared of veto players, at least until the April 2001 elections.[33] Human rights activists emerged as influential actors capable of enhancing the legitimacy of Paniagua's interim government and Alejandro Toledo's succeeding elected government. They advocated a truth commission and successfully lobbied the government of Paniagua, known to be supportive of human rights initiatives. He commissioned an inter-institutional working group to design the truth commission. Five ministries, the human rights ombudsman's office, the Coordinadora, and religious leaders joined the working group. They held planning sessions with hundreds of civil society groups, as well as national and international experts, for over three months.[34] Paniagua adopted the draft decree proposed by the working group with minor revisions.

Mandate

Just like its Chilean counterpart, the Peruvian truth commission was created by presidential decree rather than legislative action to sidestep potential veto players. The advance in the transitional justice process could face a setback, as the April 2001 presidential election led to a runoff between Alejandro Toledo, who was in principle supportive of the commission and had no personal reason to oppose human rights initiatives, and Alan García, whose earlier administration (1985–1990) had been marked by an escalation of violence and serious human rights violations. Just as in Chile, the urge to sidestep a potential veto point proved strong in Peru, and Paniagua hurried to establish the commission with a presidential decree (Supreme Decree 065-2001-PCM) in June 2001, just a month before the runoff. Either way the fears voiced by the human rights community were not realized, as García lost to Toledo. The new president revised the mandate of the commission in

September 2001, making two important changes. He increased the number of commissioners from seven to twelve, and renamed the body "Truth *and Reconciliation* Commission."

The commission was mandated to investigate "disappearances, massacres, extrajudicial executions, torture, prison conditions, prosecutions under the anti-terrorist statutes, and so on,"[35] committed by state agents, the Shining Path and Túpac Amaru Revolutionary Movement (MRTA) insurgencies, and civilian self-defense units (*rondas campesinas*, as well as their legalized version, Self-Defense Committees) between 1980 and 2000. The mandate left the decision to identify (or not) moral, political, and/or criminal responsibility to the commission's discretion. The commission was asked to present cases to the attorney general's office for criminal investigation.[36]

Composition

Peru's truth commission comprised Paniagua's original list of seven commissioners and five additional individuals, appointed by President-elect Alejandro Toledo in mid-2001.[37] Paniagua did not try to strike a numerical balance between adversaries while designating the commissioners.[38] Instead, he worked closely with the human rights movement during the selection process. As a result, the composition reflected the expectations of the human rights movement: the commissioners were social scientists, human rights activists, members of the clergy,[39] and a retired general. Unlike the Chilean commission, where the legal profession dominated the composition, the Peruvian commission was presided over by a professor of philosophy, Salomón Lerner, and the commissioners included an anthropologist, two sociologists, and one political analyst. Only two members had law degrees. Therefore, the commission was prepared to move beyond forensic investigation and develop a broader sociological-historical analysis of the conditions that made violence and authoritarianism possible in Peru.

The composition of the commission should be analyzed not merely as a function of professional background, but also in its sociological dimension. Limeños dominated the commission. Only Alberto Morote, former provost of the University of San Cristóbal at Huamanga, and Carlos Iván Degregori and Carlos Tapia (professors at the same university) had spent a considerable amount of time in Ayacucho, where political violence hit hardest. All the other commissioners were based in Lima. The geographic bias went hand in hand with an ethnocultural bias, as none of the commissioners were of indigenous origin.

The salience of Lima-based criollo intellectuals (social scientists and human rights activists in particular) among the commissioners and staff demonstrates that the truth commission was imagined to be a bridge between the political and cultural center of the nation and the periphery. Salomón Lerner, the president of the commission, was a professor of moral philosophy at the prestigious Catholic University. He was known to be an intellectual with a record of moral integrity who saw in the commission the task of self-less devotion to the people, deriving from Levinas's ethics of the Other.[40] Thus, the commission reflected urban intellectuals' aspiration to explain and transform the Peruvian reality through social-scientific analysis and moral commitment to substantive equality.

Some of the commissioners had been participating in social and political struggles since the 1960s. The commission reflected in part the historical trajectory of the human rights movement in Peru: it was spearheaded by the militant leftists of the 1960s who, in the face of government repression in the late 1970s, adopted the human rights discourse and internalized it throughout the armed conflict in the 1980s and 1990s. The right-wing opposition kept accusing the commission of a leftist bias, in an effort to establish ideological and organic links between the Shining Path and the commission in order to delegitimize the latter. However, the leftist vision adopted by most of the commissioners was completely different from the Shining Path ideology; in fact, these two visions constructed themselves in opposition to each other.[41] While the origins of the human rights movement was to be found in urban student and guerrilla activism inspired by the Guevarist model, the Shining Path took Mao's Cultural Revolution as its inspiration. The urban and distinctively Limeño character of the former was countered by the Shining Path strategy to create a cadre of provincial elites through recruiting from provincial high schools and universities.[42] Even if the leftists of the 1960s and 1970s did not rule out violence as a necessary means of social transformation, none of them shared the Shining Path leadership's fascination with violence as a constructive social force per se. The "blood quota" rhetoric[43] had separated the Shining Path from the members and ex-members of the Vanguardia Revolucionaria, Patria Roja, and other Marxist organizations since the early days of the Shining Path's armed insurgency.

Finally, it should be noted that all commissioners were Peruvian citizens, which left out viable foreign candidates who had contributed so much to the defense of human rights in Peru, like Hubert Lansier and Pilar Coll.[44] This national bias notwithstanding, the Peruvian commission was a transnational effort in terms of staff participation, consultancy, and funding.[45]

Chile's Commission Process

The Human Rights Investigation

The Chilean commission's mandate obliged the commission to investigate all cases of death and disappearance perpetrated by the state's security forces, as well as deaths caused by the armed resistance to the dictatorship.[46] The commission adopted a legalistic notion of truth that prioritized written documents as evidence, while testimonies were reduced to secondary status. The composition of the commission partly explains the legalistic bias: except for Mónica Jiménez, a social assistant, all commissioners had law degrees. The absence of precedents may be an important explanatory factor, too: the testimonial methodology became popular only later, thanks to the ritualistic public hearings of the South African Truth and Reconciliation Commission.[47] Another motivation for the commission's decision seems to be the fear that overreliance on victims' and relatives' testimonies would jeopardize the unbiased and impartial character of the commission in the eyes of pro-military sectors.[48]

The human rights archive at the human rights branch of the Catholic Church, Vicaría de la Solidaridad, was the most frequently consulted source of written documents. The list of disappeared individuals had been frequently updated by the Vicaría, thanks to the arduous labor of the Association of Relatives of the Disappeared (AFDD after its Spanish acronym) that operated in the Vicaría's premises during the dictatorship.[49] Furthermore, the commission staff asked the victims' relatives to submit copies of initial court records, as well as reports from other governmental or nongovernmental organizations that had already investigated their case.

In July 1990, the commission began to schedule interviews with those relatives who requested a testimony session. The interviews were set up to obtain additional information, offer an opportunity for family members to narrate their suffering, and create a database for the reparations program. Following the initial success of the sessions in the Metropolitan Region of Santiago, teams of social workers and lawyers traveled to regional and provincial centers from July to September 1990 to receive small groups of relatives. These interview sessions, while falling short of the public hearings that would revolutionize truth-finding methodology in the South African commission, nevertheless yielded beneficial results, according to the final report: "For many [relatives of the victims], this was the first gesture made by the Chilean government to acknowledge their situation."[50] Furthermore, the organization of the meetings as small-group gatherings enabled the victims to narrate their stories and support each other.[51] The commission collected about 3,500 testimonies from the victims' relatives and victim-survivors. Because the commission lacked subpoena power and did not offer incentives for the participation of perpetrators, it failed to collect perpetrator testimonies except for a handful of repenting agents of the infamous secret service (DINA after its Spanish acronym), such as Marcia Merino, Luz Arce, and Ingrid Olderock.

The commission made sure that all agencies willing to contribute relevant information could do so. It asked all military, business, labor, and professional organizations, as well as political parties, to provide lists of victims. A wide array of organizations, ranging from the military and the police (Carabineros) to human rights groups, the Revolutionary Left Movement (MIR), and the Communist Party, prepared lists that included the names of their members killed during the military regime. Furthermore, in every case of violation that implicated the members of the military or the police as alleged perpetrators, the commission sought to engage those institutions in the fact-finding process by contacting the corresponding branch. While the final report points to the high response rate (the Carabineros responded to almost every request, while the army responded to about two-thirds), the typical response was evasive: it either stated that the records were burned or destroyed in accordance with laws and regulations, or that the institution did not possess any further information, or that it was legally prohibited from disclosing information on matters of intelligence.[52]

Instead, the army provided the commission with four volumes of information and a video to justify the military coup and to document attacks by armed opposition groups that resulted in the deaths of security personnel and civilians.[53] The institution refused to share any information concerning the fate or whereabouts of the disappeared. In a way, the army affirmed the importance of not excluding itself from the task of illuminating the history of political violence, but employed a mixed strategy that combined nonco-operation in cases of human rights violations with selective cooperation to justify the dictatorship.

Findings

The commission received 3,428 cases of death and disappearance and quali-fied that 2,279 of them fell within its mandate; 2,115 people had been mur-dered by state agents and 164 by armed opposition groups. The commission also stated that extrajudicial murder, forced disappearance and torture were institutional and systematic practices. Using its only judicial power, "in all relevant cases the commission has sent the respective items of evidence to the courts."[54] The final report established the moral responsibility of the Chilean state, which "does not have any legal effects other than to lay the groundwork for measures of reparations."[55] It assigned institutional, moral, and historical responsibilities to political parties and other institutions, most notably the military and police.[56] Although the individual perpetrators were not named, the commission did not refrain from announcing those institutions and organizations responsible for the human rights viola-tions. However, it is not clear from the final report how historical or moral responsibilities should be assumed. Finally, the commission suggested, again without clear definitions or guidelines, that the entire society could assume responsibility.

Recommendations

The Rettig Commission presented a recommendations plan encompassing reparations for victims and political-institutional reform. The recommenda-tions were not legally binding on the government. In the area of reparations, the commission suggested a comprehensive program including social secu-rity, health, educational, and housing benefits, as well as special medical care for the victims of repression.[57] The clear message of the political-institutional recommendations was the need to strengthen the rule of law guarantees to prevent the recurrence of human rights violations. One suggested measure was to make the constitution and the military code of justice compatible with international human rights law. Another recommendation was the creation of the office of the human rights ombudsman. In terms of improving the human rights conduct of the judiciary and the military, the commission emphasized education and training. The emphasis on education suggests that the commissioners thought at least some of the perpetrators and connivers were not sufficiently aware of the theory and practice of human rights. Ignorance was prioritized over intentionality as the chief explanation of perpetrators' behavior. The final report also recommended public commemoration and education campaigns to cultivate a culture of human rights in Chile.

The silences of the recommendations chapter should also be noted. The Rettig Commission did not demand the demotion and removal of military and civilian personnel implicated in human rights violations; did not push for the derogation of the 1978 Amnesty Law; did not develop a road map for criminal investigations; and certainly did not mention the need to overcome poverty, inequality, social exclusion, or any other structural failure that may have been the root cause for political violence. Since it concerned itself exclusively with the institutional and ideological crisis at the onset of the military coup, its recommendations were limited to institutional reform and consciousness-raising through education. The self-restrained and uncontroversial nature of the recommendations increased the likelihood of their implementation, but at the risk of amnesia concerning the deeper causes for violence and violations.

Limited institutional reform put emphasis on the need to strengthen and legitimize the state to achieve the goals of political transition. The weight of legal-administrative reform signaled the concentration of power in the hands of the executive, to the exclusion of civil society participation.[58] The initial arrangement that established the commission accounts for this state-centric bias. Aylwin did not envision a truth commission that would facilitate cooperation between civil society and the state. Rather, the Rettig Commission was mandated to make a gesture toward the victims of the dictatorship and convince the pro-Pinochet political class of the need for minimal consensus on historical facts. The fundamental idea was to relegitimize the state in its capacity to govern more effectively and in line with the ethical obligations of civility and human rights, and the commission worked toward that end when it sought to overcome what it identified as the proximal cause of the problem, namely the institutional breakdown and political polarization of 1973.[59] The consequence, as we shall see, was the relative insignificance of the Rettig Commission for human rights mobilization.

Peru's Commission Process

The Human Rights Investigation

The Peruvian commission is credited for the rigorous and comprehensive study of international human rights law and international humanitarian law. The commissioners needed precise definitions to identify the nature of the conflict between the Shining Path and the government, the violations committed by each party to the conflict, and the responsibilities and obligations assigned to individuals and organizations, as well as to the Peruvian state.[60] The commission agreed to describe the period of violence and violations as "internal armed conflict."

Preceding truth commissions, especially those in South Africa and Guatemala, had provided the Peruvian one with a toolkit of methodological options. The commissioners realized that the experiences of internal armed conflict and ethnic discrimination/marginalization had much in common with the South African and Guatemalan experiences. Moreover, these exemplary commissions, especially the South African one, had revolutionized the field of transitional justice through a variety of technologies to discover and disseminate the facts of human rights violations. In terms of testimonial methodology, the South African public hearings opened a new space for victims and relatives to publicize their quest for recognition and reparation to a broad audience. The extensive testimonies challenged the wisdom of earlier truth commissions that used oral sources only as input for factual information, and added *truth telling* to the repertoire of symbolic reparations. In terms of quantitative methodology, the development of large-scale human rights information management systems[61] allowed researchers to make relatively precise estimations of the number of victims in settings where accurate data collection was not possible. The Peruvian commission made use of all of these methods.

At the inception of their work, the commissioners engaged in a theoretical discussion concerning the nature of the truth they were trying to construct. They could adopt a notion of truth finding more in line with the courtroom model (*judicial truth*) or produce a social history of violence in

Peru (*historical truth*). The weight of social scientists in the commission shifted the discussion in favor of the latter option. In the end, "this discussion was not solved necessarily by means of formal decision-making by the different bodies of the Commission, but rather under the conditions of its evolving engagement with Peruvian society."[62] As the testimonial process unfolded, especially during the victims' hearings that began in April 2002, the commissioners realized that "victim after victim demanded that the criminals be punished. In the victims' view, only after criminal justice was achieved, would other forms of reparation be asked for and reconciliation attained."[63] Attending to the demand for justice, the CVR decided not to forgo juridical standards of fact-finding. The Special Investigations Unit was established as the commission's legal team. In August 2002, the attorney general's office and the CVR signed an agreement for further cooperation. Accordingly, the commissioners agreed to refer all information on criminal responsibility to the attorney general.

Thanks to an ambitious outreach effort, the commission succeeded in collecting over 17,000 testimonies in two years.[64] It made ample use of the archives maintained by various human rights organizations throughout the conflict. Commissioners and staff members met victim-survivors and victims' relatives; visited prisons to contact the leadership and rank and file of insurgent organizations; called upon the active-duty and retired members of the armed forces and the police; and invited top politicians of the violent period to give testimonies. Despite their best efforts, the commissioners knew that they could not recover all the relevant information. Reaching the peasant communities of the Andean highlands posed serious practical difficulties, and many victims were reluctant to give testimonies after decades of fear.[65] There were no material incentives for presumed perpetrators to testify. Among political parties, the American Revolutionary Popular Alliance (APRA) had a relatively cooperative attitude, and its leader Alan García testified before the commission. Other relevant parties, and especially the supporters of Alberto Fujimori, refused to collaborate with the commission in any meaningful way.

Findings

The CVR was able to identify 18,397 dead and disappeared persons by full name. The deficiencies in information collection led the commission to employ a statistical estimation technique to infer the total number of victims.[66]

On the basis of the available data, the Multiple Systems Estimation approximated the number of dead to be 69,280 within a 95 percent confidence interval.[67] Slightly more than half the murders were attributed to the Shining Path, and around 30 percent to the agents of the state. A small percentage of the remaining deaths were attributed to the MRTA, while the perpetrators could not be identified in a large number of cases.

Commentators note that the commission's estimation of such a high death toll shocked the Peruvian public. Vociferous critics questioned the merits of statistical approximation. From the statistician's point of view, the estimation is a reasonable (and moderate)[68] inference that has no intrinsic political implication, but the introduction of the 69,280 figure (or its rounded-down version, 69,000) into national and international press coverage, political debates, and the consciousness of citizens turned it into a monumental symbol for the nation's history. Although the CVR had extensive information on other forms of violations as well, the death toll appeared to represent victimhood in numeric terms.[69]

The final report also noted that 75 percent of the victims of the internal armed conflict and authoritarianism were members of indigenous communities that make up less than 25 percent of the total population.[70] While the conflict was not caused by ethnic separatism, the unequal distribution of victimhood along ethnic lines was an alarming indication that centuries of neglect, exclusion, and marginalization had taken its toll on vulnerable populations. In geographical terms, violence hit the department of Ayacucho the hardest, followed by Junín, Huanuco, Huancavelica, and Apurimac. Lima and its surroundings suffered violence briefly, as a result of the Shining Path's strategy to extend its operations to the capital in 1989. The final report makes an interesting digression to explain the experience of violence in the provinces in terms intelligible to the audiences in Lima: "If we were all from Ayacucho," that is to say, if Peru's total number of dead per population ratio were equal to that of Ayacucho, the total number of dead would have been 1.2 million, with the number approaching 340,000 in Lima's metropolitan region or, in terms understandable to the imagined Limeño audience: "the total population of Lima's San Isidro, Miraflores, San Borja and La Molina districts."[71] Not surprisingly, the CVR found that the human rights violations committed by state agents, as well as the Shining Path, were systematic in nature. Earlier in the conflict the army did not distinguish between combatants, insurgent sympathizers, and bystanders; in time, warfare became more selective. However, massacres of civilians continued throughout the internal conflict.

The final report was adopted with unanimity, but commissioner Luis Arias Graziani signed the final document with a reservation. A letter to the president of the republic specified the retired general's reservation, which stated that the armed forces had complied with their duty, and that some of the facts in the final report remained unproven.

Recommendations

Volume 9 of the final report contains a recommendations plan consisting of eighty-five items. The bulk of the recommendations concerned political-institutional reform and a victim-oriented reparations program. Added to these were issues of commemoration, a burial program for the murdered, and the prosecution of human rights violators. Furthermore, the sociohistorical conclusions of the CVR made it necessary to view reform in a more profound light, including, in the words of one of its members, the "modification of com-monsense [notions] and conceptions of the country that many of us have."[72] In other words, the Peruvian commission saw in the emerging consciousness around human rights a transformative potential to reform political institutions and the political culture, restitute the victims' rights, and ensure that fundamental rights would never be violated again. The historical evolution of the state-society relations in Peru led the commissioners to pay close attention to the inadequacies of merely demanding respect for rights in a society where many people lacked, in Hannah Arendt's words, "the right to have rights." The rights discourse, they realized, made little contribution to the lives of those deprived of such basic access to the state as an ID card.[73] In the words of the final report, what was needed was nothing short of a "new social contract" (*nuevo pacto social*) in which all Peruvians would be recognized as first-class citizens.

Chile's Truth Commission Impact

Reception of the Final Report

The final report of the Rettig Commission did not transform the political landscape. Parties of the governing coalition, human rights organizations, and victims' relatives endorsed the report, while the political Right and the armed forces were united in their rejection. President Aylwin endorsed the report with a historic speech on March 19, 1991, in which he asked pardon of the victims' relatives.[74]

Despite the designation of individuals associated with the military regime as commissioners, the armed forces and their civilian allies expressed disillusionment with the findings. The air force issued a somewhat cautious statement in which it neither endorsed nor rejected the report, and the air force commander in chief Fernando Matthei expressed sorrow for the loss of lives. The other branches of the military condemned the commission's work in stronger terms. The Carabineros saw in the final report an effort to weaken the police force in their struggle against leftist terrorism. The army and the navy issued statements conveying serious disagreement three weeks after Aylwin's public endorsement. The commission had refuted many of the Pinochetista myths that together created the social memory of this sector, especially the notion that the military coup and subsequent abuses were justified because Chile was undergoing an internal war.[75] The military's fury was directed not only at the historical narrative but also the finding that the violations were the consequence of a systematic policy rather than sporadic excesses. The commissioners had adopted a strategy that emphasized facts rather than historical narratives. The armed forces and their allies—to this day—could not refute the facts of human rights violations in a convincing manner.[76]

The political Right chose to maintain its alliance with the military by rejecting the commission's findings. Aylwin's strategy of including right-wing commissioners did not result in the kind of national reconciliation he had envisioned. As the right-wing commissioners were not representatives of the two right-wing parties, RN and UDI, these parties' leaders found it relatively easy to ignore the facts of institutional and systematic extermination and disappearance.[77] The assassination of UDI's leader Jaime Guzmán on April 1, 1991, by the Manuel Rodríguez Patriotic Front created the appropriate excuse to reject the commission's work altogether. Among the civilian sectors, the Supreme Court went furthest in denial, threatening that the final report was putting the institutional stability of the new democracy in jeopardy.

Direct Political Impact

The Chilean truth commission generated high direct political impact. The president endorsed the commission's final report, and the government successfully implemented a victim-oriented reparations policy, published the final report, and established a follow-up institution to monitor the progress on the reparations program. The only ignored recommendation was the creation of the human rights ombudsman.

As the criminal proceedings against alleged perpetrators did not advance, President Aylwin turned to reparations as a mechanism of restitutive justice for the victims. Creating a database of recipients required a longer investigation than the one conducted by the nine-month-long truth commission. Therefore, Aylwin authorized the National Reparation and Reconciliation Corporation (CNRR in Spanish acronym) in 1992 to investigate the pending cases and establish a reparations program on the basis of additional information. The CNRR produced a list of victims and administered the reparations program.[78] When the CNRR investigation came to an end in 1996, the total number of dead was found to be 3,197.[79] The families of the disappeared and executed received reparations in the form of monthly payments, exemption from military service, and tuition scholarships. A parallel initiative, the Program of Reparations and Comprehensive Health Care (PRAIS in Spanish acronym), continues to provide free general and mental health care.[80] The formation of the CNRR enhanced not only administrative efficiency, but also extended the official recognition of victimhood through reparations. The reparations policy was accompanied by the construction of a Memorial Wall in the General Cemetery of Santiago in 1997 to display the names of the dictatorship's victims—a commemorative gesture that solidified the Chilean state's victim-oriented approach to transitional justice.

Aside from the Memorial Wall, memorialization has advanced in great part thanks to initiative on the part of individuals, victims' groups, and neighborhood associations. The central government has left decision-making powers to the local authorities, and the lack of coordination between the government and nongovernmental efforts is noted.[81] The transformation of Villa Grimaldi, previously a secret detention and torture center, into the Park for Peace in 1997 stands out as the chief accomplishment of victims' groups and neighborhood assemblies sensitive to the human rights issue.[82] Memorialization did not come about as a direct result of truth commission recommendations or civil society mobilization around the commission, but the Rettig Commission contributed to the process in two ways: first, by raising awareness about extrajudicial killings, forced disappearances, and torture, and, second, by providing a list of victims whose names are displayed at the Memorial Wall.

Civil Society Mobilization

The human rights community in Chile had managed to survive the early violent and authoritarian phase of Pinochet's rule, and "resourceful social actors sought out and *created* 'opportunity'—through personal networks embedded in historically linked social, political, and institutional networks— where none seemed forthcoming," a process that accelerated toward the end of the dictatorship.[83] Despite this history of activism, however, there was no civil society pressure on the government to implement truth commission recommendations, and the human rights movement suffered a period of retrenchment in the wake of the commission. In other words, the truth commission generated little civil society mobilization, partly as a result of the government's endorsing posture and partly as a result of the mistrust on the part of the human rights community (especially the victims' relatives).

The commission failed to mobilize the human rights movement to monitor compliance with the recommendations. The movement saw the truth commission as a positive, yet incomplete step.[84] The government's quick adoption of some of the recommendations and the commission's failure to advocate key items on the human rights agenda, such as the derogation of the Amnesty Law, limited the mobilization of influential victims' associations and human rights organizations around the commission. In addition, the government attended to victims and their relatives *as victims* through the reparations program, but did not consider them important civil society partners in policy formation. The alignment between the victims' groups and the Communist Party further strained the former's relation with the centrist Concertación. For example, AFDD's "peace and reconciliation" proposal in October 1995, delineating concrete measures to promote an agenda of reconciliation through justice, did not receive any consideration from the government.

Furthermore, the post-commission period was marked by the disarticulation of the human rights coalition that kept the issue alive since the early days of the dictatorship. The Catholic Church closed the Vicaría in 1992, much to the dismay of the relatives of the victims who had found shelter in it for sixteen years. The church officials argued that the Vicaría was meant to be an emergency measure when other civilian initiatives were violently repressed and the courts were not fulfilling their duties. As democracy and the rule of law were restored in Chile, the church would divest from this service to devote its resources to other areas of social work.[85] For the victims' relatives in the AFDD, the closure of the Vicaría was much more than the loss of a critical ally: they had to move out of the premises of the Vicaría,[86] and refashion themselves as a professional NGO within Chile's new civic sector—a task for which they were unprepared.

A further blow came in the same year as a result of the long-standing tensions among the victims' relatives: many decided to leave the AFDD to start their own organization, which they called AFDD–Línea Fundadora (Founding Line). The tension that had remained dormant throughout the dictatorship was one of ideological commitment and priorities between AFDD's earlier members (who in 1992 called themselves the "Founding Line") and the members from the Communist Party.[87] The common struggle against the dictatorship prevented the internal disagreements from surfacing during the dictatorship. But soon after the return to democracy and the frustration of the shared hope that the whereabouts of the disappeared would be discovered and perpetrators would face justice, a small group of relatives without Communist Party affiliation split definitively.[88] They did not succeed in carrying the majority along with them; therefore, the outcome was two weakened relatives' associations.

Accompanying the AFDD's own divisions was the broader phenomenon of civil society retrenchment. The lawyers and activists who were employed by the Vicaría, and later the truth commission, found jobs in the government sector. Human rights organizations lacked the resources to pay for comparable salaries. Furthermore, the precariousness of the struggle for justice, combined with the closure of the Vicaría, threatened the very existence of a human rights sector autonomous from the government. International donors divested from Chile, which they considered a normalized and peaceful country.[89] For those who could not find jobs in the government's human rights sector, they still had to seek additional employment, which reduced the full-time staff. It was painfully clear that the human rights movement, for which Chile was famous,[90] could not convert itself to a network of professional NGOs. The post-commission process looked like the end of human rights activism in Chile, rather than an era of renewal. This trend would only be reversed after Pinochet's London arrest in October 1998 and the subsequent process of civil society reinvigoration, especially around the issue of torture under the dictatorship.[91]

Peru's Truth Commission Impact

Reception of the CVR

The responses to the Chilean commission were institutional and more or less predictable. The striking feature of the Peruvian experience was that the CVR generated enormous controversy in the public sphere, yet few institutional responses. President Toledo received the final report with an attitude of endorsement. His rhetorical support and positive attitude toward the commission and the commissioners remained constant throughout his presidency. He attended seminars organized by the CVR, and he asked forgiveness in the name of the state. However, the attitude of endorsement did not usher in a coherent policy of incorporating the recommendations and conclusions into institutional reform and a reparations program.

The Council of Ministers did not issue a public statement, although some of its members, like Anel Townsend, minister of women and social development, declared willingness to promote institutional mechanisms to turn the CVR recommendations into policy. The Congress, the judiciary, and other state institutions did not take an explicit position. Despite the commission's call for self-reflection, the three political forces that were in government between 1980 and 2000, Acción Popular, APRA, and Fujimoristas respectively, failed to assume political responsibility for the violations attributed to the agents of the state. The leader of APRA, Alan García, lent measured support while expressing disagreements with some sections of the report.[92] The leaderships of the Acción Popular and Fujimorista parties, as well as many members of APRA, were openly hostile to the commission, insinuating links between some of the commissioners and the Shining Path. Among those political parties that bore no responsibility for the violations, responses were varied. Sometimes one leading figure of a party would endorse the report, while another would reject its findings.[93] All in all, politicians tended to address the CVR in a personal, and not institutional, capacity.[94]

The final report's attribution of political and criminal responsibility to leading political figures, and especially ex-presidents, politicized the debate.

The most divisive cases were those of former presidents Alan García and Alberto Fujimori. The CVR attributed to García political, but not criminal, responsibility for the 1986 prison massacre at "El Frontón." Many human rights groups and García's political rivals concurred in criticizing the CVR for this weak notion of responsibility. The politics of the case brought Fujimori's supporters in bitter conflict with the CVR, as Fujimori was singled out as the only ex-president found to bear criminal responsibility for acts under his rule.

Fear of criminal accountability was not the only reason for criticizing the CVR. The characterization of the violent period as an internal armed conflict rather than war against terrorism and the overall condemnation of this dark period in a way that disqualified narratives of heroism generated discontent among certain political sectors and the military. Some even claimed that the CVR itself, to the extent that it sought to weaken the military, was part of the subversive strategy. The CVR's stress on social exclusion, marginalization, and poverty as the root causes of the conflict led conservatives to accuse commissioners of speaking the same language of social justice as the Shining Path. Among the business community, appreciation of the CVR was rare and always with qualifications.[95]

The army did not accept that the human rights violations were "systematic and generalized";[96] at most, there was mention of "excesses." Retired generals were more vocal in their rejection of the findings.[97] Forty-two ex-generals announced their rejection of the CVR. In fact, the CVR provided an opportunity for the mobilization of active-duty and retired officers as much as it did for the human rights community. The institutional image and morale of the armed forces had been seriously damaged in 2000, due to revelations that implicated the military leadership with the Fujimori-Montesinos corruption network. The accusations of the CVR gave the negative impulse to dispel the air of disintegration among the military family. Some of the retired generals initiated libel claims against the commission.

The responses from the church deserve special attention. Many members of the Catholic and Protestant churches sympathized with the truth and reconciliation project, and two members of the clergy served as commissioners. However, the Catholic Church hierarchy that had been based in Ayacucho during the conflict had openly opposed all human rights efforts and condoned violations committed by state agents. This sector of the Catholic Church, represented by Cardinal Luis Cipriani, faced harsh criticism in the final report, and, in return, directed a virulent public campaign against the CVR.

Direct Political Impact

The Peruvian truth commission generated limited political impact. Initially, the Toledo government expressed willingness to implement the recommendations,[98] but the ex-commissioners, as well as the human rights ombudsman Walter Alban, pointed out that rhetorical support was not accompanied by action. Sofía Macher's 2007 evaluation of compliance with recommendations, a balance sheet of the Toledo presidency, reveals that some progress had been achieved in the areas of health-care reparations and human rights trials, while all other reforms had fallen short of satisfactory results. A 2009 study reveals that the recommendations were by and large ignored.[99] Besides, the expectation that the main political actors reflect on the nation's history to transform their attitudes found little support from the political elite.[100]

In terms of reparations, the significant advance was the July 2005 legislation (Law 28592) that formalized the Comprehensive Reparations Plan (Plan Integral de Reparaciones). The law put the High Level Multisector Commission (CMAN in Spanish acronym) in charge of the reparations program, and created the Reparations Council (Consejo de Reparaciones) in charge of the list of victims eligible for reparations. Article 4 of the law stipulated that members of subversive organizations were not eligible for reparations. In other words, the law was guided less by the human rights norm, which defines violation regardless of the prior moral and legal acts of the harmed individual, than a moralized notion of innocent victimhood.

The choice of cooperation with the Reparations Council posed a Faustian bargain for the human rights advocates. On the one hand, the law enabled civil society cooperation with the state to secure reparations for thousands of victims, which was better than nothing. On the other, the law established a criterion of exclusion that deviated from the human rights norm and would leave out many individuals otherwise entitled to redress. In the end, Sofía Macher, a former CVR member and human rights defender, accepted President Toledo's invitation to head the council. Accompanying her was Pilar Coll, a Spanish national known for her devoted service to human rights advocacy in Peru's prisons. Other members included representatives of the military, the business community, and advocates of indigenous rights and development. The chief task was to produce a list of individuals certified as victims on the basis of information from earlier lists (the CVR list being the most comprehensive) and collecting new testimonies from those who had not appeared in earlier lists. The disqualification of suspected terrorists and military personnel implicated in human rights violations generated serious disagreements that slowed down the certification process.[101] Also, many more victims than expected testified before the underfinanced and understaffed Reparations Council, which received more testimonies than the CVR. This reveals that even if the CVR failed to reach all the victims during its two-year mandate, it overcame the fears associated with truth telling and contributed to local projects of consciousness-raising and civil society mobilization to such an extent that the follow-up Reparations Council succeeded in collecting many more testimonies. Other enabling factors were the confidentiality of the council's testimonial process and the expectation that giving testimonies would result in tangible benefits.

The election of Alan García into presidency in 2006 further slowed down the processes of reparations and reform. García's APRA, while acknowledging the CVR's validity, had always been critical of what it perceived as the anti-APRA sentiment of the findings. The commission's revelations of various human rights violations under García's first term, including numerous massacres in the Andean highlands and the extrajudicial killing of prisoners in Lima's "El Frontón" prison, made the new government an unlikely ally. Furthermore, the wider coalition around which the new APRA government was formed included individuals and political groups that held extremely hostile positions concerning human rights and the CVR. The designation as vice president of Luis Giampietri, one of the suspects of "El Frontón" and a vocal critic of the CVR, was a clear indication of the difficulties. The human rights community began to perceive outright hostility in the area of compliance with the CVR recommendations. The sense of measured optimism was giving way to alarm.

There has been some progress with collective reparations: more than 7,000 communities have been listed as beneficiaries of collective reparations, and over 1,600 have received funding for public projects between 2007 and 2011.[102] One of the criticisms about the way collective reparations are handled is that the national and regional governments have presented them as public works in order to expand the voter base through patronage rather than emphasizing the affected communities' *right* to reparations.[103] In administering individual reparations, the lack of political will and the consequent lack of resources ruled out any possibility that the list of victims would be prepared quickly, let alone that the benefits would be distributed.[104] At times, national and international civil society groups funded local reparations efforts to substitute for state responsibility.[105] In many localities, the Reparations Council managed to supply the victims with certification papers in emotional ceremonies that brought victims together with local authorities, the council staff, and the local human rights community. Yet the question remains: "Oh, why should I remember all of that again? From the top of my head to the bottom of my feet, from the bottom of my feet to the top of my head—I've told what happened here so many times. And for what? Nothing ever changes."[106]

Civil Society Mobilization

The human rights movement endorsed the CVR. They were aware of the need to reorganize quickly to muster the political will and public financing necessary to move forward with the institutional recommendations, individual and collective reparations, criminal proceedings, and the exhumations program.[107] The early post-commission efforts focused on pressuring President Toledo to make a bold statement in support of the CVR. As the judicial and forensic institutions were reluctant to work with the findings, and powerful congressional actors were by and large in denial, strong backing from the president would boost the commission's legitimacy. In a similar vein, former CVR members demanded the creation of a follow-up commission staffed by civil society actors—again, demonstrating the trust they placed on human rights activism in the face of inaction by politicians.[108]

The diffusion of the conclusions was another major concern, as the final report, comprising nine volumes, simply could not serve that purpose. Human rights organizations, development NGOs, and research institutes published shorter books that focused on one geographical region or one topic of research (for instance, the universities during the armed conflict) at a time.[109] The abridged version of the final report, *Hatun Willakuy*, was published in February 2004 by the CVR staff. When the initial 20,000 copies were sold out, the second edition was prepared in 2008 by the joint effort of a research institute (IDEHPUCP in Spanish acronym) affiliated with the Catholic University, the ombudsman's office, and the German Catholic Bishops' Organisation for Development Cooperation (MISEREOR). The diffusion effort demonstrates the extent to which the truth commission became a mobilizing force for the civil society, while the state by and large ignored its responsibility to disseminate the findings and conclusions. The incorporation of the final report into the national educational curriculum suffered a similar setback: educational authorities in Peru chose not to make explicit reference to the findings and recommendations of the CVR, arguing that there was nothing new in the content of the final report, that these findings and recommendations were already "implicitly" contained in the national educational curriculum, and that the controversial nature of the CVR made its incorporation difficult.[110] Nongovernmental efforts accomplished a degree of incorporation at the local level.[111]

In part thanks to its unrelenting enemies, the CVR occupied a central position in public debates for a longer time than most other truth commissions around the globe. One commentator likened the CVR experience to the Dreyfus Affair for its capacity to accentuate political divisions.[112] Daily newspapers *La República* and *El Comercio* provided extensive coverage of the early post-commission process. *La Razón* and *Expreso* gave voice to the criticisms of the CVR, which typically paid less attention to the content of the findings than the commission's perceived weak spots, such as the prior political commitments of the members and the commission's budget. At times the detractors put into doubt the factual basis of the human rights investigation, especially the death toll estimated by the CVR and the methodology used. Overall, the public opinion was highly supportive of the CVR. In an editorial, *La República* declared, citing survey results that yielded a consistent majority approval for the CVR, that the commission "has won the battle over public opinion."[113]

Chile's Truth Commission Impact from a Long-term Perspective

The Rettig Commission's final report did not serve the government's purpose of national reconciliation between the perpetrators and the victims.[114] The unflinching attitude of the military, the Supreme Court, and the political Right revealed that neither the participation of conservative individuals in the commission process nor the undeniable facts of human rights violations overcame denial. In fact President Aylwin's apology, which was meant to initiate a "ritual of reconciliation,"[115] only put the pressure off those who had much to apologize for.

The opposition blocked the incorporation of the final report into the educational curriculum. After the assassination of Jaime Guzmán, the government suspended its earlier decision to disseminate the report,[116] and this spectacle of vengeful violence appeared to destroy hopes that some degree of self-reflection, dialogue, and consensus would be achieved. The dissemination of the report was further undermined when the minister of education Ricardo Lagos's proposal to use the final report in textbooks was rejected in the face of Senate opposition. The report found its place on public library shelves in 1997 for the first time.[117]

Was the assassination of Guzmán such a determining factor for the human rights issue? While there is broad consensus that the incident made it more difficult to advance truth and justice, it should not be singled out as the chief cause for the halt. Sociologist Manuel Antonio Garretón argues that the importance of the truth commission notwithstanding, it was not part of a clear political strategy. Rather, the government wanted to first gauge other political actors' reactions to the commission before developing its own human rights strategy. The assassination had such drastic effect on the reception of the Rettig Commission and human rights policy only as a result of this reluctance to develop a consistent plan for action.[118]

Commentators agree that the publication of the final report was meant to be the last, rather than the first, official mechanism to address the legacy of the dictatorship in the early years of the transition. Although Chile did not suffer cycles of violence in the democratic period, one cannot argue that the transformation of the political culture and mentalities through the truth commission accounts for this change. Refusal to learn from history, especially on the part of former perpetrators, is best illustrated by the constant military-civilian tensions that bordered twice on coup threats between 1990 and 1994. The Aylwin presidency always remained committed to the defense of human rights in rhetoric, but the worsening civilian-military relations led Aylwin to adopt a cautious approach, which he described as "justice within the possible." Truth and justice were further compromised under Eduardo Frei-Tagle's presidency (1994–2000), which treated the human right issue as a closed matter, at least until Pinochet's London arrest. A "culture of forgetfulness" dominated Chilean politics throughout the 1990s.[119]

The self-perceived success of democratic transition and national reconciliation permeated political discourse until October 16, 1998,[120] when the triumphalism of the Chilean political elite dissolved in the face of Augusto Pinochet's arrest in London, which drew international attention back to

Chile's pending human rights issue.[121] Serious generational, institutional, and political-cultural transformations would begin to shake Chilean politics around 1998,[122] and even then, the initial rift introduced at the truth commission process separated the participants of government initiatives from the grassroots human rights movement.

Chile's participatory truth commission was the 2003 National Commission on Political Imprisonment and Torture, and interestingly, it was less a follow-up to the Rettig Commission than a reaction to its shortcomings. Torture under the military regime was discussed in general terms in the Rettig Commission's final report, but the commission was not mandated to draw a list of torture victims. The fact that governments did not formulate a policy of retributive justice or reparations throughout the 1990s meant that torture victims found no place in the official transitional justice framework. However, Pinochet's arrest in London and the subsequent human rights trials at home generated increasing awareness around the issue of torture in the early 2000s. Victims' associations successfully lobbied the government to create the torture commission, known as the Valech Commission after its chair, Sergio Valech. Mandated to investigate torture, as well as sexual violence and mistreatment of minors, the Valech Commission served to extend official recognition and reparations to victims who were excluded by the Rettig Commission. Thus, the activism around the Valech Commission sought to overcome the limitations of the previous panel.

Peru's Truth Commission Impact from a Long-Term Perspective

The tendency to ignore the broader message of the CVR has shaped Peruvian politicians' choices in dealing with human rights violations and social grievances.[123] Recent incidents offer insights: the disagreements between the government and the indigenous populations of the Peruvian Amazon over the use of indigenous lands and natural resources resulted in the outbreak of violence in the community of Bagua on June 5, 2009, when a series of armed confrontations between the locals and the police left dozens dead and injured. Similar social conflicts have become common in the context of Peru's recent resource-driven economic boom. The political economy of the unrest and the pattern and duration of violence have close to nothing in common with the internal conflict. However, there is an alarming similarity: grievances formulated by marginalized communities are heeded by the political center only if the conflict turns violent, claims lives, and grabs national and international media attention. The history of poverty and exclusion, reinforced along ethnolinguistic lines, still casts its shadow on the present, and the CVR's call for overcoming poverty and marginalization, and creating a space for political articulation that makes violent spectacles unnecessary, has fallen on deaf ears.

Meanwhile, the truth commission has generated effects beyond policy change. The frustration with government inaction and hostility led human rights organizations and victims' groups to mobilize around the truth commission. The Lima-based Citizen Movement–Never Again (Movimiento Ciudadano–Para Que No Se Repita) began to function as a nationwide movement of more than seven hundred organizational members with the primary goal of promoting the commission's message.[124] In late 2006, a group of youths in their mid-twenties from the provinces of Ayacucho and Andahuaylas organized themselves as victims' associations to pressure the local and national authorities for the implementation of the recommendations.[125] Most of them were the orphans of the internal conflict, representing the aspirations of young and pragmatic community leaders to overcome the inefficacy of the earlier generation of victims' advocacy by developing a collaborative relationship with local, regional, and national governments.

The flourishing of these civil society groups was a direct result of the truth commission process.[126] When the national and international NGOs began to make inroads into Peru's provinces to expand the grassroots support for human rights advocacy and the truth commission, they faced enormous difficulties in conducting outreach campaigns. As the commission process was drawing to a close, some of these NGOs decided to offer leadership training for aspiring youths. The training involved courses on human rights, the contents of the truth commission's final report, and basic skills in human rights advocacy. The graduates of these programs found a worthy cause to put their newly acquired leadership skills in practice: the implementation of the truth commission recommendations, especially the victim-centered reparations plan.

As a first step they broke off with the "parent" victims' associations, which they found paternalistic and ineffectual. According to one of the young leaders, the older generation maintained an antagonistic attitude toward the state, which made it impossible to strike bargains and achieve positive results. Despite hurtful accusations on the part of the "parent" associations, these youths secured themselves a seat at the negotiation table and forced the local politicians to take them seriously—so much so that the elders had to admit to their efficacy and adopt their tactics. In short, the truth commission process brought into life a new model for human rights advocacy in Peru.

Conclusion

Chile's Rettig Commission was established with a mandate that reflected President Aylwin's goals, as well as those of an internationally renowned human rights lawyer, José Zalaquett. The wording of the mandate and the designation of the commissioners embodied the balancing approach to truth, justice, and reconciliation. The main task of the commission was to establish an undeniable basis of factuality concerning death and forced disappearance under the military regime. It was not asked to produce an account of the underlying causes for violence and violations, as such an effort would deepen the divisions over social memory. Instead, the commission was motivated by the responsibility to make political and institutional recommendations in order to prevent the recurrence of the political radicalization and institutional breakdown of 1973, which had provoked the military coup. The commission did deliver on those promises, as it established the facts concerning death and disappearance, presented an account of the immediate causes of the military coup (i.e., the political and institutional crisis of 1973), and proposed institutional reform. It suggested a reparations program as the mechanism for the recognition of victimhood and the reintegration of victims' families into society. The government endorsed the final report and adopted most of its policy recommendations. Despite the government's efforts to portray the commission as a platform for national reconciliation, the military and the right-wing sectors by and large chose to ignore the facts and discredit the report. Thus, the commission did not serve reconciliation in the way understood by its creators. Finally, it did not generate civil society mobilization; to the contrary, the Rettig Commission was conceived as the last step for some influential actors (such as the Catholic Church), and the subsequent process of dissolution aggravated the irrelevance of the human rights issue until Pinochet's London arrest in October 1998.

In contrast, the organization of the Peruvian Truth and Reconciliation Commission brought human rights activists and intellectuals on the political scene at a historical juncture when none of the traditional political actors or state institutions had the power and legitimacy to steer the democratic transition. The mandate granted the commissioners discretion over the kind of truth they would produce and the way in which their conclusions would be incorporated into political practice. The lack of political restrictions, the designation of commissioners from the human rights community and social sciences, and the experiences of prior truth commissions all contributed to a comprehensive, even ambitious, notion of truth that combined volumes of historical, anthropological, and sociological analysis with an elaborate investigation of several categories of human rights violations. The Peruvian commission did not single out ideological polarization and institutional breakdown as causes of the conflict, like the Chilean one. Instead, it took a wider view of the shortcomings of the social organization that perpetuated poverty, exclusion, and marginalization. This analysis guided the ambitious recommendations chapter. In the end, this tremendous civil society initiative was endorsed and defended by civil society actors. August 28, the day President Toledo received the final report in 2003, is commemorated every year as a day of respect for victims, and human rights groups across the nation hold meetings and demonstrations on this anniversary.[127] Successive governments, however, were unwilling to take the lessons from history and convert them into policy or a vision of national reconstruction. The hostility of the political class has led one commentator to label the CVR a "moral triumph," yet "political failure," four years after it completed its work.[128] There was at best rhetorical support, but the CVR always remained the project of civil society actors, and the state chose not to make the truth its own.

The commission creation process is the key juncture that explains the variation across commissions, as described in the chapter. Yet, alternative explanations of variation need to be taken into consideration. It can be argued that the difference between the commissions results from the balance of power during their respective political transitions. After all, Chile's transitional justice model had to take into consideration the ongoing influence of the Pinochetistas, while the Peruvian truth commission enjoyed the lack of organized opposition in its early months. I show that the nature of the transition does not determine a commission's mandate, composition, operation, and outcomes in light of thirteen other truth commission experiences in Chapter 6. The cases of Chile and Peru offer insights into why this is the case: the balance of power before and during the commission process can influence the commission's work and findings only *indirectly*. Whether the commission establishment process is tightly controlled or highly inclusive is not determined directly by the balance of power. While establishing the commission, the balance of power influences who can possibly sit at the table (i.e., who is likely to author the commission's mandate) but does not determine who ends up making the key decisions, or whether the decision-making procedure is participatory. For example, as discussed above, President Aylwin had to renegotiate the composition of the Chilean commission once his initial plan was frustrated; the composition reflected one of many possible outcomes rather than the necessary outcome of a negotiated transition. Therefore, the balance of power may have an indirect effect on a commission's mandate and composition, but this effect is not deterministic, that is, one type of political transition does not necessarily produce one type of commission.

It can also be argued that the Peruvian commission was more comprehensive because it drew upon the conceptual and methodological innovations of commission experiences throughout the 1990s. The transformation of what it means to create a truth commission is undeniable, and most of the more comprehensive commissions were established in the mid-1990s and 2000s. However, as Chapter 6 shows, there were relatively more comprehensive commissions in the early 1990s (e.g., the commission in Nepal), and relatively more circumscribed commissions in the late 1990s (e.g., the commission in Nigeria). The timing of a commission does have an effect, but just like with the nature of a political transition, that effect is nondeterministic and exerts itself indirectly, that is, through the commission creation process.

What does the comparison of truth commissions in Chile and Peru reveal about truth commission impact in general? Chapter 6 explores this question in light of all transitional truth commission experiences.

Explaining Variation in Truth Commission Impact (II): Evidence from Thirteen Countries

The detailed description of the pre-commission, commission, and post-commission processes in Chile and Peru in Chapter 5 reveals the complexity of interactions between politicians, state bureaucracies, civil society actors, and commission members. This chapter zooms out to explore how these dynamics influence commissions' mandate, composition, goals, modes of operation, and outcomes in thirteen other societies that have lived through political transitions from authoritarianism to democracy and/or violent conflict to peace. There is enormous cross-national variation with respect to commissions' impact on policy, judicial behavior, and social norms, as well as the sources of impact (i.e., political will to implement reforms, domestic civil society mobilization, and support form international organizations and NGOs).

The twists and turns that determine a commission's fate are fascinating—and sometimes disappointing. As argued earlier, the peculiar position of truth commissions as quasi-official truth-finding panels with strong connections to organized civil society makes their impact dependent on continued political support and civil society mobilization. Added to the dynamic interactions between transitional actors is commissions' own agency that often unsettles narrow political agendas. Short- and long-term commission impact can be conceptualized as a mixture of change driven by political will and change resulting from civil society pressure. In some countries one source of change dominates the other, whereas in other cases political and societal forces reinforce each other to generate either high or low impact.

The chapter is organized as follows: the first section demonstrates that the initial source of cross-national variation in truth commission impact is the inclusivity of the commission creation process. *Exclusionary* processes (when the government or an international organization establishes the commission singlehandedly) tend to result in commissions that are dependent on political will to generate impact. By contrast, *participatory* processes (when a number of political and social actors, including the political opposition, former armed resistance groups, and domestic and international human rights organizations take part in the initial negotiation process to set up the panel) usually result in civil society mobilization during and after the commission's work, although the enhanced agency of the latter kind of commissions may strain their political endorsement. This section also shows that alternative explanations of truth commission impact have limited or no explanatory power.

The following sections present case histories for all transitional commissions that completed their work as of 2014 to illustrate the complex interactions that shape the creation, operation, and outcomes of commissions. First, I provide detailed descriptions of truth commissions in Argentina, Uganda, Chad, El Salvador, Sri Lanka, and Nigeria, countries with exclusionary commission creation processes. I then describe commissions resulting from participatory processes in Nepal, Haiti, South Africa, Guatemala, Timor-Leste, Sierra Leone, and Liberia. These case histories do not cover all aspects of the countries' truth commissions; rather, the short and focused histories are structured around the question of how the creation and operation of a commission influences the impact it generates. The conclusion section explores whether there are deviations from this highly path-dependent story of pre-commission, commission, and post-commission processes. Evidence from various countries does affirm the presence of twists and turns in the creation, operation, and reception of truth commissions, but the basic pattern remains: the commission creation process structures the subsequent processes powerfully, even if it does not determine them.

Comparing Truth Commission Impact Around the Globe

Based on the measures for political impact and civil society mobilization described in Chapter 4 (see Table 4), I codify impact scores for every country that had a completed truth commission during its political transition in

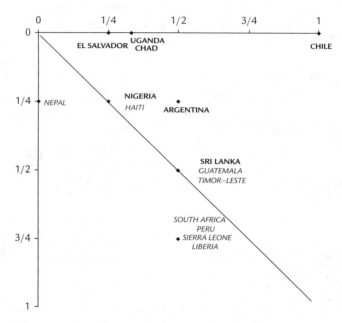

Figure 1. Commission creation process and truth commission impact.
Government-led exclusionary commission creation process: Uganda, Chad, Chile,
Nigeria, Argentina, and Sri Lanka. UN-led exclusionary commission creation
process: El Salvador. Participatory commission creation process: Nepal, Haiti,
Guatemala, Timor-Leste, South Africa, Peru, Sierra Leone, and Liberia.

Figure 1.[1] Direct political impact increases from left to right in the graph,
and impact driven by civil society mobilization increases from top to bottom. Boldfaced country names represent an exclusionary commission creation process, that is, where the government (and the United Nations in the
case of El Salvador) controlled the mandate and composition tightly, and the
italicized countries have had a participatory commission creation process.

There is a tendency for boldfaced countries to cluster in the upper triangle, where direct political impact dominates civil society mobilization, and
italicized countries to cluster in the lower triangle, where impact through civil
society pressure is dominant. Most exclusionary commission creation pro-

cesses have produced politically driven impact in the post-commission period, and most participatory negotiation processes have led to civil society mobilization around the truth commissions in the end.

To put in historical context: most early truth commissions came into existence as a result of exclusionary creation processes and generated political impact ranging anywhere between low (Uganda and Chad) to high (Chile), and no serious civil society mobilization. Most later truth commissions brought together a number of political leaders, armed groups, and domestic and transnational civil society actors. Those commissions generated (with the exception of Haiti) a high degree of civil society mobilization, which enhanced their overall impact in the long term. The presence of low-political-impact commissions created through exclusionary (Uganda, Chad, Nigeria) or near-exclusionary (El Salvador) processes suggests that dependence on the goodwill of the government (or an international organization) might result in relatively efficacious commissions, as in Argentina, Chile, and Sri Lanka, but it is also likely that the resulting commissions serve little more than as window dressing, finding no governmental or nongovernmental channels to materialize their goals.

The timing of a truth commission appears to be important. Truth commissions have become more participatory, and truth commission impact more civil society–driven, in later commissions, but there are notable exceptions. Truth commissions in Nepal and Haiti were pioneers in terms of high civil society mobilization (domestic groups in Nepal and international ones in Haiti). Nigeria's Oputa Panel, by contrast, came into existence in the late 1990s, when most commissions tended to prompt high levels of nongovernmental participation, but it was created through an exclusionary process.

The cases of Haiti and El Salvador teach valuable lessons in structuring truth commissions through international intervention. In Haiti, North America–based diaspora communities and domestic politicians initiated a relatively participatory commission creation process, and in El Salvador the United Nations set an investigatory panel singlehandedly in the context of a peace agreement. The differences in terms of inclusivity notwithstanding, both commissions faced a similar problem: once international funding and attention enabled the project, the lack of communication with the political leadership and the local human rights movement left those commissions completely dependent on ongoing international support. When the commission processes came to an end, the commissions were left without the necessary political endorsement or domestic activism to have their

Table 5. Type of Transition and Inclusivity of the Commission Creation Process

	Exclusionary Commission Creation Process	*Participatory Commission Creation Process*
Transition by collapse	Argentina, Uganda, Chad	Haiti, Peru
Negotiated transition	Chile, Nigeria, Sri Lanka	Nepal, El Salvador, South Africa, Guatemala, Sierra Leone, Timor-Leste, Liberia

recommendations incorporated into policy.[2] Hence, low direct political impact was accompanied by low civil society mobilization, demonstrating that civil society–driven change is only possible with ongoing communication and mutual support between national and transnational actors.

Does the nature of the transition, understood as the de facto and de jure strength of outgoing regime forces during the transition, shape how a commission is structured? In other words, can cross-national variation in impact be reduced to the type of transition?[3] Transition type certainly influences who sits at the table and what kinds of threats the transitional justice process is facing. However, there is no systematic relationship between the strength of the outgoing regime and the initial negotiation process that establishes the truth commission. Table 5 demonstrates that negotiated transitions are more likely to produce participatory commission creation processes. Nevertheless, for each type of transition (collapse versus negotiated) there is considerable cross-national variation in terms of truth commission inclusivity. In other words, transition type does have a limited effect on the inclusivity of the commission creation process, but the effect is not systematic and is particularly weak for transitions by collapse.

The commission creation process shapes a commission's trajectory, but contextual factors may lead to deviations from this general path. A change in government is likely to affect official reactions to a commission's findings and recommendations. Gradual transformations in laws and judges' attitudes have implications for a commission's judicial impact. Events that could not be foreseen by the sponsors and members of a truth-finding panel, like politically motivated assassinations or renewed civil conflict, may drive its work to irrelevance. The case histories in the following section demonstrate the variety of social, political, and legal factors that makes each truth commission context unique. Yet, despite the large number of parameters, the overall pattern holds: its initial creation process shapes the ways in which a truth commission produces impact in politics and society.

Case Histories of Exclusionary Truth Commissions

Argentina (1983–1984)

The National Commission on the Disappeared was the classic case of a tightly controlled commission creation process, in which presidential discretion set the terms on the objectives, areas of investigation, and the composition. The outcome was a limited commission that adopted a forensic notion of truth, by and large ignoring the underlying causes for violence and violations. Predictably, the president endorsed the commission, and some of its recommendations were adopted into policy. The country's human rights movement disputed the findings about the death toll and what it perceived to be a bias in the commission's brief historical narrative. Thus, the government-sponsored initiative did not lead to civil society mobilization around disseminating the final report or monitoring the implementation of recommendations, especially in the area of reparations.

Human rights accountability was not addressed as a dilemma between political expediency and the demand for justice in the early years of the Argentine transition. The collapse of the military regime (1976–1983) facilitated the prosecution of the outgoing regime's leadership. President Raúl Alfonsín mandated the truth commission to discover facts of violations, rather than substitute for justice or forge reconciliation. Although Alfonsín and the human rights movement converged on the need to establish the truth about what happened, questions about how prosecutions would proceed led to disillusionment early in the transitional justice process.[4] Influential human rights groups like Mothers of Plaza de Mayo and Argentine Human Rights League Foundation had demanded a bicameral investigation commission, but Alfonsín opted for a panel created by presidential decree and autonomous from the legislature, a decision that provoked accusations of partiality and dependence on the president.[5] He asked the Chamber of Deputies to appoint three members,[6] but did not negotiate the terms on which the truth commission would be established with the legislative. Chaired by novelist Ernesto Sábato, the commission consisted of thirteen members, ten appointed by the president and three by the Chamber of Deputies.

The mandate was strictly limited to uncovering facts (including the names and whereabouts of the victims) about forced disappearances. The commission collected testimonies from about 7,000 individuals. Human rights NGOs opened their archives,[7] while the military chose not to participate in the process. The commission uncovered information about 8,960 cases of forced disappearance. It established that the policy of disappearance, including brutal acts of murder and the subsequent concealing of the crime, was intentional, systematic, institutional, and orchestrated by the military high command. The final report did not give an account of the underlying causes of political violence, except for one sentence in the prologue written by chair Sábato: "during the 1970s, Argentina was torn by terror from both the extreme right and the far left."[8]

The final report recommended reparations for the victims, a follow-up commission for the identification of the disappeared, the continuation of human rights trials, and reform in the judiciary and the education system. President Alfonsín endorsed the report, while the military condemned it. The great achievement was the government-sponsored publication of the final report: the *Nunca Más* (Never Again) report not only became a national best seller overnight, but it gave name to a whole genre of official and unofficial truth projects across Latin America. The government did not legislate reparations or set up a follow-up institution to implement other recommendations.

Military trials began soon after the publication of the final report. However, Argentina's human rights policy was by and large shaped by the legislation and revocation of amnesty laws by different legislative majorities and presidents—decisions that were unrelated to the commission's findings and recommendations. The initial wave of trials ended with sentences for top military leaders, but the Full Stop Law of 1986 and the 1989 presidential pardons granted by Carlos Menem halted the progress of human rights accountability. The findings and recommendations of the truth commission report had little impact on these decisions, but insofar as they promoted social awareness about human rights violations, they at least managed to preserve the question of accountability as a latent political problem. Only when leftist Nestor Kirshner ascended to presidency in 2003 were the amnesty laws overturned and a victim-centered reparations program launched.

As explained above, the president's decision to establish a commission autonomous from the legislative chambers had raised suspicions about impartiality and usefulness. Human rights organizations never rejected the final report, but they objected to its central findings, and did not mobilize around it. Against the commission's figure of nine thousand disappearances, victims' groups asserted that the number approximated thirty thousand. The victims' perception that the truth commission's historical narrative established moral and political equality between the leftist insurgencies of the 1970s and the military and right-wing paramilitary death squads aggravated their mistrust. Sábato's one sentence about violence committed by the extreme right and the far left was powerful enough to spark a public debate that, with ebbs and flows, has continued to this day. The mention of terrorisms of the right and left was interpreted by leftist human rights organizations, including the Mothers of the Plaza de Mayo, as an endorsement of the "Two Demons Theory," which stated that society was victimized between two illegitimate, violent options. The fact that other commissioners and commentators sought to assure the public that the sentence did not endorse the Two Demons Theory,[9] let alone justify the state terror that followed, did not stop human rights groups from mobilizing against the prologue that contained the sentence. Finally, the prologue was rewritten in 2006 in a way that erased the traces of Sábato's wording.[10]

In conclusion, the human rights movement held a distant, if not antagonistic, attitude toward the final report.[11] Groups like the Grandmothers of Plaza de Mayo joined forces with the commission to identify the disappeared.[12] However, unlike more recent commissions, where the human rights movement saw a window of opportunity in the dissemination, promotion, and monitoring of the truth commission's final report, influential victims' groups and human rights organizations in Argentina maintained their struggle without a strong attachment to the truth commission's cause. At best the commission established a public record of violations, but not a platform for mobilization. For example, the truth commission process played no role in the struggle for the reparations program, which bore fruit twenty-one years after the commission's work.

Uganda (1986–1995)

Uganda's Commission of Inquiry into Violations of Human Rights was established by the Ministry of Justice.[13] Arguably, the mandate limitations and the composition made the Ugandan commission among the least autonomous ones. The lack of international support (with the notable exception of last-resort funding by the Ford Foundation)[14] further weakened the commission. Nevertheless, even this limited commission managed to exert some degree of agency beyond political constraints, in particular by expanding its operation in ongoing conflict zones "in spite of the best efforts of [President] Museveni's supporters."[15] Nonetheless, the Ugandan commission illustrates what happens when the government, domestic social actors, and international human rights groups all fail to support the truth commission: little or no political impact, as well as no civil society–driven impact.

In the wake of the successive dictatorships of Idi Amin (1971–1979) and Milton Obote (1980–1985), the incoming government of Yoweri Museveni established the commission to uncover the abuses committed by its predecessors and showcase its commitment to the human rights cause and democracy.[16] Joanna Quinn argues that Museveni used the truth commission as a means to appease the international public opinion.[17] The commission was mandated to inquire into the "causes and consequences" of a broad range of violations. The definition of crimes under investigation was broad but vague. The periodization (1962–1986) covered the entire post-colonial period up to Museveni's government. Just like its Argentine predecessor, the commission's mandate did not emphasize healing or civic repair and was meant to be no more than a fact-finding body.

Supreme Court Justice Arthur Oder chaired the commission. The panel was a mixture of nonaffiliated judges and legal scholars, a historian, and a women's rights advocate. Two members were politically affiliated with Museveni's National Resistance Movement, and one was a longtime friend. At the end of the commission's work, five commissioners joined politics under Museveni's increasingly authoritarian regime; as a consequence, the post-commission advocacy that one may expect from the commissioners did not take place. However, despite the close links to the government, "the commission was confronted with a lack of political support."[18] It was constantly underfunded and at one point had to suspend its activities until the Ford Foundation donated funds. The police and security institutions did not collaborate in terms of information sharing. One of the ways in which the commission tried to overcome its limitations was holding public hearings, some of which were broadcast on radio and television.

The commission suggested the repeal of laws allowing detention without trial, and the incorporation of human rights education in school, university, and security training curricula. A reparations policy was neither suggested by the commission nor implemented by the government, although many victims came forward to give testimonies with this expectation. The final report is almost impossible to find.[19] The permanent Ugandan Human Rights Commission, established under the 1995 constitution, came directly from the truth commission's proposal and remains its most enduring outcome.[20] All other recommendations have been ignored—with the exception of the ratification of a number of international human rights treaties. Bureaucrats have been extremely unwilling to take the commission's findings and recommendations into consideration.[21] The regime certainly did not address remembrance, and nongovernmental projects have by and large failed to substitute for the lack of political will. For example, the commissioners established the Uganda Human Rights Education and Documentation Centre (UHEDOC), since the government lent no support. UHEDOC might have produced political impact through awareness raising, but the underfinanced organization shut down in 1997.[22]

Chad (1991–1992)

Chad's Ministry of Justice's Commission of Inquiry into the Crimes and Misappropriations Committed by the Ex-President Habré, His Accomplices, and/or Accessories received little support from the government or transnational civil society networks. The original government-appointed panel was so timid in carrying out the human rights investigation that the commission's chair had to appoint new commissioners to assert some sense of agency. The scant data on the commission suggest that the findings and recommendations produced very limited political impact, although civil society organizations mobilized later for accountability and reparations for victims.

Soon after Habré's one-party regime (1982–1990) was overthrown by insurgent forces led by the former commander in chief Idriss Déby, then interim president Déby established the truth commission. The commission was asked to investigate a broad range of human rights violations, as well as charges of embezzlement, under Habré's authoritarian and repressive rule. The periodization leaves out a longer stretch of Chad's conflict-ridden history. The twelve-member panel was headed by Chad's chief prosecutor Mahamat Hassan Akabar. It consisted of "two judges, four police officers, two administrators, two archivists, and two secretaries."[23] However, some commissioners from the initial group were replaced after six months at the request of the commission chair, who argued that some members were too afraid to take active part in the commission's work.[24]

The commission did not enjoy any meaningful government or international support, with the exception of the consultation services provided by Amnesty International. Due to lack of resources it operated in a former detention chamber, which deterred many victims who had fresh memories of abuse in the facilities. Escalating levels of political violence during the commission process set hurdles for its work as well.[25] Nonetheless, the commission managed to interview 1,726 individuals. At the end, it identified 3,780 murder victims under the Habré regime. The commissioners assumed the number of identified victims to be 10 percent of the total, and thus arrived at the rough estimate of 40,000. The final report named the perpetrators and published their photographs. Not surprisingly, Habré and the secret police under him were found responsible for the violations. The most shocking aspect of the final report was its detailed account of foreign actors' role in the conflict and violations. U.S. financial, military, and technical aid for Habré, along with a list of other collaborating nations, was condemned in the final report.[26] The commission recommended the dismissal and prosecution of the personnel of Habré's political police, the Documentation and Security Directorate. It also suggested the construction of a monument to honor the victims and the opening of a museum in a former secret detention center.

The reform of security forces was largely ignored, as the personnel of Habré's political police continued to occupy positions. The commemorative recommendations were ignored, too. The truth commission's final report enjoyed greater judicial impact overseas than inside the country. International human rights advocates used the final report in order to prosecute Habré in Senegal.[27] The president of the truth commission testified before the Dakar court in May 2000.[28]

Photographs and a movie describing the commission process were shown at the commission headquarters for several days, but the government did not make an effort to disseminate the final report.[29] The files of the commission were locked away in 1992. Human rights groups mobilized in the areas of human rights accountability and reparations for victims. The Chadian Association of Victims of Political Repression and Crime (AVCRP in French acronym) gathered testimonies from 792 victims in anticipation for criminal proceedings. Although the documentation of testimonies had no effect on judicial institutions in the 1990s, and AVCRP had to suspend its activities due to lack of funds, there was renewed interest in information that could lead to criminal justice in 1999, when, "inspired by the London arrest of General Augusto Pinochet the Chadian Association for the Promotion and Defense of Human Rights (ATPDH) requested Human Rights Watch's assistance in helping Habré's victims bring him to justice."[30] The legal battle for extradition is still unresolved, but his peaceful time in Senegal might not last: the Extraordinary African Chambers, a special Senegalese court tasked with the prosecution of international crimes committed in Chad between 1982 and 1990, charged him with crimes against humanity on July 2, 2013.

AVCRP had been advocating material and symbolic reparations for victims, a key recommendation of the truth commission. As the government failed to take action, domestic groups began to work with the France-based Association for the Victims of Repression in Exile to provide mental health care for victims of torture. The initiative, according to a 2005 Human Rights Watch report, has been a limited success.[31]

El Salvador (1992–1993)

The truth commission for El Salvador was truly international. The backing from the United Nations, the availability of foreign funding, and the autonomy of the all-foreign panel from domestic political processes could have allowed for a high degree of independence from the government. However, this UN-led effort failed to mobilize potential domestic allies, as it exaggerated the protection of the commission from Salvadoran social actors.[32] As expected, the government did not implement any of the recommendations except the removal of some perpetrators from public office. The inability to engage domestic civil society actors took its toll on long-term impact as well.

The Salvadoran commission was a product of the Mexico Peace Accords between the government and the Farabundo Martí National Liberation Front (FMLN), an umbrella organization of five rebel groups. UN sponsorship equipped the commission with adequate funding and security. The commission was mandated to investigate "serious acts of violence" and make legal, political, or administrative recommendations to promote national reconciliation and prevent the recurrence of violence. The vague notion of "serious acts" led the commissioners to ask the parties to the conflict to submit a list of the atrocities that they wished to see investigated, but soon it was clear that this approach would not produce agreement. Therefore, the commissioners took the initiative to draw up the list. In the words of one of the commissioners, "not all serious acts of violence were necessarily to be investigated. The main focus was to be on acts that had a special or broader impact on society in general."[33] Unlike most other commissions, the mandate declared the Salvadoran panel's recommendations legally binding on the parties to the peace accords that ended the conflict.

Article 5 of the Chapultepec Agreement explicitly required the Truth Commission to address human rights violations to "put an end to any indication of impunity."[34] However, the peace accords did not specify if perpetrators could be named. The commissioners exercised agency by interpreting the "complete truth" in the agreement's language to include the names of perpetrators. Although both parties to the conflict asked the commission to identify the perpetrators on all sides, the government, headed by President Alfredo Cristiani, reversed its position when it realized that prominent political and military leaders might be incriminated. FMLN did not back down from asking names to be published.

The secretary-general of the United Nations appointed three foreigners (two politicians and one human rights jurist) as commissioners. No Salvadoran was selected as a commissioner or staff member in order to ward off accusations of bias. The commissioners faced intense pressure from politicians and the military to alter the content of the final report, especially not to name perpetrators.[35] However, the final report was prepared independently of these political pressures. Commission chair Thomas Buergenthal notes that it was difficult to overcome people's fear and suspicion initially, and that the local human rights organizations were "surprisingly unprepared"[36] to assist the commission. The commission made extensive use of international human rights organizations' reports at the initial stage. The U.S. government lent limited support to the fact-finding effort.[37]

The major shortcoming of the Salvadoran truth commission was the failure of the fact-finding mission. Only 33 of the more than 22,000 cases brought before the panel were resolved, and many abuses committed by death squads were left uninvestigated. Nonetheless, the panel identified some patterns of violence. The final report attributed 85 percent of the violence to state agents and 5 percent to the FMLN; the responsibility for the rest could not be identified. It did not contain a historical context chapter, but the findings dealt with the issue of political and criminal responsibility. The Salvadoran commission named some individual perpetrators, and did not single out armed actors as the only parties responsible for the conflict: the judiciary, business and exile communities that funded death squads, and U.S. interventionism were condemned for provoking and failing to stop violence and violations.

The commission recommended the removal of almost the entire military high command and the revision of the military doctrine. Judicial and legal reform included the dismissal of conniving Supreme Court judges.[38] It also recommended material and symbolic reparations for victims. The commission suggested that 1 percent of foreign aid to El Salvador should be devoted to compensation for victims. Finally the report recommended that a forum be established to monitor the implementation of recommendations. There was no recommendation for prosecution.

The president rejected the final report, and the government did not implement most of the recommendations—a clear defection from the peace accords. The military leadership and the defense minister accused the commission of slander and sought to justify the military's war conduct. The Supreme Court was the most vociferous critic of the truth commission, reacting to the recommendation to dismiss judges implicated in obstructing justice. No follow-up organization was established to monitor the progress in legal-institutional reform. There were some dismissals from the security institutions, and the legal-judicial system underwent partial reform, especially in the area of penal law. Removals were not followed by a policy of disqualification from public office, however: even those who were dismissed from one position found other public jobs.[39] The recommendation for material and symbolic reparations was ignored completely.[40]

Five days after the release of the final report, the government passed an amnesty law amid rumors of a military coup. The findings of the report, therefore, did not produce any domestic judicial impact. Foreign and international courts were more willing to make use of the Salvadoran commission's findings. The Inter-American Court of Human Rights ruled in 1999 that the amnesty law violated international law. The Spanish High Court started investigating the murder of six Jesuit priests and two women since 2008, a case implicating the former president along with military leaders. In May 2011 Spanish judge Eloy Velasco Nuñez indicted twenty military officers related to the crime, and the commission findings could be potentially useful.

Secular and Catholic legal defense and social assistance organizations had been documenting abuses and raising consciousness about the human rights violations throughout the civil war.[41] The commission failed to build strong connections with these domestic groups during and after the truth commission process.[42] This resulted in the lack of serious civil society pressure or monitoring effort.[43] In conclusion, the exclusionary nature of the UN-backed commission creation process constrained civil society mobilization.

Sri Lanka (1994–1997, 1998–2000)

Sri Lanka had three regional Commissions of Inquiry into the Involuntary Removal or Disappearance of Persons (1994–1997) and an All Island Commission (1998–2000). They were established as a corrective to earlier government-mandated panels that sought to diffuse international criticism regarding disappearances, especially the 1991 presidential commission of inquiry. The government backed the commissions and tried to implement some of their recommendations. The mandate limit on the investigation period was the most conspicuous political constraint. Furthermore, the zonal commissions' work "halted prematurely," and as a result, the subsequent commission, established in 1998, finished the remaining work. The consequence of government discretion in the creation process was a commission with moderate political impact, but no significant social mobilization.

The commission was established in the context of an ongoing civil conflict between the government and the Liberation Tigers of Tamil Eelam. The alternation of power in the 1994 elections allowed newly elected president Chandrika Kumaratunga to establish the zonal commissions. Since the commissions operated during the conflict, they could not work in the zones where fighting restarted.[44] And since they were backward-looking, they could not monitor the ongoing human rights violations, which led some commentators to see in the commissions a political effort to conveniently ignore the issue of ongoing disappearances.[45] Three presidentially appointed regional commissions (the zonal commissions) were complemented by a fourth, the All Island Commission, mandated to address complaints not covered by the regional ones. The president of the western commission and the all-island one was Manouri Kokila Muttetuwegama, a human rights activist.

All commissions could identify perpetrators. A major limitation was that the periodization excluded the period of political violence and violations before the Liberation Tigers of Tamil Eelam started their insurgency in 1987–1988. The three zonal commissions discovered over 15,000 cases of disappearances, and the All Island Commission ascertained facts about 4,473 more. The latter commission referred an additional 16,305 cases, which it could not investigate due to mandate limitations, to the Sri Lankan Human Rights Commission.[46] Moreover, it took a bold step in arguing that intolerance to dissent fueled the conflict. All commissions suggested reparations for victims. They emphasized judicial reform, including the appointment of a human rights prosecutor, and "lay visitors" to monitor police areas.[47]

The government was partially responsive to the truth commissions' findings and recommendations.[48] "Most [recommendations], however, were either completely ignored by successive governments, or were introduced only on paper, with no genuine effort made to implement them."[49] The truth commissions' final report was published with a two-year delay, in 2002. The government issued death certificates and paid compensation to over 16,000 families of the disappeared.[50] The 2001 Presidential Commission on Ethnic Violence followed up on the truth commission's work, but the periodization was limited to the 1981–1984 era, leaving out the violations between 1984 and 1988.[51] The reparations program after the 2001 commission is considered more successful than the one that followed the earlier commissions.[52] Under the Kumaratunga presidency, there were institutional efforts to investigate disappearances and bring the perpetrators before justice. Also, the government established a Disappearances Investigations Unit in 1997 under the deputy instructor general of the police.[53] More than four hundred individuals were indicted for human rights violations.[54] One area of reform that was completely ignored was the minimization of emergency law measures.

Although the Sri Lankan Human Rights Commission began to investigate the cases referred by the truth commission, it stopped the judicial processes in July 2006 for all cases, unless "special directions are received from the Government."[55] Thanks to the Disappearances Investigations Unit of the police, working in conjunction with the Missing Persons Commissions Unit in the Attorney General's Department, there were some cases ending in sentences for human rights violators. However, the truth commissions' findings had no evidentiary status at courts.

Disappearances continued throughout the conflict. There have been various nongovernmental memorialization efforts since the early 1990s, and the civil sector keeps pressuring the judiciary for prosecutions. Yet, aside from the pressure from Amnesty International and "other rights groups" for the publication of the final report,[56] the truth commissions have not contributed to civil society mobilization.

Nigeria (1999–2002)

Nigeria's Human Rights Violations Investigation Commission (later called the Judicial Commission for the Investigation of Human Rights Violations, and also known as the "Oputa Panel" after its chair Justice Chukwudifu Oputa) adamantly defended its autonomy and efficacy in the face of court interdicts that limited its powers and a government that was primarily interested in legitimizing itself through the commission.[57] The ambiguity of the mandate allowed the commissioners to move beyond narrow political constraints, but also made it vulnerable to judicial interference. In the end, the commission managed to surprise and upset outgoing and incoming political elites, but since its findings and recommendations were not adopted by either the government or the civil sector, it generated very little impact.

Nigeria transitioned into democracy in 1999, after successive military dictatorships ruled the country for most of its postindependence period, and without interruption since 1983. Olusegun Obasanjo, who himself had ruled the country as a military dictator between 1976 and 1979, was elected president, and he established the truth commission soon after assuming power. The lack of international attention (with the exception of the Ford Foundation, which granted an initial fund) resulted in a tightly government-controlled commission creation process.

Retired Supreme Court judge Chukwudifu Oputa, a highly reputed public figure, chaired the commission. Biases with respect to religious and demographic representation, however, undermined the credibility of the seven-member panel in the eyes of some social sectors.[58] Reconciliation and putting an end to impunity were the stated objectives. The commission was initially asked to investigate violations under the previous military governments between 1984 and 1999, but pressure from the human rights community led the government to extend the periodization to cover the entire period between 1966, when the first military coup took place, and 1999.[59] The remit focused on the nature, causes, and extent of violations, in particular "mysterious deaths and assassinations."[60] However, during the hearings, the commission agreed to include a broader range of violations in its investigation. The commission did not have subpoena power initially, but later it was added to the mandate—a power that the commission never used despite serious challenges to its authority to collect information. The struggle over subpoena power reflects the commission's difficulty in expanding its authority beyond the narrow confines of the mandate, while its opponents were using courts to limit the commission even further.

The commission was understaffed and underfunded. It received more than 11,000 testimony applications, of which only 150 were heard. The commission process was a struggle between the commissioners, who wanted to expand their endeavor's visibility and public authority, and the members of the outgoing regime, who tried to obstruct the commission's work. Some influential political actors, such as former president Ibrahim Babangida, obtained court rulings that restrained the commission from compelling them to participate.[61] To generate greater publicity, the commission conducted public hearings, including two hearings with President Obasanjo. He first testified as a victim, but was summoned another time to give an account of the human rights violations under his first presidency (1976–1979).

The commission criticized military and civilian collaborators for orchestrating coups and violating fundamental rights. It recommended reparations for the victims and reform of military and police institutions. President Obasanjo endorsed the report and issued an official apology: "At this moment in history, I, as chief executive of the federation . . . wish to offer my full apology to all Nigerians in general, and to direct victims in particular, for all the misdeeds."[62] However, he also declared that no reparations would be paid to victims and chose not to publish the final report. The commission generated some judicial impact, as thirty-five cases were referred to the inspector general. The naming of Ibrahim Babangida as a likely murder suspect undermined his political prospects, even if it did not culminate in prosecution.

As the government did not release the report, civil society groups, most notably the Washington-based Nigerian Democratic Movement and Nigeria-based Civil Society Forum, took the initiative in 2005 to publish it.[63] Despite this effort, some commentators have noted that the commission could not overcome the public perception that its work was somewhat unserious,[64]

meant for public entertainment rather than truth finding.[65] Thus, it generated limited civil society mobilization at best.

Case Histories of Participatory Truth Commissions

Nepal (1990–1991)

The Commission of Inquiry to Locate the Persons Disappeared During the
Panchayat Period has received little international attention. The scant data
on the commission suggest that the interim government established the
commission without devising a comprehensive human rights policy. Civil
society pressure for truth and justice created conditions under which the
commissioners, despite the lack of international support, managed to surprise
and upset the political class by naming perpetrators and advocating criminal proceedings. Successive governments and the judiciary ignored the truth
commission, while civil society groups took the initiative for disseminating
the final report and seeking accountability. Despite the early civil society
interest in the commission, however, the outbreak of the civil war in 1996
further undermined its impact.

The truth commission emerged as a result of protests against absolutism,
which culminated in the transition to constitutional monarchy in 1990. The
transitional government of Krishna Prasad Bhattarai established the commission within the first year of the transition. The commission was mandated
to investigate the "loss of lives and damage to property" in early 1990 during
the People's Movement against the monarchy. The government had to dissolve the first commission of inquiry because the appointment procedure ref-
erenced the abolished 1962 Panchayat Constitution rather than the new
legal system. The controversial process caused two former commissioners,
both human rights defenders, to resign.[66] Then, a new set of commissioners
was appointed.

Due to lack of funding, the commission investigated no more than thirty-
five cases. Surprisingly it named many perpetrators, including high-ranking
politicians, and recommended taking action against police personnel and
politicians.[67] As a result, political parties approached the report with reserve.[68]
All commentators agree that successive governments did not implement the
recommendations, especially concerning human rights accountability.[69] Instead, the government sided with presumed perpetrators in the name of pre-

serving political order. Soon after the report's publication, a Council of Ministers decision granted de facto amnesty to the perpetrators.[70] The attorneys and high courts dismissed the commission report as judicially useless. Although no general amnesty was announced, "none of the alleged violators of human rights have been tried for their actions or punished."[71] Victims' relatives petitioned the Supreme Court in 1999 to act on the truth commission's findings, to no avail.[72]

The first elected government, taking office in May 1991, chose not to disseminate the final report. Civil society pressure forced the government to release the report in 1994,[73] which remains the only area in which the truth commission produced impact. However, only a handful of copies are available in the national library and the parliamentary secretariat.[74] The long-term impact of the truth commission process was further undermined because the country was plunged into violence once again. In 1996, the Communist Party of Nepal–Maoist started a "people's war" against the government, and the number of disappeared increased dramatically during the war.

Proposals for a new truth commission failed recently. The 2006 peace accord that ended the civil war asked for the creation of a new truth and reconciliation commission. A year later, the Supreme Court ordered the government to establish a commission of inquiry to investigate disappearances.[75] The transnational advocacy networks were better prepared for the challenge of implementing transitional justice measures than in 1990. For example, the USIP organized a series of roundtable discussions in July 2007.[76] The Ministry of Peace and Reconstruction established a Commission on Disappeared Persons and prepared a draft bill to establish a separate truth and reconciliation commission. The major parties in Nepal's parliament drafted a bill to create the commission, but the Supreme Court suspended the attempt in April 2013.

Haiti (1995–1996)

Haiti's National Truth and Justice Commission was drafted through an all-inclusive negotiation process, bringing together the Haitian exile communities in North America, international organizations, and the Aristide presidency. However, none of these actors wanted to, or could, support the commission process, and it was allowed to fail. It is disputed whether the United Nations lent ongoing and adequate support.[77] Constant disagreements with diaspora groups over the commission's design alienated domestic grassroots support. Therefore, the commission produced very little political impact or civil society mobilization.

Jean-Bertrand Aristide was reinstated as the legitimate president of Haiti in 1994, three years after a military coup had ousted him. The diaspora communities in North America and the Caribbean began to lobby for a truth commission during the transition.[78] "In fact, it was the Haitian diaspora community abroad that first conceived of the idea of establishing a truth commission in Haiti and then assisted in shaping its mandate."[79] The commission was mandated to investigate human rights violations that occurred between the military coup and the restoration of Aristide to power, which limited the commission's capacity to present a fuller picture of human rights violations in Haitian history. The panel, chaired by sociologist Françoise Boucard, consisted of four Haitians representing "parts of the government and important nongovernmental organizations" and three international jurists.[80]

The disagreements between the diaspora and the locals shaped debates over the design of the commission and the notion of truth (legal-forensic versus historical-narrative) to adopt.[81] The commission consulted the American Association for the Advancement of Science (AAAS) to devise a large-scale interviewing project. However, the commissioners and the international advisory teams stopped collaboration at the last stage of the operation.[82] Priscilla Hayner and Joanna Quinn argue that some within the Haitian NGO community decided not to work with the commission due to methodological disagreements.[83] Another major problem was the constant absenteeism of the international commissioners.

Despite these limitations and disagreements, the fieldwork was of high quality.[84] The commission identified 8,667 victims of various kinds of violations. It included special reports on sexual violence, repression against journalists, and the 1994 massacre in Raboteau. It named individual perpetrators. The database of violations stands out among the achievements of the commission. However, critical observers note that the final report did not reflect the commission's (considerably successful) forensic work. The organizational difficulties faced by the commission, combined with the disagreements among commissioners about what the final report should say, resulted in a truncated document that did not contain a narrative of the underlying causes of the last military dictatorship.[85] The final report recommended the prosecution of violators in domestic courts or an international tribunal. It also suggested the creation of a reparations commission. Finally it asked the government to enact laws against sexual violence.[86]

The Aristide government was mostly supportive, with the reservation that it did not want the perpetrators to be named. However, Aristide lost the election in 1995 and the succeeding government did not follow through with the commission's work. The government of President René Préval did not distribute the final report initially, but civil society pressure forced him to publish a small number of copies.[87] Supporters of Aristide protested the publication of only 75 copies, so an additional 1,500 copies were printed in 1997. The book was in French, which limited the domestic audience to the French-speaking elite. It was assumed that civil society initiatives would undertake the diffusion work, but none did. All in all, "a collective memory that stems from the work of the Commission is conspicuously absent"[88] as a result of low political and civil society–driven impact.

In line with the recommendations, the Office of the Public Prosecutor was created. The government did not exactly heed the commission's suggestion to enact vetting against human rights violators, but it did screen off some of the applicants to the police force. Finally, there was very limited judicial impact in the aftermath of the commission: while a few key trials, such as the Raboteau case, ended in sentences, most human rights violations remained unaddressed by courts, and there is no indication that the commission played an influential role.[89]

South Africa (1995–1998)

The South African Truth and Reconciliation Commission (TRC) is by far the most famous truth commission. The negotiated transition from apartheid set the stage for a highly participatory process, in which the African National Congress (ANC), the leadership of the outgoing regime, domestic human rights groups, and the emerging transnational network of transitional justice activists created a mandate that gave every participant something. The commissioners faced immense threats to their political autonomy before and during the investigation, which they defended to the extent possible. They used discretion in designing public hearings and thematic testimonial sessions and collaborating with quantitative information management experts. The findings, narrative, and recommendations did not satisfy any actor fully and upset the political class. While the reactions from the apartheid-era elites were expected, the ANC's mostly negative reception demonstrated the extent to which a truth commission could go against the expectations of an incoming democratic government. Ultimately, the TRC managed to generate a high degree of civil society mobilization and public debate, while the political class was reluctant to implement its recommendations and push for criminal accountability.

The South African transition to democracy was negotiated between the leadership of the outgoing apartheid regime and Mandela's African National Congress. The drafting of a new constitution and the creation of a truth commission took place simultaneously. Parliamentary debates played a key role in both processes,[90] but participation was not limited to political actors. The Legal Resources Center in Johannesburg, a nongovernmental rights organization, assisted the parliament with the draft.[91] NGOs, such as the Centre for the Study of Violence and Reconciliation, Justice in Transition (led by Alex Boraine, who later became the deputy chairperson of the TRC), and the Institute for Democracy in South Africa contacted intellectuals and practitioners to draw lessons from the successes and failures of the Latin American transitions. These NGOs participated in the commission creation process by submitting recommendations on the TRC legislation. Despite their efforts, the initial draft bill included the provision of a closed-door amnesty procedure, which was only lifted after "virtually every human rights organization in the country" signed a letter to declare that they would not participate in the commission process if the secrecy provisions were not removed.[92]

The Promotion of National Unity and Reconciliation Act pressed for reconciliation through conditional amnesty as the commission's main political objective.[93] The commission was mandated to provide "as complete a picture as possible" of the causes, nature, and extent of gross violations; facilitate an amnesty procedure in return for confession; develop a victim-centered approach (i.e., restore the human and civil dignity of survivors, find the whereabouts of victims, and recommend reparations); and publish a final report containing recommendations. Throughout the process, civil society organizations pressured for a broader definition of human rights violations.[94]

These goals shaped the committees operating under the TRC: the Human Rights Violations Committee would investigate the abuses, the Reparation and Rehabilitation Committee would design restorative justice measures, and the Amnesty Committee would grant amnesties to eligible perpetrators. The act's initial decision to set the cutoff date for investigation (and the granting of amnesty) at December 6, 1993, was revised by the parliament on the TRC's request and changed to May 10, 1994. The TRC had subpoena and search-and-seizure powers to carry out its investigation.

The legislative act granted the nation's president with the authority to appoint commissioners in consultation with the cabinet. The act imposed one significant limit: the commissioners should not have a high political profile. Mandela's preference for a broadly representative commission resulted in a crowded panel of seventeen individuals. A commentator notes that "although the commissioners' racial and gender composition was not strictly proportional to that of society at large, the selection process clearly reflected a deliberate political attempt to achieve a high degree of representivity" in terms of race, gender, and political affiliation.[95]

The commissioners decided to start with victim hearings to accentuate the victim-oriented approach of the commission. The institutions most closely associated with the apartheid-era violations, such as the Defense Forces, the National Party (NP), and the Inkatha Freedom Party, did not cooperate with the commission, despite the latter's power to subpoena. In fact, the Inkatha Freedom Party explicitly declared that it refused to collaborate. The TRC fought hard not to yield to pressures from these sectors and to avoid the accusations that it was an ANC panel. The commission's sensitivity about autonomy was best exemplified when the ANC leadership came before the Amnesty Committee to testify. The leaders emphasized that they had no personal responsibility for human rights violations, and that their testimonial act was meant to encourage mid-level ANC cadres, as well as the leadership of other parties. They were granted amnesty more or less automatically, without the public confession phase, which put into question the legitimacy and political autonomy of the whole operation, and created a rift between the TRC members and the Amnesty Committee, which was mandated to act semi-independently of the TRC. The TRC took its own Amnesty Committee to court to defend its integrity, and, consequently, the amnesty for ANC leaders was reversed.

Most, but not all, negative reactions to the TRC came from the apartheid leadership. A number of victims' groups and human rights organizations questioned the constitutionality of the amnesty procedure, thereby problematizing the TRC's entire transitional justice model. Furthermore, some NGOs were dismayed at what they perceived as "closing ranks" once the TRC began its operation.[96] Despite, or perhaps as a result of, the high degree of civil society interest in the commission, the relations between NGOs and the TRC remained tense throughout.[97]

Public hearings have been the most visible procedural innovation of the TRC. Another innovative measure was the "thematic and institutional hearings" that focused on specific incidents, contexts, and professional sectors, to give a better sense of the underlying causes and patterns of violence and violations. Again, there was variation in the willingness to cooperate: while the health sector reflected on its code of ethics under apartheid, the judiciary and the business elites were reluctant to participate in the institutional hearings.

President Mandela received the report on October 29, 1998, but only after "an eleventh-hour court interdict to block" its publication, initiated by his own party, the ANC.[98] Likewise, right-wing parties denounced the final report. During and after the commission process, a wide spectrum of political actors, ranging from the ANC to the NP, denounced what they perceived as bias on the part of the TRC. In fact, a page of the final report is "blacked out" in the face of a court interdict threat by former president Frederik Willem de Klerk, who wanted to erase the "derogatory" comments about him.[99] The ANC resorted to the same tactic after its request to meet with the commissioners was denied the night before the handover ceremony, but the case was dismissed.

The indignation on the part of the ANC limited the commission's immediate political impact. The party initially decided not to grant individual reparations, to the shock of those commissioners who had worked on the reparations plan to fulfill the mandate. This brought the governing party and the former TRC participants in bitter conflict. Later, the long wait periods for reparations applications, compared to the much faster turnaround for confessing perpetrators, created discontent among the victims, too.

Individuals who participated in the TRC converted this experience into long-standing advocacy for human rights and truth commissions at home and abroad. Charles Villa-Vicencio, the TRC's former director of research, established an NGO called the Institute for Justice and Reconciliation in Africa toward that end. The final report achieved the goal of raising widespread societal acknowledgment of human rights violations under the apartheid regime. Furthermore, the government's lack of commitment to the reparations program created incentives for civil society groups to keep mobilized.[100] As a result, the government legislated a reduced version of the reparations program in 2003.[101] There have been few advances in the area of incorporating the final report into the educational curriculum.[102] TRC is taught in grades

9 and 12, but its role in "overall educational curriculum should not be over-emphasized."[103]

Guatemala (1997–1999)

The Commission for Historical Clarification (CEH in Spanish acronym) took place under the conditions of a limited democratic opening. The United Nations, domestic human rights groups, and transnational activists had the opportunity to insert their agenda into the commission's mandate, composition, and operation. However, the military and political establishment was in a strong position to limit the commission's political impact. Nonetheless, the commission found ways to turn its weakness (i.e., a vague mandate and the lack of political and judicial impact potential) into strength by focusing on the social history of the nation and detailing institutional responsibility in Guatemala's long trajectory of poverty, racial exclusion, and marginalization. Victims' groups "forced the commission to be brave."[104] Consequently, the truth commission generated enormous social impact in terms of civil society mobilization and human rights monitoring.

The CEH was established as part of the peace accord between the Guatemalan state and the umbrella guerrilla organization Guatemalan National Revolutionary Unity (URNG in Spanish acronym). However, the mandate was "negotiated by an enervated guerrilla leadership and a triumphant army high command as part of peace talks that in 1996 finally drew the war to an official close."[105] In other words, it was a highly participatory negotiation process, but the military and the policy elites were in a strong position to block proposals against their interests. Thus, the mandate was left to be weak in its juridical attributes (no subpoena power and no power to name perpetrators or refer cases to the judiciary). Furthermore, in a conscious effort to avoid deal-breaking confrontations, the mandate left ambiguous the issues of remit, periodization, and the methodology to be used.[106] An international human rights jurist (Christian Tomuschat), a Ladino jurist (Alfredo Balsells), and a Mayan activist (Otilia Lux de Cotí) were selected as commissioners to represent Guatemala's ethnic diversity and the supportive international community.

All in all, the expectation was that the intentionally weakened Guatemalan commission would be a failure.[107] However, "this ambiguity [of the mandate], it turns out, allowed the commission to define its work broadly and to use social science and historical analysis to greater extent than did previous truth commissions."[108] The prohibition on naming individual perpetrators led the commissioners to identify the institutional and historical responsibility of the main political actors who had been dominating national politics for decades. Amy Ross claims that the communities most affected by the violence forced the commission to be bold in interpreting its mandate "for the benefit of the victims, rather than the interests of the signatories."[109] The commission combined forensic investigation with a historical-narrative notion of truth.[110] It conducted interviews but also used findings from earlier nongovernmental truth-finding processes, especially the church-based unofficial truth project that had concluded shortly before the commission's operation. There was no opportunity for public hearings because the mandate, in an effort to weaken the commission's publicity, required the testimonial process to be confidential.

The final report, called *Memory of Silence—Tz'inil Na'tab'al*, stated that 93 percent of the human rights violations were attributed to the military and its allies, and 3 percent to the guerrillas. The report estimated the death toll at around 200,000 and stated that the military campaign amounted to genocidal acts.

The Guatemalan commission stands out for its powerful historical narrative that is broad yet to the point: "The report's tremendous strength comes from its simple unity of premise: that the origin of the conflict and the overwhelming majority of violent acts were the responsibility of the Guatemalan state."[111] Furthermore, the final report took the bold step to refer to social exclusion and racism at the root of the conflict and name relevant institutional actors responsible for violations, including foreign governments.[112] The CEH narrative put forward exclusion, racism, and structural violence as the underlying causes of political violence and treated political variables as proximal causes. Finally, the truth commission did not conceive of national reconstruction as a process of truth telling and mutual reconciliation across fighting parties. Instead, it called for a radical redefinition of the nation and citizenship.

"Perhaps because of [the low expectations resulting from government-imposed resource constraints], when the CEH presented its final report in February 1999 before a packed audience in Guatemala's National Theater, its forcefulness shocked observers."[113] The contention that some of the massacres perpetrated by the military reached genocidal levels, combined with the overall emphasis on the underlying causes of political violence, went against the official state narrative and generated great controversy. President Álvaro

Arzú did not take the report from the hands of the commission's chair first, but later he endorsed the report by issuing a public apology.[114]

The Guatemalan political and military elite came out of the internal conflict with an aura of triumphalism, which went hand in hand with a tendency to overlook the human rights violations. Despite its shocking findings, the truth commission report did not change this attitude. The victory of the right-wing Guatemala Republican Front in the 2000 presidential elections reduced the possibility for direct political impact even further. Nonetheless, the suggested reparations program was put into practice with delay in 2005, and a UN Human Rights Committee document states that "as many as 24,084 victims . . . already received reparations" by 2012.[115] There have been several prosecutions in the first decade following the publication of the final report. Also the report was used as contextual background in courts, such as in the 2002 conviction of former colonel Juan Valencia Osorio for his role in the murder of Myrna Mack.[116] The fact that Ríos Montt was sentenced for genocide in May 2013 attests to the discursive power of the truth commission's report.

The government ignored the final report's educational potential, but teachers and schools have become increasingly more willing to teach topics that were treated as taboo only a few years earlier.[117] The truth commission's impact is indirect: despite civil society efforts, the final report has not been incorporated into textbooks, but the space for discussion opened up by the commission has enabled the instruction of political violence. In terms of civil society mobilization, commentators speak highly of the achievements of the strong sociohistorical narrative, which many transitional justice scholars had initially greeted with suspicion. Although the absence of public hearings reduced the potential for social impact, the recommendations became "crucial touchstones for many different social organizations,"[118] in part because the commissioners included all concerned parties in the formulation of the recommendations.[119] In conclusion, the Guatemalan truth commission has reinvigorated the struggles for truth and accountability, despite successive governments' inattention to the findings and recommendations.

Timor-Leste (2002–2005)

Timor-Leste's Commission for Reception, Truth, and Reconciliation came into existence at the same time as (if not earlier than) the independent state it was mandated to serve. Therefore, it has been the least state-dependent of all truth commission efforts. The participation of domestic NGOs and sustained support from the United Nations and transnational networks, especially the active leadership role assumed by the International Center for Transitional Justice (ICTJ), created the conditions under which the commission adopted novel procedures, produced a comprehensive final report, and made broad recommendations.

The period of violence in Timor-Leste began as a result of political polarization during the brief interregnum between the end of Portuguese colonial rule in 1974 and the Indonesian invasion of 1975. Twenty-four years of asymmetric political violence between the Indonesian army, pro-Indonesia militias, and pro-independence groups reached a peak during and after the 1999 referendum campaign on Timor-Leste's independence. After the referendum, a number of investigations, such as the ones conducted by the United Nations International Commission of Inquiry on East Timor and the Indonesian National Human Rights Commission, produced accounts of the atrocities. Nevertheless, when the UN Transitional Administration in East Timor took over administrative and judicial responsibilities to establish order in the devastated country, it decided to create a truth commission. The Transitional Administration authorized the commission, but the actual drafting of the mandate was a participatory process that brought together Timorese pro-independence groups and the United Nations.[120]

The East Timorese transitional justice experience incorporated several levels of jurisdiction: the newborn International Criminal Court (ICC), an Indonesia-based ad hoc tribunal, and a Serious Crimes Unit that would work in close cooperation with domestic courts.[121] In that context, the stated objectives of the truth commission included the provision of truth, reconciliation, and reintegration (of former militias, as well as forced exiles), while justice was reserved for the courts. The periodization covered between 1974 and 1999, which allowed for a much more comprehensive investigation than that of the previous UN-backed Commission of Inquiry, which only investigated the incidents of 1999. The commission enjoyed search-and-seizure powers and would refer serious crimes to the Office of the General Prosecutor.

The most interesting inclusion was a Community Reconciliation Procedure (CRP), which promoted reconciliation and reintegration at the community level. Perpetrator confessions and victim testimonies had to be overseen by the Office of the General Prosecutor, and if that office classified the crime as "less serious," then the deponent was allowed to participate in community-based reconciliation acts.[122] The fundamental objective was societal reconcili-ation, but the process also aimed at unburdening the country's newly established judicial system. "It is generally considered by both national and international observers that the CRP programme has been a resounding suc-cess."[123] A survey conducted by the truth commission staff in mid-process showed that the majority of community inhabitants were satisfied with the program, including reintegrated former perpetrators.[124] It is also noted, how-ever, that the deponents who testify for their crimes tend to have a more posi-tive view of the process than the victims, and inaction with respect to the "serious crimes" might delegitimize the community-level initiatives, as well.[125]

The commission consisted of seven national commissioners, chaired by a human rights activist, and twenty-nine regional commissioners. Six national commissioners came from religious or secular NGOs specializing in human rights, domestic violence awareness, and refugee issues. One commissioner had a career in civil service under the Indonesian administration. The re-gional commissioners exercised the important function of moderating the CRPs and deciding how the "acts of reconciliation" would be carried out.

"The commission held 8 national hearings, conducted 1,048 research in-terviews, and received 7,760 victim statements."[126] It found that more than 100,000 people were murdered or died of conflict-related causes under the Indonesian rule. The commission named individual perpetrators at high lev-els of the Indonesian government and military. The comprehensive histori-cal narrative "denies any aspiration to be an authoritative history, but asserts a claim to being the first Timor-centric history, one driven by a multiplicity of voices, rather than being an elite or externally driven perspective."[127] It re-jected the official Indonesian narrative of saving a weak, unviable political unit from Marxist-Leninist tyranny through military occupation, but, more important, it tried to explain the conditions under which national unity was broken and could be rebuilt.[128] It celebrated the mixture of resistance and di-plomacy that brought independence and hailed the role of international civil society. Finally, the commissioners proposed broad recommendations, including a reparations program that comprised material compensation, as well as monuments.

Politicians were not entirely convinced that remembrance was a good idea,[129] and the reparations were by and large ignored.[130] The parliament began to discuss legislation of selective recommendations only in 2010. Despite the initial hope for creating a three-tier mechanism for criminal jus-tice (the ICC, the Jakarta tribunal, and the Serious Crimes Unit), ultimately none of these channels worked as imagined. The prosecutor's 2004 decision not to issue an Interpol arrest warrant for infamous general Wiranto, and the government's subsequent decision to create a watered-down intergovernmental Commission of Truth and Friendship, revealed the lack of institutional support for criminal proceedings. The new state's precarious institutions and weak position vis-à-vis Indonesia made state-induced reform highly unlikely.

The illustrated popular version of the final report called *Chega!* was published in 2010, five years after the final report came out.[131] Originally the parliament had discussed supporting the publication, and a subcommittee had favored the decision in June 2008, but subsequent government inaction led the ICTJ to mobilize domestic and international actors around the project. Although NGOs had suspected in the very beginning that the Commission for Reception, Truth, and Reconciliation and the subsequent Commission of Truth and Friendship between Timor-Leste and Indonesia would divert resources away from retributive justice, after 2008 "NGO criticism has softened, and activists have begun to see [the final reports'] potential as advocacy and educational tools."[132] In conclusion, the East Timorese commission has generated considerably greater socially driven impact in comparison to direct political impact.

Sierra Leone (2002–2004)

Sierra Leone's Truth and Reconciliation Commission is arguably among the most successful in terms of generating both political and civil society–driven impact. The commission was part of the UN-brokered Lomé Peace Accord in 1999 that concluded the civil war between the government and the Revolutionary United Front (RUF). The first round of negotiations favored blanket amnesty, but the UN representative's last-minute inclusion of a reservation statement against amnesty for serious human rights violations created judicial ambiguity for the peace process.[133] The UN Office of the High Commissioner for Human Rights, which sponsored the initiative, circulated the draft mandate to domestic and international civil society groups.[134] The International Center for Transitional Justice provided consulting assistance.

Following the South African precedent, the commission was established through the Truth and Reconciliation Act in 2000. The remit included a broad range of violations committed between 1991 and the signing of the peace agreement. Although the reintegration of ex-combatants was a major concern during the transition to peace, the mandate did not specify any mechanism toward that end. The act left significant discretion to the commissioners in deciding whether or not the testimonies should be confidential. Like the Haitian and Guatemalan examples, the commission in Sierra Leone was a mixed panel of national and foreign commissioners. Bishop Joseph Humper, considered one of the architects of the peace accord, was appointed as the chair. Despite the high degree of support from domestic and international civil society groups, and the government's sympathetic rhetoric, the commission faced serious funding and management issues, especially in its early phase. Although international actors, operating through the United Nations Mission in Sierra Leone, seemed to dominate the commission creation process,[135] the tenacity of domestic civil society groups proved critical at this juncture.[136]

The commission operated simultaneously with the Special Court for Sierra Leone, whose task was to prosecute those with the greatest responsibility for atrocities. Commentators note that there was no clear design to ensure cooperation between the two institutions.[137] The commissioners initially promoted a legal-forensic notion of truth, and collected around eight thousand testimonies, but in time they adopted a mixture of forensic and narrative truth-telling strategies. The ambiguity about the commission's legal and political objectives shifted attention toward the symbolic and spectacular aspects.[138] For example, although the mandate did not specify a reintegration plan, highly ritualized public hearings facilitated some ex-combatants' return to their communities.

The final report was about 5,000 pages long, with 3,500 pages devoted to testimonies. It established the institutional responsibility of the RUF, the army, civil defense patrols, as well as the National Patriotic Front of Liberia headed by Charles Taylor. It named perpetrators. Corruption and the lack of checks on the executive were presented as the main factors contributing to the civil war. The recommendations were legally binding on the government. In line with its historical narrative, the commission presented a broad recommendations program, which spanned "the fight against corruption, the creation of a new Bill of Rights developed in a participatory constitutional process, the independence of the judiciary, strengthening the role of Parliament, stricter control over the security forces, decentralization and enhanced economic autonomy for the provinces as well as the government's commitment to deliver basic public services and the inclusion of youth and women in political decision-making."[139] Repeating the peace accord's recommendation, the truth commission also suggested a reparations program for victims.

The final report was released at a public ceremony in October 2004. President Ahmad Tejan Kabbah, who had testified before the commission in August 2003, did not issue strong statements in favor of or against the final report. His successor Ernest Bai Coroma apologized to the women victims in April 2010. The creation of the Human Rights Commission was the first political consequence of truth commission recommendations. The National Commission for Social Action was established to carry out the commission's recommendations. Likewise, the United Nations and the government of Sierra Leone implemented a yearlong project in 2008 to compensate the amputees, victims of sexual violence, the war wounded, children affected by war, and war widows, using a grant from the UN Peacebuilding Fund.[140]

Accounts by domestic and international civil society actors focus more on the peace process circa 2000 than the developments in the aftermath of the truth commission. Based on available data, one can argue that the truth commission managed to generate considerable civil society mobilization, partly thanks to constant international pressure and partly as a result of domestic human rights activism.[141] Human rights groups remained alert, pushing for the reparations program and the prosecution of chief perpetrators. The publication of a children's version of the final report was another successful measure, although schools have tended not to use it so far.[142] However, it is debatable whether the commission remained an elite civil society initiative or managed to serve the interests of the nonelite as well.[143]

Liberia (2006–2009)

Liberia's Truth and Reconciliation Commission came into being through an all-inclusive process that brought together parties to the civil war, as well as domestic and international human rights groups, the diaspora, and intergovernmental organizations. Overseas judicial processes, such as Charles Taylor's indictment by the Special Court for Sierra Leone, overshadowed the commission's work to some extent. Nevertheless, the mandate and civil society support empowered the commissioners to make bold recommendations, which ultimately made the commission's final report difficult to accept for the political elite. Despite notable setbacks, the pre-commission and post-commission processes generated significant civil society mobilization.

The Accra Agreement of 2003 ended a period of political instability and civil war, paving the way for transitional justice measures. As in Sierra Leone, the peace agreement stipulated the creation of a truth commission in the context of legal-institutional reforms. The Liberian experience was unique, however, in that a temporary legislative body, the National Transitional Legislative Assembly, passed the act that mandated the commission. The parties to the conflict, including presumed perpetrators, had greater access to the commission creation process than in Sierra Leone. The seventy-six-member body represented former President Charles Taylor's government, the rebels, various political parties, and civil society groups.[144] The Minnesota-based Diaspora Project also took active part in the truth commission process. ICTJ opened an office in Monrovia in 2006 to monitor the truth commission's operation and collaborated with BBC Trust to train journalists in the area of transitional justice.[145]

The mandate demanded the investigation of human rights and international humanitarian law violations and economic crimes committed between 1979 and 2003. Crimes before 1979 could also be investigated if the commission deemed it necessary.[146] The commission was asked to explain the causes and patterns of violence and identify perpetrators. In other words, the commissioners had enormous discretion over the investigation. The rehabilitation of victims and reconciliation across warring factions were the main objectives. The commission had an amnesty procedure that excluded perpetrators of crimes against humanity and violations of international humanitarian law, which in fact amounted to the majority of crimes under investigation.

The all-Liberian commission[147] was chaired by Jerome Verdier, a human rights activist and environmental lawyer. The composition brought together human rights activists, social workers, religious leaders and journalists. The major challenge was to make the Liberian commission's work compatible with the Special Court for Sierra Leone.[148] The commission collected around twenty thousand testimonies, including from diaspora Liberians. There was a public hearing procedure as well. The exclusion of civil society groups from the commission process was notable. For example, when the need to enhance accountability and transparency "resulted in the formation of a TRC Working Group" in mid-process, no civil society organization was asked to join.[149]

The truth commission published three volumes between December 2008 and December 2009. It found that the abuses were widespread and systematic on the part of all the parties to the conflict. Sexual violence and the forced recruitment of children were specifically mentioned as categories of crimes committed by all sides. The report attributed the underlying causes of the conflict to "poverty, greed, corruption, limited access to education, economic, social, civil and political inequalities; identity conflict; land tenure and distribution; the lack of reliable and appropriate mechanisms for the settlement of disputes."[150] Furthermore, the report explained the social, legal, and political implications of deep divisions between the indigenous Liberia and the settler Liberia.

The recommendations of the Liberian TRC are arguably the boldest in the history of truth commissions.[151] It included a list of individuals to be barred from public service for thirty years, including President Ellen Johnson Sirleaf. It advocated the creation of an Extraordinary Criminal Tribunal for Liberia to prosecute grave human rights and international humanitarian law violations and a traditional dispute resolution mechanism, called the National Palava Hut Forum, to offer amnesty to perpetrators of less serious crimes. Complementing general suggestions for rule-of-law reform and human rights accountability, the commission asked for a reparations program to distribute U.S.$500 million over a period of thirty years.

President Sirleaf questioned the legality of the truth commission's recommendation to remove her, among others, from public office. Meanwhile, she apologized for having financed Charles Taylor in the early 1990s. The parliament decided to suspend the decision whether or not to implement the truth commission's recommendations in mid-2009. An important advance was the creation of the Independent National Commission on Human Rights in line with the commission's recommendations.

Domestic civil society groups have sought active participation at every step of the commission process, but as evidenced in their exclusion from the working group, their success in the face of powerful national and international actors has been modest at best.[152] Despite setbacks, domestic civil society groups did mobilize around the truth commission.[153] The Transitional Justice Working Group (TJWG) of Liberia (not to be confused with the working group established during the commission process), an umbrella for human rights and peace-building organizations that played an important role in drafting the commission mandate, took upon itself the task of monitoring the government's implementation of truth commission recommendations, in particular the formation of the Independent National Commission on Human Rights. The TJWG announced its "Post TRC Transitional Justice Initiative" in June 2010 to promote truth and justice efforts in the wake of the TRC process.[154] Furthermore, the post-commission process led to the formation of new victims' advocacy organizations, such as the Lutheran Church Massacre Survivors and Victims Association, that pressured the government for reparations.[155]

Conclusion

Every truth commission, just like every past it claims to represent and every present it finds itself in, is unique. The variety of violent contexts, violations, personal and collective memories, and transitional parameters defies the neat categorization of truth commission efforts to come to terms with the past. Yet, a comparative analysis of truth commission experiences reveals clear patterns. Governments (and sometimes international organizations) try to control a truth commission's mandate and composition, but the presence of countervailing forces increases the commission's likelihood of going beyond the confines of political agenda setting. Naturally, continuous political support enables a more comprehensive (and expensive) human rights investigation and increases the commission's efficacy, but evidence shows that truth-finding initiatives cannot rely on the goodwill of politicians for success. Domestic human rights activists, if they embrace the findings and recommendations of the commission, become indispensable allies during and after the commission's work. Understanding the dynamics of local civil society participation is key to explaining truth commission impact.[156]

Another increasingly influential group of actors in establishing and operating fact-finding bodies are international organizations and NGOs. Since the mid-1990s, foreign governments, international organizations like the United Nations, nongovernmental funding agencies like the Ford Foundation, and numberless civil society activists and policy experts have been lobbying for, funding, and offering technical expertise to truth commissions around the globe. Their involvement has no doubt increased truth commissions' capacity to carry out lengthy, comprehensive, and bold investigations. All the well-funded, high-capacity truth commissions have received some kind of international and/or transnational support. The surprising and delegitimizing effects of truth commissions on the domestic political elite result in great part from the empowering influence of those nonnational actors.

However, several truth commission experiences show that overseas actors do not always produce high-autonomy and high-capacity commissions.

An international organization's failure to collaborate with domestic partners might lead to a commission creation process as exclusionary as a government-run commission, and the failure to maintain ongoing communication between domestic and international civil society activists might alienate key social actors—as in El Salvador. In Haiti a relatively high-quality commission, established under the guidance of diaspora groups, was left to oblivion, as the domestic human rights community felt left out of the commission creation process. Thus, international activism tends to broaden participation in the structuring of a truth commission, but the inclusionary and empowering effects need to be assessed, rather than assumed, for each case.

This chapter suggests a high degree of path dependence spanning pre-commission, commission, and post-commission processes. Yet, it is important to acknowledge the deviations from this trajectory. A politically controlled initial process does not always undermine truth commission agency, and a participatory process does not mean that the participants in the beginning endorse the commission's work throughout. The Nigerian commission, for example, was bold enough to surprise and delegitimize political leaders despite the tight political constraints at its inception. Civil society support at the initial stages of a commission did not prevent tense relations between human rights NGOs and the commission in Liberia. Political developments that are unrelated to a commission's work may be fateful, as the 1995 presidential elections in Haiti suggest.

Nonetheless, even these twists and turns do not change the overall relationship between a commission's creation and reception. For all its inconvenience, the Nigerian commission managed to produce more government-led responses than civil society mobilization. The love-and-hate relationship between the commission and the Liberian human rights movement did not prevent the latter from organizing around the former's message. The Haitian commission's story highlights the role of contingency as much as the importance of securing diverse sources of support in case of contingency. The commission creation process does not determine everything that happens in and around a commission, it but sets firm limits on the possibility of conflict and cooperation between key actors.

CHAPTER 7

Comparing Truth Commissions' Memory Narratives: Chile and Peru

> Ustedes que ya escucharon
> La historia que se contó
> No sigan allí sentados
> Pensando que ya pasó
> No basta sólo el recuerdo
> El canto no bastará
> No basta sólo el lamento
> Miremos la realidad
> Quizás mañana o pasado o bien
> En un tiempo más
> La historia que han escuchado
> De nuevo sucederá
>   —"Canción final"

> Gobierno palacio punkupi
> Guardia centinelaschay
> Punkuchaykita kichaykuway
> Belaundiwan rimaykusaq
> Presidentiwan parlaykusaq
>   —"Queja andina"

The enormous variation across truth commissions in terms of goals, findings, recommendations, and impact is explored in Chapters 5 and 6. Truth commissions' explanations of the underlying causes of past violence and violations exhibit considerable variation as well. No doubt some of the differences owe to the context in which violations happen, as well as the nature of the violations themselves. Yet, one often observes divergent historical narratives describing comparable historical contexts. The civil wars in El Salvador and Guatemala had much in common, but the Salvadoran Truth Commission's overall preference for avoidance and brevity shared little with the comprehensive historical narrative of Guatemala's Commission for Historical Clarification (see Chapter 3).

This chapter offers a comparative analysis of the historical narratives of the Chilean and Peruvian truth commissions to understand the conditions under which truth-finding panels are likely to produce more comprehensive and inclusionary accounts. It explores what the respective commissions include and exclude when it comes to explaining the causes and consequences of political violence. Chapter 3 identifies a number of narrative strategies (*adjudication*, *avoidance*, *giving voice*, and *transformation*) that all truth commissions use, albeit with varying degrees. This chapter seeks to explain how the commissions use those strategies and to what effect.

In line with the findings of Chapters 5 and 6, this chapter shows that the initial process that establishes a truth commission shapes its historical narrative, but this structuring effect can also empower the commissioners in some cases. The commission creation process simultaneously enables and constrains the commission through the mandate and the appointment of commissioners, which in turn shapes the forensic investigation and the historical explanation. The composition of the commission is of special significance in making sense of the historical explanation, since the commissioners' professional background, ideology, values, and experiences have direct influence on the content and exclusions of the narrative.

An exclusionary commission creation process results in a constrained mandate and a list of commissioners that reflects limited and politically convenient goals. As the example of Chile suggests, such a commission is likely to lead to a relatively narrow historical narrative that avoids politically divisive issues and shuns the opportunity to produce a comprehensive account of the underlying causes of political violence and violations. In contrast, the participation of multiple social and political actors in the commission creation process, as in Peru, is likely to enable the agency of those commissioners interested in problematizing the national history. Consequently, such a commission will tend to intervene in social memory struggles more actively, adjudicating on controversial topics and incorporating more voices and per-spectives.

A word of caution: I do not claim that participatory commission creation processes produce historical narratives that are completely free from avoid-ances, exclusions, and silences. Even the most comprehensive and inclusionary historical narrative cannot entirely escape avoiding a stance on some histori-cal controversies or leaving some alternative explanations unaddressed—as my critique of the Peruvian truth commission will make clear. Nonetheless, there are fewer avoidances and exclusions in the historical narrative follow-ing a participatory commission creation process than a narrative resulting from an exclusionary process.

In the following section, I discuss the content, inclusions and exclusions of the historical narrative in the Rettig Commission's final report and situ-ate this narrative in the field of social memory struggles in Chile. Then I offer a point of comparison by analyzing the Peruvian CVR's historical narrative and its role in that country's memory debates. The concluding section in-vites scholars and practitioners to rethink the silences and exclusions of truth commissions in general. Even if political constraints set limits on how truth commissions make sense of the past, commissions would serve their goals of preserving historical memory and preventing future violence better by producing more comprehensive historical narratives that connect the proximal and underlying causes of violent conflict, taking into consider-ation the national as well as local dynamics and paying attention to indi-vidual and collective agency without reducing historical actors to victims and perpetrators.

The Historical Narrative of Chile's Rettig Commission

Chile's Concertación government initiated the truth commission to discover and publicize information on forced disappearances and killings and to put an end to the forced silencing of experiences and memories that refuted the military government's self-justifying narratives. Throughout the military re-gime, state propaganda and influential media groups had portrayed the military coup as a heroic and selfless act of salvation against Marxism and denied allegations of extrajudicial killing, disappearance, and torture. The human rights movement had devoted enormous time, resources, and energy to documenting and denouncing the violations in the face of threats, but the judiciary refused to investigate the human rights cases, and the mainstream media, in close collaboration with the military government, marginalized the movement. Neither the judiciary nor the mainstream media changed their postures in the early years of the democratic transition; the hope for revival under democracy rested with alternative fact-finding and truth-telling projects, such as the Rettig Commission.

The commissioners adopted a unanimous decision rule to confirm the veracity of forensic data and historical explanation. Reflective of the Chilean society at large, each commissioner had a particular understanding of the onset of the coup, its justifiability, the historical role of the leftist Unidad Popular government (1970–1973) and the ways in which the Right and the Christian Democratic Party handled the political impasse of 1973. The extent of divergence within the commission presents a puzzle: How did they reach agreement while coming to grips with such a divisive legacy?

The commission's chief strategy was to leave out those aspects of history in which they "agreed to disagree."[1] As the final report states: "The Commission has refrained from taking a stand on whether the use of force on September 11, 1973, and immediately thereafter was legitimate, both by those who sought to overthrow the government of President Salvador Allende and by those who sought to defend it."[2]

However, the commissioners were well aware that complete silence on the historical context would undermine the task of learning from past mistakes in order not to repeat them: "the Commission believes it must take into account the situation of the country leading up to September 11, 1973. That situation led to a break in our institutional life and a deep division between Chileans which made it more likely that human rights would be violated. One of this Commission's assigned tasks is to propose preventive measures, that is, to suggest what should be done so as to prevent the recurrence of the kinds of infractions we have investigated."[3]

The chapter entitled "Political Context" (part 2, chapter 1) is devoted to explaining the causes of the military coup and describing the institutional and political context in which human rights violations took place. The historical narrative by and large reflects the contending positions of commissioners José Zalaquett and Gonzalo Vial. Zalaquett brought the sensitivities of a human rights advocate to the table: the accurate documentation of human rights violations, the elucidation of institutional responsibilities, the categorical exclusion of violence from political ethics and practice, and the reconstruction of the nation through respect for human rights and the rule of law. His pragmatic approach to transitional justice facilitated negotiations with various political agendas, including a conservative one.

Gonzalo Vial, an influential historian whose many volumes covered Chile's entire colonial and postcolonial periods, had opposed the socialist project and its supposed violent implications since the 1960s. He saw in the democratically elected socialist Unidad Popular government an insidious plot to destroy the traditional pillars of Chilean society and impose communist tyranny, by force if necessary. He is rumored to have edited the *White Book of the Change of Government in Chile* to justify the military coup.[4] The book, published months after the coup by the secretariat-general of the military government, claimed to reveal a conspiracy of the extreme Left, called "Plan Z," to turn Chile into a dictatorship of the proletariat. Vial also served in the military government as the minister of education. Thus, his views not only reflected, but also actually shaped, the conservative worldview. Nonetheless, his self-distancing attitude toward the military regime with respect to the latter's human rights record, rare among the military regime's allies, qualified him for the truth commission.

The commission's historical narrative should be read as a consensus played out between these two positions: categorical condemnation of the human rights violations (the human rights sensitivity advocated by Zalaquett), combined with a right-wing historiography emphasizing the political polarization of the Allende years, while passing no condemnatory judgment on the military coup itself (Vial's position).

The chapter in its Spanish original consists of nineteen pages, with the first six pages devoted to the onset of the military coup, and the rest describing the institutional framework of the military regime. There is a strong historical argument coming out of the short explanation of the coup onset, which can be called the *political polarization thesis*.[5] Accordingly, the immediate causes leading up to the military coup were of a political and ideological nature. While the text acknowledges the deeper social economic causes as subject matter for a broader explanation, it focuses on the "clashes of doctrines and attitudes in the realm of politics and ideology, as these have an immediate bearing on the issue of human rights."[6] With its focus on the immediate causes, the chapter depicts the Unidad Popular government as a period of increasing polarization along political-ideological lines that led many actors on both sides to affirm violence as a legitimate instrument to achieve political ends. The parties to the conflict are identified as "government and opposition." Some sectors of the government and its allies advocated the "armed path" to bring about socialist transformation, while the opposition political parties based their strategy on rendering the country "ungovernable," through violent means if necessary.[7]

In one of the rare moves toward historical explanation, the text sets out the broader context that caused the "destruction and deterioration of numerous points of consensus . . . and shared assumptions concerning social and political coexistence, which served to safeguard respect for human rights."[8] Chief among them was the regional polarization of the Cold War, which was aggravated after the Cuban Revolution. The consequence was a disposition toward ideological inflexibility that ruled out political negotiation even when the parties to the conflict lacked the power and legitimacy to impose their political projects. Eventually, adherence to democratic procedures began to falter.

As the democratic breakdown was imminent, other causes accelerated the crisis. First, the sense of defeat and threat on the part of the policy elites led the government of the United States to direct efforts to undermine the Unidad Popular government. Second, the domestic economic crisis of 1972–1973, resulting in middle-class disenchantment with the government, destabilized the political system even more. Third, land expropriations (*tomas*) and other radical measures by the government and its allies triggered "circumstances that could seem to justify such fears"[9] among some sectors. Finally, some media organizations acted irresponsibly by vilifying their political enemies. The text describes these processes in general terms: it does not give any example of U.S. efforts to undermine Allende's government, and it does not name those irresponsible press and broadcasting organizations. Despite its decision to avoid judgment on politically divisive themes, the memory framework that shapes the report's analysis is deeply political, but only selectively so. The text explains the political and social trauma that led to the coup with a narrative of political polarization, economic crisis, and bad governance under the Allende presidency. The periods before and after Unidad Popular are spared political, institutional, and macroeconomic analysis.

What was the military's role in all this? The report pictures the armed forces as an apolitical organization that historically respected civilian democratic rule. However, the climate of ideological polarization drew the military into political conflict, as they considered themselves the ultimate bastion of democratic rule in Chile. The commission's reconstruction of history puts emphasis on how the crisis "drew them away" from their tradition of discipline, respect for civilian rule, and political neutrality.[10] Nonetheless, the report admits that "the subsequent events to which we now turn leave no doubt that there was also an ideological tendency within the armed forces and security forces,"[11] again without specifying the actors representing those tendencies.

The contradiction that runs through the context chapter is that while it condemns the parties to the political conflict for creating an environment of violence, the commissioners declare themselves unfit to condemn or praise the actual use of violence to overthrow a democratic government. The truth commission's strategy is to remain agnostic about the legitimacy of the *choice* of using military force to overthrow a democratic government and concentrating condemnatory judgment on the human rights violations during and after the coup: "whether having recourse to weapons was justified or not, there are clear norms forbidding certain kinds of behavior in the waging of hostilities, both in international and internal armed conflicts," such as killing or torturing prisoners and violating fair trial standards.[12] In other words, the final report condemns the political-ideological environment that *may have* led to violence, fails to condemn the actual decision to use violent means to appropriate political power, but then again condemns the consequence of the decision, that is, death and disappearance.[13]

Steve Stern notes that the mandate collapsed human rights law with international humanitarian law and did not address the ethical question of legitimate armed resistance. The definitional ambiguity notwithstanding, "from practical and political points of view . . . the mandate made sense. It deferred to sensibilities of the military and the Right, and it recognized that technical distinctions regarding the transcendent value of life would not register with the larger Chilean public."[14]

The context chapter has a clear message: the Chilean society should absolutely not repeat the experience of grave human rights violations. The mechanism for prevention is twofold: one, avoiding the mistakes of radical sociopolitical transformation and polarization, embodied in the Unidad Popular project, and, two, respecting democratic procedures and the rule of law. Thus, it affirms a strictly procedural notion of democracy, excluding substantive notions of social justice and radical change for fear of political mobilization, polarization, and ultimately violence.[15] Intolerant and violent ideologies motivated by the "ethics of ends,"[16] which include both the leftist discourse of the 1960s and 1970s and virulent anticommunism, are counter-poised to the procedural, pluralist, and tolerant liberal democracy.

While Gonzalo Vial was the principal author of the context chapter,[17] it is a mistake to hold him solely responsible for its strengths and weaknesses. The final report was adopted unanimously, and other commissioners have defended its historical approach in subsequent publications and academic conferences, which points to a high degree of consensus.[18]

In Chapter 3 I argue that truth commission narratives are constituted as much by what is excluded from the text as by what appears in it. Therefore the Chilean truth commission's context chapter should be situated in the broader field of social memory struggles in the 1990s. Three hegemonic memory camps dominated public debates in the early 1990s. The Pinochetista social memory, which glorified the military coup and the military regime's policies while trivializing the human rights violations, had considerable support among conservative politicians, the business community, the mainstream media, and a significant portion of the citizenry. The socialist/communist reconstruction of the same past saw in the military coup the bloody destruction of a democratic revolution that had inspired the Chilean public for the peaceful road to socialism. Those leftist groups that were excluded from the governing center-left coalition, such as the Communist Party and victims' organizations closely affiliated with them, spearheaded this memory camp. And finally, the socialists, social democrats, and Christian Democrats who came together under the Concertación banner saw themselves as the defenders of a center-left position, having left behind the radical aspirations and political errors of the 1960s and 1970s. Constructed through encounters among political activists in Chile and in exile, the centrist social memory condemns the military regime's human rights violations but also distances itself from the Unidad Popular's dream of revolutionary change. Instead, the need to uphold democracy, the rule of law, and a market economy with minimal state intervention are prioritized as the most important lessons from history.

Right-wing circles and the military were the first to criticize the truth commission on the grounds of limited contextualization. For the Pinochetista understanding of political history, "context" meant the radicalization of socioeconomic grievances and the polarization of politics under the reformist Christian Democratic government of Eduardo Frei-Montalva (1964–1970), followed by the destruction of democracy at the hands of radical Marxists (1970–1973). It was against the backdrop of this history that the coup, receiving widespread endorsement from right-wing and Christian Democratic sectors, took place. Even though violent incidents between 1964 and 1973 were a tiny faction of what happened during and after the coup, the right-wing circles objected to the commission's investigation of the military regime only.

The Concertación politicians, for their part, left the terrain of context-related disagreements to their political rivals and instead focused on the human rights question before, during, and after the truth commission process. They insisted on the legitimacy of the limited periodization for the commission mandate and did not argue with the right-wing opposition over the legacy of the 1960s and the 1970s. The internal composition of the Concertación plays a crucial role in explaining this decision. This political coalition had its origins when Christian Democrats and the moderate sectors within the Radical and Socialist parties began to regroup in the limited political opening of the early 1980s. All relevant actors knew all too well that the Christian Democrats had initially supported the coup that explicitly sought to eliminate the political Left. Influential Christian Democrats adopted an oppositional stance against the military government only after they realized that Pinochet was consolidating power, with no democratic transition in sight, and that human rights violations had reached an intolerable level—at which point some Christian Democrats found themselves targeted by state repression, too.[19] In light of this divisive political history, the only way that the new political coalition of Christian Democrats and leftists could hold together was if the troubling past was somehow forgotten and democracy and human rights were affirmed time and again as the unifying principles of the Concertación.[20] The coup onset and the initial responses to the military rule, therefore, stood out as inappropriate topics to discuss publicly, while the human rights issue served the double function of delegitimizing the right-wing opposition and providing cohesion for the ruling coalition. Hence the commission's limited mandate.

The commission entirely ruled out discussions of the underlying historical, socioeconomic, and cultural factors that made political violence and violations possible. Chilean and North American historians, in particular those on the left, have discussed class conflict at the root of political violence at length. Accordingly, the coup coalition consisted of those sectors (including the Christian Democrats) that defended their class interests against the socialist experiment under way. It was no surprise that they welcomed the military regime that destroyed Chile's democracy, disbanded leftist organizations, and crushed popular sectors in a wave of repression and neoliberal restructuring. Thus, human rights abuses cannot be understood in isolation from the economic and political project carried out by Pinochet, the business sector, and the U.S.-trained neoclassical economists (popularly known as "Chicago Boys"), and generously supported by the American government.

This Marxist-inspired historical narrative stands in sharp contrast with the truth commission's view of the military regime as a rupture in Chile's history of democratic and peaceful political development. The narrative construction of the stark distinction between the nation's liberal democratic traditions and the Pinochet dictatorship breaks down if one pays close attention to the longer trajectory of class conflict. While the dictatorship was particularly long, bloody, and lawless, leftist historians claim that it was not an exception in Chile's long history of repression against the labor movement and other forms of social protest.[21] Pinochet was but a more radical and uninterrupted phase of this pattern of repression. It was more brutal because it developed as a response to a socialist project that had ascended to political power for the first time in Chilean history. Presenting the history of the dictatorship in contradistinction to the democracy and tolerance of previous governments, as well as the Concertación, the truth commission excludes this alternative plausible explanation of the nature of political conflict and violence in Chile, past and present.[22]

Why did the commission ignore this alternative historiography? The tightly controlled commission creation process was premised on achieving numeric balance between human rights defenders and the representatives of the political Right. The public figures who could problematize the nation's long historical trajectory of violence, bring up the question of social justice, discuss the political virtues of the Allende presidency, or make a strong statement against the political choices of the military regime were excluded.[23] The extra-parliamentary Left, represented by the Communist Party and major victims' organizations, had suffered the most from human rights violations, and they were also deeply disappointed with the early transitional experience in which the essentials of the neoliberal economy, installed by Pinochet and technocrats surrounding him, were completely maintained by the Concertación. However, they were too weak to count as major actors, and the truth commission allowed their participation only as victims, not as mandate setters or commissioners. Therefore, the Marxist conception of history was at the margins of memory politics. It reminded the public of what the hegemonic discourses were concealing, but this conception was by no means a major determinant of the truth and justice processes in Chile.[24]

The Historical Narrative of Peru's CVR

In sharp contrast, the truth commission in Peru produced a broad social history to contextualize political violence and violations. From the beginning the commissioners were aware that their narration of history would shape public debates on collective identity, memory, and justice. As the commission's chair, Salomón Lerner, states in the abbreviated version of the final report: "in a country like ours, the struggle against forgetting is a powerful form of doing justice."[25]

The composition of the commission played a crucial role in that decision: most commissioners were historians, social scientists, or political activists who had devoted themselves to understanding and transforming the social reality. Furthermore, the commissioners appointed a large group of Peruvian and foreign scholars, junior as well as senior ones, as their advisers and fieldwork researchers. The staff introduced a rich array of methodological approaches, ranging from ethnographic studies of the highlands to statistical imputation techniques.

The CVR's estimation of the death toll at 69,280 has shocked even the informed observers, including the commissioners themselves. The commission used reports from a number of human rights organizations and state institutions, and they could identify 23,969 victims as dead or disappeared. The statistical estimation revealed not only that the magnitude of violations was much larger than suspected. The gap between the number of identified and projected victims also demonstrated that governmental and civic initiatives failed to account for the overwhelming majority of the victims. Part of the failure owes to the fact that the crime of forced disappearance is intrinsically secretive. However, the enormous mismatch between numbers also points to the political and cultural center's inability to administer, let alone deliver justice to, the rural highlands.

The findings debunk wartime propaganda, much like other truth commissions. All parties to the conflict committed systematic human rights violations, although the commission held Shining Path responsible for a greater proportion of violations resulting in death than state agents. It rejects the notion that Alberto Fujimori's repressive counterinsurgency tactics were necessary, legitimate, or even effective. The final report also adjudicates between various memory narratives that had dominated public discourse throughout the conflict, some held by sectors sympathetic to the human rights cause. For example, it finds that the police had no involvement in the 1983 massacre of eight journalists in Uchuraccay—confirming the 1983 Vargas Llosa Commission's findings. Likewise, it states that it has not found sufficient evidence to attribute criminal responsibility to former president Alan García for his role in the 1986 prison massacres, much to the dismay of the human rights community.

Unlike its Chilean counterpart, the Peruvian truth commission combines forensic investigation with several volumes devoted to putting violence and violations in context. The first volume describes the kinds of violations and actors involved. The second volume deals with the parties to the conflict: the Shining Path receives the most attention, but there are chapters on the armed forces, the police, the MRTA insurgency, and self-defense patrols as well. The third volume positions all major political and social actors, from various presidents to the church, in the context of political violence.[26] Then, volumes 4 to 7 analyze different types of human rights violations and examine illustrative cases. Volume 8 goes back to social history: half the volume is devoted to the "factors that made violence possible," and the other half to the psychosocial, socioeconomic, and political effects of violence. The final volume summarizes the truth commission's recommendations, which, as described in Chapter 5, move beyond political-institutional reform to encompass wide-reaching sociocultural and political transformations.

The CVR distinguishes between the immediate and underlying causes of the conflict. The immediate cause is the Shining Path's decision to initiate a so-called "people's war" against the Peruvian state. "The historical or long-term factors that explain the conflict" can be summarized as the "unequal distribution of wealth" as well as "political and symbolic power."[27] Society is sharply divided between those "who have the right to speak" and those whose grievances go unheard. The CVR presents three sets of intersecting divisions to explain the cultural and geographical cleavages: (1) Lima and the provinces; (2) the coast (costa), the highlands (sierra), and the forest (selva); and (3) the ethnocultural categories of criollos, mestizos, cholos, and indios,[28] an enduring legacy of the colonial caste system.

The final report states that poverty and social exclusion were closely correlated with victimization during the internal conflict.[29] As historian Cynthia Milton notes, the commission makes connections between its human rights investigation and historical narrative: "The Peruvian commission firmly placed the internal conflict—1980–2000—as a period in a longer national history of racism and centralism that was both the cause and a consequence of the violence."[30] The emphasis on socioeconomic inequality, poverty, ethnocultural exclusion, and marginalization gives coherence to the final report, as these factors inform the report's main findings, narrative on the causes of conflict, and the recommendations agenda.

The Peruvian truth commission could not be further from its Chilean counterpart in its willingness to condemn a fateful political event, namely Alberto Fujimori's civilian coup on April 5, 1992: "Fujimori became an authoritarian ruler who sought to remain in power consolidating a corrupt autocracy."[31] The final report lauds the presidencies of Fernando Belaúnde and Alan García for upholding electoral democracy, but criticizes them for failing to develop a comprehensive and inclusive strategy to tackle armed violence in an effective and democratically legitimate way.[32] This analysis is in line with the truth commission's finding that the two democratic presidents should bear political, but not criminal, responsibility for the crimes committed under their governments. Moreover, it demonstrates how the mixture of willful repression and political neglect perpetuated the state's failed response to the threat from the Shining Path.

The Shining Path is responsible for the violence it inflicted on the Peruvian people to advance its totalitarian and fundamentalist agenda. The final report rejects the Shining Path's self-justificatory narrative: the insurgency reproduced the relations of racism and cultural supremacy, and its supposed "peasant war" took the form of deadly confrontations between peasants. In other words, while the final report argues that social injustice has been the major factor that aggravated the conflict, it rejects that the notion that the Shining Path promoted justice in any way. The final report also points to the "potential for genocide" in the Shining Path rhetoric, although it does not specify whether acts of violence by the insurgency in fact amounted to genocide.

The Peruvian commission was a bold intervention into public discourse on the nation's past. One of the widely circulating memory narratives reduced the internal conflict between the government forces and the Shining Path to the confrontation of the forces of good and evil. This narrative minimized the violations committed by state agents and treated any criticism of the state's conduct as collaboration with terrorists. The allies of Fujimori used media power to justify the former president's pacification policies and accuse the truth commission of collaborating with foreign donors and terrorists to destabilize Peru. Other political actors who had been involved in the internal conflict, most notably the political parties APRA and Acción Popular, were more careful not to endorse the Fujimoristas' inflammatory rhetoric and were supportive of the CVR's critique of Fujimori's dictatorial presidency, but their interpretation of the past tended to emphasize the heroic struggle against the Shining Path to the exclusion of the human rights question. The Shining Path leadership, for its part, regarded the CVR as state propaganda to denigrate their "people's war." Although many of its members testified before the commission during jail visits, the leadership of the defeated insurgency never endorsed the commission's historical narrative.

The politically motivated attacks against the CVR were at least as much about the present as about the past. The collapse of Fujimori's civilian-authoritarian regime had pushed the major parties and politicians out of the political system. Fujimori's supporters retained control of the yellow media, while APRA, under the direction of Alan García, held on to a minority in the Congress in the early years of the transition. The interim government of Valentín Paniagua and the succeeding elected government of Alejandro Toledo relied on centrist and center-left constituencies' frustration with corruption and demands for social and political transformation. These governments appointed well-known human rights advocates and academics for ministerial posts, and, as I discuss in Chapter 5, the truth commission was composed of this class of intellectuals. Its enemies, therefore, attacked the truth commission as the mouthpiece of the cultural elite that was ignorant of the Peruvian reality at best and in close collaboration with terrorism at worst. The Fujimoristas' constant invocation of the word "caviar"[33] to describe the commissioners was an attempt to persuade the public of the insurmountable cultural gap separating the commissioners from the ordinary people and to take the issues of human rights and social justice off the national agenda through antileftist and anti-intellectual rhetoric.

The Chilean truth commission presents the Pinochet dictatorship (quite problematically, as I discuss above) as a rupture in the nation's democratic and civic traditions to argue that the transition's challenge is to recover these traditions. The Peruvian truth commission, by contrast, claims to advocate an unprecedented political and sociocultural project: to overcome the centuries-long legacy of racism, inequality, and discrimination. Ironically, the democratic transition (2000–2001), as well as the truth commission that grew out of it, is one among many projects that claim to represent a new beginning in the modern history of Peru. The creation of participatory democracy from the ashes of the Aristocratic Republic (1895–1919), the mobilization unleashed by the leftist-populist APRA in the 1920s and 1930s, the first election of Fernando Belaúnde in 1963, his overthrow by a reformist military regime in 1968, the return to democracy in 1980, the first APRA electoral victory in 1985, and Fujimori's 1990 election campaign to save Peru from political and economic collapse: every single one of these political projects promised rupture with the past, was greeted with national euphoria, and ended in deep disappointment. In a way, the CVR rewrites an old trope—revolutionary new beginning against the backdrop of crisis, corruption, and collapse—with a new vocabulary. The "new social contract" advocated by the CVR requires the acknowledgment of serious human rights violations as the consequence of a long history of colonial and postcolonial exclusion, racial discrimination, and social inequality. Thus, the commission reconfigures the link between the past and the present in the interstices of immanence (i.e., the social embeddedness of the narrative trope of "new beginning") and transcendence (i.e., redefining the "new beginning" with the language of human rights and social justice).

The CVR has produced one of the most comprehensive social histories of Peru. The attentiveness to long-term sociocultural and political developments, the thorough analysis of all relevant individual and institutional actors, the incorporation of a host of factors (such as ethnic identity, gender, educational resources, and geographic variation), and the breadth of methodological approaches to explore these factors combine to make the CVR unmatched among truth commissions. Are there exclusions and silences even in such an inclusionary historiographical project?

Development analyst Javier Torres argues that the major source of bias in the truth commission's narrative was the insistence that the civilians were victims caught up between state repression and the Shining Path violence.[34] The "between two fires" (*entre dos fuegos*) discourse, characterizing the human rights movement's approach to victimhood, takes away the political agency of the peasantry for the sake of protecting them. Torres states that the "rural reality is more complex" than what the CVR's final report portrays. In fact, there was a history of microconflicts in many localities before the insurgency, and the new set of actors, such as the Shining Path, the security forces, and the self-defense patrols, interacted with the local conflicts in complex ways.[35] The already existing cleavages were redefined in the context of the new conflict.[36] Furthermore, Torres warns against the tendency to see the

Shining Path as an exogenous factor in the history of local and regional politics: "The Shining Path was not an occupation army." He reaches the conclusion that a disciplinary shift is necessary to comprehend the full picture: "anthropology helps to understand the Peruvian conflict better than sociology."

This book cannot adjudicate the debate on how much choice and agency the Peruvian peasantry exercised during the internal conflict, as such judgment would require numerous ethnographies of peasant communities. It would be unfair to say that the commission did not pay attention to microhistories, as there were numerous researchers who perhaps produced the most complete account to date of violence in the rural highlands. The criticism, to be more precise, is that the commission's broad message, embodied in the conclusions and recommendations, prioritizes broad social history (what Torres refers to as "sociology" in the interview) and adopts a "protectionist, almost paternalist" stance toward the Andean peasantry. The emphasis on vulnerability and exclusion as the cause *and* consequence of violence guides the conclusion that national reconstruction requires a new social contract based on equality, mutual respect, and social justice. The chief mechanism to achieve reconstruction is considered to be the promotion of an enlightened approach to nationhood, which will ideally transform the values and worldviews of top decision makers, as well as the urban middle classes.

Although the commission did not have indigenous members, "the sensitivity expressed by the white intellectual elite leading the transition and shaped by international indigenist sensitivities seemed at least partly to make up for the weaker role of indigenous groups."[37] The sociological imagination of the truth commission is captured in its visual representations. The abbreviated version of the final report, called *Hatun Willakuy* (which means "great story" in Quechua, although the volume was published in Spanish only),[38] has on the front cover the photo of an indigenous person, distinguishable by his dark skin color and the traditional hat, grieving over a coffin. Grabbing him by the wrist is a hand of lighter color, adorned with a shiny watch. The allegory is unmistakable: the fair-colored, urban, and educated Peruvian finally overcomes the "emotional distance"[39] imposed by centuries of racism and exclusion, offering her helping hand to the victimized indigenous man. Arguably, the helping hand represents the human rights movement and the truth commission that came out of it, or perhaps it is this movement's projection of how the urban middle classes should assume their civic obligations.

Likewise, the movie *State of Fear: The Truth About Terrorism* narrates the period of political violence and the truth commission experience in a way that stresses the urban Limeños' cathartic acknowledgment of the Peruvian reality. Although the movie is not a truth commission production, it captures the commission's spirit of benign paternalism. It singles out Beatriz Alva, the young, blonde member of the truth commission who had once served as a minister under the Fujimori regime, as a role model. The movie portrays her privileged, carefree life in sharp contrast to the process of internal conflict. As her shock at the gruesome details of violations against the mostly Quechua-speaking victims transforms her consciousness, she expresses resolve to change the conditions of life in her country and joins the truth commission: "I definitely can't be the same Beatriz anymore. I can't continue my life as it was, just thinking about business and legal matters. I have responsibilities now. I've seen a reality that I can't ignore. And if I can't do something about that reality, I'll never be happy."[40]

Conclusion

The city of Santiago woke up to a special occasion on September 4, 1990. Former president Salvador Allende was accorded a proper burial at the General Cemetery, where a number of Chilean dignitaries and public figures found eternal rest. It was a government initiative, which brought together Christian Democrats, their Socialist allies in government, and also the opposition Left (the Communist Party in particular). Allende's reburial was the first of several such commemorative activities to restore the dignity of the high-profile victims of the dictatorship, followed more than a decade later by the reburial of Pablo Neruda (2004)[41] and Victor Jara (2009).

As the official procession was under way, a choir of women outside the official protocol began to recite a Pablo Neruda poem dedicated to the victims of the 1946 massacre against communists at Plaza Bulnes. Some participants joined the recitation. This anecdote, narrated in Sola Sierra's biography, is perhaps the best metaphoric description of the way the victims' organizations and the extra-parliamentary Left participated in Chile's struggle for truth and memory: they were always the choir that was not included in the program. They were there to commemorate, but their voice came from outside the stage. Quite unlike the Greek *khoros*, they did not summarize the general plot; rather, their role was to remind the principal actors of what they might be forgetting, of the exclusions of the general plot that hegemonized the shared collective memory. And among those who occupied the center of the stage, "some participants joined the recitation" some of the time, as they were reminded and inspired. Those participants knew what memories they shared with the choir, but also they knew that they could only recite insofar as the deviation did not ruin the general plot, which was the transitional justice discourse of the new government.

The choir at the Allende reburial reminded the principal actors of a discomforting exclusion of the democratic transition discourse. Allende's death on September 11, 1973, and the subsequent human rights violations cannot be conceptualized entirely outside of the history of socioeconomic inequality and class repression in Chile. While the democratic transition wanted to exorcise violence through its unifying message "never again!" and its attentiveness to the victims of death and disappearance, forgetfulness of the underlying causes of violence became the foundational symbolic violence upon which the Chilean democracy was built. If the ones who fell at Plaza Bulnes in 1946 did not set an example to stop others from falling at La Moneda twenty-seven years later, what redemptive power do such contemporary truth and memory practices as the Allende reburial and the Rettig Commission have over the future generations? Advocates of social justice kept bringing up this question in a variety of ways throughout the democratic transition as outsiders to the political mainstream.

This chapter demonstrates that the commission creation process has implications for cross-national variation in how truth commissions reconstruct the past. The inclusions and exclusions of a truth commission narrative are best understood in terms of how the mandate and composition shape the commission's agency. Chile's Rettig Commission, established under a high degree of government control in the interest of reconciliation between rival political positions, produced a limited account of the underlying causes of political violence and violations, blaming the national tragedy on the political radicalization and polarization of the 1960s and early 1970s. It avoided taking a stance on the legitimacy of the 1973 coup. The stress on political and institutional failure informed the recommendations as well. Ultimately, the Rettig Commission's strength lies in its impeccable documentation of facts, but its narrative exclusions, reflecting the priorities and expectations of the transitional elite, have limited its capacity to take part in public debates over the meaning of the past.

By contrast, the participatory commission creation process in Peru allowed the commissioners to exercise agency in the area of historical explanation. Although the CVR's final report is not free from exclusions, it contains one of the most comprehensive truth commission narratives. It broadens the scope of historical investigation to the patterns of social exclusion and marginalization permeating the long trajectory of nation building. The final report not only emphasizes political-institutional reform but also draws attention to the need to overcome the historical legacy of poverty and racial exclusion in order to prevent the recurrence of violence and violations. In the end, the CVR aimed for greater social impact, but politically it proved more difficult to integrate into policy than its Chilean counterpart—in line with the arguments presented in Chapter 5 and 6.

The Chilean commission's narrative strategy reflects a deeper concern with how truth commissions make sense of history. Reducing historical explanation to the proximal causes of violence may be considered a clever avoidance strategy, but even the least comprehensive commission narratives receive criticism for politicizing history from hostile audiences as well as sympathetic ones. The Chilean commission's preference for avoiding divisive issues did not overcome the Pinochetistas' perception of the commission as part of a campaign to discredit the military. Comprehensive narratives face similar charges, but at least they leave behind a document that can be discussed, defended, attacked, or improved—an intervention into collective memory, to be precise.

The exclusions of truth commission narratives bring into question the construction of victimhood in transitional justice discourse. Even the most comprehensive accounts, such as the one produced by the Peruvian CVR, tend to prioritize innocent victimhood[42] at the expense of acknowledging the ideas, goals, interests, and actions of those affected by violations. Commissioners do not want to appear to be endorsing particular political ideologies and projects and realize that the public is more likely to condemn abuses if they downplay those aspects of the victims' lives that might reignite the divisions over memory. Keeping in mind the politically motivated attacks truth commissions face, this approach is perhaps prudent, but ultimately it relies on a moralization of the human rights norm, which otherwise identifies a violation regardless of the prior political and moral acts of the affected. In terms of historiography, it amounts to the silencing of experiences that would have provided key insights into national tragedy and, in many cases, reducing the complexity of political conflict and violence into artificially neat categories of victim, perpetrator, bystander, and collaborator, where they "overlap and apply to the same people or social groups."[43] Instead, "acknowledging shades of gray, not only in various forms of complicity, but also in acts of protest, resistance, and refusal"[44] would greatly strengthen truth commissions' claim to provide an evenhanded and comprehensive account of the past in light of human rights awareness.

Related to the portrayal of victimhood is the issue of scope. Commissions face the task of connecting individual suffering to national tragedy. In their attempt to discover the underlying causes of macro-level tragedy, they often fail to pay due attention to the micro-level, that is, local conflicts that have their own causes and dynamics, even if they interact with events at the national level. The vast literature on civil wars highlights the pitfalls of ignoring the local sources of violent conflict.[45] Taking these local dynamics into account requires conducting ethnographic studies of conflict and, equally important, reconsidering the trope of innocent victims getting caught between two fires. Such reconsideration may be politically and morally troubling, especially because it is feared that severing the link between victimhood and innocence would play into the hands of the authors of mass atrocities who want to obscure their moral and criminal responsibility. Yet, the benefits of exploring the local dynamics of conflict, in addition to its greater truthfulness and accuracy, cannot be missed. First, innocence is not, and should not be, the criterion of entitlement to fundamental human rights—as discussed in the paragraph above. Second, people are not merely objects of history but also its subjects; therefore, the interests, values, and ideas that play into processes of political confrontation and violence should be recovered fully. And finally, the theory and practice of peace building shows that understanding the local dynamics of conflict is necessary for the prevention of future violence—one of the core goals of transitional justice.

In conclusion, truth commissions should be willing to examine the past from various angles, in a comprehensive manner, and without fearing political implications.

PART III

Zooming Out: Coming to
Terms with the Past Through
Truth Commissions

PART I offered a broad outline of what truth commissions are, how they work, and where they are located in the political landscape of the societies in which they were born. Part II explained how specific commissions managed or failed to build lasting alliances with state and civil society actors, generate impact, and intervene into debates on social memory. Part III zooms out further to situate truth commissions in the worldwide efforts to reckon with past wrongs. Why did the *truth* about human rights violations and their underlying causes become such a salient political topic in contemporary societies? Do truth commissions challenge or undermine nationalism and nationalist historiography? Is it possible that coming to terms with the past through truth commissions and other institutional mechanisms will shape how we imagine the future of our societies? What are the overall achievements of truth commission experiences? What are their limitations? What, if anything, can be done to construct more just, inclusive, and effective truth commissions in the future?

Part III is a *critical* endeavor in the original Kantian sense of the word: it explores truth commissions' conditions of possibility, limitations, and promises. The interest in factual truth and the problematization of nationalist historiography are placed in historical context, with the aim of understanding the limits of coming to terms with the past through truth commissions (Chapter 8). Finally, the lessons drawn from more than thirty years of truth commission experiences guide the normative and practical recommendations that conclude this book.

CHAPTER 8

Nation and (Its New) Narration: A Critical Reading of Truth Commissions

> Justice seeks the truth, we might say, although concealed
> beneath that commonplace is the deeper observation
> that justice wants truth the way memory desires
> phenomena to remain (or become) unforgotten. It is the
> work of justice to bring the truth to light, to secure the
> deeds, victims, and perpetrators in alētheia, in the realm
> of memory, of the unforgotten. To forget is to live at
> once in untruth and injustice, which explains the often
> (but not exclusively) negative valuation attached to
> forgetting in the classical literature. Forgetting is
> opposed to both memory and justice. . . . In our time,
> this memory-truth-justice connection has become, if
> anything, even more compelling.
> —W. James Booth, "The Unforgotten"

In what ways do truth commissions transform the ways in which citizens of contemporary societies think and speak about historical truth, justice, reconciliation, and official historiography? Transitional justice measures, and truth commissions in particular, try to raise awareness around histories of violence and violations in the context of rebuilding state institutions and national identity.[1] Most truth commissions combine meticulous human rights investigation with a critique of the national past in order to rebuild the nation.[2] Aside from pursuing such goals as delivering a measure of justice and reconciliation, avoiding future violence, strengthening democratic institutions, and enhancing peace and stability, they also problematize the relationship

between official historiography and political legitimacy: "With the increasing investment in truth commissions, and with a worldwide celebration
of historical truth, history has moved to centre stage in the ethico-political
management of the collective past."[3]

This chapter situates truth commissions in the history of the changing
relationship between truth, memory, and politics in modern societies. Truth
commissions have opened a critical space to rethink the complex relations
between history and memory, the past and the present, and ethics and politics. Most commissions produce critical, fact-based, and national (not
nationalist) histories to restore the status of factuality in politics and reconstruct the nation and the nation-state on the basis of human rights norms.[4]
By doing so, they question many of the presumptions about the relationship
between politics and historiography. In particular they problematize historical narratives that glorify nationalism and the nation-state in an uncritical light, interpret history from the victors' perspective, and grant the state
an uncontested role in producing and disseminating official historiography.
They encourage citizens'—and especially victims'—memories of pain and
suffering to unsettle the state's claim to absolute sovereignty over official
historiography.[5] Their quest for a fact-based and self-critical national imagination often results in novel significations, such as reconciliation-*through*-
truth, memory-*as*-truth, truth-*for*-justice, and so on.[6] Nevertheless, it should
also be noted that the bold attempt to articulate a novel ethical and political
vision out of history is prone to the weaknesses and ambiguities built into
the design of truth commissions.

This chapter departs from the rest of the book, especially Part II, in that it
does not offer a close-up examination of specific truth commissions' historical narratives or policy recommendations. Instead, it is an invitation to rethink the political space truth commissions have opened *in general*. I turn to
thinkers who have explored the political implications of the modern historical
consciousness in the twentieth century, most notably Hannah Arendt, Pierre
Nora, and Jürgen Habermas. Drawing on their insights into the public use of
history, the ethics of national reconstruction, the role of memory in history,
and the place of factuality in modern politics, I present a critical perspective
on the conditions of possibility, promises, and limitations of coming to terms
with the past through truth commissions.[7]

The chapter is organized around three interrelated themes: the increasing politicization of factual truth in modernity; the problematization of nationalism and the nation-state as the organizing framework of social memory

and historiography; and the implications of the contemporary interest in factual and historical truth for political institutions and collective identity. Hannah Arendt's views on truth, lying, and modern politics elucidate the increasing moral and political salience of factual truth in contemporary societies, as evidenced in the emergence and popularity of truth commissions. Then I discuss the relation of history and memory to politics in the context of nationalism and the nation-state, since truth commissions claim to address national histories of violence and violations. Pierre Nora's reflections capture the mutual implication of nation and history that is threatened by the unsettling forces of alternative historiographies in late modernity. It is precisely the shortcoming of nationalist historiography that motivates Habermas's intervention into the Historians' Debate in the late 1980s. His writings guide the search for morality in historiography in the context of what he calls the "post-national constellation." Rereading Nora and Habermas in light of truth commission experiences, I argue that contemporary societies have been developing a new, yet ambiguous, consciousness around the role of shared historical memories in guiding political normativity. The defining feature of this consciousness, captured in truth commissions' claim on factual truth and an ethics of national reconstruction, is the presence of unresolved tensions between morality and legal norms, between broad societal participation in official historiography and state control, and between methodological nationalism and post-national value orientations.

The Politicization of Factual Truth: Arendtian Insights

Factual truth, one of the most important preoccupations of today's transitional justice discourse, has achieved this elevated political status in a particular historical context. Truth commissions have emerged against a historical backdrop that necessitated and provided the conditions of the reconstruction of political democracy on the basis of truthful and accurate knowledge of past violence and violations: "truth commissions undertake their task in a context in which the value of truth-telling has been fundamentally denied. . . . Therefore, truth commissions are valuable not only because of any truths that they bring to light, but because they represent *publicly the value of truth*."[8]

The nineteenth-century philosophy of history tradition tended to associate *truth* with the foundational Idea, the overarching pattern, or a framework within which to make sense of the contingencies and seeming discontinuities of history, rather than with the seemingly less controversial notion of facts. It was the alarming extent of misinformation and deception under the fascist and Stalinist regimes of the twentieth century that provided the historical setting for the renewed interest in simple factuality, which can be witnessed in great works like Hannah Arendt's *Origins of Totalitarianism* (1951), as well as George Orwell's *Nineteen Eighty-Four* (1949).

Arendt considers the problematic of truth and politics central to twentieth-century politics.[9] She states that the politically most relevant truths are factual and, consequently, "the chances of factual truth surviving the onslaught of power are very slim indeed."[10] What is the relation of factuality to politics? Facts set an external limit on political action, thus fulfilling a constraining and enabling function simultaneously.[11] Neither persuasion, that quintessentially political product of human intersubjectivity, nor violence can alter the factual fabric: "Facts inform opinions, and opinions, inspired by different interests and passions, can differ widely and still be legitimate as long as they respect factual truth. Freedom of opinion is a farce unless factual information is guaranteed and the facts themselves are not in dispute."[12] This constraining nature of factual truth reveals at the same time an enabling character: facts provide an element of stability in the highly unstable political realm. In a way, facts are constitutive of the *world* that Arendt sees as the condition of existence of all human activity, including political action.[13]

It appears from these reflections that Arendt considers factual truth to be essentially nonpolitical (or pre-political). In fact, in one passage Arendt banishes truth telling from the realm of politics: "the mere telling of facts leads to no action whatever."[14] Yet she complements this phenomenological account by historicizing the stature of factual truth in the course of modern political developments. Even though the untruthful conduct of politics (secrecy and deception) dates back to the beginning of recorded history, "the mass manipulation of fact and opinion" is a relatively recent phenomenon.[15] "Modern political lies" consist not so much in keeping secrets as denying publicly known facts. Denial, which Arendt construes as an effort to destroy (rather than hide) facts, gives the modern lie its intrinsically violent quality. Hiding facts is an act of deception that concerns particular information made unavailable to specific people (typically political rivals and enemies at war).[16] The destruction of the historical record, on the other hand, means that the "whole factual texture"[17] needs to be rearranged. Therefore, lying in politics has acquired a world-destructive character only in modern societies. The limited untruthfulness characterizing earlier epochs was an affront to some facts some of the time, but the modern lie aims at the notion of factuality *as such*; therefore, it threatens to destroy the foundations of political action. Furthermore, lying is no longer a matter of diplomatic or military strategy, but is at the heart of social organization. The modern lie involves the systematic creation of an alternative reality,[18] and it should deceive everyone in order to achieve its goal.

Consequently truth telling, normally considered a nonpolitical activity, takes on a radically different character when mendacity threatens the possibility of political action: "only where a community has embarked upon organized lying on principle, and not only with respect to particulars, can truthfulness as such, unsupported by the distorting forces of power and interest, become a political factor of the first order."[19] In other words, it is precisely the destructive nature and societal reach of the modern lie that explains the valorization of factual truth in a political sense.

Can factuality be restored in the age of organized lying? Arendt holds that organized and systematic mendacity cannot achieve its stated end, namely the creation of an alternative reality capable of persuading everyone. Long-term brainwashing results not in the substitution of lies for facts, but in cynicism, which is the loss of belief in truth altogether. She notes that the power of persuasion, as well as of violence, can be employed to manipulate facts, but neither can offer a substitute for the stabilizing force of factuality.[20] In this way she sets herself apart from the dystopian thinking of George Orwell, whose observations on the Spanish Civil War and the Stalinist propaganda machine leads him to arrive at the troubling conclusion that mass deception is capable of creating a relatively stable substitute for factuality.[21]

Arendt places her trust in autonomous institutions whose chief task is to ascertain factual truth. Commenting on the release of the Pentagon Papers, she states that the judiciary and the university are two such institutions, and the press fulfills this function insofar as journalists act with courage and honesty. While the political manipulation of judicial and educational institutions is quite likely, this is not a reason to dismiss them altogether. Impartiality and integrity are the essential qualities these institutions need to possess in order to uncover politically inconvenient facts.[22]

Arendt's reflections provide illuminating insights into the centrality of factual truth in contemporary societies reckoning with a violent and divisive past. She rightly suggests that historical truth has acquired political importance as a result of the massive manipulation that characterized twentieth-century politics in many parts of the world. This Arendtian insight illuminates the role of truth commissions in contemporary societies: they articulate a vision in which the investigation, recognition, and diffusion of facts about human rights violations are expected to reconstruct and legitimate politics itself in the wake of mass deception. Truth commissions, none of which Arendt lived to see and write about, are established on the premise that a morally defensible and politically stable polity can be constructed only on the basis of undisputed facts.[23] Accordingly, facts ground politics, and as such, the procedures that disclose these facts should enjoy a pre-political, and perhaps supra-political, status. The preservation of factuality is embedded in autonomous institutions that derive their legitimacy from an attitude of detachment in the face of political pressures and temptations.

Arendt's insights are less illuminating, however, in explaining the social dynamics of organized lying and truth telling. Truth commissions have been established precisely when Arendt's belief in the essential stability and ultimate recoverability of factual truth did not hold. Her claim that the outcome of organized lying is cynicism cannot explain the dynamics of polarized societies in which cynical liars succeed in cultivating deep convictions in their compatriots. Histories of class, ethnic, religious, and racial conflict across the globe suggest that significant portions of the population have been persuaded in untruthful versions of past events in the context of violent conflict, and, what is more, these versions have reinforced the sense of political belonging, common identity, and collective purpose. In a way, lying in politics has produced a dynamic that not even Arendt's alarmed premonitions could foresee: untruthfulness has not only become an instrument of systematic manipulation to be used against the citizenry at the hands of the political class, but it has permeated the social fabric, thereby forming and reinforcing collective identities. Recovering factuality in contemporary societies entails discovering facts and publicly acknowledging them in the face of denial or neglect. Therefore, the recuperation of factual truth requires not only the affirmation of *that which happened* against corrupt and mendacious politicians, but also the unpersuading of fellow citizens, the *unmaking* of the alternative reality that had constituted their worldliness for a long time. Consequently, the institutional form in which factual truth can reemerge has to take into account not only the juridical and political implications of mendacity but its sociological effects as well. That is why truth commissions, in their quest to recuperate factuality in politics, allow for a high degree of societal penetration into the writing of officially sanctioned historiography.

Arendt's trust in the judiciary, the independent press, and the university system as autonomous institutions of truth seems to reflect the American experience in the wake of the traumatic military involvement in Vietnam.[24] In most other countries, however, and especially in places where democratic protections had been suspended or destroyed, supposedly autonomous institutions have themselves become parties to violent conflicts, often producing and reproducing the same lies that they are supposed to expose. Courts have condoned and abetted serious human rights violations. Sometimes entire media groups and university departments have thrown their lot with the construction of an untruthful reality. Courageous and honest intellectuals, academics, and journalists have suffered assassinations, threats, purges, censorship, and the opprobrium of colleagues when they defended factual truth. Thus, when democracy was restored in many countries, the individual and organizational actors in defense of factual truth could not work within the existing system of institutions. The failure of conventional truth-finding institutions, such as the judiciary, the university, and the media, explains the emergence of truth commissions as a novel institutional response to the legacy of political violence.

History, Memory, and the Nation: Pierre Nora's *Mémoire-Nation* and Habermas's Intervention in the Historians' Debate

Nationalism has arguably been the most influential ideology in modern times, drawing liberal, fascist, communist, colonial, and postcolonial ideologies and political projects into its orbit. Its appeal owes in great part to the articulation of present and future political struggles in terms of the imagined, even invented, history of a collective—the nation.[25] The connection between politics, organized around the nation-state in the modern international system, and nationalist historiography has been a key feature of modernity, but this connection is increasingly challenged. The violations and injustices unleashed in the name of the nation throughout the twentieth century have led a number of professional historians, intellectuals, and concerned citizens to adopt a critical attitude toward the violent and exclusionary implications of nationalism in many parts of the world. The emergence of truth commissions should be examined in light of this historical trajectory.

Pierre Nora's writings on social memory give an account of how nation-alism and the nation-state provide an ethical and political framework to reconstruct the past. He situates the relationship between memory, history, and politics in the context of modern political developments and highlights the nation-state's capacity to organize these three domains in a mutually supportive fashion. For Nora, memory refers to the unproblematic, taken-for-granted continuity of the past in the present, as it ensures unmediated access to lived experience. History, on the other hand, signifies the "recon-struction, always problematic and incomplete, of what is no longer."[26] The attitude of self-distancing from the past promotes analysis and critique. Memory, even when nourished by multiple experiences, remains particular to individuals, social groups, or nations, whereas history makes a claim to "universal authority."[27]

Nora's definitions seem to suggest the a priori opposition of memory to history, for example, when he writes "history divests the lived past of its le-gitimacy."[28] Yet, he historicizes the relationship between collective memory and history to assert that a symbiotic relationship, even if not complete iden-tification, has linked memory to history in traditional societies, as well as modern nation-states. In fact it is the recent rupture that stands out as unpre-cedented: "The uprooting of memory, its eradication by the conquering force of history, has had the effect of a revelation, as if an ancient bond of identity had been broken, calling into question something once taken for granted: the close fit between history and memory."[29]

The nation and the nation-state deserve special attention in Nora's frame-work because "the memory-nation was . . . the last incarnation of memory-history."[30] Within the framework of the nation-state, critical history served to establish, enhance, and fortify the continuity of the past in the present, rather than rupture it. "Although [history] was intended to be 'critical,' it was in fact only a deepening of that tradition. Its ultimate goal was identification through filiation. It was in this sense that history and memory were identi-cal: history was verified memory."[31] If memory upheld tradition, history sought to deepen the tradition by holding memory accountable to critical analysis. The memory-nation (*mémoire-nation*) was thus a history-nation.[32] In turn, the nation and the nation-state provided memory with the point of orientation that preserved the transcendent reference of memory to people's lives.

The recent decline of the nation-state as the political framework organiz-ing collective temporality means that the harmony achieved by national consciousness has been replaced by the cacophony of "patrimonial" memories that retreat to singular pasts. Identity politics burst open the common national identity, as each singularity began to promote its brand of a "heritage culture" with its particular memory. A historical model, centered on what Paul Ricoeur calls the "celebrations devoted to the impersonal sovereignty of the nation-state,"[33] was displaced by a commemorative model that prioritizes local, particular, fragmented memories. The contemporary discourse on memory relies on fragments of "defunct traditions" that obliterate the healthy, organic relationship in which the past and the present intermingle in what Nora calls the social environments of memory (*milieux de mémoire*). Instead, memories are particularized as commemorative sites (*lieux de mémoire*) that displace the temporal continuity of memory by spatializing the past.[34] Thus, the emerging memorial consciousness replaces solidarity with singularized identities as the organizing principle of the past-present relation.[35] On the historiographical plane, the reduction of memory to commemoration means that memory is allowed to enter the historical operation only as an object of study, but never on its own terms. This transformation takes its toll on history as well: the demise of the history-memory-nation nexus means that history has lost its privileged role in *making* the polity. The *mémoire-nation* has been replaced by the memorial-nation.

Nora's brilliance lies in identifying two distinctive and potentially conflicting modes of engagement with the past, namely, memory and history, which depend on political imagination to develop a harmonious relationship. It was the political framework of the nation-state that, tempered with the potential for disenchantment that comes with historical critique, saw to it that the shared memories of the nation and professional historiography mutually reinforced each other and embedded the spatial representations of memory in temporal continuity. While most commentators take note of Nora's emphasis on commemorative sites, rituals, and practices as representations of memory, little attention has been paid to Nora's valorization of the political as the organizing framework of the past-present relation. In Nora's idealization, the nation and the nation-state overcame the antinomy of memorial past (assumed to be in continuous harmony with the present) and historical past (whose construction requires the assertion of critical distance in the present). This political articulation mustered institutions (of the nation-state), an ideology (nationalism), and a particular mode of historical consciousness (the history-memory-nation nexus) to bestow order and stability upon society's representation of its past. The hollowing out of this reference to the nation necessarily brought the end of the historical consciousness that had crystallized in the *mémoire-nation*. The centrifugal forces of identity politics and the emergence of a novel historical consciousness unsettled the memory-history-nation matrix irreversibly, much to Nora's dismay.

The brilliant exposition of the relationship between history, memory, and politics falls victim to Nora's own privileging of the nation-state as the last successful model to organize the past. He fails to take into account the internal contradictions of the nation-state model and the consequent moral and political catastrophes that undermined the supposed happy unity of collective memory and historical criticism. The construction of social solidarity through nationhood has generated a highly contradictory and unstable unity at best and, as numerous episodes of nation building and nation keeping suggest, almost always relied on violent practices of exclusion.[36] Beneath the presumed unity of the nation, the social cleavages that have played out in the course of modernity left entire social sectors excluded, marginalized, pauperized, and vulnerable to violent repression, even extermination. A glance at histories of nationalism around the world reveals countless episodes of massacre, genocide, terror, international war, material deprivation, discrimination, political exclusion, and social stigmatization directed at groups organized along class, political, ethnic, linguistic, racial, and gender lines. The internal tensions of the nation-state project, unraveling in such a violent historical dialectic, left no hope for a shared national memory transcending particular experiences and meaning frameworks precisely because historical truth shattered illusions of nourishing an unselfconscious, naturalized memory of the national past.[37] Historians who occupy themselves with the incorporation of bittersweet memories into national identity formation cannot claim to forge the happy unity of past and present, space and time, memory and history, the citizen and the nation, in the face of historical facts.

Furthermore, Nora is too quick to dismiss the potential for a healthy relationship between history and politics in the wake of nationalism. In the context of France, he pinpoints the origins of the breakup of this relationship as the substitution of the "coupling of state and nation" for "the coupling of state and society."[38] It is true that the emergence of society as an essentially fragmented collective actor aspiring to forge a new commemorative consciousness would inevitably destroy the unity of the memory-nation and burst open social memory as a conflictual field. It is also true that the decoupling of state and nation would mean the end of an institutional and ideological framework capable of making political sense of history and re-constructing a sense of collective memory and identity.

It is not right to argue, however, that the fragmentation of social mem-ory will necessarily terminate the quest for shared meanings, value orienta-tions, and political institutions to reconfigure the role of memory and history in post-national contexts. That the field of social memory was hopelessly frag-mented in the wake of the problematic histories of the nation-state does not mean that societies have given up on the project of reestablishing a healthy relationship with the past. The almost-global striving for truth and memory in the wake of violence and violations shows the force and determination of social actors in forging a common memory and even a common normative orientation informed by past wrongs. Post-nationalist meaning frameworks and memory tropes are unlikely to rise to the status of *the* national history since the utilization of a particular memory framework as part of a national reconstruction project meets resistance from countermemories that reject the imposed mnemonic homogenization. Nevertheless, the aspiration for shared meanings around the past is very much alive, and the institutional form of the truth commission is but the clearest expression of this orientation.

In short, late modern societies *do* try to forge social solidarity and com-mon identity in the wake of moral and political failures that put into ques-tion the idea of the nation as previously conceptualized. They resist the facile identification of historical truth with the official historiography of the nation-state and its organic historians, and instead experiment with the possibility of producing a shared historical truth out of diverse and divergent experi-ences and memories in order to reconstruct an ethical basis for living to-gether. Coming to terms with the past through truth commissions and other formal and informal mechanisms is a quest for forging a shared identity out of history. It may be less state-centric than nationalist historiography, but it is no less political.

Habermas's intervention in the Historians' Debate (*Historikerstreit*) re-flects the spirit of coming to terms with the national past in an increasingly post-national context.[39] The conservative reinterpretation of the Nazi past in the mid-1980s triggers his interest in what he calls the "public use of history."[40] As he analyzes those historians' attempt to reformulate national pride and a coherent national identity through revisionist historical accounts, Haber-mas judges that the Historians' Debate has a moral and political dimension that transcends intramural disagreements over historiography, engaging the public intellectual and the citizen as much as the professional historian: "It is not a question of Popper versus Adorno, not a question of scholarly theoretical debates or of value freedom—it is a question of the public use of history."[41] Beneath the rhetoric of scholarly disinterest, revisionist accounts of the Third Reich present a functionalism that seeks to "strengthen the forces of social integration" and "counteract suspected instabilities."[42] The call for a renewed German nationalism that would define itself with reference to the Western noncommunist alliance necessitates the appropriation of praiseworthy, heroic, and politically appealing aspects of national history, creating incentives to explain away the horrors of the Holocaust and World War II as a by-product of Bolshevik aggression and barbarism and as tragedies comparable to the suffering of Germans in the Eastern provinces.

Habermas notes that the conservative historians' strategy puts the past in the service of the nation-state and power politics. He calls this the "mandarin consciousness," the "guild" (of late nineteenth- and early twentieth-century historians), and the "veteran's perspective" in numerous essays. This conventional orientation to history privileges the nation as the primary and taken-for-granted form of collective belonging. Against this tendency, which had dominated German historiography for over a century, Habermas counterpoises the unsettling forces of universalist value orientations and plural readings of history that reveal the shortcomings of the nonreflective attitude toward the past.[43] These forces, which he treats as empirical observations and normative claims at the same time, hail the ascendance of a reflective historical consciousness that embraces the ambivalence of national traditions.[44] Like Nora, he acknowledges that "nationalism made the shared cultural heritage of language, literature and history congruent with the organizational form of the state."[45] While Nora laments the decline and dissolution of this project, Habermas sees a dialectical tension between "the universalist value orientations of democracy and the constitutional state on the one hand, and the particularism of a nation distinguishing itself from what is outside it on the other hand."[46]

Habermas formulates the dialectical unraveling of particularist value orientations in historiography as the gradual replacement of narratives that selectively convey stories of national glory and moral superiority by a critical orientation that holds every taken-for-granted reading to scholarly and public scrutiny. The uneasy tensions that play out within the discipline of history, evidenced in early modernity as the contradiction between the political complicity of the myth-producing (nationalist) historical scholarship and the demystification inherent in historical method, will be resolved in favor of critical history in late modernity, as the social integration processes of a complex society overwhelm conventional identity-formation projects. Insofar as the public use of history is concerned, Habermas points to the pluralization of historiographical approaches and critical methodologies and the increasing public scrutiny of historical works as processes heralding the emergence of a critical historical consciousness in contemporary Germany.

Habermas rules out any other possibility of confronting the German past than through relentless critique. "After Auschwitz our national self-consciousness can be derived only from the better traditions in our history, a history that is not unexamined but instead appropriated critically."[47] Again, Habermas seems to be making a statement of fact with normative weight—that critical history has been replacing uncritical, unreflective history. The context in which he delivers the essay, however, suggests that he is exercising advocacy for critical history precisely because its status is all too precarious. As a public intellectual he is aware that his immediate addressees are those scholars who refuse to accord the Holocaust a transformative significance and whose ideas resonate strongly with the German conservatives holding office in the second half of the 1980s.[48] The audience that stands in historical judgment is the greater public whose conditions of existence, shared values, and traditions cannot be severed unproblematically from the circumstances that made Auschwitz possible. And yet, the intellectual debate unfolds precisely as a means to persuade the public of the constitutive significance of Auschwitz.

Habermas's position in the Historians' Debate captures the essence of a predicament: a critical historical record needs to be defended before a larger public that may remain unconvinced about the problematic nature of its own constitutedness in that history. The hindsight of transitional justice experiences confirms what appears to be a fruitful tension in Habermas's thought. The past shapes the present, but refusal to acknowledge this fact has the power of making it irrelevant. Even though his texts predict certain defeat for "conventional" historiography in the face of facts and universalist value orientations, Habermas's performance as a worried public intellectual reveals that unreflective reconstructions of the past, far from being a historical anomaly, can in fact succeed in de-emphasizing the constitutive role of past experiences, even Auschwitz. The safeguard against uncritical history is not the supposedly irreversible progress of Enlightenment values, but rather the "public use of history" as an exercise in persuasion—contentious, precarious, and reversible.[49]

I believe that truth commissions have emerged partly as a response to this Habermasian problematic, namely, the need to confront the national past with a critical and reconstructive orientation when social opinion- and identity-formation processes do not guarantee the designation of this past as having constitutive importance. Indeed, the conditions under which the struggle for social memory takes place rule out the possibility of sharing Habermas's assertion that uncritical historiography can no longer satisfy the needs of a complex society. Truth commissions have not emerged because truthfulness and self-reflection remained as the only viable or reasonable political option in the wake of authoritarianism and human rights violations. To the contrary, their existence owes to the advocacy of those who resist the likely possibility of living in a society that denies and/or relativizes the most important moral catastrophe of its past in order to forge a renewed, and in many ways coerced, sense of social integration and collective identity.

Coming to Terms with the Past Through Truth Commissions: Truth, Institutions, and Identities

Discovering and publicizing facts about political violence and violations has become increasingly more relevant in the second part of the twentieth century. The motivation to establish truth commissions does not merely reflect the need to conduct more detailed research about incidents about which there is scant data and explanation. Rather, the primary impetus is to refute widely circulated narratives of denial. The valorization of factuality and the problematization of uncritical nationalism have been possible in late modernity thanks to the high degree of societal participation in collecting evidence of human rights violations and narrating the epoch of political violence through individual memories. The coexistence of social forces that seek recognition for past crimes and forces denying those crimes propels the institutionalization of historical memory in late modern societies. Genocide recognition laws in the presence of deniers, official apologies to reverse unapologetic historical discourses, and the small yet increasing number of human rights trials in the face of impunity and amnesty demonstrate this dynamic.

The unraveling of the nexus between modern political institutions, identity projects, and official historiography undergirds the historical dynamic in which truth commissions have come into existence. Societal mobilization in the name of recovering forensic truth and historical memory exposes the contradictions of silencing and ignoring formative experiences of suffering that constitute a nation's past in order to forge a hegemonic memory of the nation and the nation-state. Yet, truth commission experiences around the world reveal that struggles around truth and memory, far from hailing the victory of facts over lies and society-wide self-reflection over denial, are actually responses to the legal, economic, political, and cultural mechanisms that obscure a society's relationship to its past. The dialectic unraveling of modernity has opened up possibilities for reckoning with a violent and divisive past but has not made such reckoning easy, let alone inevitable.

What are the promises and limitations of coming to terms with the past through truth commissions? Have commissions built a new relationship between truth and politics? I believe that truth commissions around the world have fulfilled one of their key promises: recovering factual and historical truth in the face of organized mendacity. Commissions' attempt to uncover lies, dispel propaganda, and ultimately move the ground from under the deniers' feet has not ended discourses that deny, relativize, or rationalize past violations, but has led many citizens to question the plausibility and relevance of such discourses. Truth commissions deserve much credit if not only facts but factuality *as such* could be recuperated in the wake of mass atrocities and the accompanying official disinformation about the life and death of citizens. Thus, they have made a bold attempt to reconfigure the relationship between truth and politics.

In light of the empirical findings of this book, however, it is safe to argue that the *truth* of truth commissions has produced mixed results. Cross-national variation notwithstanding, truth commissions, at an arm's length from the state and dependent on domestic and international civil society alliances, produce modest impact precisely because the status of their truth is ambiguous. Political decision makers do not want to commit themselves fully to the inconvenient consequences of facts and alternative historical narratives. Even when decision makers acknowledge the ethical and political significance of commission findings and narratives, courts often refuse to use them as evidence on the grounds that commissions' data collection method does not conform to the evidentiary standards of conventional courtroom procedures.[50] Truth commissions sidestep conventional judicial and bureaucratic mechanisms of truth telling precisely because those mechanisms have consistently failed to document and take issue with past human rights violations. Furthermore, they enable a high degree of penetration of individual citizens and organized civil society actors into the production of official truth.

In turn, the truth of truth commissions is not granted the legal sanction that the "juridical form"[51] of truth, which has defined the relationship between truth and power in modern societies by tying truth-finding procedures to judicial institutions, enjoys. The desire for truth is not matched by the willingness to live with its consequences in contemporary societies.

Have truth commissions promoted new institutions and identities? Going back to Habermas, a strong argument in favor of reckoning with the past is that the public use of history influences how a polity understands itself.[52] Thus he projects the distinction between conventional and postconventional historical consciousness onto the ethical plane (what he repeatedly calls "value orientations" in these essays), and the terms of the debate are redefined in the opposition of nationalist particularism and post-national universalism.[53] The dispelling of nationalist myths goes hand in hand with the emergence of a postconventional orientation that asserts constitutional patriotism[54] as the primary collective identity: "This more sober political identity [i.e., constitutional patriotism] has detached itself from the background of a past centered on national history. The universalist content of a form of patriotism crystallized around the democratic constitutional state is no longer pledged to continuities filled with victories; this form of patriotism is incompatible with the secondary quasi-natural character of a consciousness that has no insight into the deep ambivalance [sic] of every tradition, into the concatenation of things for which amends cannot be made, into the barbaric dark side of all cultural achievements to the present day."[55]

Is coming to terms with the past necessary to transform collective value orientations? Can Germans develop a post-national consciousness without working through Auschwitz? Can any society adhere to democracy, constitutionalism, and universal human rights while ignoring the memories of their domestic "moral catastrophe"? Is it not possible to prevent the recurrence of violence and develop a civic identity through education, institution building, economic growth, and so on—in other words, through measures other than facing up to the past? The converse question is equally puzzling: are transformed collective identities a necessary consequence of coming to terms with the past? Can societies work through a violent and divisive past without questioning their present value orientations and political institutions?

For Habermas the public use of history and collective identity are mutually reinforcing, at least in the case of Germany: "Unfortunately, in the cultural nation of the Germans, a connection to universalist constitutional principles that was anchored in convictions could be formed only after—and through—Auschwitz."[56] The moral catastrophe of Auschwitz does not only connect the past to the present; it also serves as the moral yardstick against which to measure present identity projects: "In the identity-forming process of coming to terms with the complexity of history, the commemoration of Auschwitz performs a kind of monitoring function that demands that tradition be tested."[57]

Although Habermas addresses the German public specifically, the interconnectedness of historical consciousness and collective identity, permeating individual socialization processes as well as the structures of political decision making, calls upon each society to work through this complex interaction in imaginative ways.[58] Definitely the worldwide popularity of truth commissions, public apologies, human rights memorials, and similar memory practices shows that an increasing number of social and political actors consider coming to terms with the past to be a precondition of political and social change—keeping in mind, of course, that all these practices should be understood as efforts to persuade skeptical, hostile, and apathetic audiences.

It is less clear, however, that a self-critical and truthful attitude toward the national past leads to *new* value orientations and political institutions. Laws and policies enacted under conditions of political violence, including amnesty laws, may be legal but not legitimate. Thus, advocates of truth and justice, including members of a truth commission, invoke international human rights law, international humanitarian law, and cosmopolitan moral obligation toward fellow human beings to overcome the immanence of de facto legality to periods of past violence and violations.[59] However, even when truth projects like commissions adopt post-national legal and moral standards to transcend the nation-state's legal and moral vocabulary, this post-national orientation is used quite eclectically in order to *relegitimize* the nation and the nation-state.[60] Truth commissions take the nation as their object and addressee. It has not occurred to any commission to discard the nation (and the nation-state) as an outdated, inherently exclusionary and violent, and ultimately indefensible political construct whose presumed unity had been shattered by fratricidal violence. Commissions are expected to reconstruct the ethical and political component of what makes up a nation and reintegrate systematically excluded and victimized constituencies into the nation. Thus, truth commissions presuppose *and* performatively produce the nation.

Despite calls to establish a "global truth commission"[61] to address international or supranational issues, like the slave trade, all commissions to date have remained national in scope. The worldwide appeal of truth commissions is beyond doubt, but their findings and historical narratives have not led to the formation of a "cosmopolitan memory."[62] In fact, the supranational element has been by and large ignored in favor of national investigations, even when the nature of political repression and violations points to a high degree of cross-border coordination among perpetrators, such as in South America in the 1970s. Thus the scope reproduces the nation and the nationals as the moral and political agents of historical reflection. As a result, truth commissions have not promoted a new supranational political identity. Observers rightly state that the German apology for World War II and the Holocaust has facilitated the creation and deepening of the European Union (which, not surprisingly, was a source of inspiration for Habermas's ideal of constitutional patriotism), but public apology has not triggered supranationalism in other regions with truth-telling experiences, precisely because the goals and scope of these experiences were limited to the national level.

In conclusion, truth commissions' promises and limitations should be assessed within the framework of a novel, ambiguous, and somewhat timid effort to reconfigure the relationship between truth, political institutions, and identities in contemporary societies. Commissions find themselves policing the boundaries of past and present, ethics and politics, and deconstruction and reconstruction in politically contentious contexts. Their call for individual and social repair has produced modestly positive results, falling short of forging or legitimizing a new understanding of conducting politics or imagining identities, even though the discourse and practice of coming to terms with the past, of which truth commissions form a part, often prescribe such a transformative role. These limitations notwithstanding, truth commissions have changed the way contemporary societies understand themselves in one fundamental way: victims of past violence and injustice can no longer be excluded from official history and the national imagination unproblematically. Victims are not merely the collateral damage of history; they are its objects and subjects.

Conclusion

Facing up to the past is a dreadful experience for many of the individual, organizational, and institutional actors governing contemporary societies. Even when political decision makers entrust a body of independent-minded commissioners with the authority to make a judgment on the past, they fear the consequences of declaring the implications of such judgment binding on the political realm. Thus, truth commissions operate at an arm's length from the state and its institutions. They carry the promise of resignifying our notions of memory, history, factual truth, justice, recognition, and reconciliation. In the end, however, they enable modest transformations as a result of their built-in dependence, vulnerability, and legitimacy deficit before existing political institutions.

I speculate that part of the difficulty, going beyond the constraints of political transitions that explain truth commissions' existence, stems from their sheer novelty: truth commissions have emerged recently and in the context of an unprecedented wave of memory politics. Societies are yet to learn about, and innovate on, coming to terms with a violent and divisive past when nationalist narratives fail to provide answers. Truth commissions stand out as a brave attempt to recover factuality, narrate history in the light of testimonial memories, and construct a historically informed ethical vision, but they are quite modest, if not timid, in terms of designing politics out of history—not least because they are answerable to numerous potentially hostile audiences. They incorporate a constellation of subnational, national, international, and cosmopolitan norms and practices, yet they ultimately legitimize the nation and the nation-state as the object and audience of historical narrative and political normativity. Insofar as they are free from direct intervention by politicians and state bureaucracies, they strive to build a new political articulation that resignifies memory, historical truth, and political ethics. Yet, their dependence on political endorsement and support leaves them with little room for creating a novel space in the midst of existing political arrangements.

Conclusion

Thirty years ago nobody could have anticipated that a slightly modified inquiry commission, now called *truth commission*, would have become among the most widely used political-institutional mechanisms to come to terms with the legacies of violent and divisive periods. They have outlived the transitional justice paradigm, as consolidated democracies and nontransitioning regimes began to opt for truth commissions, too. Calls for subnational, national, and international truth commissions to investigate an ever-expanding list of past violations and injustices are found everywhere. In many countries, the supporters and opponents of a past truth commission still argue bitterly about its achievements and shortcomings years after the release of its final report.

By way of conclusion, I return to the question: what do truth commissions mean for contemporary societies? Truth commissions are not simply tools of incoming governments to be used against the ancien régime or some kind of distraction from criminal justice. Their achievements and shortcomings arise from a much more complex set of reasons. They open a contentious social space for reflection on the past. While some truth commissions may reflect the interests and expectations of influential political actors, others have delegitimized and surprised decision makers, including the politicians who established them. They defend their operational autonomy from political interests jealously almost everywhere, but their ability to influence politics and society depends on the endorsement and continued support of precisely those actors who may find their findings and recommendations inconvenient or, worse still, dangerous. Autonomy and dependence, efficacy and weakness, great expectations and modest achievements: contradiction is built into truth commissions as agents of change.

Naturally, this book on truth commission impact invites the question: what does a *successful* truth commission look like? Before making suggestions, I urge caution and modesty when thinking and writing about coming to terms with the past. Ultimately, all efforts to remedy past violations are inherently limited by the inability to recuperate irretrievable losses of life, human dignity, and social relations. An institutionalized truth-finding project cannot fully satisfy a mother who wants her son back alive, and it cannot make political dreams that were once "realistic utopias" come true. Coming to terms with the past is not a success story, but rather a solemn working and reworking of an irretrievably lost past. In Adorno's brilliant formulation, it is a constant working through (*Aufarbeitung*) rather than mastering over (*Bewältigung*).[1]

In addition, truth commissions' success cannot be assessed in isolation from the multiple interests and values that create, maintain, and validate them. For some, truth telling carries the hope for redemption, a present moment in which the irretrievably lost past moments and along with them past dreams, struggles, and beloved ones are fully recovered. Even if redemption is not of this world, truth, justice, and recognition are concrete goals worth pursuing for those who survived life-shattering experiences. Shared experiences of victimhood unite people, but the potential for disagreement over priorities, goals, and strategies cannot be ignored.

For the perpetrators and beneficiaries of past violence, a truth project is an unwelcome disruption of the orderly present. Remembering is a moral and legal inconvenience unless there are strict limits to what can be remembered, how, and with what consequences. The repentant wrongdoer whose guilty conscience breaks through the wall of denial is a much sought-after yet rarely found agent of memory. There are also those who have experienced power and powerlessness at the extremes: the presence of victim-perpetrators unsettles simplistic moral formulas in the wake of mass suffering.

And then there are countless others, political leaders and regular citizens, judges and journalists, young military officers and high-school teachers, TV viewers and newspaper readers, and people taking any other configuration of social roles imaginable. Those are the ones who hear the calls for justice and amnesty, memory and amnesia, human rights awareness and blissful ignorance, from afar. They are called the bystanders, onlookers, the unaffiliated, the audience, although it is often their voice or silence that shapes the dynamics of violent conflict, and postconflict peace and justice.

In other words, truth commissions (and transitional justice in general) are deeply *political*. Although many politicians and human rights advocates associate them with consensus, reconciliation, and nation building, truth commissions do not embody some kind of supra-political "common good" that benefits all citizens. Some individual and institutional actors, in particular the perpetrators and their allies, see their interests undermined. Many others, especially victims excluded from the commission process, feel that the commission could have done more for them. Some civil society groups espouse a commission as their own, whereas others see in the same commission a failure to incorporate diverse voices and viewpoints. In other words, a truth commission, like any other political action, produces winners and losers, which cuts across the simplistic victim-perpetrator divide. Evaluating success and failure depends critically on a truth commission's goals, the decision-making processes and power dynamics that set those goals, and the extent to which a truth commission not only satisfies the given set of goals but also triggers social struggles that challenge the constraints imposed by the politics of truth commissions.

In light of these reservations, it is clear that truth commissions should not be evaluated solely on the basis of political outcomes (which tend to be positive, albeit modest, for victims and those concerned with human rights and the rule of law). The promotion of a pluralistic and participatory space for reckoning with past wrongs should be a guiding principle as well. Given that an enormous variety of social and political actors creates and participates in truth commissions with numerous and often contradictory expectations in mind, the question becomes: should institutionalized truth and memory projects, such as truth commissions, accommodate all these agents of memory? To this normative question, my answer is a qualified yes. Yes, a project that seeks to uncover facts and construct a truthful and shared historical memory should create a safe space in which all members of society, regardless of the moral and legal status of their past actions, can participate in narrating, questioning, and revising accounts of past violence and violations. Broad-based participation should be the normative foundation for truth commissions.

Yet it is a qualified yes. A postconflict society is not J. S. Mill's "marketplace of ideas" or the Rawlsian original position in which selves unburdened by history negotiate their moral differences. In the wake of mass conflict some voices are quite loud in their denial of past wrongs, others too quiet in their refusal to even take part in the shouting match, and yet many others who need a genuine dialogue cannot say a word because of a history of victimhood, stigma, and marginalization. A truth commission should be guided by an ethics of equal participation in the face of powerful political, military, and judicial actors who seek to impose forced amnesia and impunity on society. Otherwise, it (or any other truth project) only reproduces the illegitimate power relations that cause a society to resort to the commission in the first place.

I suggest an ethics of equal participation inspired by political theorist Nancy Fraser's notion of *participatory parity*.[2] Policies with a justice and recognition orientation should take into consideration the power asymmetries involved if such acknowledgment is meant to overcome, rather than reinforce, historical injustices. For truth commissions, enabling equal participation requires an all-inclusive process that brings together individuals and social groups willing to take part but also pays special attention to the participation of those persons and groups that have been most adversely affected and marginalized by processes of political violence and violations. A commission should be open to everyone, including perpetrators, but avoid capture by powerful interests.[3] It should be victim-centered yet resist the temptation to reduce people's complex agency to disempowering narratives of victimhood.

A commission's legitimacy can be enhanced through an all-inclusive creation process that brings together politicians from all major political groupings, human rights organizations, victims' associations, other interested civil society groups, and representatives of the police, the armed forces, guerrilla groups, and so on. It is important to make sure that all those actors willing to participate can do so without dominating the process. I do not propose a specific procedure, since context-specific decision-making rules are more appropriate than one-size-fits-all solutions. Nonetheless the guiding principles should be broad-based and equal participation in which no veto player is strong enough to subvert the overall outcome.

A commission should open its doors to everyone who would like to share information. Yet, the commissioners and the staff need to be mindful of the power asymmetries within society, as many persons suffer forms of exclusion and vulnerability that might ultimately prevent them from participating in the commission. As a guiding principle, a commission should try to accommodate those who are least likely to participate as a result of socioeconomic, political, ethnic, racial, and gendered exclusion. Victims' relatives and victim-survivors, especially those in the periphery of the nation's geographic, political, and cultural centers, require special effort on the part of the commission to come forward and testify.

The participation of presumed perpetrators has long preoccupied scholars and practitioners. Evidence in this book and elsewhere suggests that powerful institutions in alliance with perpetrators often seek to undermine a commission by stripping it of key powers, such as the authority to subpoena, name perpetrators, and pass information to the judiciary. Even when they are provided with material incentives (such as reduced sentences), perpetrators do not testify in large numbers. Instead of exposing themselves as violators, they choose to take the relatively low risk of not testifying today and being summoned to court later. Since most perpetrators go unpunished, the gamble pays off for them. Repentant perpetrators remain an exception. Therefore, truth commissions should approach presumed perpetrators, but not at any cost. The option of offering incentives, such as reduced sentences and amnesties, should likewise reflect the spirit of equal participation: given the uneven playing field for victims, their individual consent should be the legitimate basis for incentivizing specific perpetrators.

Lessons Learned: What the Future Holds for Truth Commissions

The discussion above suggests that there are political and ontological limits to institutionalized truth telling that militate against the search for success stories. The following is therefore not an authoritative best-practices manual but, much more modestly, a list of lessons learned from past experiences. It does not prescribe specific policies but synthesizes lessons from past commissions to provide general principles that future commissions can use.

Sustained and Diverse Support

The single most important factor that explains a commission's long-term political and social impact is the presence or absence of a supportive government and/or active civil society groups not only during but also after the commission process. Lasting impact depends as much on governmental endorsement as on continued support by domestic and transnational civil society actors—predominantly human rights and victims' NGOs but also development agencies, women's groups, (in some cases) indigenous activists, and others. Yet, the attention span of international actors is often quite short. The expected budgets and mobilization plans cover at best the successful completion of a commission. This undermines the potential for long-term change and wastes the time and resources spent on the commission—Haiti is a case in point.

Actors with economic and political resources who want to see positive results from a truth commission should plan for sustained support in the immediate post-commission period. Even if the commissioners and the staff may not be able to fully anticipate the extent of civil society mobilization around their work, it is crucial that they secure logistical and financial support for post-commission activities (such as outreach, the dissemination of the final report, and educational campaigns) and maintain the transnational alliance that brought the commission into existence in the first place. Publishing and disseminating the final report, exerting pressure on policy makers and public officials to implement the recommendations, drawing a list of compensation recipients, attending to victims' needs and demands, and generating society-wide awareness of the human rights issue are among the many tasks that require ongoing commitment in terms of funding, political will, and activism.

Commissions supported by a variety of sources, such as the domestic government, foreign governments, international donors, and national and international NGOs, have a better chance of completing their job, getting their recommendations implemented into policy, and shaping social debates in the long run. A diverse portfolio allows the commission to survive crisis situations, such as abandonment by a key donor, election of an anti-commission government, or sudden changes in human rights policy. The long list of failed truth commission attempts offers cases in point. Furthermore, supportive agents should definitely include domestic human rights groups. No matter how well intentioned and generous a group of foreign donors may be, they cannot assure successful implementation of post-commission reforms if they lose their connection with local human rights activists—a lesson drawn from the experiences of El Salvador and Haiti.

Reasonable Expectations

Politicians, NGOs, donors, and commissioners have an obligation to fully inform citizens, and especially affected individuals, about why a commission is set up, what it can achieve, and what lies outside its mandate. There is often confusion about the official status of a truth commission, especially when a government is interested in obscuring its own failure to provide retributive and restorative justice. This leads people to project their expectations from the government onto the commission. For example, many victims expressed dissatisfaction at commissions' failure to disburse reparations in Peru, Sierra Leone, and Timor-Leste, although this is of course the government's job. Likewise, a truth commission cannot (and should not) have the last word on a society's divisions over the meaning of the past or how reconciliation can be best achieved. The goal of a truth commission is the opening of dialogue, not its closure—as the Chilean political elite had to discover in the latter part of the 1990s.

An honest attitude toward the mandate and powers of a truth commission should be extended to the expected results as well. Evidence shows that victims and perpetrators do not reconcile in the short run, although the goal of reconciliation seems to pervade the political discourse of transitional societies. Likewise, there is no evidence to suggest that truth commissions by themselves have improved the quality of democracy and human rights conduct dramatically. Their findings and recommendations, when taken seriously by politicians and public officials, can guide reform efforts and prosecutions, and the process and product of a truth commission can work toward the transformation of social values and norms in the long run, but the magnitude of these effects should be scrutinized, not taken for granted. A well-researched and comprehensive truth commission can even prompt a candid dialogue about the persistence of socioeconomic, ethnic, racial, and gendered injustices (as in Peru and Guatemala), but, again, a commission contributes to change as an enabler not an enactor.

Acknowledging the Political Limits

The commissioners and their sponsors need not worry about presenting the findings, historical narratives, and recommendations in ways acceptable to everyone. Naive assumptions about consensus and reconciliation can be damaging. Individual and institutional actors supporting perpetrators have proven extremely unwilling to acknowledge violations, no matter how grave and irrefutable they may be. As the example of Chile after Pinochet's London arrest shows, contrition begins (if at all) when perpetrators feel delegitimized and cornered, not when they are greeted with conciliatory gestures. Truth commissions can at best sway a small number of repenting rank-and-file perpetrators, but their actual achievement consists in promoting dialogue and acknowledgment between victims and those bystanders who, after remaining apathetic to the violations while they were taking place, become sensitized through the commission's work. A commission should be all-inclusive in terms of providing every person a meaningful opportunity to participate in truth telling, not in terms of satisfying every demand, how exclusionary or unjust it may be.

Perpetrators of human rights violations are rarely, if ever, moved by discourses of apology, forgiveness, and reconciliation. Therefore, expecting large numbers of perpetrators to testify in recognition of a moral obligation is quite naive. However, it is also wrong to regard perpetrators as the incarnation of evil, a group at the margins of "normal" humanity. This is not to excuse their behavior or ignore the fact that some perpetrators are simply sadistic people, but to acknowledge that their inhumane acts took place in the context of a social and political conflict that made it possible for human relations to degenerate into exercises of brutal power.

However, precisely because violent conflict is an all-too-human phenomenon, getting confessions out of perpetrators can be difficult. They often build strong political-ideological defense mechanisms to justify their acts, operate on an ethic of not telling on their comrades in arms, and tend to regard human rights defenders as enemies in civilian outfit. Furthermore, many perpetrators trust that they are backed by powerful individuals and institutions—a reasonable belief when the outgoing elite enjoy de facto power and have an interest in maintaining the bonds of complicity.

Therefore, perpetrators are unlikely to speak out in general, and even when they do, the willful omissions and lies in their narratives may frustrate the quest for truth. A combination of "carrots and sticks" (such as subpoena power and selective incentives) can succeed in taking as many perpetrator testimonies as possible, but it is advisable not to hold high expectations. Finally, the incentives, such as mitigated sentences or amnesties, should be conditional on the consent of individual victim-survivors and victims' relatives.

Comprehensive Notion of Truth

Discovering and publicizing the facts of human rights violations are the primary tasks of truth commissions. A highly accurate historical record provides background information for courts, accomplishes a minimum degree of closure for the aggrieved, pulls the ground from beneath the deniers' feet, and forces broader society to face up to the enormity of others' suffering. However, the striving for forensic truth should not lead the commissioners to downplay the need to set political violence and violations in political and historical context. Acknowledgment of past wrongs, a demand voiced by victims, their relatives, many bystanders, and even some of the perpetrators, requires an explanation of why conflict and violence took place at a massive scale.

No historical narrative, including a truth commission's, can claim to represent *the* truth once and for all. It is bound to be partial, just as with any other historical interpretation. Yet, a truth commission can construct a comprehensive account of national history by researching the facts and integrating a variety of different perspectives and narrative strategies. Truth commissions have come into existence precisely because violations go hand in hand with official propaganda and the forced silencing of alternative voices, which together obscure facts as well as legitimate historical interpretations. In line with the principle of equal participation, it is a commission's responsibility to give voice to those persons and social groups that had been excluded from public discourse. Successful examples of Guatemala and Peru show that an inclusive, truthful, and accurate historical explanation can be the lasting contribution of a commission.

Openness to Post-National Imagination

Truth commissions address national tragedy with the hope of national rebuilding. While their commitment to self-critique on the nation's behalf has its merits, commissions should not limit themselves to methodological nationalism in their human rights investigation and conclusions. The regional geopolitical context and cross-border collaboration between perpetrators should be examined to explain the causes, patterns, and consequences of political violence. Anticommunist authoritarian regimes committed the majority of human rights violations in the 1960s and 1970s in the Southern Cone and in the 1980s in Central America, and it is widely known that these regimes coordinated their repression efforts. The end of the Cold War ushered in a period of instability and state decline in much of Central Asia and sub-Saharan Africa, which demonstrates that the civil wars and internationalized civil wars of the 1990s were not strictly national phenomena. Yet, most commissions have remained nation-centered in their analyses.

Truth commissions can experiment with a post-national imagination not only with their investigation topics but with their fundamental value orientations, too. They already negotiate the boundaries of national belonging through their commitment to the cosmopolitan human rights norm, but the cosmopolitan element is often at the service of a national reconstruction project. Why not assert that the local information on past violations points to a global, and not merely national, tragedy? Even if the specific details of human suffering may be embodied in local histories, its moral import as a human rights violation, historical injustice, and manifestation of social inequality transcends the national context. I am not suggesting that truth commissions should try to forge regional or globalized conceptions of belonging, which is a much bigger task than what truth-finding panels can achieve. They can, nonetheless, leave the door open for alternative imaginations by highlighting the subnational, regional, international, and transnational implications of their findings, conclusions, and recommendations.

Final Remarks

When I started this project in mid-2007, I was worried that truth commissions would soon lose their attraction for societies, as the third wave of democratic transitions came to an end and the shift of attention to the International Criminal Court as an accountability mechanism signaled the demise of truth commissions as a suitable transitional justice model. In other words, my topic of investigation would be shelved as "history of the recent past" rather than "current affairs." As of this writing, truth commissions had lost nothing of their popularity. Brazil and Côte d'Ivoire mandated commissions recently. It will not be surprising if new truth commissions flourish in the troubled countries of the Middle East—a panel is under way in Tunisia. Civil society actors have already begun to lobby for a truth commission since peace negotiations between the Turkish government and the Kurdish rebels were announced in late 2012. Despite their many ambiguities and shortcomings, truth commissions have provided contemporary societies with a workable tool for coming to terms with their past. For scholars, practitioners, and all concerned citizens, the hope and challenge that gave birth to truth commissions is still alive: to construct future peace and justice in light of past tragedy—or, in other words, to overcome a past that constructs our being.

NOTES

Introduction

1. For details, see Larry Rohter, "Searing Indictment," *New York Times*, February 27, 1999; Jonathan D. Tepperman, "Truth and Consequences," *Foreign Affairs* 81, no. 2 (2002): 128–145; Christian Tomuschat, "Clarification Commission in Guatemala," *Human Rights Quarterly* 23, no. 2 (2001): 233–234.

2. Dorothy C. Shea, *The South African Truth Commission: The Politics of Reconciliation* (Washington, DC: U.S. Institute of Peace Press, 2000), 3.

3. "In Venezuela, Protesters Point to Their Scars," *New York Times*, April 27, 2014.

4. "La izquierda 'abertzale' pedirá hoy una 'comisión internacional de la verdad'," *El País— País Vasco*, February 25, 2012.

5. "Zimbabwe's Mugabe: Lift Sanctions, UN's Navi Pillay Urges," *BBC News*, May 25, 2012.

6. "BBC Newsline Poll: Support for Parades Commission and Peace Centre," *BBC News*, December 17, 2013.

7. Kathryn Sikkink, *The Justice Cascade: How Human Rights Prosecutions Are Changing World Politics* (New York: W. W. Norton, 2011).

8. Tricia D. Olsen, Leigh A. Payne, and Andrew G. Reiter, *Transitional Justice in Balance: Comparing Processes, Weighing Efficacy* (Washington, DC: U.S. Institute of Peace Press, 2010).

9. Derek Beach and Rasmus Brun Pedersen, "What Is Process Tracing Actually Tracing? The Three Variants of Process Tracing Methods and Their Uses and Limitations" (paper presented at the American Political Science Association annual meeting, Seattle, WA, September 2011).

10. Andrew Bennett, "Process Tracing: A Bayesian Approach," in *The Oxford Handbook of Political Methodology*, ed. Janet M. Box-Steffensmeier, Henry E. Brady, and David Collier (Oxford: Oxford University Press, 2008), 702–721.

11. Jeffrey T. Checkel, "Tracing Causal Mechanisms," *International Studies Review* 8, no. 2 (2006): 362–370.

12. I select the truth commissions in Chile and Peru to allow for maximal variation with respect to the outcome of interest, that is, truth commission impact driven by political will and civil society pressure, to develop a theory. See David Collier and James Mahoney, "Insights and Pitfalls: Selection Bias in Qualitative Research," *World Politics* 49, no. 1 (October 1996): 56–91. The main rationale is to minimize the selection bias that would arise from small-N case selection. Chile had a commission that generated politically driven impact, whereas in Peru almost all politicians ignored the commission's work.

Chapter 1. Definition and Conceptual History

1. "El informe sobre la toma del Palacio de Justicia," posted on Álvaro E. Duque's blog *Este infierno paradisíaco*, November 19, 2006, accessed January, 27, 2015, http://alvaroduque.wordpress.com/2006/11/19/el-informe-sobre-la-toma-del-palacio-de-justicia/.

2. "Amia Bombing: Argentina and Iran Agree Truth Commission," *BBC News*, January 28, 2013.

3. "Banking—Stand by for an Inquiry," *BBC News*, July 2, 2012.

4. "Jimmy Savile Scandal Prompts Flood of Calls to Abuse Victims' Groups," *Observer* (London), October 13, 2012.

5. "Head of Teachers' Union Tests Candidates' Views, *New York Times*, May 10, 2013.

6. "UCI: Truth Commission to Launch in 2014," November 13, 2013, accessed January 27, 2015, http://www.bicycling.com/news/pro-cycling/uci-truth-commission-launch-2014.

7. Giovanni Sartori, "Concept Misformation in Comparative Politics," *American Political Science Review* 64, no. 4 (1970): 1033–1053.

8. This definition draws upon conceptual work on truth commissions; see Eric Wiebelhaus-Brahm, "Truth and Consequences: The Impact of Truth Commissions in Transitional Societies" (Ph.D. diss., University of Colorado at Boulder, 2006); Mark Freeman, *Truth Commissions and Procedural Fairness* (Cambridge: Cambridge University Press, 2006); Priscilla B. Hayner, *Unspeakable Truths: Confronting State Terror and Atrocity* (New York: Routledge, 2011).

9. The publicity of the final report should not be considered in dichotomous terms, as a final report can be more or less public along a continuum. Truth commissions in Uganda and Haiti published final reports in 1996 and 1994 respectively, but no more than a handful of copies were printed. For all practical purposes, these final reports are unavailable to the public. This contrasts sharply with the publicity of Argentina's 1983–1984 truth commission, whose final report became a national best seller. I follow the existing literature in including those final reports with limited publicity in my list of truth commissions, but their special condition has to be noted.

10. Daan Bronkhorst, *Truth Commissions and Transitional Justice: A Short Guide* (Amsterdam: Amnesty International Dutch Section, 2003).

11. Uganda's Commission of Inquiry into Violations of Human Rights (1986–1994) covered a period of twenty-four years, which at the time amounted to the entire independent existence of that nation. Timor-Leste's Commission for Reception, Truth, and Reconciliation (2002–2005) accompanied the country's independence and investigated more than two decades of Indonesian invasion.

12. Freeman, *Truth Commissions and Procedural Fairness*, 17.

13. The only alteration came as a result of an impending court interdict, which forced the commissioners to agree with former president F. W. de Klerk to delete paragraphs accusing him.

14. Alexandra Barahona de Brito, "Truth and Justice in the Consolidation of Democracy in Chile and Uruguay," *Parliamentary Affairs* 46, no. 4 (1993): 590. Furthermore, the report's findings were not shared with the public, and there was no effort at dissemination. Nevertheless, Hayner, *Unspeakable Truths*, and Amnesty International list it as a truth commission, while Freeman, *Truth Commissions and Procedural Fairness*, and Barahona de Brito, "Truth and Justice," do not.

15. A prominent example to the contrary is the addition of Luis Arias Grazziani to Peru's Truth and Reconciliation Commission (2001–2003) while he was serving as adviser to President Alejandro Toledo.

16. While scholars tend to treat human rights violations committed under an undemocratic regime as "paradigmatic" for transitional justice, violations committed by democratic regimes during prolonged conflict pose complex challenges and paradoxes. See Fionnuala Ní Aoláin and Colm Campbell, "The Paradox of Transition in Conflicted Democracies," *Human Rights Quarterly* 27, no. 1 (2005): 172–213.

17. "Truth Commission: Uganda 74," United States Institute of Peace (USIP) Truth Commission Digital Collection, accessed January 27, 2015, http://www.usip.org/publications/truth-commission-uganda-74.

18. "Truth Commission: Bolivia," USIP Truth Commission Digital Collection, accessed January 27, 2015, http://www.usip.org/publications/truth-commission-bolivia.

19. "Commission of Inquiry: Zimbabwe," USIP Truth Commission Digital Collection, accessed January 27, 2015, http://www.usip.org/publications/commission-inquiry-zimbabwe.

20. "Truth Commission: Ecuador 96," USIP Truth Commission Digital Collection, accessed January 27, 2015, http://www.usip.org/publications/truth-commission-ecuador-96.

21. Timothy Garton Ash, "A Nation in Denial," *Guardian*, March 7, 2002.

22. "Truth Commission: Serbia and Montenegro," USIP Truth Commission Digital Collection, accessed January 27, 2015, http://www.usip.org/publications/truth-commission-serbia-and -montenegro.

23. Dejan Ilic, "The Yugoslav Truth and Reconciliation Commission: Overcoming Cognitive Blocks," *Eurozine*, April 23, 2004.

24. Priscilla Hayner, "Past Truths, Present Dangers: The Role of Official Truth Seeking in Conflict Resolution and Prevention," in *International Conflict Resolution After the Cold War*, ed. Paul C. Stern and Daniel Druckman (Washington, DC: National Academies Press, 2000), 369.

25. Louis Bickford, "Unofficial Truth Projects," *Human Rights Quarterly* 29, no. 4 (2007): 994–1035.

26. For example, the failure of the Uruguayan transitional government to establish an independent truth commission and the dissatisfaction with the 1985 parliamentary commission of inquiry inspired a human rights organization, Servicio Paz y Justicia—Uruguay (SERPAJ), to carry out its alternative truth project called "Uruguay Nunca Más," whose final report became a best seller overnight. "Uruguay Nunca Más" captures the enormous appeal of the notion of a truth commission in the early transition, as well as its frustration in the political process.

27. Bickford, "Unofficial Truth Projects," 1002.

28. José Zalaquett, "Balancing Ethical Imperatives and Political Constraints: The Dilemma of New Democracies Confronting Past Human Rights Violations," *Hastings Law Journal* 43 (1992): 1425–1438.

29. Martha Minow, "Between Vengeance and Forgiveness: South Africa's Truth and Reconciliation Commission," *Negotiation Journal* 14, no. 4 (1998): 319–55; Priscilla B. Hayner, "Fifteen Truth Commissions—1974 to 1994: A Comparative Study," *Human Rights Quarterly* 16, no. 4 (1994): 651; Luc Capdevila, "Le passé/présent entre dictature et transition politique dans la société paraguayenne contemporaine," *Nuevo Mundo Mundos Nuevos*, Coloquios (2008), accessed January 27, 2015, http://nuevomundo.revues.org/28802.

30. "The first countries to implement truth commissions in the mid to late 1980s did so in response to unique domestic circumstances. At the time, the international community advocated prosecutions in response to human rights abuses. The first successful truth commissions ever used—namely those in Argentina and in Uganda—were implemented as a rational response to domestic factors alone. Once this option existed, other transitioning states and international organizations and powerful states all learned about the truth commission option." Sara Lynn Parker, "Seeking Truth: The Development of an International Truth Commission Norm" (Ph.D. diss., University of Delaware, 2008), 21.

31. It may be asked if these transformations owe to the revolutionary and worldwide impact of South Africa's Truth and Reconciliation Commission. The Salvadoran commission preceded it, and the mandate of the Guatemalan commission, which would already exhibit significant procedural and ideational changes from earlier commissions, was ratified before that of the South African panel. However, some of the methodological novelties of the South African case, especially the information management system developed by Patrick Ball and his colleagues, were adopted by the Guatemalans. The impact of the South African innovations was most visible in the Peruvian commission, whose repertoire included a quantitative information management software, public hearings, and televised sessions. In short, changes in the idea of *truth commission* had already begun before the South African commission, but that commission's innovative approach and worldwide fame accelerated the change.

32. While the earlier commissions worked with a clear definition of serious violations, namely, death and forced disappearance, the Salvadoran commission took serious violations to mean those cases "that had a special or broader impact on society in general." Thomas Buergenthal, "The United Nations Truth Commission for El Salvador," *Vanderbilt Journal of Transnational Law* 27, no. 3 (1994): 500. Charles T. Call is very critical of the implications of this investigatory practice for victims, who "received little attention. Only a handful of the 75,000 victims' families received information about the fate of their loved ones, and none received psychological services or compensation, although the Truth Commission called for reparations and other steps toward reconciliation." Charles T. Call, "Democratisation, War and State-Building: Constructing the Rule of Law in El Salvador," *Journal of Latin American Studies* 35, no. 4 (2003): 852.

33. Luke Wilcox, "Reshaping Civil Society Through a Truth Commission: Human Rights in Morocco's Process of Political Reform," *International Journal of Transitional Justice* 3, no. 1 (2009): 49–68.

34. Kate Doyle, "'Forgetting Is Not Justice': Mexico Bares Its Secret," *World Policy Journal* 20, no. 2 (2003): 61–72.

35. "Philippine Court Rules Anti-Corruption Panel Illegal," *New York Times*, December 7, 2010.

36. "Nepal Court Blocks Civil War Truth Commission," *BBC News*, April 1, 2013.

37. Cath Collins, *Post-Transitional Justice: Human Rights Trials in Chile and El Salvador* (University Park: Pennsylvania State University Press, 2010).

Chapter 2. Speaking Truth to Power?

1. Richard Ned Lebow, "The Politics of Memory in Postwar Europe," in *Politics of Memory in Postwar Europe*, ed. Richard Ned Lebow, Wulf Kansteiner, and Claudio Fogu, 1–39 (Durham, NC: Duke University Press, 2006).

2. Jelena Subotić, "The Transformation of International Transitional Justice Advocacy," *International Journal of Transitional Justice* 6, no. 1 (2012): 112.

3. Kieran McEvoy, and Lorna McGregor, *Transitional Justice from Below: Grassroots Activism and the Struggle for Change* (Oxford: Hart, 2010).

4. Human rights groups have usually greeted the truth commission with enthusiasm, and more often than not, NGO initiatives have prepared the groundwork for an official commission. During Argentina's democratic transition, however, victims' associations and human rights groups approached the truth commission idea with suspicion, as they feared that a presidential commission would lack autonomy and replace criminal proceedings. Influential victims' organizations like the Mothers of Plaza de Mayo and Liga Argentina por los Derechos del Hombre demanded a governmental or bicameral investigation commission, but President Alfonsín opted for an investigative body created by presidential decree and autonomous from the legislature. Ruti G. Teitel, *Transitional Justice* (New York: Oxford University Press, 2000), 78; Elin Skaar, "Truth Commissions, Trials or Nothing? Policy Options in Democratic Transitions," *Third World Quarterly* 20, no. 6 (1999): 1109–1128; Emilio Crenzel, "Argentina's National Commission on the Disappearance of Persons: Contributions to Transitional Justice," *International Journal of Transitional Justice* 2, no. 2 (2008): 173–191. Nevertheless, once the commissions began the investigatory work, the initial suspicion gave way to critical and selective support.

5. Lucy Hovil and Moses Chrispus Okello, "Editorial Note," *International Journal of Transitional Justice* 5, no. 3 (2011): 333–344.

6. Martha Finnemore and Kathryn Sikkink, "International Norm Dynamics and Political Change," *International Organization* 52 (1998): 887–917.

7. Aaron P. Boesenecker and Leslie Vinjamuri, "Lost in Translation? Civil Society, Faith-Based Organizations and the Negotiation of International Norms," *International Journal of Transitional Justice* 5, no. 3 (2011): 345–365.

8. Mark Vasallo, "Truth and Reconciliation Commissions: General Considerations and a Critical Comparison of the Commissions of Chile and El Salvador." *University of Miami Inter-American Law Review* 33, no. 1 (2002): 155.

9. Richard A. Wilson, *The Politics of Truth and Reconciliation in South Africa: Legitimizing the Post-Apartheid State* (Cambridge: Cambridge University Press, 2001).

10. Greg Grandin, "The Instruction of Great Catastrophe: Truth Commissions, National History, and State Formation in Argentina, Chile, and Guatemala," *American Historical Review* 110, no.1 (2005): 46–67.

11. I borrow the term *elective affinity* from the Weberian sociological tradition to examine the concurrence of ideas and interests. The relationship is not one of causation, and it should not be taken as a nomothetic universal rule that holds across cases. See Richard Herbert Howe, "Max Weber's Elective Affinities: Sociology Within the Bounds of Pure Reason," *American Journal of Sociology* 84, no. 2 (1978): 366–385.

12. Richard Wilson mentions the "elective affinities between global human rights and particular social constituencies." Richard A. Wilson, "Afterword to 'Anthropology and Human Rights in a New Key': The Social Life of Human Rights," *American Anthropologist* 108, no. 1 (2006): 77–83. My approach is inspired by Wilson, but I treat elective affinities between the human rights discourse and political actors as a relationship mediated by truth commissions rather than something that fully exists prior to the commission process.

13. Ariel Dorfman, *Exorcising Terror: The Incredible Unending Trial of General Augusto Pinochet* (New York: Seven Stories Press, 2002).

14. Grandin, "Instruction of Great Catastrophe," 47.

15. Grandin, "Instruction of Great Catastrophe," 48.

16. Grandin, "Instruction of Great Catastrophe," 48.

17. Grandin, "Instruction of Great Catastrophe," 48.

18. "Prologue," in *Guatemala: Memory of Silence; Tz'inil Na'tab'al*, report of the Commission for Historical Clarification (1999).

19. "Recommendations: Introduction," in *Guatemala: Memory of Silence*.

20. It should be noted that not all truth commissions interpret the past in order to legitimize, delegitimize, or set normative standards for the present. Especially post-transitional truth commissions, established at least one decade after return to peace and democratic rule (see Chapter 1), are under less pressure to envision a national reconstruction project, as institutional transformations had already taken place in their absence. For example, the presidential mandate that established the Uruguayan Commission for Peace (2000) does not specify any political objectives except national peace among all citizens. Likewise, the final report lacks a historical narrative, arguably because there was no expectation that the commission should develop one. The truth commission does not reinforce or question the legitimating discourses of the incoming regime; it simply sidesteps the issue.

21. The reconstruction and legitimation of the state through an inclusive reparations program finds clear expression in the words of Ernesto Verdeja: "[Reparations] publicly reassert victims' moral worth and dignity; make a society reconsider its notion of the 'we' when faced with reintegrating as equals those who were violated, injured and marginalized in the past; foster the development of public trust in state institutions (important where the state is a primary violator of rights); contribute to undermining the justificatory narratives given by perpetrators by resituating victims as moral agents; and generate a public, critical interpretation of history." Ernesto Verdeja, "Reparations in Democratic Transitions," *Res Publica* 12, no. 2 (2006): 135.

22. For one of the exceptional studies that situate truth commissions in state–civil society relations, see Joanna R. Quinn, "The Politics of Acknowledgement: Truth Commissions in Uganda and Haiti" (Ph.D. diss., McMaster University, 2003).

23. Madeleine Fullard and Nicky Rousseau, "Truth Telling, Identities, and Power in South Africa and Guatemala," in *Identities in Transition: Challenges for Transitional Justice in Divided Societies*, ed. Paige Arthur (New York: Cambridge University Press, 2011), 54–86.

24. Leigh A. Payne, *Unsettling Accounts: Neither Truth nor Reconciliation in Confessions of State Violence* (Durham, NC: Duke University Press, 2008), 13–40.

Chapter 3. One Truth Among Others?

1. There are, nonetheless, exceptional studies that explore the challenges of writing national history and promoting historical justice through truth commissions in a case study, a comparison of several commissions, or a broader theoretical overview of all commission efforts. For example, see Wilson, *The Politics of Truth and Reconciliation in South Africa*; Claire Moon, Narrating Political Reconciliation: South Africa's Truth and Reconciliation Commission (Lanham, MD: Lexington Books, 2008); Grandin, "The Instruction of Great Catastrophe"; Teitel, *Transitional Justice.*

2. Anika Oettler, "Encounters with History: Dealing with the 'Present Past' in Guatemala," *European Review of Latin American and Caribbean Studies* 81 (October 2006): 16.

3. Jeffrey K. Olick, and Joyce Robbins, "Social Memory Studies: From 'Collective Memory' to the Historical Sociology of Mnemonic Practices," *Annual Review of Sociology* 24 (1998): 105–140; Aleida Assmann, "History, Memory, and the Genre of Testimony," *Poetics Today* 27, no. 2 (2006): 261–273; Kerwin L. Klein, "On the Emergence of Memory in Historical Discourse," *Representations* 69 (2000): 127–150.

4. Jacques Le Goff, *History and Memory*, trans. Steven Rendall and Elizabeth Claman (New York: Columbia University Press, 1992); Wulf Kansteiner, "Finding Meaning in Memory: A Methodological Critique of Collective Memory Studies," *History and Theory* 41, no. 2 (2002): 179–197; Claudio Fogu and Wulf Kansteiner, "The Politics of Memory and the Poetics of History," in *The Politics of Memory in Postwar Europe*, ed. Richard Ned Lebow, Wulf Kansteiner, and Claudio Fogu (Durham, NC: Duke University Press, 2006), 284–310.

5. Paul Ricoeur, *Memory, History, Forgetting*, trans. Kathleen Blamey and David Pellauer (Chicago: University of Chicago Press, 2004), 21.

6. Martin Imbleau, "Initial Truth Establishment by Transitional Bodies and the Fight Against Denial," in *Truth Commissions and Courts: The Tension Between Criminal Justice and the Search for Truth*, ed. William A. Schabas and Shane Darcy (Dordrecht: Kluwer, 2004), 168.

7. For an illuminating discussion of the South African commission's conceptions of truth, see Alex Boraine, *A Country Unmasked: Inside South Africa's Truth and Reconciliation Commission* (Oxford: Oxford University Press, 2000).

8. Chile's National Commission on Truth and Reconciliation relied heavily on the irrefutability of facts. In the words of the commission's architect José Zalaquett: "Society cannot simply black out a chapter of its history; it cannot deny the facts of its past, however differently these may be interpreted." Zalaquett, "Balancing Ethical Imperatives," 1433.

9. Elizabeth Stanley, "Torture, Silence and Recognition," *Current Issues in Criminal Justice* 16, no. 1 (2004): 5–25.

10. Commissions' moral interest in historical truth can be situated in the broader context of the transformation of the historical profession in the wake of human rights violations. For a critical account of the increasingly moralized responsibility of historians and intellectuals, see: Richard J. Evans, "History, Memory, and the Law: The Historian as Expert Witness," *History and*

Theory 41, no. 3 (2002): 326–345; Paul Muldoon, "Reconciliation and Political Legitimacy: The Old Australia and the New South Africa," *Australian Journal of History and Politics* 49, no. 2 (2003): 182–196.

11. Eduardo González Cueva, "The Contribution of the Peruvian Truth and Reconciliation Commission to Prosecutions," *Criminal Law Forum* 15 (2004): 62.

12. Sophia A. McClennen and Joseph R. Slaughter, "Introducing Human Rights and Literary Forms; or, The Vehicles and Vocabularies of Human Rights," *Comparative Literature Studies* 46, no. 1 (2009): 1–19. For a general theory of the performative and commemorative aspects of memory work, see Paul Connerton, *How Societies Remember* (New York: Cambridge University Press, 1989).

13. Eviatar Zerubavel, "Social Memories: Steps to a Sociology of the Past," *Qualitative Sociology* 19, no. 3 (1996): 283–300.

14. Some commentators hail the victim orientation in terms that resonate with the subaltern studies perspective on the epistemological and moral primacy of the marginalized: "the [South African] TRC's conscientious diffusion of the meaning of 'truth' aimed at the provisional and transitional nature of truth, a kind of empowering critical element within truth that could only come from the position of the powerless." Leigh M. Johnson, "Transitional Truth and Historical Justice: Philosophical Foundations and Implications of the Truth and Reconciliation Commission," *International Studies in Philosophy* 38, no. 2 (2006): 81.

15. Maurice Halbwachs, *On Collective Memory*, trans. Lewis A. Coser (Chicago: University of Chicago Press, 1992).

16. Verdeja, "Reparations in Democratic Transitions," 135; Johnson, "Transitional Truth and Historical Justice."

17. Alex Wilde, "Irruptions of Memory: Expressive Politics in Chile's Transition to Democracy," *Journal of Latin American Studies* 31 (1999): 473–500.

18. Jay Winter, *Sites of Memory, Sites of Mourning: The Great War in European Cultural History* (Cambridge: Cambridge University Press, 1995).

19. For the challenges of writing victim-centered histories, especially the danger of overidentification with the victim and the traumatic narrative, see Dominick LaCapra, *Writing History, Writing Trauma* (Baltimore: Johns Hopkins University Press, 2001).

20. *Guatemala: Memory of Silence*, para. 24.

21. Comisión para la Paz [Commission for Peace, Uruguay], *Informe Final* (Montevideo: La Comisión, 2003), para. 46, accessed January 27, 2015, http://www.presidencia.gub.uy/noticias /archivo/2003/abril/Informe_final.doc.

22. This belief, accompanied by the Cold War fear that the Cuban government actively supported the insurgency, was central to the military strategy developed in the early years of the conflict, when General Clemente Noel took charge of the military-political administration of the department of Ayacucho.

23. Comisión de la Verdad y Reconciliación [CVR, Peru], *Informe Final* (Lima: CVR, 2003), vol. 2, chap. 1, pp. 15–16 (hereafter, CVR, *Informe Final*)

24. Carlos Iván Degregori, *El Surgimiento de Sendero Luminoso: Ayacucho 1969–1979* (Lima: Instituto de Estudios Peruanos, 1990); Orin Starn, "Maoism in the Andes: The Communist Party of Peru-Shining Path and the Refusal of History," *Journal of Latin American Studies* 27 (1995): 399–421; Gustavo Gorriti, *Shining Path: A History of the Millenarian War in Peru*, trans. R Kirk (Chapel Hill: University of North Carolina Press, 1999).

25. "Prologue," in *Nunca Más: Informe de la Comisión Nacional sobre la Desaparición de Personas* (Buenos Aires: EUDEBA, 1984), translated as *Nunca Más (Never Again): Report of CONADEP (National Commission on the Disappearance of Persons)*, accessed January 27, 2015, http://web.archive.org/web/20031004074316/nuncamas.org/english/library/nevagain/nevagain _001.htm.

26. Steve J. Stern, *Reckoning with Pinochet: The Memory Question in Democratic Chile, 1989–2006* (Durham, NC: Duke University Press, 2010), 82.

27. In countries that have undergone more than one truth commission process, the later commission may correct the historical inadequacies of the earlier one. Chile's 2003 Commission on Political Imprisonment and Torture devotes part of its context chapter to refuting the thesis that a state of civil war existed before the coup. The earlier National Commission on Truth and Reconciliation (or "Rettig Commission," after its president) is ambiguous on the subject: it rejects that an actual civil war took place in Chile, but it also notes that "the objective conditions for a civil war" were present in 1973. The later commission rejects the "objective conditions" argument, as well. Not surprisingly, the discussion included a harsh critique of the *White Book of Change of Government in Chile*, a propaganda book published in 1973 to draw support for the military regime, and presumably written by Gonzalo Vial, who had participated in the Rettig Commission! Vial was quick to respond to the revisions of the 2003 commission in a series of opinion pieces published in the daily *La Segunda*.

28. Charles S. Maier, "Doing History, Doing Justice: The Narrative of the Historian and of the Truth Commission," in *Truth v. Justice: The Morality of Truth Commissions*, ed. Robert I. Rotberg and Dennis Thompson (Princeton, NJ: Princeton University Press, 2000), 267.

29. The final report of El Salvador's 1992 Commission on the Truth acknowledges that "the causes and conditions which generated the large number of serious acts of violence in El Salvador derive from very complex circumstances." Yet, "the Commission was not called upon to deal with all these factors, nor could it do so. Instead, it focused on certain considerations which prompted it to formulate its basic recommendations in such a way that this situation might be fully understood." "Recommendations," in *From Madness to Hope: The 12-Year War in El Salvador; Report of the Commission on the Truth for El Salvador* (New York: United Nations, 1993), accessed January 27, 2015, www.usip.org/sites/default/files/file/ElSalvador-Report.pdf.

30. *Report of the Chilean National Commission on Truth and Reconciliation*, vol. 1, trans. Phillip E. Berryman (Notre Dame, IN: University of Notre Dame Press, 1993), 64.

31. *Report of the Chilean National Commission on Truth and Reconciliation*, 31.

32. Brandon Hamber, "The Need for a Survivor-Centered Approach to the Truth and Reconciliation Commission," *Community Mediation Update* (Community Dispute Resolution Trust, Johannesburg, South Africa) 9 (1996).

33. This is not to say that the testimonial procedures are free from the effects of socioeconomic, cultural, and political inequalities. Unequal access to the public sphere, a condition that precedes the testimonial process, inevitably creates "narrative inequality." Jan Blommaert, Mary Bock, and Kay McCormick, "Narrative Inequality in the TRC Hearings: On the Hearability of Hidden Transcripts," *Journal of Language and Politics* 5, no. 1 (2006): 37–70. Furthermore, the complex interaction between the interviewer and the interviewee engenders another layer of power relations. Elizabeth Nannelli, "Memory, Records, History: The Records of the Commission for Reception, Truth, and Reconciliation in Timor-Leste," *Archival Science* 9, nos. 1–2 (2009): 35.

34. Laurel E. Fletcher and Harvey M. Weinstein, "Violence and Social Repair: Rethinking the Contribution of Justice to Reconciliation," *Human Rights Quarterly* 24, no. 3 (2002): 573–639.

35. Fiona C. Ross, "On Having Voice and Being Heard: Some After-Effects of Testifying Before the South African Truth and Reconciliation Commission," *Anthropological Theory* 3, no. 3 (2003): 326.

36. Elizabeth Lira, "Remembering: Passing Back Through the Heart," in *Collective Memory of Political Events: Social Psychological Perspective*, ed. James W. Pennebaker, Darío Páez, and Bernard Rimé (Mahwah, NJ: Lawrence Erlbaum Associates, 1997), 229.

37. Lisa J. Laplante and Kimberly S. Theidon, "Truth with Consequences: Justice and Reparations in Post-Truth Commission Peru," *Human Rights Quarterly* 29, no. 1 (2007): 238.

38. Payne, *Unsettling Accounts*. For a critical take on the practice of incentivizing perpetrators to testify, see Moon, Narrating Political Reconciliation, 91–114.

39. Pablo de Greiff, ed., *The Handbook of Reparations* (Oxford: Oxford University Press, 2006); see also Roy L. Brooks, "Reflections on Reparations" and Sharon F. Lean, "Is Truth Enough? Reparations and Reconciliation in Latin America," both in *Politics and the Past: On Repairing Historical Injustices*, ed. John Torpey (Lanham, MD: Rowman and Littlefield, 2003), 103–114 and 169–191.

40. Juan E. Méndez, "Derecho a la verdad frente a las graves violaciones a los derechos humanos," in *La aplicación de los tratados sobre derechos humanos por los tribunales locales*, ed. Martín Abregú and Christian Courtis (Buenos Aires: Del Puerto-CELS, 1997), 517–540; Yasmin Naqvi, "The Right to the Truth in International Law: Fact or Fiction?" *International Review of the Red Cross* 88, no. 862 (2006): 245–273.

41. *Guatemala. Memory of Silence*, 122.

42. Grandin, "Instruction of Great Catastrophe."

43. The Salvadoran truth commission, facing a case in which "three U.S. nuns and a lay worker had been raped by soldiers before they were killed," reported only that they were "abducted and killed" because the commission could not determine if the cases of rape fell within the scope of politically motivated acts, or they were committed at the initiative of the soldiers. Hayner, *Unspeakable Truths*, 87.

44. Diane Orentlicher, "Independent Study on Best Practices, Including Recommendations, to Assist States in Strengthening Their Domestic Capacity to Combat All Aspects of Impunity," UN Doc. E/CN.4/2004/88, February 27, 2004, para. 19(f).

45. For an excellent account of the "technologies of truth" employed by the South African TRC, see Wilson, *Politics of Truth and Reconciliation*, 33–61.

46. Elizabeth Stanley, "Truth Commissions and the Recognition of State Crime," *British Journal of Criminology* 45, no. 4 (2005): 582–597.

47. Mahmood Mamdani, "Amnesty or Impunity? A Preliminary Critique of the Report of the Truth and Reconciliation Commission of South Africa," *Diacritics* 32, nos. 3–4 (2002): 38.

48. Vasuki Nesiah, "Gender and Truth Commission Mandates," Paper presented at Open Society Institute Forum on Gender and Transitional Justice, New York, February 7, 2006.

49. The parliamentary act that created the truth commission in Liberia mandates the investigation of the period between 1979 and 2003. Yet, aware of the limits of periodization, it allows the commissioners to explore events before the start date, if necessary.

50. Hakeem O. Yusuf, *Transitional Justice, Judicial Accountability and the Rule of Law* (New York: Routledge, 2010), 42–43.

51. González Cueva, "Contribution of the Peruvian Truth and Reconciliation Commission"; Cynthia E. Milton, "At the Edge of the Peruvian Truth Commission: Alternative Paths to Recounting the Past," *Radical History Review* 98 (2007): 3–33.

52. United States Institute of Peace, "Truth Commission: Chad," accessed January 27, 2015, http://www.usip.org/publications/truth-commission-chad.

53. Stanley, "Truth Commissions and the Recognition of State Crime," 590.

54. Audrey R. Chapman, and Patrick Ball, "The Truth of Truth Commissions: Comparative Lessons from Haiti, South Africa, and Guatemala," *Human Rights Quarterly* 23, no. 1 (2001): 41; Audrey R. Chapman, "Truth Finding in the Transitional Justice Process" in *Assessing the Impact of Transitional Justice: Challenges for Empirical Research*, ed. Hugo van der Merwe, Victoria Baxter, and Audrey R. Chapman (Washington, DC: U.S. Institute of Peace Press, 2009), 104–105. Others have noted the potential for producing detailed oral histories through truth commissions. See

Bronwyn Leebaw, review of *Truth and Reconciliation in South Africa: Did the TRC Deliver?* ed. Audrey R. Chapman and Hugo van der Merwe, *Human Rights Quarterly* 31, no. 2 (2009): 535.

55. Hugo van der Merwe and Audrey R. Chapman, "Did the TRC Deliver?" in *Truth and Reconciliation in South Africa: Did the TRC Deliver?*, ed. Audrey R. Chapman and Hugo van der Merwe (Philadelphia: University of Pennsylvania Press, 2008), 249.

56. Diana Sankey, "Towards Recognition of Subsistence Harms: Reassessing Approaches to Socioeconomic Forms of Violence in Transitional Justice," *International Journal of Transitional Justice* 8 (2014): 121–140.

57. Mamdani, "Amnesty or Impunity?," 57; original emphasis.

58. Peter Winn, ed., *Victims of the Chilean Miracle: Workers and Neoliberalism in the Pinochet Era, 1973–2002* (Durham, NC: Duke University Press, 2004).

59. Andreas Wimmer and Nina Glick Schiller define methodological nationalism as "the assumption that the nation/state/society is the natural social and political form of the modern world." Andreas Wimmer and Nina Glick Schiller, "Methodological Nationalism and Beyond: Nation-State Building, Migration and the Social Sciences," *Global Networks* 2, no. 4 (2002): 302.

60. Truth commissions in Chad and Guatemala are an exception to this rule, as they elaborate on the role of foreign governments and individuals in explaining political violence.

61. Marita Eastmond and Johanna Mannergren Selimovic, "Silence as Possibility in Postwar Everyday Life," *International Journal of Transitional Justice* 6, no. 3 (2012): 502–524.

62. Pilar Riaño-Alcalá and Erin Baines, "The Archive in the Witness: Documentation in Settings of Chronic Insecurity," *International Journal of Transitional Justice* 5, no. 3 (2011): 412–433.

63. Wilson, *Politics of Truth and Reconciliation*, xvi.

64. Aryn Bartley, "Violence of the Present: *David's Story* and the Truth and Reconciliation Commission," *Comparative Literature Studies* 46, no. 1 (2009): 103–124.

Chapter 4. Truth Commission Impact

1. James L. Gibson, *Overcoming Apartheid: Can Truth Reconcile a Divided Nation?* (New York: Russell Sage Foundation, 2004).

2. Not all accounts assess commissions' worth in terms of political outcomes. The investigation of human rights violations and remembrance of the past in an institutionalized setting may be desirable and morally defensible independently of political transformations, which I discuss elsewhere in the book. This chapter, however, is devoted to truth commissions' impact on politics and society. See James W. Booth, "The Unforgotten: Memories of Justice," *American Political Science Review* 95, no. 4 (2001): 777–791; Jonathan Allen, "Balancing Justice and Social Unity: Political Theory and the Idea of a Truth and Reconciliation Commission," *University of Toronto Law Journal* 49, no. 3 (2001): 315–353.

3. Martha Minow, *Between Vengeance and Forgiveness: Facing History After Genocide and Mass Violence* (Boston: Beacon Press, 1998).

4. André du Toit, "The Moral Foundations of the South African TRC: Truth as Acknowledgment and Justice as Recognition," in *Truth v. Justice: The Morality of Truth Commissions*, ed. Robert I. Rotberg and Dennis Thompson (Princeton, NJ: Princeton University Press, 2000), 122–140; de Greiff, *The Handbook of Reparations*.

5. Fiona C. Ross, "On Having Voice and Being Heard," 326; Molly Andrews, "Grand National Narratives and the Project of Truth Commissions: A Comparative Analysis," *Media, Culture & Society* 25, no. 1 (2003): 45.

6. Lisa J. Laplante, "On the Indivisibility of Rights: Truth Commissions, Reparations, and the Right to Develop," *Yale Human Rights & Development Law Journal* 10 (2007): 141–177; Minow, *Between Vengeance and Forgiveness*.

7. Lisa Magarrell, "Reparations for Massive or Widespread Human Rights Violations: Sorting out Claims for Reparations and the Struggle for Social Justice," *Windsor Yearbook of Access to Justice* 22 (2003): 85.

8. Zalaquett, "Balancing Ethical Imperatives," 1433.

9. Amnesty International, "Truth, Justice and Reparation: Establishing an Effective Truth Commission," POL 30/009/2007, June 11, 2007.

10. Brian Grodsky, 'International Prosecutions and Domestic Politics: The Use of Truth Commissions as Compromise Justice in Serbia and Croatia,' *International Studies Review* 11, no. 4 (2009): 687–706. Since the early days of transitional justice scholarship, the specific applications of a state's duty to prosecute have fueled disagreements. For a summary of the debates on the duty to prosecute at the 1988 Aspen Institute Conference, one of the meetings that framed the field of transitional justice, see Paige Arthur, "How 'Transitions' Reshaped Human Rights: A Conceptual History of Transitional Justice," *Human Rights Quarterly* 31, no. 2 (2009): 321–354.

11. It should be noted that most of the studies cited in this chapter explore the effects of a number of transitional justice measures and not solely those of truth commissions. This book has an admittedly narrower yet (hopefully) more precise focus: the specific contributions of truth commissions.

12. Office of the United Nations High Commissioner for Human Rights, "Rule of Law Tools for Post-Conflict States: Truth Commissions," HR/PUB/06/1 (New York: United Nations, 2006); Amnesty International, "Truth, Justice and Reparation"; David Bloomfield, Teresa Barnes, and Luc Huyse, eds. *Reconciliation After Violent Conflict: A Handbook* (Stockholm: IDEA, 2003).

13. Eric Wiebelhaus-Brahm, *Truth Commissions and Transitional Societies: The Impact on Human Rights and Democracy* (New York: Routledge, 2010); Hunjoon Kim and Kathryn Sikkink, "Explaining the Deterrence Effect of Human Rights Prosecutions for Transitional Countries," *International Studies Quarterly* 54, no. 4 (2010): 939–963; Olsen, Payne, and Reiter, *Transitional Justice in Balance.*

14. Jack Snyder and Leslie Vinjamuri, "Trials and Errors: Principle and Pragmatism in Strategies of International Justice," *International Security* 28, no. 3 (2003): 5–44; Wiebelhaus-Brahm, *Truth Commissions and Transitional Societies.*

15. James L. Gibson and Amanda Gouws, "Truth and Reconciliation in South Africa: Attributions of Blame and the Struggle over Apartheid," *American Political Science Review* 93, no. 3 (1999): 501–517; James L. Gibson, "The Contributions of Truth to Reconciliation: Lessons from South Africa," *Journal of Conflict Resolution* 50, no. 3 (2006): 409–432.

16. James L. Gibson, "Truth, Reconciliation, and the Creation of a Human Rights Culture in South Africa," *Law & Society Review* 38, no. 1 (2004): 5–40.

17. Examples include but are not limited to Wilson, *The Politics of Truth and Reconciliation in South Africa*; William J. Long and Peter Brecke, *War and Reconciliation: Reason and Emotion in Conflict Resolution* (Cambridge, MA: MIT Press, 2003); Brahm, "Truth and Consequences"; and Emily Brooke Rodio, "More than Truth: Democracy and South Africa's Truth and Reconciliation Commission" (Ph.D. diss., Syracuse University, 2009).

18. Charles D. Kenney and Dean E. Spears, "Truth and Consequences: Do Truth Commissions Promote Democratization?," paper presented at the Annual Meeting of the American Political Science Association, Washington, DC, September 1–4, 2005; Kim and Sikkink, "Explaining the Deterrence Effect"; Olsen, Payne, and Reiter, *Transitional Justice in Balance.*

19. Oskar N. T. Thoms, James Ron, and Roland Paris, "State-Level Effects of Transitional Justice: What Do We Know?," *International Journal of Transitional Justice* 4, no. 3 (2010): 329–354.

20. Olsen, Payne, and Reiter, *Transitional Justice in Balance*, 153–154.

21. Kim and Sikkink "Explaining the Deterrence Effect."

22. Wiebelhaus-Brahm, *Truth Commissions and Transitional Societies.*

23. David Mendeloff, "Truth-Seeking, Truth-Telling, and Postconflict Peacebuilding: Curb the Enthusiasm?" *International Studies Review* 6, no. 3 (2004): 355–380, cites several Amnesty International reports to conclude that truth commissions do not contribute to human rights progress; while Carmen González Enríquez, Alexandra Barahona de Brito, and Paloma Aguilar Fernández, *The Politics of Memory: Transitional Justice in Democratizing Societies* (Oxford: Oxford University Press, 2001), puts into question the democracy-promotion effects of truth commissions based on four case studies. .

24. Emilie M. Hafner-Burton and James Ron, "Seeing Double: Human Rights Impact Through Qualitative and Quantitative Eyes," *World Politics* 61, no. 2 (2009): 360–401.

25. Olsen, Payne and Reiter, *Transitional Justice in Balance*, 181–188.

26. Freeman, *Truth Commissions and Procedural Fairness*, counts twenty-eight commissions, excluding five panels that appear as truth commissions in Hayner's first edition of *Unspeakable Truths* (2001). Wiebelhaus-Brahm, *Truth Commissions and Transitional Societies*, includes twenty-nine panels as truth commissions until 2006. Hayner's 2011 edition of *Unspeakable Truths* counts a total of forty truth commissions, including six new ones since 2006, and thirty-four commissions for the period covered by Freeman's and Wiebelhaus-Brahm's accounts.

27. Eric Wiebelhaus-Brahm, "Uncovering the Truth: Examining Truth Commission Success and Impact," *International Studies Perspectives* 8, no. 1 (2007): 16–35.

28. Snyder and Vinjamuri, "Trials and Errors," 20.

29. Paul Collier, Anke Hoeffler, and Måns Söderbom, "Post-Conflict Risks," CSAE WPS/2006-12 (Oxford: Centre for the Study of African Economies, Department of Economics, University of Oxford, 2006); Barbara Walter, "Does Conflict Beget Conflict? Explaining Recurring Civil War," *Journal of Peace Research* 41, no. 3 (2004): 371–388.

30. Stephen van Evera, *Guide to Methods for Students of Political Science* (Ithaca, NY: Cornell University Press, 1997).

31. For the distinction between product- and process-driven impact, see Hayner, "Past Truths, Present Dangers."

32. For example, the payment of reparations is an important step for the progress of transitional justice, but the meager amounts allocated to individual victims put into question the actual success. See Lisa Schlein, "War Reparations Program in Sierra Leone Needs Money," *Voice of America*, April 24, 2010.

33. It is important to note that these four categories can be considered *indicators* of impact, as they demonstrate a government's capacity and willingness to implement policies in line with a commission's recommendations, as well as *measures* of impact, since they indeed capture the public effect of a commission.

34. "Truth Commission: Argentina," USIP Truth Commission Digital Collection, accessed January 27, 2015, http://www.usip.org/publications/truth-commission-argentina.

35. "Truth Commission: Chile 90," USIP Truth Commission Digital Collection, accessed January 27, 2015, http://www.usip.org/publications/truth-commission-chile-90; Zalaquett, "Balancing Ethical Imperatives," 1435.

36. In the case of South Africa, the issue of endorsement heightened the tension within the executive: President Mandela endorsed the final report despite opposition from the governing ANC. Shea, *The South African Truth Commission*, 3.

37. "Truth Commission: Guatemala," USIP Truth Commission Digital Collection, accessed January 27, 2015, http://www.usip.org/resources/truth-commission-guatemala.

38. Elizabeth Knight, "Facing the Past: Retrospective Justice as a Means to Promote Democracy in Nigeria," *Connecticut Law Review* 35 (2002): 867–914.

39. Joanna R. Quinn, "Constraints: The Un-Doing of the Ugandan Truth Commission," *Human Rights Quarterly* 26, no. 2 (2004): 419.

40. Teivo Teivainen, "Truth, Justice and Legal Impunity: Dealing with Past Human Rights Violations in Chile," *Nordic Journal of Latin American and Caribbean Studies* 30, no. 2 (2000): 72.

41. Anna Neistat, *Recurring Nightmare: State Responsibility for "Disappearances" and Abductions in Sri Lanka* (New York: Human Rights Watch, 2008).

42. Joanna R. Quinn, "Haiti's Failed Truth Commission: Lessons in Transitional Justice," *Journal of Human Rights* 8, no. 3 (2009): 270.

43. "Truth Commission: Timor-Leste (East Timor)," USIP Truth Commission Digital Collection, accessed January 27, 2015, http://www.usip.org/publications/truth-commission-timor-leste-east-timor.

44. "Truth Commission: Sierra Leone," USIP Truth Commission Digital Collection, accessed January 27, 2015, http://www.usip.org/publications/truth-commission-sierra-leone.

45. Paul James-Allen, Aaron Weah, and Lizzie Goodfriend, *Beyond the Truth and Reconciliation Commission: Transitional Justice Options in Liberia* (New York: International Center for Transitional Justice, 2010), 27–28.

46. Cath Collins, "State Terror and the Law: The (Re)judicialization of Human Rights Accountability in Chile and El Salvador," *Latin American Perspectives* 35, no. 5 (2008): 33.

47. Yusuf, *Transitional Justice, Judicial Accountability*, 45.

48. There are ongoing efforts in Liberia, which have not yet changed policy. See "Liberia's First Victims Group Holds Workshop in Monrovia," *New Liberian*, May 27, 2009.

49. Wiebelhaus-Brahm, *Truth Commissions and Transitional Societies*, 9; Amnesty International, "Truth, Justice and Reparation."

50. Charles Beitz, "What Human Rights Mean," *Daedalus* 132, no. 1 (2003): 36–46.

51. Margaret E. Keck and Kathryn Sikkink, *Activists Beyond Borders: Advocacy Networks in International Politics* (Ithaca, NY: Cornell University Press, 1998); Andrew Moravcsik, "The Origins of Human Rights Regimes: Democratic Delegation in Postwar Europe," *International Organization* 54, no. 2 (1997): 217–252; Alejandro Anaya, "Transnational and Domestic Processes in the Definition of Human Rights Policies in Mexico," *Human Rights Quarterly* 31, no. 1 (2009): 35–58.

52. Beth Simmons, *Mobilizing for Human Rights: International Law in Domestic Politics* (Cambridge: Cambridge University Press, 2009), 154.

53. Hayner, *Unspeakable Truths*: 166–167; David Backer, "Watching a Bargain Unravel? A Panel Study of Victims' Attitudes About Transitional Justice in Cape Town, South Africa," *International Journal of Transitional Justice* 4, no. 3 (2010): 443–456; Christopher J. Colvin, "Overview of the Reparations Program in South Africa," in *The Handbook of Reparations*, ed. Pablo de Greiff (Oxford: Oxford University Press, 2006).

54. Oettler, "Encounters with History."

55. The Peruvian reparations law was passed in 2005, but the actual payments to individuals did not begin until 2011. For the role of civil society groups in pressuring for the legislation and implementation of the reparations program in Peru, see Laplante and Theidon, "Truth with Consequences."

56. "Sierra Leone: Truth and Reconciliation Commission," accessed January 27, 2015, http://www.justiceinperspective.org.za/africa/sierra-leone/truth-and-reconciliation-commission.html.

57. Domestic and international groups have successfully lobbied for the 2012 National Reparations Programme Bill. See Amnesty International, *Timor-Leste: Remembering the Past; Recommendations to Effectively Establish the "National Reparations Programme" and "Public Memory Institute"* (London: Amnesty International, 2012).

58. "Over the next few years, Amnesty International and local human rights groups repeatedly urged the government to publish the commission's report and ensure that any persons

implicated in human rights violations be brought to justice." Hayner, *Unspeakable Truths*, 244–245. Also see "Commission of Inquiry: Nepal 90," USIP Truth Commission Digital Collection, accessed January 27, 2015,http://www.usip.org/resources/commission-inquiry-nepal-90.

59. For Sri Lanka, see Hayner, *Unspeakable Truths*, 247–248.

60. The final report "was not made public until a year later [1997], after considerable pressure from rights groups." Hayner, *Unspeakable Truths*, 53, 54. The report enjoyed limited publicity as a result of the fact that the publication was in French, rather than Creole, and few copies were available to the public.

61. "Finally, in January 2005, after pushing for the release of the report for over two and a half years, several civil society organizations independently released the report by placing it on the internet." Hayner, *Unspeakable Truths*, 250.

62. For the case of Timor-Leste, see "Timor-Leste: Illustrated Version of Truth Report," ICTJ Features, August 31, 2010.

63. Furthermore, new civil society organizations were formed in South Africa, Peru, Sierra Leone, and Liberia to monitor the progress of reforms in the wake of the truth commissions.

64. The commission was nonetheless helpful in drawing the lists of beneficiaries: "To receive payment, victims had to be listed in the final report of the National Commission on the Disappearance of Persons (Conadep), or have been reported to the state's Human Rights Office and confirmed as disappeared or killed. The total tally of potential beneficiaries includes family members of about 15,000 disappeared persons." Verdeja, "Reparations in Democratic Transitions," 129.

65. For the data on vetting, see Hayner, *Unspeakable Truths*, 280–284; Olsen, Payne, and Reiter, *Transitional Justice in Balance*, 181–188.

66. Many violators who were dismissed from one position found other public jobs in El Salvador. See Mike Kaye, "The Role of Truth Commissions in the Search for Justice, Reconciliation and Democratisation: The Salvadorean and Honduran Cases," *Journal of Latin American Studies* 29 (1997): 693–716.

67. Mark Freeman and Priscilla B. Hayner, "Truth-Telling," in Bloomfield, Barnes, and Huyse, *Reconciliation After Violent Conflict*, 126–127; Paige Arthur, " 'Fear of the Future, Lived Through the Past': Pursuing Transitional Justice in the Wake of Ethnic Conflict," in Arthur, *Identities in Transition*, 289–290; Fullard and Rousseau, "Truth Telling, Identities, and Power," 88; Stephan Landsman, "Alternative Responses to Serious Human Rights Abuses: Of Prosecution and Truth Commissions," *Law and Contemporary Problems* 59, no. 4 (1996): 89; Wiebelhaus-Brahm, *Truth Commissions and Transitional Societies*, 12.

68. In Guatemala, Bishop Juan Gerardi was assassinated in April 1998, soon after the publication of a church-backed human rights report under his direction. In Peru, threats against the truth commission staff, most notably against its president Salomón Lerner, have been reported several times.

69. Wiebelhaus-Brahm, *Truth Commissions and Transitional Societies*, 13.

70. José Zalaquett, "Confronting Human Rights Violations Committed by Former Governments: Applicable Principles and Political Constraints," *Hamline Law Review* 13, no. 3 (1990): 629.

71. Minow, *Between Vengeance and Forgiveness*.

72. Olsen, Payne, and Reiter, *Transitional Justice in Balance*.

73. Payne, *Unsettling Accounts*.

74. James L. Gibson stands out in explaining the causal mechanism for how historiography may have promoted attitudes toward reconciliation in the context of the South African transition. Accordingly, the publication of historical facts by the truth commission creates cognitive dissonance in individual and group perceptions of apartheid. The need to mitigate "collective dogmatism" forces individuals to rethink their past actions and to renounce earlier self-justifications that interpreted political conflict in terms of absolute evil and absolute good. Gibson, "Truth, Reconciliation."

75. Brandon Hamber and Richard A. Wilson, "Symbolic Closure Through Memory, Reparation and Revenge in Post-Conflict Societies," *Journal of Human Rights* 1, no. 1 (2002): 35–53.

76. Susan Dwyer, "Reconciliation for Realists," *Ethics and International Affairs* 13, no. 1 (2006): 81–98.

77. This does not imply that not instituting a truth commission would facilitate consensus building. As the example of Bosnia and Herzegovina suggests, the absence of society-wide truth-telling procedures might delay reconciliation further, as widely divergent accounts of why a violent conflict started and who the perpetrators were inhibit dialogue and consensus between ethnic and political groups. See Roland Kostic, "Nationbuilding as an Instrument of Peace? Exploring Local Attitudes Towards International Nationbuilding and Reconciliation in Bosnia and Herzegovina," *Civil Wars* 10, no. 4 (2008): 384–412.

78. Ernesto Verdeja, "Derrida and the Impossibility of Forgiveness," *Contemporary Political Theory* 3, no. 1 (2004): 23–47; Colleen Murphy, *A Moral Theory of Political Reconciliation* (New York: Cambridge University Press, 2010).

79. David Gairdner, *Truth in Transition: The Role of Truth Commissions in Political Transition in Chile and El Salvador* (Bergen: Chr. Michelsen Institute, 1999); Oettler, "Encounters with History."

80. Impact on social norms refers to the acceptance of a commission's findings and its capacity to foster acknowledgment of and responsibility for past abuses and not mere exposure to the commission; exposure to an idea does not lead to its automatic internalization. See Chapman, "Truth Finding in the Transitional Justice Process." My modest assumption is that awareness of a truth commission's work (as opposed to no exposure whatsoever) increases a person's likelihood of adopting its central message.

81. Elizabeth Oglesby, "Historical Memory and the Limits of Peace Education: Examining Guatemala's *Memory of Silence* and the Politics of Curriculum Design," in *Teaching the Violent Past: History Education and Reconciliation*, ed. Elizabeth A. Cole (New York: Rowman and Littlefield, 2007), 175–202.

82. Jason S. Abrams and Priscilla B. Hayner, "Documenting, Acknowledging and Publicizing the Truth," in *Post-Conflict Justice*, ed. M. Cherif Bassiouni (Ardsley, NY: Transnational Publishers, 2002), 283–293; Amnesty International, "Truth, Justice and Reparation."

83. I do not separate positive judicial impact *with* and *without* civil society mobilization because in all observed cases of impact, significant civil society activism on the part of domestic and international actors has been a major intervening factor.

84. Freeman, *Truth Commissions and Procedural Fairness.*

85. Peter Harris and Ben Reilly, eds., *Democracy and Deep-Rooted Conflict: Options for Negotiators* (Stockholm: International Institute for Democracy and Electoral Assistance, 1998); Priscilla Hayner, "Truth Commissions: Exhuming the Past," *NACLA Report on the Americas* 32, no. 2 (1998): 30–32.

86. Jon Elster, *Closing the Books: Transitional Justice in Historical Perspective* (Cambridge: Cambridge University Press, 2004): 116–117.

87. Mark J. Osiel, "Why Prosecute? Critics of Punishment for Mass Atrocity," *Human Rights Quarterly* 22, no. 1 (2000): 118–147.

88. "In transitional justice circles, the indistinction between forgiveness and amnesty has been rendered murkier by the fact that the one instance where binding amnesty decisions were made by a truth commission, South Africa, was also an instance where the idiom of forgiveness played a central role." Rebecca Saunders, "Questionable Associations: The Role of Forgiveness in Transitional Justice," *International Journal of Transitional Justice* 5, no. 1 (2011): 125.

89. The temptation to establish truth commissions in order to avoid justice has provoked normative debates over the nature of the relationship between truth, justice, and reconciliation. Juan Méndez argues against counterpoising truth and justice, as well as reconciliation and justice, as

binary opposites. Instead, he claims: "Truth commissions are important in their own right, but they work best when conceived as a key component in a holistic process of truth-telling, justice, reparations, and eventual reconciliation." Juan E. Méndez, "National Reconciliation, Transnational Justice, and the International Criminal Court," *Ethics & International Affairs* 15, no. 1 (2001): 29. Likewise, Ernesto Verdeja resists the appropriation of reconciliation as a pretext for impunity and amnesia. He argues for a notion of reconciliation understood as "mutual respect among former enemies" that implies truth telling, accountability, victim recognition, and the rule of law as fundamental tenets. Ernesto Verdeja, *Unchopping a Tree: Reconciliation in the Aftermath of Political Violence* (Philadelphia: Temple University Press, 2009).

90. Carla del Ponte, prosecutor for the International Criminal Tribunal for the Former Yugoslavia (ICTY), for instance, helped stop the formation of a truth commission for Bosnia because she feared a commission would undermine judicial accountability. Charles T. Call, "Is Transitional Justice Really Just?," *Brown Journal of World Affairs* 11, no. 1 (2004): 112 n. 14.

91. For data on judicial impact, see Hayner, *Unspeakable Truths*, 280–284; Hunjoon Kim and Kathryn Sikkink, "Detailed Description of Human Rights Prosecutions: Domestic Transitional Human Rights Prosecution (By Country)."

92. For the specific case of Guatemala, see Oglesby, "Historical Memory," in *Teaching the Violent Past*: 199.

93. Hayner, *Unspeakable Truths*, 280.

94. Hayner, *Unspeakable Truths*, 247. Also see "Chad: Minister of Justice's Commission of Inquiry on the Crimes Committed by the Hissène Habré Regime," accessed January 27, 2015, http://www.justiceinperspective.org.za/africa/chad/minister-of-justices-commission-of -inquiry-on-the-crimes-committed-by-the-hissene-habre-regime.html.

95. Elizabeth M. Evenson, "Truth and Justice in Sierra Leone: Coordination Between Commission and Court," *Columbia Law Review* 104, no. 3 (2004): 730–767.

96. Max Pensky, "Amnesty on Trial: Impunity, Accountability, and the Norms of International Law," *Ethics & Global Politics* 1, nos. 1–2 (2008), accessed January 27, 2015,http:// www.ethicsandglobalpolitics.net/index.php/egp/article/view/1816.

97. In the case of Liberia, the commission was mandated to recommend, not grant, amnesty to presumed perpetrators. The commission mandate is available at http://trcofliberia.org/about /trc-mandate (accessed January, 27, 2015).

98. Data available at http://www.justice.gov.za/trc/amntrans/index.htm (accessed January, 27, 2015).

99. In fact, the South African TRC exposed many presumed perpetrators whose applications for amnesty were rejected. However, "none recommended by the TRC were prosecuted." Hayner, *Unspeakable Truths*, 281.

100. "The [TRC]'s work was confidential, and both the [Special Court for Sierra Leone] (SCSL) and the TRC made clear that there would be no sharing of information. Thus nothing from the TRC was utilized by the SCSL. Also, the Lomé Accord amnesty precluded domestic prosecutions." E-mail communication with Beth Dougherty, professor of international relations, October 11, 2011.

101. The UN representative at the Sierra Leonean peace process introduced a last-minute disclaimer: "The United Nations holds the understanding that the amnesty and pardon in Article IX of the agreement shall not apply to international crimes of genocide, crimes against humanity, war crimes and other serious violations of international humanitarian law." Quoted from Priscilla B. Hayner, *Negotiating Peace in Sierra Leone: Confronting the Justice Challenge* (Geneva: Centre for Humanitarian Dialogue, 2007), 5.

102. Margaret Popkin, and Naomi Roht-Arriaza, "Truth as Justice: Investigatory Commissions in Latin America," *Law & Social Inquiry* 20, no. 1 (1995): 79–116.

103. "The most damaging false understanding about the TRC [in Sierra Leone] was that it would provide immediate support to victims, the idea that the TRC was going to give people money or supplies." Gearoid Millar, "Assessing Local Experiences of Truth-Telling in Sierra Leone: Getting to 'Why' Through a Qualitative Case Study Analysis," *International Journal of Transitional Justice* 4, no. 3 (2010): 491.

104. Alison Bisset, *Truth Commissions and Criminal Courts* (Cambridge: Cambridge University Press, 2012), 6.

Chapter 5. Explaining Variation in Truth Commission Impact (I)

Note to epigraph: Lerner's comments are quoted from John E. Drabinski, "'That Gesture of Recognition': An Interview with Salomón Lerner Febres," *Humanity: An International Journal of Human Rights, Humanitarianism, and Development* 4, no. 1 (2013): 171–180.

1. Ascanio Cavallo argues that the truth commission idea originated with a report submitted by Zalaquett to the human rights commission of Aylwin's "presidential program group." Ascanio Cavallo, *La historia oculta de la transición* (Santiago: Grijalbo, 1998), 19.

2. Comité de Cooperación para la Paz en Chile was created in October 1973 by various religious denominations to provide legal and social assistance to the victims of human rights violations. It operated under the most repressive phase of the dictatorship and was forced to dissolve in November 1975. The Catholic Church continued the assistance and documentation work in the Vicaría de la Solidaridad from 1976 onward.

3. The Concertación was the electoral coalition of socialist, social democratic, and Christian democratic parties that put an end to Augusto Pinochet's military regime and ruled between 1990 and 2010.

4. Patricio Aylwin, interviewed by Margarita Serrano and Ascanio Cavallo, in Margarita Serrano and Ascanio Cavallo, *El poder de la paradoja: 14 lecciones políticas de la vida de Patricio Aylwin* (Santiago: Norma, 2006).

5. The Concertación won the majority of elected seats in both houses, but the addition of nine unelected senators designated by Pinochet and his allies shifted the balance in favor of right-wing sectors.

6. Teivainen, "Truth, Justice and Legal Impunity."

7. Roberto Garretón notes that although a law would be preferable over a presidential decree to establish such a commission, the right-wing Senate majority that "did not emanate from popular will" and "did not accept the truth during the dictatorship" made such an initiative impossible. Roberto Garretón, "Política de derechos humanos del gobierno democrático," *Política y Espíritu* 46, no. 391 (1992): 23.

8. Domestic human rights defenders and international human rights NGOs sharply criticized the decision not to include torture cases. See Amnesty International, *Chile: El legado de los derechos humanos*, AI: AMR 22/01/91/s (Madrid: Editorial Amnistía Internacional, 1991), 4.

9. The only crime excluded from amnesty was the assassination of Orlando Letelier, a politician and diplomat during the Allende government, and his assistant Ronni Moffitt, in Washington, DC, on September 21, 1976.

10. Felipe Portales, *Chile: Una democracia tutelada* (Santiago: Editorial Sudamericana Chilena, 2000), 69.

11. For an overview of the political and legal context in the early years of the transition, see Rebecca Evans, "Pinochet in London—Pinochet in Chile: International and Domestic Politics in Human Rights Policy," *Human Rights Quarterly* 28, no. 1 (2006): 207–244.

12. Zalaquett, "Balancing Ethical Imperatives."

13. *Report of the Chilean National Commission on Truth and Reconciliation*, vol. 1, trans. Phillip E. Berryman (Notre Dame, IN: University of Notre Dame Press, 1993), 7.

14. The Chilean military did not reveal any information regarding deaths and disappearances, as its members were not coerced to testify before the commission and no amnesty-for-confession mechanism was in place.

15. Supreme Decree No. 355, art. 8, para. 2.

16. *Report of the Chilean National Commission*, 23.

17. *Report of the Chilean National Commission*, 18.

18. Jaime Castillo Velasco, from Aylwin's Christian Democratic Party, was the only member with ongoing party affiliation.

19. There are various interpretations for why the right-wing politicians declined. Sergio Onofre Jarpa, the president of the RN in 1990, argued that the better strategy for a truth commission would be to recruit "independent persons" who were not active party members. "Jarpa: Renovación apoya comisión de la verdad, pero . . . ," *El Fortin*, April 24, 1990. Miguel Otero, the vice president of the RN, gave deeper insights into the nature of the party's refusal when he declared that the negotiations with the government failed for the following reasons: first, the time period covered by the mandate of the commission (1973–1990) ran counter to the RN's suggestion to include the pre-1973 period of political polarization. Second, in his view the commission was devoted to replacing the judiciary rather than clarifying issues that could not be covered by courts, such as the "causes and origins of violence in Chile, those responsible for [violence], victims, and how to solve the problems caused by violence." Finally, he argued that the RN was against using the commission to initiate a campaign against the armed forces. In other words, the political Right envisioned a commission that would emphasize how the military had to take action to save the country from political and economic collapse in 1973 and preferably keep silent about the human rights violations. See Andrés Allamand, "Verdad a medias," *La Tercera*, April 29, 1990.

20. Martín was a senator designated by the outgoing regime when appointed to the commission. He took part in the military government as the president of a government-appointed human rights commission analyzing exile. Cea was a professor of law. Vial served in the military government as minister of education.

21. Interview with journalist Hugo Mery, February 3, 2009.

22. Despite his cautious approach, Aylwin admits that representatives of the military had objected to the designation of human rights defenders like José Zalaquett and Jaime Castillo Velasco. Serrano and Cavallo, *El poder de la paradoja*, 149–150.

23. Zalaquett notes that the numerical balance of commissioners and the unanimity rule in making decisions enhanced the credibility of the commission. Interview with José Zalaquett, January 20, 2009.

24. The agency of the right-wing commissioners deserves special attention. Although some members, like Gonzalo Vial, pulled the commission toward a more conservative stance, especially in contextualizing political violence, there were occasions in which right-wing commissioners acted as the harshest critics of the military and judiciary during the dictatorship: "The report's stinging descriptions of law and the judiciary's failure—in civilian as well as military courts, at the Supreme Court level as well as lower levels—came from the likes of Ricardo Martín, a former Supreme Court justice, and José Luis Cea, a constitutional scholar." Stern, *Reckoning with Pinochet*, 81. This demonstrates that constraints on a commission's mandate and composition delimit its capacity to exercise agency, but even restrictive commissions produce surprising results.

25. Jo-Marie Burt, *Political Violence and the Authoritarian State in Peru: Silencing Civil Society* (Chicago: University of Chicago Press, 2003).

26. Alberto Fujimori was elected president in 1990. Two years later he suspended democratic institutions in a self-coup and ruled Peru for eight more years with a mixture of nominal elections, draconian emergency and antiterrorism measures, and corruption.

27. Furthermore, the domestic human rights movement was articulating the need for a truth commission before transnational actors began to promote the idea: "the TRC in Peru was the result of an internal process fed by external factors." Coletta Youngers, of the Washington Office on Latin America (WOLA), quoted in Parker, "Seeking Truth," 232–233.

28. For Fujimori, the Roundtable was a convenient maneuver to appease the democratic opposition and international public opinion; therefore he appointed four representatives of the government. Interview with Beatriz Alva, June 10, 2009.

29. The participants from the human rights movement were Jorge Santistevan de Noriega, the human rights ombudsman, Luis Bambarén, the president of the Peruvian Episcopal Conference, and Sofía Macher, the executive secretary of the Coordinadora.

30. Rafael Roncagliolo, "Procesos post conflicto y Comisiones de la Verdad" (presented at "De la negación al reconocimiento," Seminario Internacional Procesos Post Comisiones de la Verdad, Lima, June 4–6, 2003).

31. Andrew F. Cooper and Thomas Legler, "A Tale of Two Mesas: The OAS Defense of Democracy in Peru and Venezuela," *Global Governance* 11, no. 4 (2005): 438.

32. Several human rights defenders served as ministers and high-level bureaucrats in the early years of the transition, but the alliance between the state and human rights organizations came to an end under the Toledo and García presidencies. Interviews with civil society activist and politician Susana Villarán, May 19, 2009, and human rights activist Pablo Rojas, April 22, 2009.

33. The Peruvian commission was not the outcome of a peace accord between the government and the armed insurgency, as the Shining Path had already been defeated militarily by 2000. The outgoing authoritarian government did not enjoy the de facto political power that Pinochet's allies did in Chile, as the Fujimori regime ended in collapse. The military was seriously demoralized, in great part because a number of top generals had been captured taking bribes from Fujimori's secret service chief, Vladimiro Montesinos, in a series of embarrassing video recordings. An important organizational actor that survived the internal armed conflict and authoritarianism was the American Revolutionary Popular Alliance (APRA), a long-standing political party led by Alan García after he returned from exile in January 2001. However, the party lost the 2001 presidential election and was a minority in the Congress.

34. Rebecca Root, "Through the Window of Opportunity: The Transitional Justice Network in Peru," *Human Rights Quarterly* 31, no. 2 (2009): 452–473.

35. Juan E. Méndez and Javier Mariezcurrena, review of *Unspeakable Truths: Facing the Challenge of Truth Commissions*, by Priscilla B. Hayner, *Human Rights Quarterly* 25, no. 1 (2003): 248.

36. An external boost to the commission's juridical work came from the Inter-American Court of Human Rights: on March 14, 2001, the international court declared the Amnesty Law of 1995 without legal effect in the decision *Barrios Altos v. Peru*. The ruling triggered criminal proceedings against Alberto Fujimori, Vladimiro Montesinos, and the infamous death squad La Colina. As a result, the findings of the newly founded CVR enjoyed increased potential for judicial impact.

37. The most controversial addition was the retired lieutenant general of the air force Luis Arias Graziani. His inclusion generated discontent within the commission because he was an adviser to President Toledo at the time of his appointment. The Ayacucho-based victims' association ANFASEP opposed the designation of Arias Graziani on the grounds of his military background. Commissioner Carlos Tapia argued that the inclusion of a presidential adviser was incompatible with the autonomy of the CVR, but the president of the commission, Salomón Lerner, endorsed the new member.

38. The only commissioner who had participated in the Fujimori regime was Beatriz Alva, and, not surprisingly, her inclusion sparked serious controversy around June 2001. She was a latecomer to the Fujimori cabinet and was unscathed by the corruption scandal. In her own words, the commissioners slowly accepted her presence thanks to her "good work." Interview with Beatriz Alva, June 10, 2009.

39. Three members came from religious institutions, all known for their support for human rights defense: Gastón Garatea, José Antunez de Mayolo, and Humberto Lay. Luis Bambarén was an observer.

40. Interview with Salomón Lerner, June 3, 2009.

41. Carlos Basombrío Iglesias, "Sendero Luminoso and Human Rights: A Perverse Logic That Captured the Country," in *Shining and Other Paths: War and Society in Peru, 1980–1995*, ed. Steve J. Stern (Durham, NC: Duke University Press, 1998), 425–446.

42. Interview with José Coronel, coordinator of the CVR in Ayacucho, July 2, 2009.

43. Gustavo Gorriti, *Shining Path: A History of the Millenarian War in Peru*, trans. Robin Kirk (Chapel Hill: University of North Carolina Press, 1999).

44. Hubert Lansier (1929–2003) was a Belgian priest known for his advocacy of persons wrongly accused of terrorism during Peru's internal conflict. Pilar Coll (1929–2012), a Spanish national, defended the fundamental rights of prisoners and was the executive secretary of the Coordinadora between 1987 and 1992.

45. Roughly two-thirds of the commission budget was funded by the Peruvian government, while several foreign governments and international organizations covered the remainder. See the commission's website, accessed January 27, 2015, http://www.cverdad.org.pe/lacomision /ifinanciera/pdfs/01financ.pdf.

46. Sectors of the Left and human rights groups opposed the inclusion of civilian attacks resulting in the death of security personnel, arguing that those cases were already judged in courts, and therefore did not require further investigation. José Iván Colorado García, "Violaciones a los derechos humanos y transición a la democracia en Chile (1990–1994)" (presented at I Encuentro de Jóvenes Investigadores en Historia Contemporánea de la Asociación de Historia Contemporánea, Zaragoza, September 26–28, 2007).

47. It is worth noting that despite the decision to hold public hearings, the South African Truth and Reconciliation Commission separated the healing function of the testimonies from the actual task of finding facts. The testimonies were not used as data for verifying victims. See Wilson, *The Politics of Truth and Reconciliation in South Africa*, 41.

48. However, the legal/positivistic approach to truth finding did not alter the negative perceptions of the commission's right-wing critics. Jaime Guzmán, leader of the UDI in 1990, commented that the commission provided the presumed perpetrators with no incentives to collaborate, as "accused persons would . . . not accept presenting their defense before a commission that, however respectable its members could be, is not a competent tribunal of justice for this purpose." "Deben respetarse las funciones propias del poder judicial," *El Mercurio*, April 7, 1990, my translation.

49. As of 1988, the AFDD list contained 763 cases of disappearance.

50. *Report of the Chilean National Commission*, 17.

51. The minutes of these meetings are not available to the public.

52. Although the commission worked in the absence of meaningful cooperation from the military and the police, a confidential official request for each identified case of disappearance was sent to the respective institution in order to obtain further information on the fate and whereabouts of these persons. However, this last attempt at engaging the repressive institutions was likewise fruitless: "Although almost all of these requests were answered, none of the answers offered any information that could substantially serve [the] purpose [of determining what had

happened to those persons identified as disappeared]." *Report of the Chilean National Commission*, 21–22.

53. "Ejército entregó amplio informe a comisión Rettig," *El Mercurio*, August 7, 1990.

54. *Report of the Chilean National Commission*, 43.

55. *Report of the Chilean National Commission*, 33.

56. *Report of the Chilean National Commission*, 34–35.

57. Mark Ensalaco, "Truth Commissions for Chile and El Salvador: A Report and Assessment," *Human Rights Quarterly* 16, no. 4 (1994): 664.

58. Hernán Vidal, *Política cultural de la memoria histórica* (Santiago: Mosquito Comunicaciones, 1997).

59. Zalaquett notes that the commissioners "agreed to disagree" on the justifiability of the coup itself. Interview with José Zalaquett, January 20, 2009.

60. Coletta Youngers, "En busca de la verdad y la justicia: La Coordinadora Nacional de Derechos Humanos del Perú," in *Historizar el pasado vivo en América Latina*, ed. Anne Pérotin-Dumon, 26, available at http://www.historizarelpasadovivo.cl (accessed January 27, 2015).

61. The system was set up by Patrick Ball and his colleagues, and employed by several investigatory bodies, including the truth commissions in South Africa, Guatemala, and Peru.

62. González Cueva, "Contribution of the Peruvian Truth and Reconciliation Commission to Prosecutions," 62.

63. González Cueva, "Contribution," 62.

64. Interview with Iris Jave, May 19, 2009.

65. Interview with Carlos Landeo, April 13, 2009; interview with Susana Cori, April 20, 2009.

66. Annex 2 in the final report describes the estimation methodology. The Peruvian version was developed by Patrick Ball, Jana Asher, David Sulmont, and Daniel Manrique.

67. Patrick Ball, Jana Asher, David Sulmont, and Daniel Manrique, *How Many Peruvians Have Died?* (Washington, DC: American Association for the Advancement of Science, 2003).

68. David Sulmont notes that the estimation was based on data collected from the CVR, the ombudsman's office, and various human rights NGOs. As the baseline number of verified victims in this database has been increasing with new testimonies, the approximated number is likely to shift upward, as well. Interview with David Sulmont, May 27, 2009. Many victims and victims' relatives who had not testified before the truth commission have registered with the Reparations Council. Based on the new baseline level, the estimation of the death toll might exceed 100,000. "Serían 100 mil las víctimas de la guerra interna en el Perú," *El Comercio*, October 7, 2011.

69. The CVR was much more sensitive to the gender aspect of human rights violations than its Chilean counterpart—although not without its problems. Interview with Bettina Valdez, May 18, 2009; also see Michele Leiby, "Digging in the Archives: The Promise and Perils of Primary Documents," *Politics & Society* 37, no. 1 (2009): 75–100. There was a separate section on sexual violence in the CVR's final report that put the number of victims, women and men, at 531. The sensitivity to gender demonstrates in part the evolution of truth commissions in the 1990s. While the Argentine and Chilean commissions by and large ignored the gender factor in explaining human rights violations, "commissions in Guatemala, South Africa, and Peru paid particular attention to gender even though their mandates were formally gender neutral. They interpreted mandate language regarding torture and ill treatment as the legal channels to address sexual violence." Nesiah, "Gender and Truth Commission Mandates."

70. *Informe Final*, 161.

71. *Informe Final*, 162.

72. Sofía Macher, *Recomendaciones vs. realidades: Avances y desafíos en el post-CVR Perú* (Lima: Instituto de Defensa Legal, 2007), 11; translation mine.

73. Interview with Eduardo Toche, May 14, 2009.

74. It is important to note that Aylwin did not argue for a political or juridical mechanism for forgiveness of the kind that was later employed in South Africa. "I cannot forgive for another. Forgiveness is not imposed by decree. Forgiveness requires repentance on one hand, and generosity on the other." Aylwin, quoted in Human Rights Watch, *Human Rights Watch World Report 1992: Events of 1991* (New York: Human Rights Watch, 1992), 162.

75. The army had insisted on justifying the deaths as casualties of war during and after the military regime. When the first discovery of a clandestine grave in the northern town on Pisagua shocked the nation in June 1990, the army was quick to issue a statement calling the dead "casualties of war." Ascanio Cavallo notes that during the first National Security Meeting following Aylwin's public endorsement of the final report, generals reacted in general to the "historical framework" of the final report, especially its rejection of the internal war thesis. Cavallo, *La historia oculta de la transición*, 92.

76. Of the 1,198 cases of disappeared persons investigated by the Rettig Commission and the follow-up National Reparation and Reconciliation Corporation only a handful were found to contain errors.

77. The liberal wing of the RN, represented by figures such as Andrés Allamand, had a more positive attitude toward the final report than their conservative colleagues. Gregory Weeks, *The Military and Politics in Postauthoritarian Chile* (Tuscaloosa: University of Alabama Press, 2003), 74.

78. The fact that the CNRR did not have the authority to discover the whereabouts of the disappeared individuals elicited criticism from victims' organizations.

79. It is important to note, however, that victims of torture did not receive compensation because the commission was not mandated to investigate individual torture cases. This omission animated a civil society campaign that resulted in the 2003 torture commission and subsequent reparations for torture victims.

80. Elizabeth Lira, "Human Rights in Chile: The Long Road to Truth, Justice, and Reparations," in *After Pinochet: The Chilean Road to Democracy and the Market*, ed. Silvia Borzutzky and Lois Hecht Oppenheim (Gainesville: University Press of Florida, 2006).

81. Teresa Meade, "Holding the Junta Accountable: Chile's 'Sitios de Memoria' and the History of Torture, Disappearance, and Death," *Radical History Review* 79 (Winter 2001): 123–139.

82. The recuperation of Villa Grimaldi as a material and symbolic site began in the early 1990s with the initiative of one individual, Pedro Alejandro Matta. He had been detained and tortured by DINA in 1976 and went into exile afterward. Upon his return to Chile, he conducted an independent investigation of the abuses committed at Villa Grimaldi and discovered many more cases of disappearance than previously assumed. Later, Matta took part in the creation of the Association of Former Political Prisoners of Villa Grimaldi (Agrupación de ex-Prisioneros Políticos de Villa Grimaldi). The association's activism bore fruits, as the municipality granted them the permission to build a park at the site of the former torture center. Interview with Pedro Alejandro Matta, October 6, 2008; interview with Ana Torrealba, October 20, 2008.

83. Mara Loveman, "High-Risk Collective Action: Defending Human Rights in Chile, Uruguay, and Argentina," *American Journal of Sociology* 104, no. 2 (1998): 496; original emphasis.

84. "Realizan balance a 10 años de Informe Rettig," *El Mercurio*, March 3, 2001.

85. Interview with Juana Guerra, March 6, 2009; interview with María Paz Vergara, March 6, 2009.

86. Interview with Viviana Díaz, November 28, 2008.

87. The first wave of selective violence organized by the DINA took place in 1974 and 1975, and its victims were the members of the Revolutionary Left Movement (MIR), a leftist organization popular among the university youth. The relatives of the disappeared MIRistas (mostly mothers) did not necessarily share their children's zeal for political activism; in fact, many of them were not even aware that their relatives participated in resistance against the dictatorship. The

disappearance of their relatives at the hands of the secret police forced them to take action, for the first time in life for many of them, that required political organization and confrontation with state agents. While they were struggling with this life-transforming experience, the dictatorship's second wave of targeted repression hit the Communist Party in 1976. The victims were not only the inexperienced militants; the party's leadership was disarticulated as well. The Communist Party was much older and institutionalized than the MIR: founded in 1922, the party was known to generate a strong sense of identity among its members, and it had already survived a wave of repression and clandestine existence between 1948 and 1958. In other words, the relatives of the Communist Party victims were often members of the party themselves, well aware of the risks of political action under the dictatorship, and prepared to participate in opposition politics (including human rights activism). They held together thanks to a strong party identity that they continued to cultivate in their new regroupings. When they arrived at the Vicaría in 1976, they found it relatively easy to occupy leadership positions among the victims' relatives, transform the organizational structure along the Communist Party model, and oblige other members to follow their vision of political action. Vidal, *Política cultural de la memoria histórica*, 78–79; interview with Norma Matus, March 11, 2009.

88. Interview with Roberto D'Orival, November 20, 2008.

89. Hugo Fruhling, "Nonprofit Organizations as Opposition to Authoritarian Rule: The Case of Human Rights Organizations in Chile," in *The Nonprofit Sector in International Perspective*, ed. Estelle James (New York: Oxford University Press, 1989), 372.

90. Randy B. Reiter, M. V. Zunzunegui, and Jose Quiroga, "Guidelines for Field Reporting of Basic Human Rights Violations," Human Rights Quarterly 8, no. 4 (1986): 628–653.

91. Not surprisingly, victims' groups like AFDD led the prosecutions abroad, once the domestic route to justice was closed off. Cath Collins, "Grounding Global Justice: International Networks and Domestic Human Rights Accountability in Chile and El Salvador," *Journal of Latin American Studies* 38, no. 4 (2006): 711–738.

92. The APRA published its official position vis-à-vis the CVR. See Partido Aprista Peruano, Comité Ejecutivo Nacional, "El APRA y la Comisión de la Verdad," statement no. 26-2003, adopted August 13, 2003, Lima.

93. The contrasting positions within the Unidad Nacional were embodied by Lourdes Flores, who by and large expressed support for the CVR, and Rafael Rey, who not only condemned the final report but also insinuated some commissioners' links to terrorism.

94. A number of Congress members, led by APRA's Edgar Núñez, sued the commission for breach of impartiality, but the prosecutor dropped the case in February 2010.

95. Confederación Nacional de Instituciones Empresariales Privadas (CONFIEP), "Pronunciamiento en torno a las conclusiones del Informe de la Comisión de la Verdad y la Reconciliación," September 26, 2003.

96. *Informe Final*, 8:323.

97. To this end, the Defenders of Democracy Against Terrorism Association (Asociación Defensores de la Democracia Contra el Terrorismo [ADDCOT]) and the Retired Generals and Admirals Association of Peru (Asociación de Oficiales Generales y Almirantes en Retiro del Perú [ADOGEN]) were established.

98. The Toledo government entertained the hope of using the findings on poverty and violations to receive aid from the European Commission. Foreign affairs minister Manuel Rodríguez Cuadros asked for international cooperation to alleviate poverty among "those most affected by violence" at the presentation of the final report before international diplomats. "Cancillería difundirá informe de la CVR," *La República*, February 24, 2004.

99. International Federation for Human Rights, "Observatory for the Protection of Human Rights Defenders Annual Report 2009—Peru," June 18, 2009, accessed January 27, 2015, http://www.unhcr.org/refworld/docid/4a5f301723.html.

100. Pundit Santiago Pedraglio talks about the final report as an "orphan" in political terms insofar as "no significant political power has adopted it," and comments that "the CVR has not succeeded in unsettling any actor's initial point of view, that is to say, the one they had before and during the armed conflict." Santiago Pedraglio, "Un informe huérfano," *Perú 21*, August 29, 2004; translation mine.

101. Interview with Sofía Macher, June 2, 2009.

102. Cristián Correa, *Reparations in Peru: From Recommendations to Implementation* (New York: International Center for Transitional Justice, 2013), 12.

103. Interview with Carlos Landeo, April 13, 2009.

104. In June 2009, only an approximated 27 percent of the victims had been registered in the department of Ayacucho. A more encouraging process was under way in Andahuaylas, where successful lobbying by the organizations of the affected culminated in a much more focused registry process carried out by the regional government. Interview with Mario Zenitagoya, July 1, 2009; interview with José Carlos Alca, June 26, 2009 (interviewed by the author and Ponciano del Pino). A total of 160,429 victims were registered by the end of 2012. However, in January 2013, Minister of Justice Eda Rivas declared that the identification of victims was still incomplete and that the government would prioritize collective reparations over individual ones. Correa, *Reparations in Peru*, 10; "Reparaciones colectivas serán prioridad," *Perú 21*, January 11, 2013.

105. In the city of Huamanga, Ayacucho, for example, one of the three Reparations Council offices had been operated for a year by Paz y Esperanza, a Peruvian Protestant organization with links to German funds. When the German Development Fund (DED in German acronym) financing for the project expired in April 2009, the office had to close. Interview with Omar Bengoa, June 30, 2009.

106. Justiniana Huamán, quoted in Laplante and Theidon, "Truth with Consequences," 229.

107. The CVR identified 2,444 actual burial sites (where human remains had been found) and about 2,200 potential burial sites.

108. Nicolás Lynch, "Politicemos la CVR," *La República*, February 29, 2004.

109. Interview with Javier Torres, April 27, 2009.

110. Rocío Trinidad, *El informe final de la Comisión de la Verdad y el reto de la diversificación curricular en Ayacucho* (Lima: Asociación SER, 2006); Pablo Sandoval, *Educación, ciudadanía y violencia en el Perú: Una lectura del Informe de la CVR* (Lima: TAREA and IEP, 2004).

111. An intergovernmental development agency, Fondo Contravalor Perú–Alemania, states that collaboration with Peruvian development and human rights NGOs resulted in the incorporation of the memory of political violence into the educational curricula in parts of Huancavelica and Ayacucho. Karin Apel, "Resultados de las Convocatorias 'Fortalecimiento de la Democracia y Reparaciones en Huancavelica y norte de Ayacucho,' C 03–2005–L1 C 03–2006– L1 (adicional)" (December 2007), accessed January 27, 2015, http://www.fcpa.org.pe/archivos/file/Sistematizacion _ApoyoalPIR.pdf.

112. Mirko Lauer, "Necesaria CVR," *La República*, August 6, 2006.

113. "Informe CVR y silencios," *La República*, September 28, 2003.

114. Claudio Fuentes, "Partidos políticos en Chile: Entre pactos y proyectos," in *El modelo chileno: Democracia y desarrollo en los Noventa*, ed. Paul Drake and Ivan Jaksic (Santiago: LOM Ediciones, Colección sin Norte, 1999).

115. Norbert Lechner and Pedro Güell, "Construcción social de las memorias en la transición chilena," in *La caja de Pandora: El retorno de la transición chilena*, ed. Amparo Menéndez-Carrión and Alfredo Joignant (Santiago de Chile: Planeta/Ariel, 1999), 185–210.

116. Hayner, "Fifteen Truth Commissions," 622.

117. Felipe Portales, "Concertación y violaciones a derechos humanos de la dictadura" (2006), 5, accessed January 27, 2015, http://www.archivochile.com/Chile_actual/09_p_concert/chact _pconcert0002.pdf.

118. Manuel Antonio Garretón, "La redemocratización política en Chile: Transición, inauguración, y evolución," *Estudios Públicos* 42 (Autumn 1991): 129.

119. Brian Loveman and Elizabeth Lira, *Las suaves cenizas del olvido: Vía chilena de reconciliación política, 1814–1932* (Santiago: LOM Ediciones/DIBAM, 2000).

120. Interview with Roberto Garretón, March 5, 2009.

121. Interview with Jorge Contesse, March 5, 2009.

122. Onur Bakiner, "From Denial to Reluctant Dialogue: The Chilean Military's Confrontation with Human Rights (1990–2006)," *International Journal of Transitional Justice* 4, no. 1 (2010): 47–66.

123. Michael Shifter and Vinay Jawahar, "Reconciliation in Latin America: A Fine Balance," *Brown Journal of World Affairs* 11, no. 1 (2004): 131.

124. Interview with Rosa Villarán, June 2, 2009.

125. The information presented in this section is based on interviews by the author and Ponciano del Pino with José Carlos Alca, June 26, 2009, and Daniel Roca, June 29, 2009. Also see Frente Regional de Organizaciones de Base por la Verdad y Justicia (FROBAVEJ)–Ayacucho, "Pronunciamiento: El Frente Regional de Organizaciones de Base por la Verdad y Justicia" (2004),

126. Julie Guillerot and Lisa Magarrell, *Reparación en la transición peruana: Memorias de un proceso inacabado* (Lima: APRODEH, 2006).

127. The regional government of Andahuaylas declared August 28 as the Day of Honoring to the Victims in 2006.

128. Nicolás Lynch, "CVR: Fracaso político," *La República*, August 30, 2007.

Chapter 6. Explaining Variation in Truth Commission Impact (II)

1. *Direct political impact* is captured by the following policy changes taking place within the first two years of the commission's work: (1) the implementation of a reparations program (if recommended by the truth commission); (2) the publication of the final report; (3) the official endorsement of the commission's work; and (4) the creation of a follow-up body to implement recommendations. *Civil society mobilization* refers to: (1) the delayed implementation of a reparations program as a result of civil society pressure; (2) the delayed publication of the final report as a result of civil society pressures; (3) the emergence of new human rights NGOs and victims' associations to monitor the progress of post-commission reforms; and (4) nongovernmental efforts to disseminate the findings and recommendations of the commission. For each variable, the value of the dependent variables is the number of impact measures fulfilled as a fraction of the total impact measures. Thus, each country scores between 0 (no impact) and 1 (perfect impact) for each category of impact. See Chapter 4, Table 4.

2. For a discussion of the relationship between domestic and international actors, see Catherine Turner, "Delivering Lasting Peace, Democracy and Human Rights in Times of Transition: The Role of International Law," *International Journal of Transitional Justice* 2, no. 2 (2008): 126–151; Luc Huyse, "Reconciliation: The People," in *Reconciliation After Violent Conflict: A Handbook*, ed. David Bloomfield, Teresa Barnes, and Luc Huyse (Stockholm: IDEA, 2003).

3. It is important to note that the title "transitional" is problematic. Commissions that were established during a political opening are called "transitional" throughout this book, but this opening toward peace and democracy can be quite brief and incomplete, as the "transitions" in Uganda (1986) and Sri Lanka (1994) show.

4. Crenzel, "Argentina's National Commission on the Disappearance of Persons."

5. Elin Skaar, *Human Rights Violations and the Paradox of Democratic Transition: A Study of Chile and Argentina* (Bergen, Norway: Chr. Michelsen Institute, 1994), 100.

6. The Senate was likewise asked to appoint three members, but it failed to do so. See "Truth Commission: Argentina," USIP Truth Commission Digital Collection, accessed January 27, 2015, http://www.usip.org/publications/truth-commission-argentina.

7. Hayner, "Fifteen Truth Commissions," 615.

8. "Prologue," in *Nunca Más*.

9. Greg Grandin notes that the commission process and the subsequent politics of human rights were characterized by silence about the underlying causes of political violence: "the intellectuals who designed Argentina's post dictatorship human rights policy, while understanding political violence to be rooted in psychological and cultural patterns deeply entrenched in national history, refrained from making any historical judgment in either the trials or in the final report of the Comisión Nacional sobre la Desaparición de Personas (CONADEP)." Grandin, "The Instruction of Great Catastrophe," 49.

10. Oliver Galak, "Controversia por el prólogo agregado al informe 'Nunca más': Rechaza la teoría de los dos demonios," *La Nación*, May 19, 2006.

11. Hayner, *Unspeakable Truths*, 224–225.

12. David Backer, "Civil Society and Transitional Justice: Possibilities, Patterns and Prospects," *Journal of Human Rights* 2, no. 3 (2003): 297–313. Also see Rebecca Lichtenfeld, "Accountability in Argentina: 20 Years Later, Transitional Justice Maintains Momentum," International Center for Transitional Justice Case Studies Series, August 2005.

13. Uganda has a tradition of setting up commissions of inquiry, following the 1914 Commissions of Inquiry Act, concerning a broad range of issues, including human rights. An earlier human rights body, the Commission of Inquiry into the Disappearances of People in Uganda Since 25 January 1971, was established by Idi Amin in 1974. The final report, never made public, was highly critical of Idi Amin, and the commissioners suffered reprisals after the publication of the report. See "Truth Commission in Uganda," in *Track Impunity Always* blog, accessed January 27, 2015, http://www.trial-ch.org/index.php?id=962&L=5.

14. The Ford Foundation granted $93,300 to the commission in 1987. However, given the enormity of the task, and the absence of accompanying funds, the grant did not satisfy the need. Hayner, "Fifteen Truth Commissions," 619.

15. Quinn, "Constraints," 421.

16. Joshua B. Rubongoya, *Regime Hegemony in Museveni's Uganda: Pax Musevenica* (New York: Palgrave Macmillan, 2007).

17. Quinn, "Constraints," 417.

18. "Truth Commission: Uganda 86," USIP Truth Commission Digital Collection, accessed January 27, 2015, http://www.usip.org/resources/truth-commission-uganda-86.

19. Trudy H. Peterson, *Final Acts: A Guide to Preserving the Records of Truth Commissions* (Washington, DC: Woodrow Wilson Center Press; Baltimore: Johns Hopkins University Press, 2005), 79.

20. Quinn, "Constraints," 419.

21. Quinn, "Constraints," 420.

22. Quinn, "Constraints," 423.

23. Human Rights Watch, "Chad: The Victims of Hissène Habré Still Awaiting Justice," *Human Rights Watch* 17, no. 10(A) (July 2005): 14. The CIA supported Habré's regime as an ally against the Gaddafi regime in the last phase of the Cold War.

24. "Chad-Commission of Inquiry into the crimes and misappropriations committed by ex-President Habré, his accomplices and/or accessories," in *Track Impunity Always* blog, accessed January 27, 2015, http://www.trial-ch.org/en/resources/truth-commissions/africa/chad.html.

25. The final report states: "Within the Commission, some members judged the task too hazardous and disappeared altogether. Others reappeared only at the end of the month to pick up their pay and vanished again." Quoted from Hayner, "Fifteen Truth Commissions," 624.

26. Human Rights Watch, "Chad," 15.

27. "Chad: Minister of Justice's Commission of Inquiry on the Crimes Committed by the Hissène Habré Regime," accessed January 27, 2015, http://www.justiceinperspective.org.za/africa /chad/minister-of-justices-commission-of-inquiry-on-the-crimes-committed-by-the-hissene -habre-regime.html.

28. Reed Brody, "The Prosecution of Hissène Habré—an African Pinochet," *New England Law Review* 35 (2000): 321–336.

29. Human Rights Watch, "Chad," 32.

30. Human Rights Watch, "Chad," 18.

31. Human Rights Watch, "Chad," 30.

32. David Holiday and William Stanley, "Building the Peace: Preliminary Lessons from El Salvador," *Journal of International Affairs* 46, no. 2 (1993): 415–438.

33. Buergenthal, "The United Nations Truth Commission for El Salvador," 500.

34. Buergenthal, "The United Nations Truth Commission for El Salvador," 500.

35. "On 18 November 1992, General Ponce and the Minister of the Presidency, Oscar Santamaria, wrote to the Truth Commission underlining the importance of omitting the names of individuals from the final report. President Cristiani stated publicly in March 1993 that 'there will be violence' if individuals were named in the Commission's report, and he privately lobbied several countries to pressure UN officials on his behalf." Kaye, "The Role of Truth Commissions in the Search for Justice, Reconciliation and Democratisation," 707–708.

36. Buergenthal, "The United Nations Truth Commission for El Salvador," 513.

37. Buergenthal is extremely critical of some Americans' reluctance to provide information. Many requests for information were denied on national security grounds, and subsequently declassified documents (by the Clinton Administration) show that the information withheld by the interagency group "could have greatly facilitated the Commission's truth-finding task without endangering U.S. national security or intelligence sources." Buergenthal discovered that part of the information was withheld to protect some Salvadorans from investigation, and not for national security reasons. Nevertheless, he thinks the decision was not official U.S. policy, but that some individual officials used discretion. Buergenthal, "The United Nations Truth Commission for El Salvador," 508.

38. Vasallo, "Truth and Reconciliation Commissions," 176.

39. "Joaquin Villalobos and Ana Guadalupe Martinez became leader of the Partido Demócrata and Vice President of the Legislative Assembly respectively, despite being named as participating in the murders of several civilian mayors. Similarly, General Ponce was appointed head of the Administración Nacional de Telecomunicaciones (ANTEL) after being removed as Defence Minister, and Mauricio Gutierrez was nominated and elected to serve on the OAS Inter-American Judicial Committee." Kaye, "Role of Truth Commissions," 705.

40. Collins, "State Terror and the Law," 33.

41. Jean Boler, "The Mothers Committee of El Salvador: National Human Rights Activists," *Human Rights Quarterly* 7, no. 4 (1985): 541–556.

42. Reed Brody, "The United Nations and Human Rights in El Salvador's Negotiated Revolution," *Harvard Human Rights Journal* 8 (1995): 153.

43. Alexander Segovia, "The Reparations Proposals of the Truth Commissions in El Salvador and Haiti: A History of Noncompliance," in de Greiff, *The Handbook of Reparations*, 159.

44. Priscilla B. Hayner, "Commissioning the Truth: Further Research Questions," *Third World Quarterly* 17, no. 1 (1996): 19–30.

45. Sri Lanka had already established a presidentially mandated monitoring commission in 1991 that did not investigate crimes before its date of operation, in line with the tradition of establishing commissions of inquiry, under the Commissions of Inquiry Act (1948) and the Special Presidential Commissions of Inquiry Law (1978). From time to time, such commissions "have been used more as a means of victimizing political opponents than as a means of finding or

acknowledging the truth." Mario Gomez, "Sri Lanka's New Human Rights Commission," *Human Rights Quarterly* 20, no. 2 (1998): 292. Also see Wasana Punyasena, "The Façade of Accountability: Disappearances in Sri Lanka," *Boston College Third World Law Journal* 23 (2003): 115–158.

46. "Commissions of Inquiry: Sri Lanka," USIP Truth Commission Digital Collection, accessed January 27, 2015, http://www.usip.org/resources/commissions-inquiry-sri-lanka.

47. "Summary of Recommendations" (chap. 12), in *Final Report of the Commission of Inquiry into Involuntary Removal and Disappearance of Certain Persons (All Island)*, 2002.

48. World Organisation Against Torture et al., *State Violence in Sri Lanka: An Alternative Report to the United Nations Human Rights Committee* (Geneva: World Organisation Against Torture, 2004).

49. Neistat, *Recurring Nightmare*, 22–23.

50. Neistat, *Recurring Nightmare*, 24.

51. Neistat, *Recurring Nightmare*, 24.

52. Anonymous, "Against the Grain: Pursuing a Transitional Justice Agenda in Postwar Sri Lanka," *International Journal of Transitional Justice* 5, no. 1 (2011): 43.

53. Neistat, *Recurring Nightmare*, 21.

54. "Sri Lanka: Presidential Truth Commission on Ethnic Violence," in *Justice in Perspective*, accessed January 27, 2015, http://www.justiceinperspective.org.za/asia-a-australasia/sri-lanka/presidential-truth-commission-on-ethnic-violence.html.

55. Neistat, *Recurring Nightmare*, 21.

56. Hayner, *Unspeakable Truths*, 247–248.

57. "The Commission was fundamentally flawed from the outset by a deliberate ploy on the part of the government that initiated the Commission to weaken and undermine its effectiveness." Hakeem O. Yusuf, "Travails of Truth: Achieving Justice for Victims of Impunity in Nigeria," *International Journal of Transitional Justice* 1, no. 2 (2007): 268.

58. Yusuf notes that five members, including the chair, were Christians in a country where more than half the population is Muslim and the religious divide is politically salient. Yusuf, "Travails of Truth," 281.

59. Yusuf, "Travails of Truth," 271.

60. Obiora Chinedu Okafor, *Legitimizing Human Rights NGOs: Lessons from Nigeria* (Trenton, NJ: Africa World Press, 2006), 184.

61. Amnesty International, *Nigeria: Time for Justice and Accountability* (London: International Secretariat, 2000).

62. Quoted from Knight, "Facing the Past," 887.

63. Hayner, *Unspeakable Truths*, 250.

64. Bickford, "Unofficial Truth Projects," 1027.

65. "Yes, it was a huge entertainment for a people previously starved of fun for so many years. There were jeers, there were boos; and there were emotions as there were sophistry on free display." Mike Ikhariale, "The Oputa Reports: An Unfinished Job" (May 2002).

66. "Commission of Inquiry: Nepal 90," USIP Truth Commission Digital Collection, accessed January 27, 2015, http://www.usip.org/resources/commission-inquiry-nepal-90.

67. Tafadzwa Pasipanodya, "A Deeper Justice: Economic and Social Justice as Transitional Justice in Nepal," *International Journal of Transitional Justice* 2, no. 3 (2008): 378–397.

68. Even the Communist Party of Nepal (the Unified Marxist-Leninists), which had promised to implement the commission's recommendations once elected, supported a candidate whose name was cited as a perpetrator in the final report. Binod Bhattarai et al., *Impunity in Nepal: An Exploratory Study* (Kathmandu: Asia Foundation, 1999), 3.

69. "The report and recommendations of the commission were not only not executed by the interim government and the first elected government, but were also dismissed as a half-finished job." Bhattarai et al., *Impunity in Nepal*, 3.

70. The Council of Ministers decision (2047/3/18) reads as follows: "Because of the faulty system even if there have been police excesses, in order to keep the morale of the police high and because the police are responsible for all internal security, and taking into account that the police will have a major role to ensure that the forthcoming elections are peaceful, no action will be taken based on the Commission's report." Quoted from Bhattarai et al., *Impunity in Nepal*, 10.

71. Bhattarai et al., *Impunity in Nepal*, 3.

72. Human Rights Watch, *Waiting for Justice: Unpunished Crimes from Nepal's Armed Conflict* (New York: Human Rights Watch, 2008), 18, accessed January 27, 2015, http://www.unhcr.org/refworld/docid/48ca22942.html.

73. Hayner, *Unspeakable Truths*, 244–245.

74. "Commission of Inquiry: Nepal 90," USIP Truth Commission Digital Collection, accessed January 27, 2015, http://www.usip.org/resources/commission-inquiry-nepal-90.

75. "Nepal: Commission of Inquiry to Locate the Persons Disappeared during the Panchayet Period," in Justice in Perspective, accessed January 27, 2015, http://www.justiceinperspective.org.za/asia-a-australasia/nepal/commission-of-inquiry-to-locate-the-persons-disappeared-during-the-panchayet-period.html.

76. "USIP Rule of Law Advisor Scott Worden, conflict resolution specialist Karon Cochran-Budhathoki, and consultant Shobakhar Budhathoki met with representative groups from civil society, victims of the ten-year armed conflict, the media, and government and political party representatives." Karon Cochran-Budhathoki and Scott Worden, "Transitional Justice in Nepal: A Look at the International Experience of Truth Commissions" (USIP Policy Brief, 2007), accessed January 27, 2015, available at http://www.usip.org/resources/transitional-justice-nepal-look-international-experience-truth-commissions.

77. Joanna Quinn notes that the joint UN/OAS International Civilian Mission in Haiti refused to support the commission, although the UN website argues the opposite. Quinn, "Haiti's Failed Truth Commission," 275.

78. Laura A. Young, and Rosalyn Park, "Engaging Diasporas in Truth Commissions: Lessons from the Liberia Truth and Reconciliation Commission Diaspora Project," *International Journal of Transitional Justice* 3, no. 3 (2009): 341–361.

79. Quinn, "Haiti's Failed Truth Commission," 267.

80. Chapman and Ball, "The Truth of Truth Commissions," 17.

81. The degree of grassroots participation has generated controversy among scholars. Fanny Benedetti notes the strong response of grassroots organizations to the commission's call: "These groups reacted promptly and efficiently in notifying the populace of the presence of the Commission in various localities. The results were greater than many observers had expected. A strong willingness to testify about human rights abuses was the rule rather than the exception even though a significant number of victims expressed anxiety about the present of past perpetrators of human rights violations in the surrounding areas." Fanny Benedetti, "Haiti's Truth and Justice Commission," Human Rights Brief, Center for Human Rights and Humanitarian Law, Washington College of Law, American University (1996), accessed January 27, 2015, http://www.wcl.american.edu/hrbrief/v3i3/haiti33.htm. Joanna Quinn disagrees strongly: "the Commission failed to win the popular support of Haitians, by ignoring local nongovernmental organizations (NGOs) and failing to tell ordinary Haitians about the purpose of the Commission." Quinn, "Haiti's Failed Truth Commission," 269.

82. "Unfortunately, in the last stages of the process, the commissioners discarded almost all the work the field investigators did and substituted a chronology of the *de facto* regime. The commissioners never informed the AAAS of their reasons for not using the regional data; although the statistical analyses were presented, the tables omitted most of the content and the translations into French were inadequate." Patrick Ball and Herbert F. Spirer, "The Haitian National Commission for Truth and Justice: Collecting Information, Data Processing, Database

Representation, and Generating Analytical Reports," in *Making the Case: Investigating Large Scale Human Rights Violations Using Information Systems and Data Analysis*, ed. Patrick Ball, Herbert F. Spirer, and Louise Spirer (Washington, DC: American Association for the Advancement of Science, 2000).

83. Hayner, *Unspeakable Truths*; Quinn, "Haiti's Failed Truth Commission."

84. Chapman and Ball, "The Truth of Truth Commissions," 24.

85. Chapman and Ball, "The Truth of Truth Commissions," 31.

86. "Truth Commission: Haiti," USIP Truth Commission Digital Collection, accessed January 27, 2015, http://www.usip.org/resources/truth-commission-haiti.

87. Hayner, *Unspeakable Truths*, 54.

88. Quinn, "Haiti's Failed Truth Commission," 279.

89. "Truth Commission: Haiti," USIP Truth Commission Digital Collection, accessed January 27, 2015, http://www.usip.org/resources/truth-commission-haiti.

90. Johnny de Lange, "The Historical Context, Legal Origins and Philosophical Foundation of the South African Truth and Reconciliation Commission," in *Looking Back Reaching Forward: Reflections on the Truth and Reconciliation Commission of South Africa*, ed. Charles Villa-Vicencio and Wilhelm Verwoerd (Cape Town, South Africa: Cape Town University Press, 2000).

91. Hayner, *Unspeakable Truths*, 224.

92. Shea, *The South African Truth Commission*, 10–11. Also see Priscilla B. Hayner, "International Guidelines for the Creation and Operation of Truth Commissions: A Preliminary Proposal," *Law and Contemporary Problems* 59 (1996): 173–180.

93. Shea, *The South African Truth Commission*, 5.

94. The Center for Applied Legal Studies, for example, "argued that the definition of 'severe ill-treatment' should be interpreted to include apartheid abuses such as forced removals, pass law arrests, alienation of land and breaking up of families." Quoted from Mamdani, "Amnesty or Impunity?," 39.

95. Shea, *The South African Truth Commission*, 25.

96. Shea, *The South African Truth Commission*, 26–32.

97. Hayner, *Unspeakable Truths*, 225–226.

98. Shea, *The South African Truth Commission*, 3.

99. Shea, *The South African Truth Commission*, 37.

100. See Colvin, "Overview of the Reparations Program in South Africa."

101. Backer, "Watching a Bargain Unravel?"

102. Elizabeth A. Cole, "Transitional Justice and the Reform of History Education," *International Journal of Transitional Justice* 1, no. 1 (2007): 115–137.

103. Elizabeth A. Cole and Karen Murphy, "History Education Reform, Transitional Justice, and the Transformation of Identities," in Arthur, *Identities in Transition*, 356.

104. Amy Ross, "The Creation and Conduct of the Guatemalan Commission for Historical Clarification," *Geoforum* 37, no. 1 (2006): 79.

105. Grandin, "The Instruction of Great Catastrophe," 58.

106. Ross, "Creation and Conduct of the Guatemalan Commission," 80.

107. Elizabeth Oglesby, "Historical Memory and the Limits of Peace Education: Examining Guatemala's *Memory of Silence* and the Politics of Curriculum Design," in *Teaching the Violent Past: History Education and Reconciliation and History Education*, ed. Elizabeth A. Cole (New York: Rowman and Littlefield, 2007), 175–202

108. Grandin, "The Instruction of Great Catastrophe," 58.

109. Ross, "Creation and Conduct of the Guatemalan Commission," 79.

110. "Commission researchers incorporated history, anthropology, sociology, economics, and military science into the analysis." Chapman and Ball, "The Truth of Truth Commissions," 10.

111. Chapman and Ball, "The Truth of Truth Commissions," 33.

112. "The CEH's analysis of the Central Intelligence Agency's (CIA) 1954 coup that ended this democratic decade stands in opposition to the Rettig Commission, which blamed Allende's 1973 ouster on Cold War polarization." Grandin, "The Instruction of Great Catastrophe," 60.

113. Oglesby, "Historical Memory," 179.

114. "Truth Commission: Guatemala," USIP Truth Commission Digital Collection, accessed January 27, 2015, http://www.usip.org/resources/truth-commission-guatemala.

115. UN Human Rights Committee, Major Progress Made in Human Rights Protections Since Guatemala's Peace Accords 15 Years Ago, Although Much Work Remains, Human Rights Committee Told," UN Doc. HR/CT/744, March 19, 2012.

116. Oglesby, "Historical Memory," 199.

117. Oglesby, "Historical Memory," 183.

118. Oglesby, "Historical Memory," 194.

119. Tomuschat, "Clarification Commission in Guatemala," 253.

120. Catherine Jenkins, "A Truth Commission for East Timor: Lessons from South Africa?" *Journal of Conflict and Security Law* 7, no. 2 (2002): 233–252.

121. Patrick Burgess notes that the ICC option never became a realistic possibility, while the Jakarta ad hoc tribunal failed due to lack of political will on the part of the Indonesian government. The Dili-based Serious Crimes Unit worked with greater efficiency and political will, but its failure to arrest leading Indonesian suspects set limits on its capacity to deliver justice. Patrick Burgess, "Justice and Reconciliation in East Timor: The Relationship Between the Commission for Reception, Truth and Reconciliation and the Courts," *Criminal Law Forum* 15 (2004): 141.

122. Fausto Belo Ximenes, "The Unique Contribution of the Community-Based Reconciliation Process in East Timor" (paper prepared for the Transitional Justice Fellowship Program of the International Center for Transitional Justice and the Institute for Justice and Reconciliation, May 2004).

123. Burgess, "Justice and Reconciliation in East Timor," 151.

124. Burgess, "Justice and Reconciliation in East Timor," 151.

125. Lia Kent, "Unfulfilled Expectations: Community Views on CAVR's Community Reconciliation Process" (report prepared for the Judicial System Monitoring Programme, Dili, East Timor, August 2004), 45.

126. "Truth Commission: Timor-Leste (East Timor)," USIP Truth Commission Digital Collection, accessed January 27, 2015, http://www.usip.org/publications/truth-commission-timor-leste-east-timor.

127. David Webster, "History, Nation and Narrative in East Timor's Truth Commission Report," *Pacific Affairs* 80, no. 4 (2007): 582.

128. "The imperatives of a diplomatically driven struggle saw the East Timorese move away from the language of revolution and towards the language of human rights. *Chega!* simultaneously notes this shift, celebrates it, and is a product of it." Webster, "History, Nation and Narrative," 587.

129. Post-independence president Xanana Gusmao, criticizing what he perceived as a foreign imposition to remember past violence and conduct human rights trials, said during his presidential campaign: "On the basis of [East Timorese] traditions, the return to harmony and the burying of the past constitute the factors which, combined with the political component of reconciliation, are the foundation for the process so far implemented." Quoted from Frederick Rawski, "Truth-Seeking and Local Histories in East Timor," *Asia-Pacific Journal on Human Rights & Law* 3, no. 1 (2002): 77.

130. Simon Robins, "Challenging the Therapeutic Ethic: A Victim-Centred Evaluation of Transitional Justice Process in Timor-Leste." *International Journal of Transitional Justice* 6, no. 1 (2012): 97; Elizabeth F. Drexler, "Fatal Knowledges: The Social and Political Legacies of Collaboration and Betrayal in Timor-Leste," *International Journal of Transitional Justice* 7, no. 1 (2013): 85 n. 42.

131. "Timor-Leste: Illustrated Version of Truth Report," ICTJ Features, August 31, 2010.

132. Lia Kent, "Local Memory Practices in East Timor: Disrupting Transitional Justice Narratives," *International Journal of Transitional Justice* 5, no. 3 (2011): 450.

133. The last-minute disclaimer reads: "The United Nations holds the understanding that the amnesty and pardon in Article IX of the agreement shall not apply to international crimes of genocide, crimes against humanity, war crimes and other serious violations of international humanitarian law." Quoted from Hayner, *Negotiating Peace in Sierra Leone*, 5.

134. Beth K. Dougherty, "Searching for Answers: Sierra Leone's Truth & Reconciliation Commission," *African Studies Quarterly* 8, no. 1 (2004): 41. Also see Michael O'Flaherty, "Sierra Leone's Peace Process: The Role of the Human Rights Community," *Human Rights Quarterly* 26, no. 1 (2004): 29–62.

135. Parker, "Seeking Truth," 244.

136. Several scholars point to the high degree of international involvement in the commission and the potential for discrepancy between the commission's objectives and local approaches to justice. See William Schabas, "The Sierra Leone Truth and Reconciliation Commission," in *Transitional Justice in the Twenty-First Century: Beyond Truth Versus Justice*, ed. Naomi Roht-Arriaza and Javier Mariezcurrena (Cambridge: Cambridge University Press, 2006); Rosalind Shaw, "Rethinking Truth and Reconciliation Commissions: Lessons from Sierra Leone" (United States Institute of Peace, Special Report 130, February 13, 2005). Nonetheless, the role of domestic NGOs cannot be ignored: "In Sierra Leone, local nongovernmental organizations (NGOs) and human rights activists not only pushed for the [truth commission's] creation, but also maintained interest during the delay in setting it up and helped with important tasks such as sensitization." Dougherty, "Searching for Answers," 41.

137. The court had the power to force the commission to share information at its disposal, but the prosecutor emphatically rejected the possibility. Evenson, "Truth and Justice in Sierra Leone," 745, 756.

138. Tim Kelsall, "Truth, Lies, Ritual: Preliminary Reflections on the Truth and Reconciliation Commission in Sierra Leone," *Human Rights Quarterly* 27, no. 2 (2005): 361–391.

139. "Truth Commission: Sierra Leone," USIP Truth Commission Digital Collection, accessed January 27, 2015, http://www.usip.org/resources/truth-commission-sierra-leone.

140. "Sierra Leone: Truth and Reconciliation Commission, accessed January 27, 2015, http://www.justiceinperspective.org.za/africa/sierra-leone/truth-and-reconciliation-commission.html.

141. O'Flaherty, "Sierra Leone's Peace Process."

142. Julia Paulson, "The Educational Recommendations of Truth and Reconciliation Commissions: Potential and Practice in Sierra Leone," *Research in Comparative and International Education* 1, no. 4 (2006): 346.

143. Commentators criticize the commission's failure to explain its goals and procedures and publicize its final report, especially among the illiterate. Andrew R. Iliff, "Root and Branch: Discourses of 'Tradition' in Grassroots Transitional Justice," *International Journal of Transitional Justice* 6, no. 2 (2012): 262; Gearoid Millar, "Expectations and Experiences of Peacebuilding in Sierra Leone: Parallel Peacebuilding Processes and Compound Friction," *International Peacekeeping* 20, no. 2 (2013): 189–203.

144. "Civil society's role in the peace process was largely driven by church-based organizations including the Catholic Bishops' Conference, the Liberia Council of Churches and the Inter-Faith Mediating Committee, comprising both Muslims and Christians. Another group that impacted the process included the Liberia Leadership Forum, a coalition of Diaspora and local organizations." Ezekiel Pajibo, "Civil Society and Transitional Justice in Liberia: A Practitioner's Reflection from the Field," *International Journal of Transitional Justice* 1, no. 2 (2007): 293.

145. "Liberia: BBC Trust, ICTJ Training Journalists," *Analyst* (Monrovia), August 8, 2008.

146. Most observers hail the broad periodization, but a critical commentator notes that the designation of 1979 as the starting date shifts all the blame toward the post-Americo-Liberian era, as the last ruler of American-born ancestry was overthrown with a coup in 1979. Lansana Gberie, "Truth and Justice on Trial in Liberia," *African Affairs* 107, no. 428 (2008): 456.

147. "Liberia's Commission includes nine national members who have the support of international advisors, which seems a good way to benefit from foreign expertise without compromising the indigenous nature of the enterprise." Erin Daly, "Truth Skepticism: An Inquiry into the Value of Truth in Times of Transition," *International Journal of Transitional Justice* 2, no. 1 (2008): 28 n. 14.

148. Matiangai V. S. Sirleaf, "Regional Approach to Transitional Justice? Examining the Special Court for Sierra Leone and the Truth and Reconciliation Commission for Liberia," *Florida Journal of International Law* 21 (2009): 209–285.

149. Pajibo, "Civil Society and Transitional Justice in Liberia," 291.

150. "Truth Commission: Liberia," USIP Truth Commission Digital Collection, accessed January 27, 2015, http://www.usip.org/publications/truth-commission-liberia.

151. According to Aaron Weah, "the courage of the TRC was perceived not only to vindicate the Commission from its previous mishaps and its timidity during the public hearings but also to render the report's shortcomings a nonissue." Aaron Weah, "Hopes and Uncertainties: Liberia's Journey to End Impunity," *International Journal of Transitional Justice* 6, no. 2 (2012): 335.

152. Hayner also notes the disillusionment on the part of human rights and church-based organizations "when the truth commission failed to engage them in any sustained manner." Hayner, *Unspeakable Truths*, 226.

153. "[The commission's] impact has been widespread. Within the first six months of the report's release, it generated a national conversation across the country. [Radio] stations organized sustained phone-in talk shows which generated conversations with ordinary Liberians from across the country. I even saw portions of the TRC report cut and kept in wallets and posted alongside calendars in households." E-mail communication with Aaron Weah, October 7, 2011.

154. "TJWG Launches Transitional Justice Initiative Project," *Analyst*, June 29, 2010.

155. "TJWG Launches Transitional Justice Initiative Project," *Analyst*, June 29, 2010.

156. Lydiah Kemunto Bosire and Gabrielle Lynch, "Kenya's Search for Truth and Justice: The Role of Civil Society," *International Journal of Transitional Justice* 8 (2014): 259.

Chapter 7. Comparing Truth Commissions' Memory Narratives

Notes to epigraphs: Lyrics of "Canción final" (Final Song), in *Santa María de Iquique, Cantata Popular*, composed by Luis Advis (1970); translation mine:

You who have now heard
The story that was told
Do not just sit there
Thinking it is all over
Remembrance by itself is not enough
The *canto* will not be enough
Mourning by itself is not enough
Let's look at the reality
Perhaps sooner or later
Or even further away
The story you have heard
Will happen again.

Fortunato Galindo, "Queja Andina" (Andean Complaint), recorded as title track of Edwin Montoya y Los Heraldos's first LP for Sello Odeon in 1966. Lyrics quoted from Rodrigo Montoya, Luis Montoya, and Edwin Montoya, *Urqukunapa Yawarnin: La sangre de los cerros* (Lima:

CEPES, Mosca Azul Editores, and UNMSM., 1987); courtesy of Ponciano del Pino; re-translation from Spanish mine:

> In the door of the government palace
> My sentinel guard
> Please open the door for me
> I'm going to talk to Belaúnde
> I'm going to speak with the president.

1. Interview with José Zalaquett, January 20, 2009.

2. *Report of the Chilean National Commission on Truth and Reconciliation* (1993), 31.

3. *Report of the Chilean National Commission*, 32.

4. Vial's views on the justifiability of the military coup are not limited to this highly propagandistic piece with no identifiable authors. In his account of the history of Chile, he writes: "Finally, all these evils deepened in the thousand days of Unidad Popular, whose regime and supporters encouraged violence, steering the country toward a shattering crisis. The divisions of civic life threatened to reproduce themselves within the Armed Forces, which finally chose to hear the voice of the vast majority of the country that wished the end of the Allende regime. In that sense, September 11 [1973] was not any barrack conspiracy [*cuartelazo*] or military coup, but rather constituted a military uprising in the face of the crisis that was threatening the very soul of Chileanhood." Gonzalo Vial Correa, *Historia de Chile, 1891–1973*, vol. 2 (Santiago de Chile: Editorial Santillana del Pacífico, 1981), 315; translation mine.

5. In one of the rare studies of the Chilean truth commission's historical narrative, Daniela Cuadros Garland argues that the contextual chapter privileged consensus-building over historical veracity. Daniela Cuadros Garland, "La Commission Rettig: Innovation, silences et contestations d'une mise en récit 'consensuelle' des violations des droits de l'homme au Chili" (2006), accessed January 27, 2015, http://cuadros.free.fr/militantisme_fichiers/cuadrosrettig2006.pdf.

6. *Report of the Chilean National Commission*, 47.

7. *Report of the Chilean National Commission*, 51.

8. *Report of the Chilean National Commission*, 47.

9. *Report of the Chilean National Commission*, 68.

10. *Report of the Chilean National Commission*, 70.

11. *Report of the Chilean National Commission*, 57.

12. *Report of the Chilean National Commission*, 31.

13. The commission's strict adherence to the human rights norm to separate justifiability of the decision to use violence from the acts and effects of violence reaches an impasse: the commission includes the deaths resulting from confrontations between security forces and armed resistance movements as "human rights violations." In other words, combat deaths are covered by the human rights investigation, but the commission declares itself unfit to make a judgment on the first and most destructive combat (i.e., the military coup itself).

14. Stern, *Reckoning with Pinochet*, 84.

15. See Grandin, "The Instruction of Great Catastrophe," for a critique of this position.

16. Interview with José Zalaquett, January 20, 2009.

17. Stern, *Reckoning with Pinochet*, 82.

18. For example, Zalaquett reiterates the basic argument of the context chapter when interviewed by historian Greg Grandin: "[The Rettig Report] is the history of doctrinary justification of ethically unacceptable means in political action." Grandin, "The Instruction of Great Catastrophe," 56 n. 40.

19. Hugo Fruhling and Frederick Woodbridge, Jr., "Stages of Repression and Legal Strategy for the Defense of Human Rights in Chile: 1973–1980," *Human Rights Quarterly* 5, no. 4 (1983): 521.

20. One example is Patricio Aylwin's 1993 speech entitled "La Concertación de Partidos por la Democracia: Desafíos y perspectivas," in Patricio Aylwin Azócar, *Crecimiento con equidad: Discursos escogidos, 1992–1994* (Santiago: Editorial Andres Bello, 1994).

21. Historian Sergio Grez names the Santa María School massacre in the north province of Iquique (1907), the massacre against workers in Marusia, Antofagasta (1925), and the criminalization of the Communist Party (1948) as examples of class repression throughout the early twentieth century, and the systematic repression of the indigenous Mapuches in the South. Interview with Sergio Grez, February 23, 2009.

22. The erasure of class conflict is not unique to the Chilean transitional justice model. Critics have taken issue with existing transitional justice models for failing to challenge the neoliberal status quo in general. Lisa J. Laplante, "Transitional Justice and Peace Building: Diagnosing and Addressing the Socioeconomic Roots of Violence Through a Human Rights Framework," *International Journal of Transitional Justice* 2, no. 3 (2008): 331–355.

23. Contrast the government's and the Rettig Commission's failure to recognize the victims' political agency during the Unidad Popular experience with this statement by Sola Sierra, a leading figure of the AFDD: "We loved [our disappeared relatives] because they were free in their thinking and just in their decisions [*determinaciones*]. We loved them because they were leaders of popular political parties, because they were union leaders." Quoted in Sandrine Lefranc, "Aquello que no se conmemora: ¿Democracias sin un pasado compartido?" *Revista de Ciencia Política* 23, no. 2 (2003): 231–240; translation mine.

24. Several left-leaning historians published a document called *The Historians' Manifesto* in January 1999 as a rejoinder to Augusto Pinochet's "Letter to Chileans," released a month earlier. The *Manifesto* does not mention the truth commission but heavily criticizes Gonzalo Vial's interpretation of Chile's political history. Sergio Grez and Gabriel Salazar, comps., *Manifiesto de historiadores* (Santiago de Chile: LOM, 1999).

25. "Prefacio," in *Hatun Willakuy: Versión abreviada del Informe final de la Comisión de la Verdad y Reconciliación, Perú* (Lima: Comisión de la Verdad y Reconciliación, 2004); translation mine.

26. Interview with Ricardo Caro, May 25, 2009.

27. *Hatun Willakuy*, chap. 6.

28. These terms have their origins in the colonial caste (*casta*) system, which established racial hierarchies based on perceived purity of race in the Spanish empire. *Criollos* refers to people of pure European descent. *Mestizos* refers to people of mixed European and native ancestry. *Cholos* may refer to various degrees of native ancestry and is still used as a derogatory word for the native populations of Peru and Bolivia. *Indios* refers to people of pure indigenous ancestry.

29. CVR, *Informe Final*, conclusion 4. The "General Conclusions" of the final report are translated into English and are available at www.cverdad.org.pe.

30. Milton, "At the Edge of the Peruvian Truth Commission," 149.

31. CVR, *Informe Final*, conclusion 36.

32. CVR, *Informe Final*, conclusion 38.

33. Several interviewees mention that *caviar* is used as an adjective to insult the CVR and the human rights movement in general. Although a precise definition is lacking, *caviar* denotes a group of intellectuals who act against the nation's best interest to obtain foreign funds and lead extravagant lives. Interview with Salomón Lerner, June 3, 2009; interview with Susana Villarán, May 19, 2009; interview with Rocio Santisteban, May 20, 2009.

34. This and the following quotes are taken from the interview with Javier Torres, April 27, 2009.

35. Stathis Kalyvas warns against the tendency in civil war studies to reduce the dynamics of local and private conflicts to those of the master cleavage. Stathis N. Kalyvas, "The Ontology of 'Political Violence': Action and Identity in Civil Wars," *Perspectives on Politics* 1, no. 3 (2003): 475–494.

36. For examples of recent scholarship that incorporates micro-level conflicts, see Edgar Alberto Tucno Rocha, "Guerra Popular! O Microconflictos: Los comites de autodefensa en el distrito de Vinchos," in *Reflexiones en Ayacucho desde las ciencias sociales* (Editorial UNSCH-CEISA, Ayacucho, 2003); Ponciano del Pino H., "Family, Culture, and 'Revolution': Everyday Life with Sendero Luminoso," in Stern, *Shining and Other Paths*.

37. Ruth Rubio-Marín, Claudia Paz y Paz Bailye, and Julie Guillerot, "Indigenous Peoples and Claims for Reparation: Tentative Steps in Peru and Guatemala," in Arthur, *Identities in Transition*.

38. The CVR sensitized the human rights groups to the use of Quechua. Several books and reports published after the commission process had Quechua names, although they were written in Spanish. Elizabeth Jelin, "Silences, Visibility, and Agency: Ethnicity, Class, and Gender in Public Memorialization," in Arthur, *Identities in Transition*, 194–196.

39. Interview with Susana Villarán, May 19, 2009.

40. More information about the *State of Fear* is available at http://skylight.is/films/state-of -fear/ (accessed January 27, 2015).

41. Neruda presumably died of ill health two weeks after the military coup and, soon after, soldiers raided his house. Controversy around the circumstances of his death led to the exhumation of his grave in 2013. Even if he was not a direct victim of the dictatorship in the strict sense, his funeral in 1973 took place under heavy police surveillance, which explains the motivation behind the reburial in 2004.

42. Kimberly Susan Theidon, "Histories of Innocence: Postwar Stories in Peru," in *Localizing Transitional Justice: Interventions and Priorities After Mass Violence*, ed. Rosalind Shaw and Lars Waldorf, with Pierre Hazan (Stanford, CA: Stanford University Press, 2010).

43. Murphy, *A Moral Theory of Political Reconciliation*, 166.

44. Bronwyn Leebaw, *Judging State-Sponsored Violence, Imagining Political Change* (New York: Cambridge University Press, 2011), 147.

45. See, for example, Kalyvas, "The Ontology of 'Political Violence'"; and Séverine Autesserre, *The Trouble with the Congo: Local Violence and the Failure of International Peacebuilding* (Cambridge: Cambridge University Press, 2010).

Chapter 8. Nation and (Its New) Narration

1. In addition to truth commissions, writing history can assume a central role in other justice initiatives, such as domestic courts, foreign courts prosecuting nonnationals, and international criminal trials. See Christiane Wilke, "Staging Violence, Staging Identities: Identity Politics in Domestic Prosecutions," in Arthur, *Identities in Transition*, 133; Wilson, *The Politics of Truth and Reconciliation in South Africa*; Hannah Arendt, *Eichmann in Jerusalem: A Report on the Banality of Evil* (New York: Penguin Books, 2006).

2. José Zalaquett, "Moral Reconstruction in the Wake of Human Rights Violations and War Crimes," in *Hard Choices: Moral Dilemmas in Humanitarian Intervention*, ed. Jonathan Moore (Lanham, MD: Rowman and Littlefield, 1998).

3. Berber Bevernage, "Writing the Past Out of the Present: History and the Politics of Time in Transitional Justice," *History Workshop Journal* 69, no. 1 (2010): 111.

4. Two caveats are in order. First, even if all truth commissions discover and publicize facts about human rights violations, not all of them write extensive historical narratives. I elaborate on the variation across commissions in the extent to which they make public use of history in Chapter 7. The analytical approach in this chapter is therefore more general and abstract. Second, the commissioners and staff are rarely selected from professional historians and social scientists. As I argue in Chapter 3, commissions address the general public, which leads them to pay close attention to public debates on social memory, even if they also make use of academic

scholarship. Therefore, commissions produce "public" but not necessarily "professional" histories. In the words of Antoon De Baets, they are "archive-producers and protohistorians." Antoon De Baets, "Resistance to the Censorship of Historical Thought in the Twentieth Century," in *Making Sense of Global History: The 19th International Congress of Historical Sciences, Oslo 2000, Commemorative Volume*, ed. Sølvi Sogner (Oslo: Universitetsforlaget, 2001), 402.

5. Charles Maier writes about this notion in mildly optimistic terms: a truth commission "suggests that societies and historians can establish narratives that are emancipatory and not simply efforts to control history or to channel the transition from one dominating culture to another. But a truth commission itself does not complete this narrative task; it only offers us the possibility—an advance, to be sure, but hardly a guarantee either of justice or democracy." Maier, "Doing History, Doing Justice," 273.

6. Aletta Norval notes, in the context of the South African Truth and Reconciliation Commission, that the struggle over the interpretation of history and politics is "over the very identity and character of post apartheid South Africa" and "is played out in the contestations around its nodal points—justice, reconciliation, truth and memory." Aletta Norval, "Truth and Reconciliation: The Birth of the Present and the Reworking of History," review article, *Journal of Southern African Studies* 22 (1999): 504.

7. I do not aim to provide full textual analyses of any of these thinkers, nor do I claim that truth commissions have emerged as a direct response to their texts on the ethics of public historiography. However, I do assume that the philosophical import of these texts supersedes the contexts in which they were written. Thus, I use these texts as an opportunity to rethink the relationship between history and politics in modernity, a process that culminated in a distinctive historical consciousness embodied in practices of coming to terms with the past in the late twentieth century.

8. Rhiana Chinapen, and Richard Vernon, "Justice in Transition," *Canadian Journal of Political Science* 39, no. 1 (2006): 129; emphasis mine.

9. John S. Nelson, "Politics and Truth: Arendt's Problematic," *American Journal of Political Science* 22, no. 2 (1978): 270–301.

10. Hannah Arendt, "Truth and Politics," in *Between Past and Future: Eight Exercises in Political Thought* (New York: Penguin Books, 1977), 239.

11. Patrick Riley notes that for Arendt, politics is not about finding eternal moral truth in the Platonic sense, but rather about forming "general, impartial, 'enlarged' public opinion" through persuasion and judgment. Consequently, "politics should respect that truth which stands outside the political realm altogether, even if the *polis* is not truth 'realized.'" Patrick Riley, "Hannah Arendt on Kant, Truth and Politics," in *Essays on Kant's Political Philosophy*, ed. Howard L. Williams (Chicago: University of Chicago Press, 1992), 318.

12. Arendt, "Truth and Politics," 238.

13. From her preoccupation with nuclear destruction to the analysis of the totalitarian impulse for constant mobilization and politicization, Arendt has tirelessly repeated the need to preserve the stability of the world, that is, the totality of objects and relationships that we experience as our given environment. Forgetfulness of the human embeddedness in the world (what Arendt calls "world-alienation") unhinges action from its worldliness and transforms the otherwise creative human activity into mindless destruction processes. While Arendt does not invoke the *world* in the essays on factual truth, it is clear that she situates facts as the condition of possibility of any meaningful action, the starting point (the past) from which to initiate something new (the future). Arendt, "Truth and Politics," 258. I suggest there are some parallels between Arendt's interpretation of how lawmaking was conceptualized in Greek antiquity and her notion of facts in the later essays. Laws, "like the wall around the city," secured a space in which human action could take place for the Greeks. Hannah Arendt, *The Human Condition* (Chicago: University of Chicago Press, 1998), 194. Facts likewise constitute an external constraint, thereby enabling a space for communication in which persuasion over opinion can take place.

14. Arendt, "Truth and Politics," 251.

15. Arendt, "Truth and Politics," 252.

16. Arendt, "Truth and Politics," 252–253.

17. Arendt, "Truth and Politics," 253.

18. Arendt's favorite example in this regard is the complete erasure of Leon Trotsky from Soviet history under Stalinist rule. While she takes note that totalitarian subversion of politics is more likely to rely on, and more capable to carry out, a policy of massive deception than any other regime type, she does not qualify the "modern lie" as an exclusively totalitarian (or authoritarian) project.

19. Arendt, "Truth and Politics," 251.

20. Arendt, "Truth and Politics," 257–258.

21. Even before writing *Nineteen Eighty-Four*, Orwell's observations about the Spanish Civil War led him to warn his readers about the possibility that the idea of "objective truth" might be in danger. Commenting on fascist propaganda during the war, he writes: "This kind of thing is frightening to me, because it often gives me the feeling that the very concept of objective truth is fading out of the world." George Orwell, "Looking Back on the Spanish War," in *George Orwell: A Collection of Essays* (Garden City, NY: Doubleday, 1954), 203.

22. Arendt, "Truth and Politics," 251.

23. Commentators have noted the liberating element of publicizing factual truth through truth commissions. In the specific context of the South African Truth and Reconciliation Commission, Leigh M. Johnson writes: "Embedded in the power regime of apartheid was an elaborate structure of lies, and the TRC aimed to resist the perpetuation of both those lies and the oppressive form of power that they generated. . . . The TRC's conscientious diffusion of the meaning of 'truth' aimed at the provisional and transitional nature of truth, a kind of empowering critical element within truth that could only come from the position of the powerless." Johnson, "Transitional Truth and Historical Justice," 81.

24. See Arendt, "Truth and Politics," 260, 261. Also see Hannah Arendt, "Lying in Politics," in *Crises of the Republic* (New York: Harcourt Brace Jovanovich, 1972), 44–45.

25. Benedict Anderson, *Imagined Communities: Reflections on the Origin and Spread of Nationalism* (London: Verso, 1991); Eric Hobsbawm and Terence Ranger, eds., *The Invention of Tradition* (Cambridge: Cambridge University Press, 1983).

26. Pierre Nora, "General Introduction: Between Memory and History," in *Realms of Memory: The Construction of the French Past*, vol. 1, *Conflicts and Divisions*, ed. Lawrence D. Kritzman, trans. Arthur Goldhammer (New York: Columbia University Press, 1996), 3.

27. Pierre Nora, "Between Memory and History: Les Lieux de Mémoire," *Representations* 26 (1989): 9.

28. Nora, "General Introduction," 3.

29. Nora, "General Introduction," 2.

30. Nora, "General Introduction," 6.

31. Pierre Nora, "The Era of Commemoration," in *Realms of Memory: The Construction of the French Past*, vol. 3, *Symbols*, ed. Lawrence D. Kritzman, trans. Arthur Goldhammer (New York: Columbia University Press, 1998), 626.

32. Nancy Wood, *Vectors of Memory: Legacies of Trauma in Postwar Europe* (Oxford: Berg, 1999), 16.

33. Ricoeur, *Memory, History, Forgetting*, 91.

34. Nora, "General Introduction," 1.

35. Ricoeur, *Memory, History, Forgetting*, 406.

36. The collaborative project of rethinking the French nation, compiled in several volumes under Nora's direction, reflects the exclusions of a nation-centered framework. Hue-Tam Ho Tai alerts the readers of *Les lieux de mémoire* to the complete absence of colonialism in the seven vol-

umes devoted to the history of the French nation. Hue-Tam Ho Tai, "Remembered Realms: Pierre Nora and French National Memory," *American Historical Review* 106, no. 3 (2001): 906–922.

37. Benedict Anderson formulates the violent unfolding of national history in his discussion of *fraternity* and *fratricide*. Characterizing political violence as fratricide already assumes that one is imagining a sense of fraternity, represented in the writings of Ernest Renan and Jules Michelet: "the imagining of that fraternity, *without which the reassurance of fratricide can not be born*, shows up remarkably early, and not without a curious authentic popularity." Anderson, *Imagined Communities*, 202; emphasis mine.

38. Nora, "General Introduction," 11.

39. Jürgen Habermas, *The New Conservatism: Cultural Criticism and the Historians' Debate*, trans. Shierry Weber Nicholsen (Cambridge, MA: MIT Press, 1990).

40. In particular, Habermas addresses the writings of Ernst Nolte, Andreas Hillgruber, and Michael Stürmer.

41. Habermas, *The New Conservatism*, 237.

42. Habermas, *The New Conservatism*, 209.

43. Habermas, *The New Conservatism*, 226–227.

44. German historiography underwent significant transformations in the 1960s. The first young generation to be born in the Bundesrepublik promoted "a democratic ethos" that "began to replace the old forms of authoritarian nationalism." Georg G. Iggers, "Nationalism and Historiography, 1789–1996: The German Example in Historical Perspective," in *Writing National Histories: Western Europe Since 1800*, ed. Stefan Berger, Mark Donovan, and Kevin Passmore (London: Routledge, 1999), 23.

45. Habermas, *The New Conservatism*, 253.

46. Habermas, *The New Conservatism*, 254.

47. Habermas, *The New Conservatism*, 234.

48. Drawing on Nora's work, Ross Poole refers to this as the "tension within historical practice" and argues that Habermas's position in the Historians' Debate reflects such a tension: "History . . . wears the guise of disinterested scholarship, treats the nation as just another historical contingency, and investigates other social formation (classes, mentalities, geographical areas, etc.) that have equal or greater historical interest. But it also has a public existence, in which it is at the service of various projects to transform or preserve the nation's understanding of itself: it speaks to and for our country. In its academic existence, it often strives to speak in the third person and to achieve a certain value neutrality. In its public role, however, it adopts the first person, and cannot escape the values and commitments implicit in this identification." Ross Poole, "Memory, History and the Claims of the Past," *Memory Studies* 1 (2008): 161.

49. Paul Ricoeur's treatment of the Historians' Debate is illuminating here. He is guided by the question: "is a historiographical treatment of the unacceptable possible?" The disagreement between Habermas and Nolte over the moral and historical significance of the Holocaust ultimately centers on its uniqueness and comparability. Ricoeur states that only "an enlightened public opinion" can establish the "exemplary singularity" insofar as citizens transform the retrospective judgment "into a pledge to prevent [the crime's] reoccurrence." Ricoeur, *Memory, History, Forgetting*, 326–333.

50. Freeman, *Truth Commissions and Procedural Fairness*.

51. Michel Foucault, "Truth and Juridical Forms," in *Power*, vol. 3 of *Essential Works of Foucault, 1954–1984*, ed. James D. Faubion, series ed. Paul Rabinow (New York: New Press, 2000).

52. Booth, "The Unforgotten," 786.

53. Habermas's strong defense of post-national identity in the course of the Historians' Debate has not gone uncontested among the left-leaning scholars. Mary Nolan observes that many historians associated with the history of the everyday (*Alltagsgeschichte*) tradition have directed the resistance to nationalism toward local and oppositional identities. Mary Nolan, "The Historikerstreit and Social History," *New German Critique* 44 (1988): 51–80.

54. It is interesting to note that Habermas uses the notion "constitutional patriotism" for the first time in the course of the Historians' Debate. Patchen Markell, "Making Affect Safe for Democracy? On 'Constitutional Patriotism,'" *Political Theory* 28, no. 1 (2000): 38–63.

55. Habermas, *The New Conservatism*, 257. For an excellent discussion of the connection between constitutional morality and memory in the German context, see Jan-Werner Müller, "On the Origins of Constitutional Patriotism," *Contemporary Political Theory* 5, no. 3 (2006): 278–296.

56. Habermas, *The New Conservatism*, 227.

57. Jürgen Habermas, "The Finger of Blame: The Germans and Their Memorial," in *Time of Transitions*, ed. and trans. Ciaran Cronin and Max Pensky (Cambridge: Polity Press, 2006), 44.

58. Benjamin Robinson, "Against Memory as Justice," *New German Critique* 33, no. 2 (2006): 135–160.

59. Likewise, the use of local traditional and religious conceptions of justice and reconciliation, such as *ubuntu* in South Africa, can be seen as the expression of an alternative framework to think about the nation.

60. Furthermore, truth commissions do not necessarily provide the impetus for novel institutions, national or post-national. Most commissions were not accompanied by new, post-authoritarian constitutions (South Africa being a major exception). In fact, many suspect that the absence of a "constitutional moment" during a political transition may have popularized truth commissions for political elites as a nonbinding (therefore ineffectual) spectacle of national reconstruction.

61. Barry K. Gills, "'Empire' Versus 'Cosmopolis': The Clash of Globalizations," *Globalizations* 2, no. 1 (2005): 5–13.

62. Daniel Levy and Natan Sznaider, "Memory Unbound: The Holocaust and the Formation of Cosmopolitan Memory," *European Journal of Social Theory* 5, no. 1 (2002): 87–106.

Conclusion

1. Adorno's famous 1959 essay, titled "What Does Coming to Terms with the Past Mean?," begins with the observation that West German society has achieved the miraculous transition to democracy at the cost of citizens' emotional detachment and alienation from politics. Adorno's terminology is instructive in grasping the subtleties of the general notion of *coming to terms with the past*. He prefers the German word *Aufarbeitung* (working through) over *Bewältigung* (mastering over) throughout the essay. The former connotes an active work of engagement with the past, without necessarily reaching an end point where working through is no longer necessary, whereas the latter signifies the possibility that mastery over the past, once and for all, is achievable. Theodor W. Adorno, "What Does Coming to Terms with the Past Mean?" in *Bitburg in Moral and Political Perspective*, ed. Geoffrey H. Hartman (Bloomington: Indiana University Press, 1986), 114–129.

2. Developed as an ethic of recognition by Nancy Fraser, *participatory parity* grounds the discourse of cultural recognition in struggles for equality and justice. Fraser demonstrates the pitfalls of reducing progressive politics to the acknowledgment of cultural difference at the expense of emancipatory projects of eliminating socioeconomic domination. Nancy Fraser, "Recognition Without Ethics?," *Theory, Culture & Society* 18, nos. 2–3 (June 2001): 21–42. Also see Nancy Fraser, "From Redistribution to Recognition? Dilemmas of Justice in a 'Post Socialist' Age," in *Theorizing Multiculturalism: A Guide to the Current Debate*, ed. Cynthia Weller (Oxford: Blackwell, 1998), 19–49; Nancy Fraser "Rethinking Recognition: Overcoming Displacement and Reification in Cultural Politics," *New Left Review* 2, no. 3 (2000): 110–111.

3. The tensions between truth commissions' striving for an accurate historical record and an inclusive process are explored in Bronwyn Leebaw, "The Irreconcilable Goals of Transitional Justice," *Human Rights Quarterly* 30, no. 1 (2008): 95–118.

BIBLIOGRAPHY

Abrams, Jason S., and Priscilla B. Hayner. "Documenting, Acknowledging and Publicizing the Truth." In *Post-Conflict Justice*, ed. M. Cherif Bassiouni, 283–293. Ardsley, NY: Transnational Publishers, 2002.

Adorno, Theodor W. "What Does Coming to Terms with the Past Mean?" In *Bitburg in Moral and Political Perspective*, ed. Geoffrey H. Hartman, 114–129. Bloomington: Indiana University Press, 1986.

Alexander, Jeffrey C., Ron Eyerman, Bernard Giesen, Neil J. Smelser, and Piotr Sztompka. *Cultural Trauma and Collective Identity*. Berkeley: University of California Press, 2004.

Allamand, Andrés. "Verdad a medias." *La Tercera*, April 29, 1990.

Allen, Jonathan. "Balancing Justice and Social Unity: Political Theory and the Idea of a Truth and Reconciliation Commission." *University of Toronto Law Journal* 49, no. 3 (2001): 315–353.

"Amia Bombing: Argentina and Iran Agree Truth Commission." *BBC News*, January 28, 2013.

Amnesty International. *Chile: El legado de los derechos humanos.* AI: AMR 22/01/91/s. Madrid: Editorial Amnistía Internacional, 1991.

——. *Nigeria: Time for Justice and Accountability.* London: International Secretariat, 2000.

——. *Timor-Leste: Remembering the Past; Recommendations to Effectively Establish the "National Reparations Programme" and "Public Memory Institute."* London: Amnesty International, 2012.

——. "Truth, Justice and Reparation: Establishing an Effective Truth Commission." POL 30/009/2007, June 11, 2007.

Anaya, Alejandro. "Transnational and Domestic Processes in the Definition of Human Rights Policies in Mexico." *Human Rights Quarterly* 31, no. 1 (2009): 35–58.

Anderson, Benedict. *Imagined Communities: Reflections on the Origin and Spread of Nationalism.* London: Verso, 1991.

Andrews, Molly. "Grand National Narratives and the Project of Truth Commissions: A Comparative Analysis." *Media, Culture & Society* 25, no. 1 (2003): 45–65.

Anonymous. "Against the Grain: Pursuing a Transitional Justice Agenda in Postwar Sri Lanka." *International Journal of Transitional Justice* 5, no. 1 (2011): 31–51.

Apel, Karin. "Resultados de las Convocatorias 'Fortalecimiento de la Democracia y Reparaciones en Huancavelica y norte de Ayacucho,' C03–2005–L1 C03–2006–L1 (adicional)." December 2007. Available at http://www.fcpa.org.pe/archivos/file/Sistematizacion_ApoyoalPIR .pdf

Arendt, Hannah. *Eichmann in Jerusalem: A Report on the Banality of Evil.* New York: Penguin Books, 2006.

——. *The Human Condition.* Chicago: University of Chicago Press, 1998.

——. "Lying in Politics." In *Crises of the Republic*, 1–48. New York: Harcourt Brace Jovanovich, 1972.

——. *The Origins of Totalitarianism.* New York: Harcourt, Brace, 1951.

———. "Truth and Politics," in *Between Past and Future: Eight Exercises in Political Thought*. New York: Penguin Books, 1977.

Arthur, Paige. "'Fear of the Future, Lived Through the Past': Pursuing Transitional Justice in the Wake of Ethnic Conflict." In *Identities in Transition: Challenges for Transitional Justice in Divided Societies*, ed. Paige Arthur, 271–302. New York: Cambridge University Press, 2011.

———. "How 'Transitions' Reshaped Human Rights: A Conceptual History of Transitional Justice." *Human Rights Quarterly* 31, no. 2 (2009): 321–354.

———, ed. *Identities in Transition: Challenges for Transitional Justice in Divided Societies*. New York: Cambridge University Press, 2011.

Ash, Timothy Garton. "A Nation in Denial." *Guardian*, March 7, 2002.

Assmann, Aleida. "History, Memory, and the Genre of Testimony." *Poetics Today* 27, no. 2 (2006): 261–273.

Autesserre, Séverine. *The Trouble with the Congo: Local Violence and the Failure of International Peacebuilding*. Cambridge: Cambridge University Press, 2010.

Aylwin Azócar, Patricio. "La Concertación de Partidos por la Democracia: Desafíos y perspectivas." In *Crecimiento con equidad: Discursos escogidos, 1992–1994*. Santiago: Editorial Andres Bello, 1994.

Backer, David. "Civil Society and Transitional Justice: Possibilities, Patterns and Prospects." *Journal of Human Rights* 2, no. 3 (2003): 297–313.

———. "Watching a Bargain Unravel? A Panel Study of Victims' Attitudes About Transitional Justice in Cape Town, South Africa." *International Journal of Transitional Justice* 4, no. 3 (2010): 443–456.

Baer, Ulrich. *Remnants of Song: Trauma and the Experience of Modernity in Charles Baudelaire and Paul Celan*. Stanford, CA: Stanford University Press, 2000.

Bakiner, Onur. "From Denial to Reluctant Dialogue: The Chilean Military's Confrontation with Human Rights (1990–2006)." *International Journal of Transitional Justice* 4, no. 1 (2010): 47–66.

Ball, Patrick, Jana Asher, David Sulmont, and Daniel Manrique. 2003. *How Many Peruvians Have Died?* Washington, DC: American Association for the Advancement of Science, 2003.

Ball, Patrick, and Herbert F. Spirer. "The Haitian National Commission for Truth and Justice: Collecting Information, Data Processing, Database Representation, and Generating Analytical Reports." In *Making the Case: Investigating Large Scale Human Rights Violations Using Information Systems and Data Analysis*, ed. Patrick Ball, Herbert F. Spirer, and Louise Spirer, 27–40. Washington, DC: American Association for the Advancement of Science, 2000.

"Banking—Stand for an Inquiry." *BBC News*, July 2, 2012.

Barahona de Brito, Alexandra. "Truth and Justice in the Consolidation of Democracy in Chile and Uruguay." *Parliamentary Affairs* 46, no. 4 (1993): 579–593.

Bartley, Aryn. "The Violence of the Present: *David's Story* and the Truth and Reconciliation Commission." *Comparative Literature Studies* 46, no. 1 (2009): 103–124.

Basombrío Iglesias, Carlos. "Sendero Luminoso and Human Rights: A Perverse Logic That Captured the Country." In *Shining and Other Paths: War and Society in Peru, 1980–1995*, ed. Steve J. Stern, 425–446. Durham, NC: Duke University Press, 1998.

"BBC Newsline Poll: Support for Parades Commission and Peace Centre." *BBC News*, December 17, 2013.

Beach, Derek, and Rasmus Brun Pedersen. "What Is Process Tracing Actually Tracing? The Three Variants of Process Tracing Methods and Their Uses and Limitations." Paper presented at the Annual Meeting of the American Political Science Association, Seattle, WA, September 2011.

Beitz, Charles. "What Human Rights Mean." *Daedalus* 132, no. 1 (2003): 36–46.

Bell, Christine. "Transitional Justice, Interdisciplinarity and the State of the 'Field' or 'Non-Field.'" *International Journal of Transitional Justice* 3, no. 1 (2009): 5–27.

Benedetti, Fanny. "Haiti's Truth and Justice Commission." Human Rights Brief, Center for Human Rights and Humanitarian Law, Washington College of Law, American University, 1996. http://www.wcl.american.edu/hrbrief/v3i3/haiti33.htm.

Bennett, Andrew. "Process Tracing: A Bayesian Approach." In *The Oxford Handbook of Political Methodology*, ed. Janet M. Box-Steffensmeier, Henry E. Brady, and David Collier, 702–721. Oxford: Oxford University Press, 2008.

Beverage, Berber. "Writing the Past Out of the Present: History and the Politics of Time in Transitional Justice." *History Workshop Journal* 69, no. 1 (2010): 111–131.

Bhattarai, Binod, Mohan Mainali, Jogendra Ghimere, and Akhilesh Upadhyay. *Impunity in Nepal: An Exploratory Study*. Kathmandu: Asia Foundation, 1999.

Bickford, Louis. "Unofficial Truth Projects." *Human Rights Quarterly* 29, no. 4 (2007): 994–1035.

Bisset, Alison. *Truth Commissions and Criminal Courts*. Cambridge: Cambridge University Press, 2012.

Blakeley, Georgina. "Digging Up Spain's Past: Consequences of Truth and Reconciliation." *Democratization* 12, no. 1 (2005): 44–59.

Blommaert, Jan, Mary Bock, and Kay McCormick. "Narrative Inequality in the TRC Hearings: On the Hearability of Hidden Transcripts." *Journal of Language and Politics* 5, no. 1 (2006): 37–70.

Bloomfield, David, Teresa Barnes, and Luc Huyse, eds. *Reconciliation After Violent Conflict: A Handbook*. Stockholm: IDEA, 2003.

Blustein, Jeffrey. *The Moral Demands of Memory*. Cambridge: Cambridge University Press, 2008.

Boesenecker, Aaron P., and Leslie Vinjamuri. "Lost in Translation? Civil Society, Faith-Based Organizations and the Negotiation of International Norms." *International Journal of Transitional Justice* 5, no. 3 (2011): 345–365.

Boler, Jean. "The Mothers Committee of El Salvador: National Human Rights Activists." *Human Rights Quarterly* 7, no. 4 (1985): 541–556.

Booth, W. James. "Communities of Memory: On Identity, Memory, and Debt." *American Political Science Review* 93, no. 2 (1999): 249–263.

———. "The Unforgotten: Memories of Justice." *American Political Science Review* 95, no. 4 (2001): 777–791.

Boraine, Alex. *A Country Unmasked: Inside South Africa's Truth and Reconciliation Commission*. Oxford: Oxford University Press, 2000.

Bosire, Lydiah Kemunto, and Gabrielle Lynch. "Kenya's Search for Truth and Justice: The Role of Civil Society." *International Journal of Transitional Justice* 8 (2014): 256–276.

Brody, Reed. "The Prosecution of Hissène Habré—an African Pinochet." *New England Law Review* 35 (2000): 321–326.

———. "The United Nations and Human Rights in El Salvador's Negotiated Revolution." *Harvard Human Rights Journal* 8 (1995): 153–178.

Bronkhorst, Daan. *Truth Commissions and Transitional Justice: A Short Guide*. Amsterdam: Amnesty International Dutch Section, 2003.

Brooks, Roy L. "Reflections on Reparations." In *Politics and the Past: On Repairing Historical Injustices*, ed. John Torpey, 103–114. Lanham, MD: Rowman and Littlefield, 2003.

Buergenthal, Thomas. "The United Nations Truth Commission for El Salvador." *Vanderbilt Journal of Transnational Law* 27, no. 3 (1994): 497–544.

Burgess, Patrick. "Justice and Reconciliation in East Timor: The Relationship Between the Commission for Reception, Truth and Reconciliation and the Courts." *Criminal Law Forum* 15 (2004): 135–158.

Burt, Jo-Marie. *Political Violence and the Authoritarian State in Peru: Silencing Civil Society.* Chicago: University of Chicago Press, 2003.

Caivano, Joan M., and Thayer Hardwick. "Latin American Women in Movement: Changing Politics, Changing Minds." In *Civil Society and Social Movements: Building Sustainable Democracies in Latin America,* ed. Arthur Domike, 265–300. Washington, DC: Inter-American Development Bank, 2008.

Call, Charles T. "Democratisation, War and State-Building: Constructing the Rule of Law in El Salvador." *Journal of Latin American Studies* 35, no. 4 (2003): 827–862.

———. 2004. "Is Transitional Justice Really Just?" *Brown Journal of World Affairs* 11, no. 1 (2004): 101–114.

"Cancillería difundirá informe de la CVR." *La República*, February 24, 2004.

Capdevila, Luc. "Le passé/présent entre dictature et transition politique dans la société paraguayenne contemporaine." *Nuevo Mundo Mundos Nuevos,* Coloquios, 2008. http://nuevomundo .revues.org/28802.

Cavallo, Ascanio. *La historia oculta de la transición.* Santiago: Grijalbo, 1998.

Chapman, Audrey R. "Truth Commissions as Instruments of Forgiveness and Reconciliation." In *Forgiveness and Reconciliation: Religion, Public Policy, and Conflict Transformation,* ed. Raymond G. Helmick and Rodney L. Peterson. Philadelphia: Templeton Foundation Press, 2001.

———. "Truth Finding in the Transitional Justice Process." In *Assessing the Impact of Transitional Justice: Challenges for Empirical Research,* ed. Hugo van der Merwe, Victoria Baxter, and Audrey R. Chapman. Washington, DC: U.S. Institute of Peace Press, 2009.

Chapman, Audrey R., and Patrick Ball. "The Truth of Truth Commissions: Comparative Lessons from Haiti, South Africa, and Guatemala." *Human Rights Quarterly* 23, no. 1 (2001): 1–43.

Chapman, Audrey R., and Hugo van der Merwe. "Introduction: Assessing the South African Transitional Justice Model." In *Truth and Reconciliation in South Africa: Did the TRC Deliver?,* ed. Audrey R. Chapman and Hugo van der Merwe, 1–19. Philadelphia: University of Pennsylvania Press, 2008.

Checkel, Jeffrey T. "Tracing Causal Mechanisms." *International Studies Review* 8, no. 2 (2006): 362–370.

Chinapen, Rhiana, and Richard Vernon. "Justice in Transition." *Canadian Journal of Political Science* 39, no. 1 (2006): 117–134.

Cochran-Budhathoki, Karon, and Scott Worden. "Transitional Justice in Nepal: A Look at the International Experience of Truth Commissions." *USIP Policy Brief* (2007). Available at http://www.usip.org/resources/transitional-justice-nepal-look-international-experience -truth-commissions.

Cole, Elizabeth A. "Transitional Justice and the Reform of History Education." *International Journal of Transitional Justice* 1, no. 1 (2007): 115–137.

Cole, Elizabeth. A., and Karen Murphy. "History Education Reform, Transitional Justice, and the Transformation of Identities." In *Identities in Transition: Challenges for Transitional Justice in Divided Societies,* ed. Paige Arthur, 334–367. New York: Cambridge University Press, 2011.

Collier, David, and James Mahoney. "Insights and Pitfalls: Selection Bias in Qualitative Research." *World Politics* 49, no. 1 (1996): 56–91.

Collier, Paul, Anke Hoeffler, and Måns Söderbom. "Post-Conflict Risks." CSAE WPS/2006-12. Oxford: Centre for the Study of African Economies, Department of Economics, University of Oxford, 2006.

Collins, Cath. "Grounding Global Justice: International Networks and Domestic Human Rights Accountability in Chile and El Salvador." *Journal of Latin American Studies* 38, no. 4 (2006): 711–738.

———. *Post-Transitional Justice: Human Rights Trials in Chile and El Salvador.* University Park: Pennsylvania State University Press, 2010.

———. "State Terror and the Law: The (Re)judicialization of Human Rights Accountability in Chile and El Salvador." *Latin American Perspectives* 35, no. 5 (2008): 20–37.

Colorado García, José Iván. "Violaciones a los derechos humanos y transición a la democracia en Chile (1990–1994)." Presented at I Encuentro de Jóvenes Investigadores en Historia Contemporánea de la Asociación de Historia Contemporánea, Zaragoza, September 26–28, 2007.

Colvin, Christopher J. "Overview of the Reparations Program in South Africa." In *The Handbook of Reparations*, ed. Pablo de Greiff, 176–214. Oxford: Oxford University Press, 2006.

Comisión para la Paz [Commission for Peace, Uruguay]. *Informe Final.* Montevideo: La Comisión, 2003.

Comisión de la Verdad y Reconciliación [CVR, Peru]. *Informe Final.* Lima: CVR, 2003.

Commission for Reception, Truth, and Reconciliation Timor-Leste (CAVR). *Chega! Final Report of the Commission for Reception, Truth and Reconciliation in East Timor, 2005.* New York: International Center for Transitional Justice, 2005.

Confederación Nacional de Instituciones Empresariales Privadas (CONFIEP). "Pronunciamiento en torno a las conclusiones del Informe de la Comisión de la Verdad y la Reconciliación." September 26, 2003.

Connerton, Paul. *How Societies Remember.* New York: Cambridge University Press, 1989.

Cooper, Andrew F., and Thomas Legler. "A Tale of Two Mesas: The OAS Defense of Democracy in Peru and Venezuela." *Global Governance* 11, no. 4 (2005): 425–444.

Correa, Cristián. *Reparations in Peru: From Recommendations to Implementation.* New York: International Center for Transitional Justice, 2013.

Cosamalón Aguilar, Jesús A. "Combatir contra el olvido: El oficio de historiador después del Informe de la CVR." *Páginas* 30, no. 196 (2005): 48–58.

Crenzel, Emilio. "Argentina's National Commission on the Disappearance of Persons: Contributions to Transitional Justice." *International Journal of Transitional Justice* 2, no. 2 (2008): 173–191.

Cuadros Garland, Daniela. "La Commission Rettig: Innovation, silences et contestations d'une mise en récit 'consensuelle' des violations des droits de l'homme au Chili." 2006. Available at http://cuadros.free.fr/militantisme_fichiers/cuadrosrettig2006.pdf.

Daly, Erin. 2008. "Truth Skepticism: An Inquiry into the Value of Truth in Times of Transition." *International Journal of Transitional Justice* 2, no. 1 (2008): 23–41.

Dancy, Geoff. "Impact Assessment, Not Evaluation: Defining a Limited Role for Positivism in the Study of Transitional Justice." *International Journal of Transitional Justice* 4, no. 3 (2010): 355–376.

De Baets, Antoon. "Resistance to the Censorship of Historical Thought in the Twentieth Century." In *Making Sense of Global History: The 19th International Congress of Historical Sciences, Oslo 2000, Commemorative Volume*, ed. Sølvi Sogner, 389–409. Oslo: Universitetsforlaget, 2001.

"Deben respetarse las funciones propias del poder judicial." *El Mercurio*, April 7, 1990.

Degregori, Carlos Iván. *El surgimiento de Sendero Luminoso: Ayacucho, 1969–1979.* Lima: Instituto de Estudios Peruanos, 1990.

Degregori, Carlos Iván, and Pablo Sandoval. "La antropología en el Perú: Del estudio del otro a la construcción de un nosotros diverso." *Revista Colombiana de Antropología* 43 (2007): 299–334.

de Greiff, Pablo. "Habermas on Nationalism and Cosmopolitanism." *Ratio Juris* 15, no. 4 (2002): 418–438.

———, ed. *The Handbook of Reparations.* Oxford: Oxford University Press, 2006.

de Lange, Johnny. "The Historical Context, Legal Origins and Philosophical Foundation of the South African Truth and Reconciliation Commission." In *Looking Back Reaching Forward:*

Reflections on the Truth and Reconciliation Commission of South Africa, ed. Charles Villa-Vicencio and Wilhelm Verwoerd, 14–31. Cape Town, South Africa: Cape Town University Press, 2000.

del Pino H., Ponciano. "Family, Culture, and 'Revolution': Everyday Life with Sendero Luminoso." In *Shining and Other Paths: War and Society in Peru, 1980–1995*, ed. Steve J. Stern, 158–192. Durham, NC: Duke University Press, 1998.

Dorfman, Ariel. *Exorcising Terror: The Incredible Unending Trial of General Augusto Pinochet.* New York: Seven Stories Press, 2002.

Dougherty, Beth K. "Searching for Answers: Sierra Leone's Truth & Reconciliation Commission." *African Studies Quarterly* 8, no. 1 (2004): 39–56.

Doyle, Kate. "'Forgetting Is Not Justice': Mexico Bares Its Secret." *World Policy Journal* 20, no. 2 (2003): 61–72.

Drabinski, John E. "'That Gesture of Recognition': An Interview with Salomón Lerner Febres." *Humanity: An International Journal of Human Rights, Humanitarianism, and Development* 4, no. 1 (2013): 171–180.

Drexler, Elizabeth F. "Fatal Knowledges: The Social and Political Legacies of Collaboration and Betrayal in Timor-Leste." *International Journal of Transitional Justice* 7, no. 1 (2013): 74–94.

du Toit, André. "The Moral Foundations of the South African TRC: Truth as Acknowledgment and Justice as Recognition." In *Truth v. Justice: The Morality of Truth Commissions*, ed. Robert I. Rotberg and Dennis Thompson, 122–140. Princeton, NJ: Princeton University Press, 2000.

Dwyer, Susan. "Reconciliation for Realists." *Ethics and International Affairs* 13, no. 1 (2006): 81–98.

Eastmond, Marita, and Johanna Mannergren Selimovic. "Silence as Possibility in Postwar Everyday Life." *International Journal of Transitional Justice* 6, no. 3 (2012): 502–524.

"Ejército entregó amplio informe a comisión Rettig." *El Mercurio*, August 7, 1990.

"El informe sobre la toma del Palacio de Justicia." Posted on Álvaro E. Duque's blog *Este infierno paradisíaco*, November 19, 2006. Available at http://alvaroduque.wordpress.com/2006/11/19 /el-informe-sobre-la-toma-del-palacio-de-justicia/.

Elster, Jon. *Closing the Books: Transitional Justice in Historical Perspective.* Cambridge: Cambridge University Press, 2004.

Ensalaco, Mark. "Truth Commissions for Chile and El Salvador: A Report and Assessment." *Human Rights Quarterly* 16, no. 4 (1994): 657–675.

Evans, Rebecca. "Pinochet in London—Pinochet in Chile: International and Domestic Politics in Human Rights Policy." *Human Rights Quarterly* 28, no. 1 (2006): 207–244.

Evans, Richard J. "History, Memory, and the Law: The Historian as Expert Witness." *History and Theory* 41, no. 3 (2002): 326–345.

Evenson, Elizabeth M. "Truth and Justice in Sierra Leone: Coordination Between Commission and Court." *Columbia Law Review* 104, no. 3 (2004): 730–767.

Final Report of the Commission of Inquiry into Involuntary Removal and Disappearance of Certain Persons (All Island) [Sri Lanka]. 2001.

Finnemore, Martha, and Kathryn Sikkink. "International Norm Dynamics and Political Change." *International Organization* 52, no. 2 (1998): 887–917.

Fletcher, Laurel E., and Harvey M. Weinstein. "Violence and Social Repair: Rethinking the Contribution of Justice to Reconciliation." *Human Rights Quarterly* 24 (2002): 573–639.

Fogu, Claudio, and Wulf Kansteiner. "The Politics of Memory and the Poetics of History." In *The Politics of Memory in Postwar Europe*, ed. Richard Ned Lebow, Wulf Kansteiner, and Claudio Fogu, 284–310. Durham, NC: Duke University Press, 2006.

Foucault, Michel. "Truth and Juridical Forms." In *Power*, vol. 3 of *Essential Works of Foucault, 1954–1984*, ed. James D. Faubion, series ed. Paul Rabinow. New York: New Press, 2000.

Fraser, Nancy. "From Redistribution to Recognition? Dilemmas of Justice in a 'Post Socialist' Age." In *Theorizing Multiculturalism: A Guide to the Current Debate*, ed. Cynthia Willett, 19–49. Oxford: Blackwell, 1998.

———. "Recognition Without Ethics?" Theory, Culture and Society 18, nos. 2–3 (2001): 21–42.

———. "Rethinking Recognition: Overcoming Displacement and Reification in Cultural Politics." *New Left Review* 2, no. 3 (2000): 107–120.

Freeman, Mark. *Truth Commissions and Procedural Fairness*. Cambridge: Cambridge University Press, 2006.

Freeman, Mark, and Priscilla B. Hayner. "Truth-Telling." In *Reconciliation After Violent Conflict: A Handbook*, ed. David Bloomfield, Teresa Barnes, and Luc Huyse, 122–144. Stockholm: IDEA, 2003.

Freeman, Mark, and Joanna R. Quinn. "Lessons Learned: Practical Lessons Gleaned from Inside the Truth Commissions of Guatemala and South Africa." *Human Rights Quarterly* 25, no. 4 (2003): 1117–1149.

Frente Regional de Organizaciones de Base por la Verdad y Justicia (FROBAVEJ)–Ayacucho. "Pronunciamiento: El Frente Regional de Organizaciones de Base por la Verdad y Justicia." 2004.

From Madness to Hope: The 12-year War in El Salvador; Report of the Commission on the Truth for El Salvador. New York: United Nations, 1993. Available at www.usip.org/sites/default/files/file/ElSalvador-Report.pdf.

Fruhling, Hugo. "Nonprofit Organizations as Opposition to Authoritarian Rule: The Case of Human Rights Organizations in Chile." In *The Nonprofit Sector in International Perspective*, ed. Estelle James. New York: Oxford University Press, 1989.

Fruhling, Hugo, and Frederick Woodbridge, Jr. "Stages of Repression and Legal Strategy for the Defense of Human Rights in Chile: 1973–1980." *Human Rights Quarterly* 5, no. 4 (1983): 510–533.

Fuentes, Claudio. "Partidos políticos en Chile: Entre pactos y proyectos." In *El modelo chileno: Democracia y desarrollo en los Noventa*, ed. Paul Drake and Ivan Jaksic. Santiago: LOM ediciones, Colección sin Norte, 1999.

Fullard, Madeleine, and Nicky Rousseau. "Truth Telling, Identities, and Power in South Africa and Guatemala." In *Identities in Transition: Challenges for Transitional Justice in Divided Societies*, ed. Paige Arthur, 54–86. New York: Cambridge University Press, 2011.

Gairdner, David. *Truth in Transition: The Role of Truth Commissions in Political Transition in Chile and El Salvador*. Bergen: Chr. Michelsen Institute, 1999.

Galak, Oliver. "Controversia por el prólogo agregado al informe 'Nunca más': Rechaza la teoría de los dos demonios." *La Nación*, May 19, 2006.

Garretón, Manuel Antonio. "La redemocratización política en Chile: Transición, inauguración, y evolución." *Estudios Públicos* 42 (1991): 101–133.

Garretón, Roberto. "Política de derechos humanos del gobierno democrático." *Política y Espíritu* 46, no. 391 (1992): 21–25.

Gberie, Lansana. "Truth and Justice on Trial in Liberia." *African Affairs* 107, no. 428 (2008): 455–465.

Gibson, James L. "The Contributions of Truth to Reconciliation: Lessons from South Africa." *Journal of Conflict Resolution* 50, no. 3 (Transitional Justice) (2006): 409–432.

———. *Overcoming Apartheid: Can Truth Reconcile a Divided Nation?* (New York: Russell Sage Foundation, 2004).

———. "Truth, Reconciliation, and the Creation of a Human Rights Culture in South Africa." *Law & Society Review* 38, no. 1 (2004): 5–40.

Gibson, James L., and Amanda Gouws. "Truth and Reconciliation in South Africa: Attributions of Blame and the Struggle over Apartheid." *American Political Science Review* 93, no. 3 (1999): 501–517.

Gills, Barry K. "'Empire' Versus 'Cosmopolis': The Clash of Globalizations." *Globalizations* 2, no. 1 (2005): 5–13.

Gomez, Mario. "Sri Lanka's New Human Rights Commission." *Human Rights Quarterly* 20, no. 2 (1998): 281–302.

González Cueva, Eduardo. "The Contribution of the Peruvian Truth and Reconciliation Commission to Prosecutions." *Criminal Law Forum* 15 (2004): 55–66.

González Enríquez, Carmen, Alexandra Barahona de Brito, and Paloma Aguilar Fernández. *The Politics of Memory: Transitional Justice in Democratizing Societies.* Oxford: Oxford University Press, 2001.

Gorriti, Gustavo. *Shining Path: A History of the Millenarian War in Peru.* Trans. Robin Kirk. Chapel Hill: University of North Carolina Press, 1999.

Grandin, Greg. "The Instruction of Great Catastrophe: Truth Commissions, National History, and State Formation in Argentina, Chile, and Guatemala." *American Historical Review* 110, no. 1 (2005): 46–67.

Grez, Sergio, and Gabriel Salazar, comps. *Manifiesto de historiadores.* Santiago de Chile: LOM, 1999.

Grodsky, Brian. "International Prosecutions and Domestic Politics: The Use of Truth Commissions as Compromise Justice in Serbia and Croatia." *International Studies Review* 11, no. 4 (2009): 687–706.

Guatemala: Memory of Silence; Tz'inil Na'tab'al. Report of the Commission for Historical Clarification, Guatemala, 1999. Available at www.aaas.org/sites/default/files/migrate/uploads/mos _en.pdf

Guillerot, Julie, and Lisa Magarrell. *Reparación en la transición peruana: Memorias de un proceso inacabado.* Lima: APRODEH, 2006.

Habermas, Jürgen. "The Finger of Blame: The Germans and Their Memorial." In *Time of Transitions,* ed. and trans. Ciaran Cronin and Max Pensky. Cambridge: Polity Press, 2006.

———. *The New Conservatism: Cultural Criticism and the Historians' Debate.* Trans. Shierry Weber Nicholsen. Cambridge, MA: MIT Press, 1990.

———. *The Postnational Constellation: Political Essays.* Trans., ed., and with an introduction by Max Pensky. Cambridge, MA: MIT Press, 2001.

Hafner-Burton, Emilie M., and James Ron. "Seeing Double: Human Rights Impact Through Qualitative and Quantitative Eyes." *World Politics* 61, no. 2 (2009): 360–401.

Halbwachs, Maurice. *On Collective Memory.* Trans. Lewis A. Coser. Chicago: University of Chicago Press, 1992.

Hamber, Brandon. "The Need for a Survivor-Centered Approach to the Truth and Reconciliation Commission." *Community Mediation Update* (Community Dispute Resolution Trust, Johannesburg, South Africa) 9 (1996).

Hamber, Brandon, and Richard A. Wilson. "Symbolic Closure Through Memory, Reparation and Revenge in Post-Conflict Societies." *Journal of Human Rights* 1, no. 1 (2002): 35–53.

Harris, Peter, and Ben Reilly, eds. *Democracy and Deep-Rooted Conflict: Options for Negotiators.* Stockholm: International Institute for Democracy and Electoral Assistance, 1998.

Hatun Willakuy: Versión abreviada del Informe final de la Comisión de la Verdad y Reconciliación, Perú. Lima: Comisión de la Verdad y Reconciliación, 2004.

Hayner, Priscilla B. "Commissioning the Truth: Further Research Questions." *Third World Quarterly* 17, no. 1 (1996): 19–30.

———. "Fifteen Truth Commissions—1974 to 1994: A Comparative Study." *Human Rights Quarterly* 16, no. 4 (1994): 597–655.

———. *Negotiating Peace in Sierra Leone: Confronting the Justice Challenge.* Geneva: Centre for Humanitarian Dialogue, 2007.

———. "Past Truths, Present Dangers: The Role of Official Truth Seeking in Conflict Resolution and Prevention." In *International Conflict Resolution After the Cold War*, ed. Paul C. Stern and Daniel Druckman, 338–382. Washington, DC: National Academies Press, 2000.

———. "Truth Commissions: Exhuming the Past." *NACLA Report on the Americas* 32, no. 2 (1998): 30–32.

———. "Truth Commissions: A Schematic Overview." *International Review of the Red Cross* 88, no. 862 (2006): 295–310.

———. *Unspeakable Truths: Confronting State Terror and Atrocity*. New York: Routledge, 2011.

"Head of Teachers' Union Tests Candidates' Views." *New York Times*, May 10, 2013.

Hobsbawm, Eric, and Ranger, Terence, eds. *The Invention of Tradition*. Cambridge: Cambridge University Press, 1983.

Holiday, David, and William Stanley. "Building the Peace: Preliminary Lessons from El Salvador." *Journal of International Affairs* 46, no. 2 (1993): 415–438.

Hovil, Lucy, and Moses Chrispus Okello. "Editorial Note." *International Journal of Transitional Justice* 5, no. 3 (2011): 333–344.

Howe, Richard Herbert. "Max Weber's Elective Affinities: Sociology Within the Bounds of Pure Reason." *American Journal of Sociology* 84, no. 2 (1978): 366–385.

Human Rights Watch. "Chad: The Victims of Hissène Habré Still Awaiting Justice." *Human Rights Watch* 17, no. 10(A), July 2005.

———. *Human Rights Watch World Report 1992: Events of 1991*. New York: Human Rights Watch, 1992.

———. *Waiting for Justice: Unpunished Crimes from Nepal's Armed Conflict*. New York: Human Rights Watch, 2008.

Humphrey, Michael. "From Victim to Victimhood: Truth Commissions and Trials as Rituals of Political Transition and Individual Healing." *Australian Journal of Anthropology* 14, no. 2 (2003): 171–187.

Huntington, Samuel P. *The Third Wave: Democratization in the Late Twentieth Century*. Norman: University of Oklahoma Press, 1991.

Huyse, Luc. "Reconciliation: The People." In *Reconciliation After Violent Conflict: A Handbook*, ed. David Bloomfield, Teresa Barnes, and Luc Huyse. Stockholm: IDEA, 2003.

Iggers, Georg G. "Nationalism and Historiography, 1789–1996: The German Example in Historical Perspective." In *Writing National Histories: Western Europe Since 1800*, ed. Stefan Berger, Mark Donovan, and Kevin Passmore, 15–29. London: Routledge, 1999.

Ikhariale, Mike. "The Oputa Reports: An Unfinished Job." May 2002. Available at http://www.nigerdeltacongress.com/oarticles/oputa_reports.htm.

Ilic, Dejan. "The Yugoslav Truth and Reconciliation Commission: Overcoming Cognitive Blocks." *Eurozine*, April 23, 2004.

Iliff, Andrew R. "Root and Branch: Discourses of 'Tradition' in Grassroots Transitional Justice." *International Journal of Transitional Justice* 6, no. 2 (2012): 253–273.

Imbleau, Martin. "Initial Truth Establishment by Transitional Bodies and the Fight Against Denial." In *Truth Commissions and Courts: The Tension Between Criminal Justice and the Search for Truth*, ed. William A. Schabas and Shane Darcy, 159–192. Dordrecht: Kluwer, 2004.

"Informe CVR y silencios." *La República*, September 28, 2003.

International Federation for Human Rights. "Observatory for the Protection of Human Rights Defenders Annual Report 2009—Peru." June 18, 2009. Available at http://www.unhcr.org/refworld/docid/4a5f301723.html.

"In Venezuela, Protesters Point to Their Scars." *New York Times*, April 27, 2014.

James-Allen, Paul, Aaron Weah, and Lizzie Goodfriend. *Beyond the Truth and Reconciliation Commission: Transitional Justice Options in Liberia.* New York: International Center for Transitional Justice, 2010.

"Jarpa: Renovación apoya comisión de la verdad, pero. . . ." *El Fortin*, April 24, 1990.

Jeffery, Anthea. *The Truth About the Truth Commission.* Johannesburg: South African Institute of Race Relations, 1999.

Jelin, Elizabeth. "Silences, Visibility, and Agency: Ethnicity, Class, and Gender in Public Memorialization." In *Identities in Transition: Challenges for Transitional Justice in Divided Societies*, ed. Paige Arthur, 187–214. New York: Cambridge University Press, 2011.

———. *State Repression and the Labors of Memory.* Trans. Judy Rein and Marcial Godoy-Anativia. Minneapolis: University of Minnesota Press, 2003.

Jenkins, Catherine. "A Truth Commission for East Timor: Lessons from South Africa?" *Journal of Conflict and Security Law* 7, no. 2 (2002): 233–252.

"Jimmy Savile Scandal Prompts Flood of Calls to Abuse Victims' Groups." *Observer* (London), October 13, 2012.

Johnson, Leigh M. "Transitional Truth and Historical Justice: Philosophical Foundations and Implications of the Truth and Reconciliation Commission." *International Studies in Philosophy* 38, no. 2 (2006): 69–105.

Kalyvas, Stathis N. "The Ontology of 'Political Violence': Action and Identity in Civil Wars." *Perspectives on Politics* 1, no. 3 (2003): 475–494.

Kansteiner, Wulf. "Finding Meaning in Memory: A Methodological Critique of Collective Memory Studies." *History and Theory* 41, no. 2 (2002): 179–197.

Kaye, Mike. "The Role of Truth Commissions in the Search for Justice, Reconciliation and Democratisation: The Salvadorean and Honduran Cases." *Journal of Latin American Studies* 29, no. 3 (1997): 693–716.

Keck, Margaret E., and Kathryn Sikkink. *Activists Beyond Borders: Advocacy Networks in International Politics.* Ithaca, NY: Cornell University Press, 1998.

Kelsall, Tim. "Truth, Lies, Ritual: Preliminary Reflections on the Truth and Reconciliation Commission in Sierra Leone." *Human Rights Quarterly* 27, no. 2 (2005): 361–391.

Kenney, Charles D., and Dean E. Spears. "Truth and Consequences: Do Truth Commissions Promote Democratization?" Paper presented at the Annual Meeting of the American Political Science Association, Washington, DC, September 1–4, 2005.

Kent, Lia. "Local Memory Practices in East Timor: Disrupting Transitional Justice Narratives." *International Journal of Transitional Justice* 5, no. 3 (2010): 434–455

———. "Unfulfilled Expectations: Community Views on CAVR's Community Reconciliation Process." Report prepared for the Judicial System Monitoring Programme, Dili, East Timor, August 2004.

Kim, Hunjoon, and Kathryn Sikkink. "Explaining the Deterrence Effect of Human Rights Prosecutions for Transitional Countries." *International Studies Quarterly* 54, no. 4 (2010): 939–963.

Klein, Kerwin L. "On the Emergence of Memory in Historical Discourse." *Representations* 69 (2000): 127–150.

Knight, Elizabeth. "Facing the Past: Retrospective Justice as a Means to Promote Democracy in Nigeria." *Connecticut Law Review* 35 (2002): 867–914.

Kostic, Roland. "Nationbuilding as an Instrument of Peace? Exploring Local Attitudes Towards International Nationbuilding and Reconciliation in Bosnia and Herzegovina." *Civil Wars* 10, no. 4 (2008): 384–412.

LaCapra, Dominick. "Revisiting the Historians' Debate: Mourning and Genocide." *History and Memory* 9, nos. 1–2 (1997): 80–112.

———. *Writing History, Writing Trauma.* Baltimore: Johns Hopkins University Press, 2001.

"La izquierda 'abertzale' pedirá hoy una 'comisión internacional de la verdad.'" *El País—País Vasco*, February 25, 2012.

Landsman, Stephan. "Alternative Responses to Serious Human Rights Abuses: Of Prosecution and Truth Commissions." *Law and Contemporary Problems* 59, no. 4 (1996): 81–92.

Laplante, Lisa J. "On the Indivisibility of Rights: Truth Commissions, Reparations, and the Right to Develop." *Yale Human Rights & Development Law Journal* 10 (2007): 141–177.

———. "Transitional Justice and Peace Building: Diagnosing and Addressing the Socioeconomic Roots of Violence Through a Human Rights Framework." *International Journal of Transitional Justice* 2, no. 3 (2008): 331–355.

Laplante, Lisa J., and Kimberly S. Theidon. "Truth with Consequences: Justice and Reparations in Post-Truth Commission Peru." *Human Rights Quarterly* 29, no. 1 (2007): 228–250.

Lauer, Mirko. "Necesaria CVR." *La República*, August 6, 2006.

Lean, Sharon F. "Is Truth Enough? Reparations and Reconciliation in Latin America." In *Politics and the Past: On Repairing Historical Injustices*, ed. John Torpey, 169–191. Lanham, MD: Rowman and Littlefield, 2003.

Lebow, Richard Ned. "The Politics of Memory in Postwar Europe." In *The Politics of Memory in Postwar Europe*, ed. Richard Ned Lebow, Wulf Kansteiner, and Claudio Fogu, 1–39. Durham, NC: Duke University Press, 2006.

Lebow, Richard Ned, Wulf Kansteiner, and Claudio Fogu, eds. *The Politics of Memory in Postwar Europe*. Durham, NC: Duke University Press, 2006.

Lechner, Norbert, and Pedro Güell. "Construcción social de las memorias en la transición chilena." In *La caja de Pandora: El retorno de la transición chilena*, ed. Amparo Menéndez-Carrión and Alfredo Joignant, 185–210. Santiago de Chile: Planeta/Ariel, 1999.

Leebaw, Bronwyn. "The Irreconcilable Goals of Transitional Justice." *Human Rights Quarterly* 30, no. 1 (2008): 95–118.

———. *Judging State-Sponsored Violence, Imagining Political Change*. New York: Cambridge University Press, 2011.

———. Review of *Truth and Reconciliation in South Africa: Did the TRC Deliver?*, ed. Audrey R. Chapman and Hugo van der Merwe. *Human Rights Quarterly* 31, no. 2 (2009): 530–537.

Lefranc, Sandrine. "Aquello que no se conmemora: ¿Democracias sin un pasado compartido?" *Revista de Ciencia Política* 23, no. 2 (2003): 231–240.

Le Goff, Jacques. *History and Memory*. Trans. Steven Rendall and Elizabeth Claman. New York: Columbia University Press, 1992.

Leiby, Michele. "Digging in the Archives: The Promise and Perils of Primary Documents." *Politics & Society* 37, no. 1 (2009): 75–100.

Levy, Daniel, and Natan Sznaider. "Memory Unbound: The Holocaust and the Formation of Cosmopolitan Memory." *European Journal of Social Theory* 5, no. 1 (2002): 87–106.

"Liberia: BBC Trust, ICTJ Training Journalists." *Analyst* (Monrovia), August 8, 2008.

"Liberia's First Victims' Group Holds Workshop in Monrovia." *New Liberian*, May 27, 2009.

Lichtenfeld, Rebecca. "Accountability in Argentina: 20 Years Later, Transitional Justice Maintains Momentum." International Center for Transitional Justice Case Study Series, August 2005.

Lira, Elizabeth. "Human Rights in Chile: The Long Road to Truth, Justice, and Reparations." In *After Pinochet: The Chilean Road to Democracy and the Market*, ed. Silvia Borzutzky and Lois Hecht Oppenheim. Gainesville: University Press of Florida, 2006.

———. "Remembering: Passing Back Through the Heart." In *Collective Memory of Political Events: Social Psychological Perspective*, ed. James W. Pennebaker, Darío Páez, and Bernard Rimé, 223–235. Mahwah, NJ: Lawrence Erlbaum Associates, 1997.

Long, William J., and Peter Brecke. *War and Reconciliation: Reason and Emotion in Conflict Resolution*. Cambridge, MA: MIT Press, 2003.

Loveman, Brian, and Elizabeth Lira. *El espejismo de la reconciliación política: Chile 1990–2002.* Santiago: LOM Ediciones/DIBAM, 2002.

———. *Las suaves cenizas del olvido: Vía chilena de reconciliación política, 1814–1932.* Santiago: LOM Ediciones/DIBAM, 2000.

Loveman, Mara. "High-Risk Collective Action: Defending Human Rights in Chile, Uruguay, and Argentina." *American Journal of Sociology* 104, no. 2 (1998): 477–525.

Lynch, Nicolás. "CVR: Fracaso político." *La República*, August 30, 2007.

———. "Politicemos la CVR." *La República*, February 29, 2004.

Macher, Sofía. *Recomendaciones vs. realidades: Avances y desafíos en el post-CVR Perú.* Lima: Instituto de Defensa Legal, 2007.

Magarrell, Lisa. "Reparations for Massive or Widespread Human Rights Violations: Sorting Out Claims for Reparations and the Struggle for Social Justice." *Windsor Yearbook of Access to Justice* 22 (2003): 85–98.

Maier, Charles S. "Doing History, Doing Justice: The Narrative of the Historian and of the Truth Commission." In *Truth v. Justice: The Morality of Truth Commissions*, ed. Robert I. Rotberg and Dennis Thompson, 261–278. Princeton, NJ: Princeton University Press, 2000.

Mamdani, Mahmood. "Amnesty or Impunity? A Preliminary Critique of the Report of the Truth and Reconciliation Commission of South Africa." *Diacritics* 32, nos. 3–4 (2002): 33–59.

Manzi, Jorge, Soledad Ruiz, Mariane Krause, Alejandra Meneses, Andrés Haye, and Edmundo Kronmüller. "Memoria Colectiva del Golpe de Estado de 1973 en Chile." *Revista Interamericana de Psicología* 38, no. 2 (2004): 153–169.

Markell, Patchen. "Making Affect Safe for Democracy? On 'Constitutional Patriotism.'" *Political Theory* 28, no. 1 (2000): 38–63.

McClennen, Sophia A., and Joseph R. Slaughter. "Introducing Human Rights and Literary Forms; or, The Vehicles and Vocabularies of Human Rights." *Comparative Literature Studies* 46, no. 1 (2009): 1–19.

McEvoy, Kieran, and Lorna McGregor, eds. *Transitional Justice from Below: Grassroots Activism and the Struggle for Change.* Oxford: Hart, 2010.

Meade, Teresa. "Holding the Junta Accountable: Chile's 'Sitios de Memoria' and the History of Torture, Disappearance, and Death." *Radical History Review* 79 (Winter 2001): 123–139.

Mendeloff, David. "Truth-Seeking, Truth-Telling, and Postconflict Peacebuilding: Curb the Enthusiasm?" *International Studies Review* 6, no. 3 (2004): 355–380.

Méndez, Juan E. "Derecho a la verdad frente a las graves violaciones a los derechos humanos." In *La aplicación de los tratados sobre derechos humanos por los tribunales locales*, ed. Martín Abregú and Christian Courtis, 517–540. Buenos Aires: Del Puerto-CELS, 1997.

———. "National Reconciliation, Transnational Justice, and the International Criminal Court." *Ethics & International Affairs* 15, no. 1 (2001): 25–44.

Méndez, Juan E., and Javier Mariezcurrena. Review of *Unspeakable Truths: Facing the Challenge of Truth Commissions*, by Priscilla B. Hayner. *Human Rights Quarterly* 25, no. 1 (2003): 237–256.

Millar, Gearoid. "Assessing Local Experiences of Truth-Telling in Sierra Leone: Getting to 'Why' Through a Qualitative Case Study Analysis." *International Journal of Transitional Justice* 4, no. 3 (2010): 477–496.

———. "Expectations and Experiences of Peacebuilding in Sierra Leone: Parallel Peacebuilding Processes and Compound Friction." *International Peacekeeping* 20, no. 2 (2013): 189–203.

Milton, Cynthia E. "At the Edge of the Peruvian Truth Commission: Alternative Paths to Recounting the Past." *Radical History Review* 98 (2007): 3–33.

Minow, Martha. *Between Vengeance and Forgiveness: Facing History After Genocide and Mass Violence.* Boston: Beacon Press, 1998.

———. "Between Vengeance and Forgiveness: South Africa's Truth and Reconciliation Commission." *Negotiation Journal* 14, no. 4 (1998): 319–355.

———. "The Hope for Healing: What Can Truth Commissions Do?" In *Truth v. Justice: The Morality of Truth Commissions*, ed. Robert I. Rotberg and Dennis Thompson. Princeton, NJ: Princeton University Press, 2000.

Montoya, Rodrigo, Luis Montoya, and Edwin Montoya. *Urqukunapa Yawarnin: La sangre de los cerros*. Lima: CEPES, Mosca Azul Editores, and UNMSM, 1987.

Moon, Claire. Narrating Political Reconciliation: South Africa's Truth and Reconciliation Commission. Lanham, MD: Lexington Books, 2008.

Moravcsik, Andrew. "The Origins of Human Rights Regimes: Democratic Delegation in Postwar Europe." *International Organization* 54, no. 2 (1997): 217–252.

Muldoon, Paul. "Reconciliation and Political Legitimacy: The Old Australia and the New South Africa." *Australian Journal of History and Politics* 49, no. 2 (2003): 182–196.

Müller, Jan-Werner. "On the Origins of Constitutional Patriotism." *Contemporary Political Theory* 5, no. 3 (2006): 278–296.

Murphy, Colleen. *A Moral Theory of Political Reconciliation*. New York: Cambridge University Press, 2010.

Nalepa, Monika. *Skeletons in the Closet: Transitional Justice in Post-Communist Europe*. New York: Cambridge University Press, 2010.

Nannelli, Elizabeth. "Memory, Records, History: The Records of the Commission for Reception, Truth, and Reconciliation in Timor-Leste." *Archival Science* 9, nos. 1–2 (2009): 29–41.

Naqvi, Yasmin. "The Right to the Truth in International Law: Fact or Fiction?" *International Review of the Red Cross* 88, no. 862 (2006): 245–273.

Neistat, Anna. *Recurring Nightmare: State Responsibility for "Disappearances" and Abductions in Sri Lanka*. New York: Human Rights Watch, 2008.

Nelson, John S. "Politics and Truth: Arendt's Problematic." *American Journal of Political Science* 22, no. 2 (1978): 270–301.

"Nepal Court Blocks Civil War Truth Commission." *BBC News*, April 1, 2010.

Nesiah, Vasuki. "Gender and Truth Commission Mandates." International Center for Transitional Justice, 2006. Available at http://www.ictj.org/static/Gender/0602.GenderTRC.eng .pdf.

Ní Aoláin, Fionnuala, and Colm Campbell. "The Paradox of Transition in Conflicted Democracies." *Human Rights Quarterly* 27, no. 1 (2005): 172–213.

Nietzsche, Friedrich W. *Untimely Meditations*. Ed. Daniel Breazeale, trans. R. J. Hollingdale. Cambridge: Cambridge University Press, 1997.

Nolan, Mary. "The Historikerstreit and Social History." *New German Critique* 44 (1988): 51–80.

Nora, Pierre. "Between Memory and History: Les Lieux de Mémoire." *Representations* 26 (1989): 7–24.

———. "The Era of Commemoration." In *Realms of Memory: The Construction of the French Past*, vol. 3, *Symbols*, ed. Lawrence Kritzman, trans. Arthur Goldhammer, 609–637. New York: Columbia University Press, 1998.

———. "General Introduction: Between Memory and History." In *Realms of Memory: The Construction of the French Past*, vol. 1, *Conflicts and Divisions*, ed. Lawrence Kritzman, trans. Arthur Goldhammer, 1–20. New York: Columbia University Press, 1996.

Norval, Aletta. "Truth and Reconciliation: The Birth of the Present and the Reworking of History." Review article, *Journal of Southern African Studies* 22, no. 3 (1999): 499–519.

Nowrojee, Binaifer. "Making the Invisible War Crime Visible: Post-Conflict Justice for Sierra Leone's Rape Victims." *Harvard Human Rights Journal* 18 (2005): 85–106.

Nunca más: Informe de la Comisión Nacional sobre la Desaparición de Personas (Buenos Aires: EUDEBA, 1984) translated as *Nunca Más (Never Again): Report of CONADEP (National Commission on the Disappearance of Persons)*. Available at http://web.archive.org/web /20031004074316/nuncamas.org/english/library/nevagain/nevagain_001.htm.

Nwogu, Nneoma V. *Shaping Truth, Reshaping Justice: Sectarian Politics and the Nigerian Truth Commission*. Lanham, MD: Rowman and Littlefield, 2007.

O'Donnell, Guillermo A., Philippe Schmitter, and Laurence Whitehead. *Transitions from Authoritarian Rule: Comparative Perspectives*. Baltimore: Johns Hopkins University Press, 1986.

Oettler, Anika. "Encounters with History: Dealing with the 'Present Past' in Guatemala." *European Review of Latin American and Caribbean Studies* 81 (October 2006): 3–19.

Office of the United Nations High Commissioner for Human Rights. "Rule of Law Tools for Post-Conflict States: Truth Commissions." HR/PUB/06/1. New York: United Nations, 2006.

O'Flaherty, Michael. "Sierra Leone's Peace Process: The Role of the Human Rights Community." *Human Rights Quarterly* 26, no. 1 (2004): 29–62.

Oglesby, Elizabeth. "Historical Memory and the Limits of Peace Education: Examining Guatemala's *Memory of Silence* and the Politics of Curriculum Design." In *Teaching the Violent Past: History Education and Reconciliation*, ed. Elizabeth A. Cole, 175–202. Lanham, MD: Rowman and Littlefield, 2007.

Okafor, Obiora Chinedu. *Legitimizing Human Rights NGOs: Lessons from Nigeria*. Trenton, NJ: Africa World Press, 2006.

Olick, Jeffrey K., and Joyce Robbins. "Social Memory Studies: From 'Collective Memory' to the Historical Sociology of Mnemonic Practices." *Annual Review of Sociology* 24 (1998): 105–140.

Olsen, Tricia D., Leigh A. Payne, and Andrew G. Reiter. *Transitional Justice in Balance: Comparing Processes, Weighing Efficacy*. Washington, DC: U.S. Institute of Peace Press, 2010.

Orentlicher, Diane. "Independent Study on Best Practices, Including Recommendations, to Assist States in Strengthening Their Domestic Capacity to Combat All Aspects of Impunity." UN Doc. E/CN.4/2004/88, February 27, 2004.

Orwell, George. "Looking Back on the Spanish War." In *George Orwell: A Collection of Essays*. Garden City, NY: Doubleday, 1954.

Osiel, Mark J. "Why Prosecute? Critics of Punishment for Mass Atrocity." *Human Rights Quarterly* 22, no. 1 (2000): 118–147.

Pajibo, Ezekiel. "Civil Society and Transitional Justice in Liberia: A Practitioner's Reflection from the Field." *International Journal of Transitional Justice* 1, no. 2 (2007): 287–296.

Parker, Sara Lynn. "Seeking Truth: The Development of an International Truth Commission Norm." Ph.D. diss., University of Delaware, 2008.

Partido Aprista Peruano, Comité Ejecutivo Nacional. "El APRA y la Comisión de la Verdad" Statement no. 26-2003. Adopted August 13, 2003, Lima.

Pasipanodya, Tafadzwa. "A Deeper Justice: Economic and Social Justice as Transitional Justice in Nepal." *International Journal of Transitional Justice* 2, no. 3 (2008): 378–397.

Paulson, Julia. "The Educational Recommendations of Truth and Reconciliation Commissions: Potential and Practice in Sierra Leone." *Research in Comparative and International Education* 1, no. 4 (2006): 335–350.

Payne, Leigh A. *Unsettling Accounts: Neither Truth nor Reconciliation in Confessions of State Violence*. Durham, NC: Duke University Press, 2008.

Pedraglio, Santiago. "Un informe huérfano." *Perú 21*, August 29, 2004.

Pensky, Max. "Amnesty on Trial: Impunity, Accountability, and the Norms of International Law." *Ethics & Global Politics* 1, nos. 1–2 (2008). Available at http://www.ethicsandglobalpolitics .net/index.php/egp/article/view/1816.

Peterson, Trudy H. *Final Acts: A Guide to Preserving the Records of Truth Commissions*. Washington, DC: Woodrow Wilson Center Press; Baltimore: Johns Hopkins University Press, 2005.

"Philippine Court Rules Anti-Corruption Panel Illegal." *New York Times*, December 7, 2010.

Poole, Ross. "Memory, History and the Claims of the Past." *Memory Studies* 1, no. 2 (2008): 149–166.

Popkin, Margaret, and Naomi Roht-Arriaza. "Truth as Justice: Investigatory Commissions in Latin America." *Law & Social Inquiry* 20, no. 1 (1995): 79–116.

Portales, Felipe. *Chile: Una democracia tutelada.* Santiago de Chile: Editorial Sudamericana Chilena, 2000.

———. "Concertación y violaciones a derechos humanos de la dictadura." 2006. Available at http://www.archivochile.com/Chile_actual/09_p_concert/chact_pconcert0002.pdf.

Punyasena, Wasana. "The Façade of Accountability: Disappearances in Sri Lanka." *Boston College Third World Law Journal* 23 (2003): 115–158.

Quinn, Joanna R. "Constraints: The Un-Doing of the Ugandan Truth Commission." *Human Rights Quarterly* 26, no. 2 (2004): 401–427.

———. "Haiti's Failed Truth Commission: Lessons in Transitional Justice." *Journal of Human Rights* 8, no. 3 (2009): 265–281.

———. "The Politics of Acknowledgement: An Analysis of Uganda's Truth Commission." YCISS Working Paper no. 19. York Centre for International and Security Studies, March 2003.

———. "The Politics of Acknowledgement: Truth Commissions in Uganda and Haiti." Ph.D. diss., McMaster University, 2003.

Rawski, Frederick. "Truth-Seeking and Local Histories in East Timor." *Asia-Pacific Journal on Human Rights & Law* 3, no. 1 (2002): 77–96.

"Realizan balance a 10 años de Informe Rettig." *El Mercurio*, March 3, 2001.

Reiter, Randy B., M. V. Zunzunegui, and Jose Quiroga. "Guidelines for Field Reporting of Basic Human Rights Violations." Human Rights Quarterly 8, no. 4 (1986): 628–653.

"Reparaciones colectivas serán prioridad." *Perú 21*, January 11, 2013.

Report of the Chilean National Commission on Truth and Reconciliation. Vol. 1. Trans. Phillip E. Berryman. Notre Dame, IN: University of Notre Dame Press, 1993.

Republic of Liberia, Truth and Reconciliation Commission (TRC). *Truth and Reconciliation Commission of Liberia Final Report.* Monrovia: TRC of Liberia, 2009.

Riaño-Alcalá, Pilar, and Erin Baines. "The Archive in the Witness: Documentation in Settings of Chronic Insecurity." *International Journal of Transitional Justice* 5, no. 3 (2011): 412–433.

Ricoeur, Paul. *Memory, History, Forgetting.* Trans. Kathleen Blamey and David Pellauer. Chicago: University of Chicago Press, 2004.

Riley, Patrick. "Hannah Arendt on Kant, Truth and Politics." In *Essays on Kant's Political Philosophy*, ed. Howard L. Williams, 305–323. Chicago: University of Chicago Press, 1992.

Robins, Simon. "Challenging the Therapeutic Ethic: A Victim-Centred Evaluation of Transitional Justice Process in Timor-Leste." *International Journal of Transitional Justice* 6, no. 1 (2012): 83–105.

Robinson, Benjamin. "Against Memory as Justice." *New German Critique* 33, no. 2 (2006): 135–160.

Rodio, Emily Brooke. "More than Truth: Democracy and South Africa's Truth and Reconciliation Commission." Ph.D. diss., Syracuse University, 2009.

Rohter, Larry. "Searing Indictment." *New York Times*, February 27, 1999.

Roncagliolo, Rafael. "Procesos post conflicto y Comisiones de la Verdad." Presented at "De la negación al reconocimiento." Seminario Internacional Procesos Post Comisiones de la Verdad, Lima, June 4–6, 2003.

Root, Rebecca. "Through the Window of Opportunity: The Transitional Justice Network in Peru." *Human Rights Quarterly* 31, no. 2 (2009): 452–473.

Ross, Amy. "The Creation and Conduct of the Guatemalan Commission for Historical Clarification." *Geoforum* 37, no. 1 (2006): 69–81.

Ross, Fiona C. "On Having Voice and Being Heard: Some After-Effects of Testifying Before the South African Truth and Reconciliation Commission." *Anthropological Theory* 3, no. 3 (2003): 325–341.

Rubio-Marín, Ruth, Claudia Paz y Paz Bailye, and Julie Guillerot. "Indigenous Peoples and Claims for Reparation: Tentative Steps in Peru and Guatemala." In *Identities in Transition: Challenges for Transitional Justice in Divided Societies*, ed. Paige Arthur, 17–53. New York: Cambridge University Press, 2011.

Rubongoya, Joshua B. *Regime Hegemony in Museveni's Uganda: Pax Musevenica*. New York: Palgrave Macmillan, 2007.

Sandoval, Pablo. *Educación, ciudadanía y violencia en el Perú: Una lectura del Informe de la CVR*. Lima: TAREA and IEP, 2004.

Sankey, Diana. "Towards Recognition of Subsistence Harms: Reassessing Approaches to Socioeconomic Forms of Violence in Transitional Justice." *International Journal of Transitional Justice* 8 (2014): 121–140.

Sartori, Giovanni. "Concept Misformation in Comparative Politics." *American Political Science Review* 64, no. 4 (1970): 1033–1053.

Saunders, Rebecca. "Questionable Associations: The Role of Forgiveness in Transitional Justice." *International Journal of Transitional Justice* 5, no. 1 (2011): 119–141.

Schabas, William. "The Relationship Between Truth Commissions and International Courts: The Case of Sierra Leone." *Human Rights Quarterly* 25, no. 4 (2003): 1035–1066.

———. "The Sierra Leone Truth and Reconciliation Commission." In *Transitional Justice in the Twenty-First Century: Beyond Truth Versus Justice*, ed. Naomi Roht-Arriaza and Javier Mariezcurrena, 21–42. Cambridge: Cambridge University Press, 2006.

Schlein, Lisa. "War Reparations Program in Sierra Leone Needs Money." *Voice of America*, April 24, 2010.

Segovia, Alexander. "The Reparations Proposals of the Truth Commissions in El Salvador and Haiti: A History of Noncompliance." In *The Handbook of Reparations*, ed. Pablo de Greiff, 154–175. Oxford: Oxford University Press, 2006.

Sennett, Richard. "Disturbing Memories." In *Memory*, ed. Patricia Fara and Karalyn Patterson, 10–26. Cambridge: Cambridge University Press, 1998.

"Serían 100 mil las víctimas de la guerra interna en el Perú." *El Comercio*, October 7, 2011.

Serrano, Margarita, and Ascanio Cavallo. El poder de la paradoja: 14 lecciones políticas de la vida de Patricio Aylwin. Santiago: Norma, 2006.

Shaw, Rosalind. "Rethinking Truth and Reconciliation Commissions: Lessons from Sierra Leone." Special Report 130. United States Institute of Peace, February 13, 2005.

Shea, Dorothy C. *The South African Truth Commission: The Politics of Reconciliation*. Washington, DC: U.S. Institute of Peace Press, 2000.

Shifter, Michael, and Vinay Jawahar. "Reconciliation in Latin America: A Fine Balance." *Brown Journal of World Affairs* 11, no. 1 (2004): 127–135.

Sikkink, Kathryn. *The Justice Cascade: How Human Rights Prosecutions Are Changing World Politics*. New York: W. W. Norton, 2011.

Simmons, Beth. *Mobilizing for Human Rights: International Law in Domestic Politics*. Cambridge: Cambridge University Press, 2009.

Sirleaf, Matiangai V. S. "Regional Approach to Transitional Justice? Examining the Special Court for Sierra Leone and the Truth and Reconciliation Commission for Liberia." *Florida Journal of International Law* 21 (2009): 209–285.

Skaar, Elin. *Human Rights Violations and the Paradox of Democratic Transition: A Study of Chile and Argentina*. Bergen, Norway: Chr. Michelsen Institute, 1994.

———. "Truth Commissions, Trials or Nothing? Policy Options in Democratic Transitions." *Third World Quarterly* 20, no. 6 (1999): 1109–1128.

Smith, Anthony D. *Nationalism in the Twentieth Century*. New York: New York University Press, 1979.

Snyder, Jack, and Leslie Vinjamuri. "Trials and Errors: Principle and Pragmatism in Strategies of International Justice." *International Security* 28, no. 3 (2003): 5–44.

Soyinka, Wole. "Memory, Truth and Healing." In *The Politics of Memory: Truth, Healing, and Social Justice*, ed. Ifi Amadiume and Abdullah An-Na'im, 21–37. London: Zed Books, 2000.

Stanley, Elizabeth. "Torture, Silence and Recognition." *Current Issues in Criminal Justice* 16, no. 1 (2004): 5–25.

———. "Truth Commissions and the Recognition of State Crime." *British Journal of Criminology* 45, no. 4 (2005): 582–597.

Starn, Orin. "Maoism in the Andes: The Communist Party of Peru–Shining Path and the Refusal of History." *Journal of Latin American Studies* 27 (1995): 399–421.

Stern, Steve J. *Reckoning with Pinochet: The Memory Question in Democratic Chile, 1989–2006.* Durham, NC: Duke University Press, 2010.

———. *Remembering Pinochet's Chile: On the Eve of London, 1998.* Durham, NC: Duke University Press, 2004.

———, ed. *Shining and Other Paths: War and Society in Peru, 1980–1995.* Durham, NC: Duke University Press, 1998.

Subotić, Jelena. "The Transformation of International Transitional Justice Advocacy." *International Journal of Transitional Justice* 6, no. 1 (2012): 106–125.

Tai, Hue-Tam Ho. "Remembered Realms: Pierre Nora and French National Memory." *American Historical Review* 106, no. 3 (2001): 906–922.

Teitel, Ruti G. *Transitional Justice.* New York: Oxford University Press, 2000.

Teivainen, Teivo. "Truth, Justice and Legal Impunity: Dealing with Past Human Rights Violations in Chile." *Nordic Journal of Latin American and Caribbean Studies* 30, no. 2 (2000): 55–82.

Tepperman, Jonathan D. "Truth and Consequences." *Foreign Affairs* 81, no. 2 (2002): 128–145.

Theidon, Kimberly Susan. "Histories of Innocence: Postwar Stories in Peru." In *Localizing Transitional Justice: Interventions and Priorities After Mass Violence*, ed. Rosalind Shaw and Lars Waldorf, with Pierre Hazan, 92–110. Stanford, CA: Stanford University Press, 2010.

Thoms, Oskar N. T., James Ron, and Roland Paris. "State-Level Effects of Transitional Justice: What Do We Know?" *International Journal of Transitional Justice* 4, no. 3 (2010): 329–354.

"TJWG Launches Transitional Justice Initiative Project." *Analyst* (Monrovia), June 29, 2010.

Tomuschat, Christian. "Clarification Commission in Guatemala." *Human Rights Quarterly* 23, no. 2 (2001): 233–258.

Torpey, John. "Introduction: Habermas and the Historians." *New German Critique* 44 (1988): 5–24.

Trinidad, Rocio. El informe final de la Comisión de la Verdad y el reto de la diversificación curricular en Ayacucho. Lima: Asociación SER, 2006.

Tucno Rocha, Edgar Alberto. "Guerra Popular! O Microconflictos: Los comités de autodefensa en el distrito de Vinchos." In *Reflexiones en Ayacucho desde las ciencias sociales.* Editorial UNSCH-CEISA, Ayacucho, 2003.

Turner, Catherine. 2008. "Delivering Lasting Peace, Democracy and Human Rights in Times of Transition: The Role of International Law." *International Journal of Transitional Justice* 2, no. 2 (2008): 126–151.

United Nations Human Rights Committee. "Major Progress Made in Human Rights Protections Since Guatemala's Peace Accords 15 Years Ago, Although Much Work Remains, Human Rights Committee Told." UN Doc. HR/CT/744, March 19, 2012.

United Nations Human Rights Council. "Right to the Truth." A/HRC/5/7, June 7, 2007.

van der Merwe, Hugo, and Audrey R. Chapman. "Did the TRC Deliver?" In *Truth and Reconciliation in South Africa: Did the TRC Deliver?*, ed. Audrey R. Chapman and Hugo van der Merwe, 241–279. Philadelphia: University of Pennsylvania Press, 2008.

van Evera, Stephen. *Guide to Methods for Students of Political Science*. Ithaca, NY: Cornell University Press, 1997.

Vasallo, Mark. "Truth and Reconciliation Commissions: General Considerations and a Critical Comparison of the Commissions of Chile and El Salvador." *University of Miami Inter-American Law Review* 33, no. 1 (2002): 153–182.

Verdeja, Ernesto. "Derrida and the Impossibility of Forgiveness." *Contemporary Political Theory* 3, no. 1 (2004): 23–47.

———. "Reparations in Democratic Transitions." *Res Publica* 12, no. 2 (2006): 115–136.

———. *Unchopping a Tree: Reconciliation in the Aftermath of Political Violence*. Philadelphia: Temple University Press, 2009.

Vial Correa, Gonzalo. *Historia de Chile, 1891–1973*. Santiago de Chile: Editorial Santillana del Pacífico, 1981.

Vidal, Hernán. *Dar la vida por la vida: Agrupación Chilena de Familiares de Detenidos Desaparecidos*. Santiago: Mosquito Editores, 1996.

———. *Política cultural de la memoria histórica*. Santiago: Mosquito Comunicaciones, 1997.

Villa-Vicencio, Charles, and Wilhelm Verwoerd, eds. *Looking Back Reaching Forward: Reflections on the Truth and Reconciliation Commission of South Africa*. Cape Town, South Africa: Cape Town University Press, 2000.

Walter, Barbara. "Does Conflict Beget Conflict? Explaining Recurring Civil War." *Journal of Peace Research* 41, no. 3 (2004): 371–388.

Weah, Aaron. "Hopes and Uncertainties: Liberia's Journey to End Impunity." *International Journal of Transitional Justice* 6, no. 2 (2012): 331–343.

Webster, David. "History, Nation and Narrative in East Timor's Truth Commission Report." *Pacific Affairs* 80, no. 4 (2007): 581–591.

Weeks, Gregory. *The Military and Politics in Postauthoritarian Chile*. Tuscaloosa: University of Alabama Press, 2003.

Wiebelhaus-Brahm, Eric. "Truth and Consequences: The Impact of Truth Commissions in Transitional Societies." Ph.D. diss., University of Colorado at Boulder, 2006.

———. *Truth Commissions and Transitional Societies: The Impact on Human Rights and Democracy*. New York: Routledge, 2010.

———. "Uncovering the Truth: Examining Truth Commission Success and Impact." *International Studies Perspectives* 8, no. 1 (2007): 16–35.

———. "What Is a Truth Commission and Why Does It Matter?" *Peace and Conflict Review* 3, no. 2 (2009): 1–14.

Wilcox, Luke. "Reshaping Civil Society Through a Truth Commission: Human Rights in Morocco's Process of Political Reform." *International Journal of Transitional Justice* 3, no. 1 (2009): 49–68.

Wilde, Alexander. "Irruptions of Memory: Expressive Politics in Chile's Transition to Democracy." *Journal of Latin American Studies* 31 (1999): 473–500.

Wilke, Christiane. "Staging Violence, Staging Identities: Identity Politics in Domestic Prosecutions." In *Identities in Transition: Challenges for Transitional Justice in Divided Societies*, ed. Paige Arthur, 118–148. New York: Cambridge University Press, 2011.

Wilson, Richard A. "Afterword to 'Anthropology and Human Rights in a New Key': The Social Life of Human Rights." *American Anthropologist* 108, no. 1 (2006): 77–83.

———. *The Politics of Truth and Reconciliation in South Africa: Legitimizing the Post-Apartheid State*. Cambridge: Cambridge University Press, 2001.

———. *Writing History in International Criminal Trials*. New York: Cambridge University Press, 2011.

Wimmer, Andreas, and Nina Glick Schiller. "Methodological Nationalism and Beyond: Nation-State Building, Migration and the Social Sciences." *Global Networks* 2, no. 4 (2002): 301–334.

Winn, Peter, ed. *Victims of the Chilean Miracle: Workers and Neoliberalism in the Pinochet Era, 1973–2002*: Durham, NC: Duke University Press, 2004.

Winter, Jay. *Sites of Memory, Sites of Mourning: The Great War in European Cultural History*. Cambridge: Cambridge University Press, 1995.

Wood, Nancy. *Vectors of Memory: Legacies of Trauma in Postwar Europe*. Oxford: Berg, 1999.

World Organisation Against Torture, in collaboration with the Families of the Disappeared (Kalape Api), Human Rights and Development Centre (SETIK), and Janasansadaya (People's Forum), Sri Lanka. *State Violence in Sri Lanka: An Alternative Report to the United Nations Human Rights Committee*. Geneva: World Organisation Against Torture, 2004.

Ximenes, Fausto Belo. "The Unique Contribution of the Community-Based Reconciliation Process in East Timor." Paper prepared for the Transitional Justice Fellowship Program of the International Center for Transitional Justice and the Institute for Justice and Reconciliation, May 2004.

Young, Laura A., and Rosalyn Park. "Engaging Diasporas in Truth Commissions: Lessons from the Liberia Truth and Reconciliation Commission Diaspora Project." *International Journal of Transitional Justice* 3, no. 3 (2009): 341–361.

Young-Bruehl, Elizabeth. *Hannah Arendt: For the Love of the World*. New Haven, CT: Yale University Press, 2004.

Youngers, Coletta. "En busca de la verdad y la justicia: La Coordinadora Nacional de Derechos Humanos del Perú." In *Historizar el pasado vivo en América Latina*, ed. Anne Pérotin-Dumon. Santiago, Chile: Universidad Alberto Hurtado, Centro de Ética, 2007. Available at http://www.historizarelpasadovivo.cl.

Yusuf, Hakeem O. Transitional Justice, Judicial Accountability and the Rule of Law. New York: Routledge, 2010.

———. "Travails of Truth: Achieving Justice for Victims of Impunity in Nigeria." *International Journal of Transitional Justice* 1, no. 2 (2007): 268–286.

Zalaquett, José. "Balancing Ethical Imperatives and Political Constraints: The Dilemma of New Democracies Confronting Past Human Rights Violations." *Hastings Law Journal* 43 (1992): 1425–1438.

———. "Confronting Human Rights Violations Committed by Former Governments: Applicable Principles and Political Constraints." *Hamline Law Review* 13, no. 3 (1990): 623–655.

———. "Moral Reconstruction in the Wake of Human Rights Violations and War Crimes." In *Hard Choices: Moral Dilemmas in Humanitarian Intervention*, ed. Jonathan Moore, 211–228. Lanham, MD: Rowman and Littlefield, 1998.

Zerubavel, Eviatar. "Social Memories: Steps to a Sociology of the Past." *Qualitative Sociology* 19, no. 3 (1996): 283–300.

"Zimbabwe's Mugabe: Lift Sanctions, UN's Navi Pillay Urges." *BBC News*, May 25, 2012.

INDEX

Page numbers in boldface indicate primary discussion. Page numbers followed by *t* indicate tables; page numbers followed by *f* indicate figures.

ACKNOWLEDGMENTS

═══════

What happens to beautiful, defiant, and painful pasts? Have people already forgotten about the dreams of the generation that came before? Are we living in a continuous present? If so, can memory save us from the straitjacket of the present? Is the past to be redeemed by a "pearl diver" who knows to see the treasure hidden under heaps of history, to quote from Hannah Arendt's famous essay on Walter Benjamin?

As an academic with mixed loyalties to political theory and comparative politics, I kept wondering if I should seek answers to these questions. It all started as I was reading about the political history of the Left in Latin America in the 1960s and 1970s, especially Chile's Unidad Popular movement. One question kept bothering me: where did all these wonderful men and women, with all their ideas and struggles, admirable strengths and inevitable weaknesses, go? Someone, somewhere, should be busy remembering past struggles for a free and fair society, I thought. But then I learned: the interest in memory is indeed remarkable in contemporary societies, but the variety of ways in which individuals and social groups negotiate the past and the present, suffering and renewal, and oneself and the other, complicates the redemptive power associated with memory. This is how my initial musings about beautiful, defiant, and painful pasts evolved into this book about truth commissions, one of the chief mechanisms to come to terms with the past in contemporary societies.

I would like to thank first and foremost all the generous people who agreed to interview with me and shared their views and experiences in their different roles as victims, victims' relatives, civil society activists, politicians, lawyers, and intellectuals. I can only hope that I have done justice to their ideas, experiences, and memories.

I am grateful to Elisabeth J. Wood for her excellent mentoring, tireless support, and inspiring personality. Libby has been my role model as an academic, as an intellectual, and, most important, as a person. I also thank Seyla

Benhabib, James C. Scott, and Jeffrey Alexander for their thoughtful commentary on earlier versions of this book.

I feel lucky to have worked with Peter Agree, editor-in-chief of the University of Pennsylvania Press. His ongoing belief in this book project and thoughtful advice are much appreciated.

The fieldwork became possible thanks to the assistance of the staff at the Vicaría de la Solidaridad archive in Santiago, Chile, the Asociación Pro Derechos Humanos (APRODEH), Lima, Peru, and Centro de Información para la Memoria Colectiva y los Derechos Humanos, Lima, Peru. The Department of Political Science at the Pontificia Universidad Católica de Chile provided me with office space. Special thanks to Jacqueline Fowks and Marcela Penna, who made the fieldwork possible.

I have been fortunate enough to work closely with thoughtful and generous friends and colleagues at Yale University. My special thanks to Dessislava Kirilova, Ponciano del Pino, and Eddie Camp for their support, helpful criticism, and friendship. I express my appreciation to Gina Bateson, Sierra Bell, Lara Chausow, Ron Eyerman, Valerie Frey, Amelia Green Hoover, Corinna Jentzsch, Andrea Katz, Paul Lagunes, Xiaobo Lu, Meghan Lynch Foster, Lizbeth Leyva, Joel Middleton, Shivaji Mukherjee, Paulina Ochoa-Espejo, Celia Paris, Pia Raffler, Angelika Schlanger, Livia Schubiger, Rachel Silbermann, Paolo Spada, Jason Stearns, Susan Stokes, Peter Verovšek, and Christian Volk for their continued support and guidance.

I am thankful to the students and faculty of the School for International Studies, Simon Fraser University. Their thoughtful criticism and overall support made it possible to refine the book manuscript in its later stages. I would like to acknowledge Jeffrey Checkel's relentless encouragement in particular.

I would also like to thank the participants of the Political Philosophy Colloquium and Comparative Politics Workshop at Yale University, the Coming to Terms with the Past Conference at Yale University, the Sociology Speaker Series at Boğaziçi University, Istanbul, the Historical Justice and Memory Conference, Melbourne, Australia, and the Simon Fraser University and the University of British Columbia Latin American Studies Working Paper Series, 2011–2012, for their commentary on the book chapters.

Parts of Chapter 4 were published under the title "Truth Commission Impact: an Assessment of How Commissions Influence Politics and Society" in the *International Journal of Transitional Justice* 8, no. 1 (2014): 6–30.

I acknowledge the following research institutes and centers at Yale University for supporting my research: the MacMillan Center, the Council on Latin American and Iberian Studies, and the Council on European Studies Language Study Grant.

I dedicate this book to my parents, Sevdiye and Kemal Bakıner, and my sister Egenur for encouraging me to be the best person I can be and to imagine a world in which humankind lives like a happy family. *Sizi seviyorum!*